W9-AXI-751

A S Q C
LIBRARY

The Handbook
of
Strategic Expertise

The Handbook
of
Strategic Expertise

Over 450 Key Concepts and Techniques
Defined, Illustrated, and Evaluated
for the Strategist

Catherine L. Hayden

THE FREE PRESS
A Division of Macmillan, Inc.
NEW YORK

Collier Macmillan Publishers
LONDON

ASQC
LIBRARY

Copyright © 1986 by The Free Press
A Division of Macmillan, Inc.

All rights reserved. No part of this book may be reproduced
or transmitted in any form or by any means, electronic or
mechanical, including photocopying, recording, or by any
information storage and retrieval system, without permission
in writing from the Publisher.

The Free Press
A Division of Macmillan, Inc.
866 Third Avenue, New York, N. Y. 10022

Collier Macmillan Canada, Inc.

Printed in the United States of America

printing number

1 2 3 4 5 6 7 8 9 10

Library of Congress Cataloging-in-Publication Data

Hayden, Catherine L.

The handbook of strategic expertise.

Bibliography: p. 351
Includes index.
1. Strategic planning. I. Title.
HD30.28.H389 1986   658.4′012   86–14316
ISBN 0–02–914220–2

To
Dorothy Hayden Truscott
and
Dorothy Maloney Johnson

Contents

Preface

In 1962, Alfred Chandler defined strategy as "the determination of the basic long-term goals and objectives of an enterprise and the adoption of courses of action and the collection of resources necessary for carrying out these goals." With this definition he wove together the huge effort that preceded him and formed the basis for a tidal wave of research and development that has followed. Today strategic planning is institutionalized in nearly all large companies and touches not only senior management but managers at all levels of the organization. This explosion in interest has brought about a bewildering profusion of new concepts, procedures, and terminology. Strategic planning is evolving its own specialized language, with terms like SBUs, matrices, experience curves, mobility barriers, and value added chains, as well as borrowing and reinterpreting terms from other fields. There is also an ever-expanding literature in strategic planning, containing both chaff and wheat, which a manager must try to keep up with.

As with other sciences, there are many schools of thought and much debate. For example, there is debate over such fundamental questions as to whether there exists an encompassing concept and related techniques or whether there exists a series of groups of concepts and techniques that may or may not be applicable to a given problem. And there is debate as to specific questions as to which comes first—a goal, an objective, or a mission. These differing perspectives are all reflected in this book. Many of the entries herein have supporters as well as detractors. The purpose of including them was not to legitimize them but to allow readers to make their own assessments.

This handbook provides a single-source reference for managers who develop strategic plans at the corporate, sector, or business level; managers who evaluate the strategic plans others have developed; and managers who otherwise make decisions that require a strategic perspective. It draws on concepts in strategy developed by academics, consultants, and managers as well as concepts from related disciplines such as marketing, finance, operations management, accounting, engineering, and economics. Most important, although these definitions and examples are simplified to eliminate the need for specific expertise, they remain comprehensive from the perspective of the strategist. In short, the book collects in one place information on all the relevant terms a manager needs in order to understand and apply state-of-the-art techniques in strategic planning.

The growth of the strategic planning field and the number and variety of contributors have led to definition, redefinition, and redundant definition—such that a term may have a very precise meaning for one user and a very general meaning for another. To this end, the handbook provides an eclectic view to which readers may add their own judgments to those made by current practitioners.

Finally, the handbook has been structured to be used in three general ways. The first is as a reference book both for understanding material on strategic planning that others have developed and as a reference for developing new material. Second, the book is cross-referenced within context so that the reader can either begin with the first term or start at any point of particular interest and pursue it in as much depth and breadth as needed. Third, the book can be used as a source for materials on other disciplines that would be of interest to a strategist under particular circumstances.

Acknowledgments

These concepts and techniques have been suggested, researched, developed, refined, expanded on, and tested by managers at all levels of organizations; by professionals in accounting firms; by management consultants; by academics in the fields of mathematics, economics, and business administration in organizations around the world. In addition to those noted in the bibliography, a number of firms contributed to this manuscript through materials and conversations with associates or their clients. They include Arthur Andersen & Company; Arthur D. Little Inc.; A. T. Kearney Inc.; Bain & Company; Booz, Allen & Hamilton, Inc.; Boston Consulting Group Inc.; Cambridge Associates Inc.; Coopers & Lybrand; Cresap, McCormick and Paget; Greenwich Research Associates; Harbridge House, Inc.; Hayes/Hill Inc.; Index Systems, Inc.; Kurt Salmon Associates, Inc.; The LEK Partnership; Management Analysis Center, Inc.; Marakon Associates; McKinsey & Company Inc.; Monitor Company; Nolan, Norton and Company, Inc.; Peat, Marwick; Price Waterhouse & Company; Resource Planning Associates; Stanford Research Institute; Strategic Planning Associates; Strategic Planning Institute; Temple Barker & Sloane, Inc.; Theodore Barry & Associates; Touche Ross and Company; and Towers, Perrin, Forster and Crosby.

And I, like anyone else who writes in the field of strategic management, must acknowledge the work of Michael Porter. His contributions both as an individual and together with colleagues and practitioners has had a significant impact on the frameworks and vocabulary of the field.

I would especially like to thank Richard E. Caves, who reviewed major portions of the manuscript, and Jane Kenney Austin, who read and commented on the entire manuscript.

I would also like to thank Emily Feudo and Jill Pellarin, who managed the production of the manuscript, and my editor, Robert Wallace.

The Science of Strategy—
A Historical Overview

The concepts and techniques of strategy have evolved over time as the ends and the means of organizations have changed. These changes in the strategies of organizations are reflections of changes in the structure of the economy in which these organizations compete.

In the 1700s, the U.S. economy consisted of two basic types of businesses: those that produced products and those that did everything else. Products were either grown on family farms and plantations or manufactured in small one- or a few-person shops, or they were imported. The efforts of these producers were linked by all-purpose general merchants, who were very often exporter, manufacturer, wholesaler, retailer, transporter, distributor, banker, and underwriter all in one. Many theorists believe that the key to success at this time was having, in the first case, a family large enough to produce what was needed and, in the second case, a family large enough to provide trusted agents wherever needed.

In the 1800s a trend toward specialization developed, leading to an economy composed of a number of different types of business that focused on specific functions (such as jobbing as opposed to either retailing or wholesaling) or on one or two types of products or services. This specialization engendered a variety of goods, which were sold to wider markets involving many separate businesses, each trying to make a profit on its transactions. By the mid-1800s, with the coming of the railroad and telegraph, businesses were larger and more complex. These new organizations needed middle managers and senior executives to run them, and CAPITAL MARKETS—rather than family fortunes—to finance them. The STRATEGIES that resulted from the combination of investors and managers were different from those of the family business in both ends and means. The creation of ECONOMIC VALUE for the shareholder was the new goal and management concepts and techniques were developed as the means to that end.

Until the depression of the 1870s, growth was the key goal of business, and management's focus was on developing organizations that could be efficiently expanded and on learning the principles of mass production and mass marketing. By the end of the century, attention turned toward greater efficiency through coordination and control and VERTICAL INTEGRATION when necessary. Management concepts of that time dealt with the development of INFORMATION SYSTEMS and techniques such as order numbers and routing slips and the development of INCENTIVE SYSTEMS geared to either piece- or daywork.

In 1911, the management theory pioneer Frederick Taylor wrote *The Principles of Scientific Management*. Maintaining that the key challenge that companies faced was the increase of national efficiency, he pointed out that not only were forests vanishing, waterpowers going to waste, soil eroding, and supplies of coal and iron diminishing, but there was an even larger waste of human effort due to poor direction and inefficiency. He noted that in the past the belief had been that captains of industry were born, not made; success in the future would depend on eliminating inefficiency by melding the interests of employees and employers through SCIENTIFIC MANAGEMENT.

In 1924, Mary Parker Follet presented her theories of CONSTRUCTIVE CONFLICT at a conference series entitled "Scientific Foundations of Business Administration." Follet agreed with Taylor on the importance of integrating the interests of management and employees but emphasized the need for competitive analysis as well. She believed that successful management depends on controlling the potentially conflicting interests of employees and competing businesses.

Throughout the early 1900s, managers increasingly recognized that, regardless of changing political climates, social values, or geographic boundaries, organizations needed effective managers to be successful. Accordingly, the concept of management as science began to be explored by academics in the fields of BUSINESS POLICY and administration and applied by managers in an ever-increasing range of industries. This was the beginning of the continuing relationship between theorists and practitioners that has led to today's STRATEGY concepts and techniques. It was also the beginning of another field of business, that of the management consultant. Consultants, considered by many to be a hybrid of theorists and practitioners, have undeniably made their share of contributions to management science. Their changing interests reflect the changes in the economy over time.

From 1900 to the 1920s, the goal of management was ever-increasing profits, and the means included the manipulation of securities or the control of suppliers, distributors, and competitors or both. There was an emphasis on MERGERS and VERTICAL INTEGRATION. This era saw beginnings of global competition. Everyone worked on administrative theories regarding the management of the flow of materials and funds through the increasingly complex and diverse VALUE ADDED CHAINS.

The recession from 1920–1922 made many companies recognize the need for effective planning over and above day-to-day operations management. Managers placed new emphasis on inventory control, FORECASTING demand, and building ORGANIZATIONAL STRUCTURES that could respond to change. This trend marked the beginning of multifunctional divisions whose performance was monitored by top management. In order to measure that performance, top management began to build advisory staffs to study the BUSINESS CYCLE, build MEASUREMENT SYSTEMS, and compare actual performance with FORECASTS.

The drastic decline in national income in the 1930s led to an increasing interest in DIVERSIFICATION for risk reduction and in PRODUCT INNOVATION for growth. Although ACQUISITIONS were sometimes used to achieve DIVERSIFICATION, the major emphasis was on internal development. MANAGEMENT SYSTEMS had to be enhanced to allow not only for quick measurement of and response to market changes but also for a RESOURCE ALLOCATION process that balanced the short-term cost of investing against potential long-term returns.

The demands of industry made by World War II taught many more industries about management systems in forecasting, accounting, and inventory control, as well as new techniques like OPERA-

TIONS RESEARCH. After the war, twenty years of steady DEMAND growth provided a huge mass market that provided the resources for overseas expansion and stimulated the growth of new organizational forms such as MATRIX ORGANIZATIONS.

The trend toward increasingly complex STRATEGIES and STRUC-TURES continued into the 1950s. During this time companies began to perceive a mismatch between the products they were attempting to sell and the changing needs and demands of their would-be customers. Managers began to look for an understanding of their buyers' HIERARCHY OF NEEDS and ways to avoid MARKETING MYOPIA as the basis for new STRATEGIES.

By the 1960s, top management delegated many operating responsibilities and began to focus on the future. This focus usually took the form of long-range plans. Businesses were asked to develop ten-year plans for submission to top management. Top management reviewed the plans with an emphasis on consolidating them in order to meet corporate goals. Pursuit of growth through DIVERSIFICATION became an increasingly popular management activity. The extreme form of this phenomenon was the CONGLOMERATE with its narrowly defined CORPORATE STRATEGY. But CONGLOMERATES as well as other diversified companies had the same problem of how to allocate resources among different businesses, in different industries, pursuing different strategies, with different time horizons.

Most companies responded with one of two related answers to this problem. The first involved techniques for discriminating among businesses in order to maximize performance and was often based on PORTFOLIO APPROACHES and illustrated with MATRICES. The second response involved integrating the businesses with each other in order to maximize performance and was often based on the development of SYNERGY. The PIMS PROGRAM, the Boston Consulting Group's concept of the GROWTH/SHARE MATRIX, and the McKINSEY SCREEN are considered by many to be the most effective portfolio techniques developed. SYNERGY did not fare as well. Although most everyone agreed that it must exist and that it offered huge potential, there did not seem to be any way to conceptualize it such that it could be exploited.

In the 1970s, management's main concern became protecting profits from rising costs, TECHNOLOGICAL CHANGE, and new competitors. INFLATION was eroding margins, distorting accounting, masking real growth, attracting ENTRY, and financing new competing technologies. This, together with the rising COST OF CAPITAL, led to a focus on the creation of real and increasing ECONOMIC VALUE. By the end of the decade a huge range of concepts and techniques had evolved for understanding the CAPITAL MARKETS, analyzing and controlling INDUSTRY STRUCTURE, evaluating competitors, and formulating strategies that used STRENGTHS AND WEAKNESSES to protect against THREATS and take advantage of competitors' weaknesses.

In the 1980s, management continues to wrestle with finding the optimal combination of structure and strategy, measuring performance, allocating resources, analyzing buyers, protecting profits, and especially finding new OPPORTUNITIES and new ways to compete. Time horizons have shortened and competition has intensified to the point where an OPPORTUNITY not taken advantage of quickly becomes a threatening imperative. The emphasis has shifted to using STRATEGIC MANAGEMENT to build and sustain COMPETITIVE ADVANTAGES. A huge range of concepts and techniques has evolved for anticipating and exploiting opportunities. The problem of synergy is being effectively conceptualized with FIELD THEORY, CONCEPTS OF FIT, BUSINESS SYSTEMS, and HORIZONTAL STRATEGY. And there is an increased emphasis on implementation of strategies in two ways: The first is providing techniques like the VALUE CHAIN for understanding what actually has to be done to carry out a strategy; the second is providing management theories like the SEVEN-S FRAMEWORK for understanding how organizations can be changed.

These techniques and theories are allowing strategists to change their approach fundamentally. Strategists used to believe the first and most important step in STRATEGIC PLANNING was to develop a consensus of the big picture and the purpose of the enterprise; followed by specifics as to STRATEGIES, TACTICS, and, finally, implementation. Many strategists are now reversing this process with what some have called the "mother's milk approach." That is, they start with a basic understanding of what the business is currently doing and then implement incremental improvements that build up to a more profitable and effective company. However the latter does not mean that the focus of strategy is narrowing. To the contrary, many of the challenges now faced by managers come from abroad and an important task for today's strategist is to incorporate the lessons learned in this new and wider arena in developing a GLOBAL PERSPECTIVE. The field continues to evolve.

The Handbook
of
Strategic Expertise

Concepts
and Techniques

Note on Definitions

In this book a business, an industry, and a company have simple but specific definitions.

A business sells products. Those products may be services, but they are always refered to as products. A business competes in an industry.

An industry is a group of businesses that make similar products and close SUBSTITUTE PRODUCTS.

A company is a firm made up of one or more businesses. The mix of businesses can provide more or less DIVERSIFICATION. Companies compete in the CAPITAL MARKETS for funds to invest in their portfolios of businesses.

The entries are alphabetized letter by letter; for example, MARKETING CERTAINTY MATRIX comes before MARKET PRICE. In case the reader has difficulty following this method of alphabetizing, the index clearly shows the order of entries in the text.

2

A

Acquisition: the purchase of a company or part thereof by another company. A company's approach to acquisition is usually defined as part of its CORPORATE STRATEGY. Companies look for ACQUISITION CANDIDATES that will increase the ECONOMIC VALUE of the company. Some strategists believe that there are five characteristics of a good ACQUISITION CANDIDATE: growing market, market leader, sufficient sales base, ROI in excess of HURDLE RATE, and strong management. These strategists evaluate candidates on such criteria as current returns, MARKET VALUE, and stock price. Other strategists believe that these criteria are old news, that there are very few companies with the five characteristics just mentioned, and that any companies with these characteristics that were for sale would be too expensive. Instead, this second group of strategists argues that a successful acquisition, if one assumes that it meets other criteria, is made by beating the ACQUISITION MARKET. They point out that acquisitions take place in a bidding market with a floor price at the PRESENT VALUE of the ongoing concern.

Furthermore, they say that this bidding market for companies is becoming a more EFFICIENT MARKET. Increasing press coverage and increasingly sophisticated intermediaries are leading to aggressive, well-informed sellers and more and more buyers. As a result, buyers are paying significant premiums over the market price of acquisitions. The strategists point to three ways of beating that market: identifying market imperfections; anticipating disequilibrium in the candidates' INDUSTRY STRUCTURE; or exploiting a distinct ability to build STRATEGIC LEVERAGE through FINANCIAL FIT, FORMULA FIT, or FUNCTIONAL FIT. In the first case, market imperfections can result in a low floor price because the owner wants to sell, has an undercapitalized business, or has a NO-FIT that is misunderstood. Market imperfections can also result in a low market price when the seller has noneconomic goals such as prestige, the buyer has special information, there is an economic downturn, or the seller's business appears to be in trouble. A buyer can get more out of an acquisition than was paid for if industry disequilibrium can be anticipated. For example, a buyer's ADJACENT EXPERIENCE may indicate the possibility of structural change in a supplier's industry, technological change in a process, PRODUCT INNOVATION, new ways of selling, the fact of undermarketing, an emerging channel, or changing buyer needs. And finally, a buyer can get more than was paid for from an acquisition that allows that buyer to build valuable BUSINESS INTERRELATIONSHIPS.

Acquisition Analysis: the process by which a company determines the needs to be met and the OPPORTUNITIES to be gained by purchasing another business or company. An ACQUISITION may provide an entrée into a new geographic region or access to new channels of distribution. In the course of the analysis, management sets criteria for evaluating ACQUISITION CANDIDATES and establishes an ACQUISITION SCREENING process.

Purchases aimed at enhancing or creating STRATEGIC LEVERAGE and ECONOMIC VALUE must be considered in the light of a company's CORPORATE STRATEGY and especially its CONCEPT OF FIT. Management's review of corporate strategy is likely to identify more possibilities for developing new forms of STRATEGIC LEVERAGE if the company has been relying on just one or even two CONCEPTS OF FIT in the past. This type of review should be ongoing both in support of the acquisition process as well as in support of new product development to the extent that the latter fits with the company's CONCEPT OF ASSEMBLY.

From this analysis the strategist can develop a list of companies or types of companies to be considered in the ACQUISITION SCREENING process as well as a set of criteria to use to screen the candidates during each step of the process.

Acquisition Candidate: a company or part of a company that is being considered for purchase by another. Usually, companies base their search for acquisition candidates on a list of needs and OPPORTUNITIES generated by their ACQUISITION ANALYSIS. Candidates are then identified and reviewed for acceptability in the process of ACQUISITION SCREENING. Sometimes, however, candidates come to the attention of an acquirer through brokers and finders or through other unanticipated sources.

One method of classifying ACQUISITION CANDIDATES is based on these two criteria: whether the candidate is an entire company or just part of a company and whether or not it is to be kept intact after the purchase.

The type of ACQUISITION CANDIDATE and its relationship to ex-

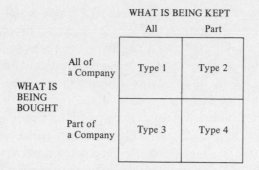

isting businesses influence the ease with which the acquirer can integrate it into its own management structure, operating systems, and CORPORATE STRATEGY. As a result, some companies have a definite preference for one type of candidate over the others.

A Type 1 candidate is a company that the acquirer plans to keep in its entirety. The acquirer may choose to reorganize the candidate to fit better with the acquirer's CONCEPT OF MANAGEMENT or to reposition the candidate's businesses within its industries. Nevertheless, the acquirer has the option of allowing the company to continue to operate much as it had been before.

A Type 2 candidate is a company of which the acquirer plans to retain only part; this type is often called a PORTFOLIO-CLEANUP candidate. With this type, the acquirer retains the candidate's businesses that fit with the company's CORPORATE STRATEGY and divests those that do not. These businesses are called NO-FITS. Calculating the cost of acquiring a PORTFOLIO-CLEANUP candidate can be difficult because the unknown revenue from selling the candidate's NO-FITS must be considered.

Type 3 and Type 4 candidates are parts of other companies rather than entire companies. To gauge the attractiveness or importance of these target businesses or divisions from the perspective of their parents, acquirers sometimes construct a GROWTH/SHARE MATRIX or a PENETRATION CHART for the parent. Targets which are clearly NO-FITS from the parent's perspective may be available at an attractive price. However, a Type 4 candidate is also a PORTFOLIO CLEAN-UP candidate and brings with it the added uncertainty of unknown revenues from future divestitures.

Type 3 candidates can vary widely in terms of the changes necessary to integrate them into the new parent. Divisions which operated independently may continue to do so under a new parent whereas those which relied heavily on an old parent will place greater demands on the new parent as well.

Depending on the size and complexity of the Type 4 candidate, the acquirer may plan to divest an entire business, to dispose of some plants, or simply to discontinue low-return products. These plans often resemble FIX PLANS.

Many other characteristics of ACQUISITION CANDIDATES can be used to classify them. The method just described is one which gives some insight into the difficulty of integrating a new acquisition and the uncertainties connected with later divestments. Another scheme for classifying candidates is based on whether the products sold and the markets targeted by the acquisition would represent a departure from the acquiring company's current activities. MARKETING CERTAINTY MATRICES are often used for this type of classification. This classification method also provides insight into the challenge posed by the integration of the candidate into the company's current portfolio of businesses.

Acquisition Screening: the process of identifying and evaluating businesses which are to be considered for purchase. The objective is to generate a short list of ACQUISITION CANDIDATES and to rank them according to ECONOMIC VALUE. ECONOMIC VALUE is a function of the cost of the ACQUISITION and the expected return once the candidate has been effectively integrated into the company. Both factors are measured and compared during the screening process.

It is often difficult to determine what characteristics or criteria should be used to screen candidates because there is no single set of screening criteria that is relevant to all companies. Therefore, a strategist must formulate screening criteria to suit the CORPORATE STRATEGY of each company (particularly the CONCEPT OF FIT). The criteria must allow the company to measure the expected cost of the acquisition, including the cost of integrating and improving the acquired company, and the return the company can expect to generate from the acquisition.

A company whose CORPORATE STRATEGY is based on diversifying into related businesses and integrating them into a tightly managed organization is likely to have more specific criteria than a company comprised of a portfolio of unrelated businesses. Calculating the expected return for a related acquisition is also likely to be more complex. A related acquisition is more likely to affect the profitability of the company's other businesses, and so the impact of the performance of the entire company must be evaluated to determine the candidate's contribution to ECONOMIC VALUE. Conceptually, the expected return can be divided into the return the candidate currently earns and the net effect on that return of effectively integrating the acquisition with the company. For example, take the case of a company that manufactures and sells building supplies. It is considering the acquisition of a regional company which manufactures a new building supply product and is earning a 10 percent return on sales. The acquirer has excess sales force capacity and expects to improve the candidate's 10 percent return by eliminating the cost of its sales force. The acquirer's nationwide sales force is also expected to increase the distribution of the candidate's product and thereby increase CAPACITY UTILIZATION and develop ECONOMIES OF SCALE. Therefore, the acquirer should adjust the return the candidate currently earns to take into account the potential for creating STRATEGIC LEVERAGE.

Most companies have a screening process that implicitly or explicitly involves four steps. As the process moves from step one through step four, the criteria and the analysis become more complex, and the number of candidates under consideration is reduced. The obvious first step is to generate a list of candidates. The company can do this in a variety of ways: by contacting finders and brokers, by generating lists of companies with a given SIC CODE and of a specific size, and even by using the DELPHI METHOD. At this point, most companies also screen for current return, using combinations of such measures as MARKET SHARE, sales growth, return on sales, RETURN ON INVESTMENT, and asset turnover.

In step two the list is whittled down, eliminating companies which would require too large an outlay or which would be too big to absorb. Initial criteria for screening the cost of the acquisition usually include a sales volume and the size of the asset base, on the assumption that candidates above a certain size would be too expensive to acquire. In addition, many companies do not consider acquiring companies that are bigger than they are because of the difficulty of absorbing a large candidate. Many companies apply rules of thumb regarding the size of the ACQUISITION CANDIDATE. For example, one company may eliminate ACQUISITION CANDIDATES over one-twentieth its size. In step two of the process, most companies take a closer look at the COMPETITIVE FORCES in the industries in which each candidate competes in order to get an idea of the potential returns in those industries and the candidate's COMPETITIVE PO-

SITION. Companies also begin to consider changes in operations or strategy they would make to position the candidate differently after an acquisition.

The third step is a much tighter screen that reduces the list to a small number of finalists. During this step the criteria for screening the cost of the acquisition usually require an assessment of the FAIR MARKET VALUE of the ACQUISITION CANDIDATE and a sense of whether the candidate would be available at that price. Using the industry and competitive information collected in step two, the company then estimates the expected future returns of each candidate on the basis of current returns and anticipated changes in the way the candidate operates or positions itself.

Finally, the fourth step is an in-depth analysis to determine the relative attractiveness of the finalists considering both the cost of the acquisition and the expected future returns for each candidate. Estimates of the cost of each candidate are refined and reflect the optimal financial deal or financing arrangements available for each remaining candidate. Estimates of expected future returns are scrutinized one last time to identify key ASSUMPTIONS and the critical areas of uncertainty for each candidate. Once the expected return and the cost of acquisition for each candidate are compared, the relative rank of each candidate can be determined in terms of contribution to ECONOMIC VALUE.

Adjacent Experience: familiarity and INSIGHT into competing in a particular industry gained indirectly, often through participation in related industries, contact with relevant customer groups, or exposure to similar operating systems and distribution channels. A company is often considered to be a likely entrant into an industry when it has a significant amount of ADJACENT EXPERIENCE. Such experience often allows the company to lower the cost or risk of ENTRY. It may also be the basis for creating STRATEGIC LEVERAGE and increasing returns after ENTRY.

ADL Matrix: another name for the STRATEGIC CONDITION MATRIX, developed by the Arthur D. Little Company. The LIFE CYCLE MATRIX is also a version of the approach identified with Arthur D. Little.

Affordable Growth: *see* SUSTAINABLE GROWTH.

Alliance: *see* COALITION.

Alternative Cost: *see* OPPORTUNITY COST.

Alternative Plan: a second or substitute framework (or STRATEGIC PLAN) for carrying out a STRATEGY. ALTERNATIVE PLANS are considered in order to evaluate the tactical options available to a business.

Ancillary Products: products that are used or consumed jointly with another product. Many services such as repairs and installation are ancillary products. Ancillary products may or may not be COMPLEMENTARY PRODUCTS.

Some businesses derive COMPETITIVE ADVANTAGE by expanding their COMPETITIVE SCOPE to include ancillary products. Other businesses find it advantageous to CHERRY-PICK among the ancillary products and not offer the basic product.

Assumption: a supposition about the future that is the basis for a planned action. ASSUMPTIONS may range from explicit estimates of quantifiable phenomena, such as national economic growth, to vaguely articulated notions about the dynamics of an industry. These ASSUMPTIONS are important to strategists in two ways. First, they are the foundation for FORECASTS of future events and the SCENARIOS built around these FORECASTS.

Second, ASSUMPTIONS play an important role in analyzing the behavior of a business or a company. Strategists ask what ASSUMPTIONS the management must be making about its business and industry that would explain its behavior. Often these ASSUMPTIONS reflect examples of CONVENTIONAL WISDOM, such as the belief that a product is a COMMODITY and cannot be differentiated or that buyers in the industry are not susceptible to TRADING-UP.

It is important for strategists to consider the ASSUMPTIONS of their own managers as well as those of their competitors. Challenging the ASSUMPTIONS held by one's own managers can be the key to changing their behavior. Recognizing the ASSUMPTIONS that competitors are making can be crucial to anticipating their future actions.

Average Cost Pricing: determining the amount to be charged for a particular product by distributing the expenses incurred while producing a line of products. Many strategists worry about this practice in their own businesses because they feel that it can both cover up OPPORTUNITIES and make the business vulnerable to THREATS. Take, for example, a business that has an average cost per product of $8 for a line of three products, A, B, and C. The company prices the whole line at $10 to earn an average return on sales of 20 percent.

A COST ANALYSIS of each product may reveal costs of $7, $8, and $9 and margins of 30, 20, and 10 percent respectively for products A, B, and C. In this situation, the business may be missing opportunities to cut back on the lower-margin product C and to increase sales of the higher-margin product A. In a more extreme case, the AVERAGE COST PRICING method may even hide unprofitable products. The business may also be vulnerable to a competitor who chooses to focus on product A by underpricing it and taking only a 25 percent margin. Without changing its PRODUCT MIX or its PRICING POLICY, the business will be unable to match the competitor's prices without reducing its overall return on sales.

On the other hand, AVERAGE COST PRICING can be used deliberately to create a CROSS SUBSIDY. The higher margins on some products can compensate for lower margins on others for a company that is developing a full product line in its efforts to build MARKET SHARE.

B

Backward Integration: *see* VERTICAL INTEGRATION.

Bad Competitor: *see* GOOD COMPETITOR.

BCG Matrix: another name for the GROWTH/SHARE MATRIX developed by the Boston Consulting Group. Many other BUBBLE CHARTS are derivatives of the BCG MATRIX.

Beta: a measure of the tendency of the return on a security to move in parallel with the return on the stock market as a whole. BETA (β) is derived by REGRESSION ANALYSIS of past variations in the return of the individual security relative to the movement of the stock market as a whole or to the movement of an index such as the Standard & Poor's 500. The volatility in the return on a security associated with the volatility of the stock market as a whole is called SYSTEMATIC RISK. A stock with a BETA of 1.0 tends to rise and fall as the Standard & Poor's 500 index rises and falls. Therefore, a stock with a BETA of 1.0 has the same level of SYSTEMATIC RISK as the market as a whole. Stocks with BETAS greater than 1.0 are sensitive to market changes. They tend to rise and fall by a greater percentage than the market and have a high level of SYSTEMATIC RISK. Conversely, stocks with BETAS less than 1.0 have a low level of SYSTEMATIC RISK and are less sensitive to market changes.

BETA is an important element of the CAPITAL ASSET PRICING MODEL (CAPM), a theory which explains how investors value securities. It can be used to derive the COST OF EQUITY for a company.

Blind Spot: the inability of a business to perceive a salient aspect of its environment. BLIND SPOTS can arise because management accepts CONVENTIONAL WISDOM, because it does not receive adequate information, or because its attention and responsibility for key aspects of the business are divided.

In the first case, an ASSUMPTION that a product can be sold only in one type of outlet, that a product is a COMMODITY and BRAND IDENTIFICATION is impossible, or that the process for producing the product cannot be automated may cause management to discount potential competitors or to ignore a rival's moves. In the second case, MEASUREMENT SYSTEMS may not provide timely or detailed enough information to alert management to changes in competitors' activities. For example, some companies have inadequate systems for tracking MARKET SHARE. If a particular product under attack is part of a broad line, the MEASUREMENT SYSTEM may not single it out for attention. If the system provides only total sales by product on a national level, the company may be vulnerable to a market-by-market attack. The aggressor can then achieve a strong position in smaller or isolated markets while minimizing the effect on the overall sales of the competitor. By the time the competitor notices all this, the battle is well along on many fronts.

Finally, its ORGANIZATIONAL STRUCTURE may hamper a business when it is devising or implementing a response to changes in an industry. For example, the separation of quality control and production management responsibilities within some businesses has blunted their response to foreign competitors with innovative products.

Because BLIND SPOTS, no matter how they arise, make a business vulnerable, strategists are interested in identifying them in their competitors. A competitor's BLIND SPOT allows a company to take action aimed at improving its COMPETITIVE POSITION while minimizing the risk that the competitor will retaliate.

Blocking Position: an OPERATING POLICY, product market, business, or COALITION that can be used to obstruct or hinder a competitor or otherwise protect against THREATS. For example, a BUSINESS UNIT might let it be known that R & D has a new technology ready to respond to a competitor's increase in PRODUCT QUALITY. A business might carry a full line of products or enter a geographic area to obstruct strategic beachheads. Or a company might compete in a given business because it discourages a MULTIPOINT COMPETITOR with a profitable competing business.

Book Value: the worth of an asset as it is stated in a company's accounting records; that is, the original cost of the asset minus the accumulated depreciation. The BOOK VALUE of an asset is determined by accounting conventions and may not be at all related to the value of that asset to the company or to a potential buyer. The SUPPLY and DEMAND for the asset and the REPLACEMENT VALUE of that asset are more likely to be reflected in its MARKET PRICE.

The BOOK VALUE of a company is often calculated by adding up the BOOK VALUE of all that company's assets minus its current liabilities and long-term debt. The MARKET-TO-BOOK RATIO is used to compare the MARKET VALUE of a company with the BOOK VALUE.

Bottlenecks: *see* CRITICAL PATH METHOD.

Bottom-up Planning: an approach to STRATEGIC PLANNING that gives responsibility for formulating STRATEGIC PLANS to individuals at the "bottom" of the ORGANIZATIONAL HIERARCHY. The idea behind BOTTOM-UP PLANNING is that the managers who are most familiar with the businesses and who will be charged with implementing the plans should formulate them.

Strategists who favor this approach usually employ a PLANNING PROCESS that begins with a meeting between the corporate manager and the line managers of each division. In that meeting, the corporate staff outlines what is expected of the division in broad general terms. The staff encourages the division to consider the FIVE COMPETITIVE FORCES which drive its businesses as well as the activities of their competitors when devising a STRATEGY. After that meeting, the line managers are left to identify those parts of the division which face the same constellation of competitors, suppliers, buyers, and substitutes and then to develop a COMPETITIVE STRATEGY for each of these BUSINESS UNITS. The corporate staff provides no further direction and helps only if asked. Top management's involvement is usually limited to reviewing the plans. A corporate planning staff may be used to facilitate that review process.

Strategists who do not favor the BOTTOM-UP approach argue that the line managers may be too close to their own businesses to spot the THREATS and OPPORTUNITIES emerging for the industry as a whole. For example, line managers often see their competitors as the line managers of companies making competing products. They assume that these competitors are pursuing the same objectives that they are and making their decisions on the basis of the same information. If these competitors were viewed as parts of a corporation with a different set of OBJECTIVES and a different decision-making process, the line managers might make different and more accurate predictions about their competitors' behavior. Furthermore, critics argue that good information does not flow naturally upward in an organization and that it takes explicit INTEGRATING SYSTEMS to overcome the tendencies of managers to guard information and to inform the top selectively about what's going on at the bottom. Finally, critics argue that unless higher-level management intervenes, the sum of the BOTTOM-UP PLANS is more likely to be a book of meaningless reports than an agenda for future actions.

OPPORTUNITY-BASED PLANNING is a modified BOTTOM-UP approach, and TOP-DOWN PLANNING is the opposite.

Brand Extension: a new product marketed under the BRAND NAME of a current product in order to exploit the brand image associated with the current product.

Introducing a new product as a BRAND EXTENSION rather than as a new brand requires only incremental advertising in contrast to the effort and high cost of establishing a new BRAND. BRAND EXTENSION also reduces the cost of failure that results from the fact that advertising expenditures on failed products have no salvage value. For example, the $40 million that was spent to promote the failed Real brand of cigarettes is an irretrievable loss. At least in a BRAND EXTENSION, some of that money would have been spent on further awareness of the original brand name. However, if a new product fails as a BRAND EXTENSION, that failure may damage the original brand identity.

Some brand identities are very narrow and offer little possibility for BRAND EXTENSION whereas others are more transferable. Some strategists use a narrow identity to provide an especially high ENTRY

BARRIER. For example, consumers can ask for Charmin by name and get what they asked for. The same cannot be said for Scott. In the same way, the introduction of other flavors of diet soda under the Tab name would make it more difficult to ask for a Tab and may lower the MOBILITY BARRIERS Coca-Cola has built around its diet cola.

A product line extension is occasionally defined more narrowly than a BRAND EXTENSION to include only new forms or shapes of the original product. However, the distinction can be subtle. For example, the addition of Chapstick with sun protection to the Chapstick line of lip balms is probably a product line extension. But what about the addition of Quencher nail polish to the line of Quencher lipsticks? The nail polish is also a line extension if the Quencher franchise is positioned to cover a full line of cosmetics. On the other hand, Woolite Rug Shampoo is probably a BRAND EXTENSION, as is Alka-Seltzer Cold Medicine. That is because both of these attempt to extend the coverage of the original BRAND IDENTITY to include a new type of product.

Brand Identification: the use of a word, mark, symbol, or design to identify a product and to distinguish the products of one company from those of another.

Strategists use BRAND IDENTIFICATION to create and maintain their buyers' loyalty to their company's products with the promise of their product's continuing UTILITY. This tactic contributes to profitability because it can reduce both RIVALRY and BUYER POWER in an industry. Brand identification can diminish RIVALRY by stabilizing MARKET SHARES and reducing PRICE COMPETITION, and it can also decrease BUYER POWER by lowering PRICE SENSITIVITY and creating PULL THROUGH. For example, all aspirin is chemically identical. One might expect that aspirin manufacturers would compete on price and that buyers would purchase on the basis of price. However, Bayer Aspirin has created a brand image of high PRODUCT QUALITY and persuaded buyers to pay premium prices over other products despite the fact that there are no actual PRODUCT DIFFERENCES.

There are three types of brand names: corporate/family brands, individual brands, and private label brands. Corporate/Family Brands identify the product with the name of the company or division of the company that produces the product, such as Johnson & Johnson's Baby Shampoo or Buick Oldsmobile. Individual brands identify the product with a specific name that is neither the company's name nor that of a division, such as Tide detergent, which is made by Procter & Gamble. Private label brands identify the product with the name of the distributor or retailer rather than the manufacturer, such as the Sears Coffee Pot, which is sold by Sears but made by West Bend Industries.

A brand name can also be categorized as a regional, national, or international brand name, depending on the geographic scope of the markets in which it is promoted. Some companies promote the same product under different brand names in different locations, a practice called using multiple brand names. Language differences in international markets can make multiple brand names necessary. For example, the NOVA, a domestic car, could not be effectively marketed under that brand name in Spanish-speaking countries, where it meant "no go."

Some strategists use BRAND EXTENSIONS to take advantage of ECONOMIES OF SCALE in building BRAND IDENTIFICATION. Other strategists use COMPETING BRANDS to build MOBILITY BARRIERS.

Break-even Analysis: a method for determining the additional sales that must be generated by an investment to leave a company at least as profitable as it would have been without the investment. BREAK-EVEN ANALYSIS is used to assess the risk involved in making an investment in areas including advertising, promotion, new equipment, and R&D by focusing attention on the probability of achieving the break-even sales level. The basic tenet of BREAK-EVEN ANALYSIS— that a risky investment is one with a high probability of not breaking even—seems fairly obvious, but the exercise of carrying out the analysis is often revealing. Break-even analysis highlights four aspects of the investment decision: FIXED COSTS, VARIABLE COSTS, price, and unit sales. The analysis compares the total costs, fixed and variable, of producing and selling at each level of unit sales with the revenues generated at a given price for each level. Take, for an example, a business that is thinking of investing $100 to make a new product that will cost $.50 per unit to produce and that the business hopes to sell at $1.00 per unit. Management can plot the total costs incurred and the revenues generated at each level of unit sales on a graph like that on the following page.

Total cost is equal to the fixed cost plus the variable costs times the number of units [Fixed costs + (variable costs × units)]. Total revenues are equal to the price times the number of units (price × units). For this investment the break-even volume is at 200 units, the

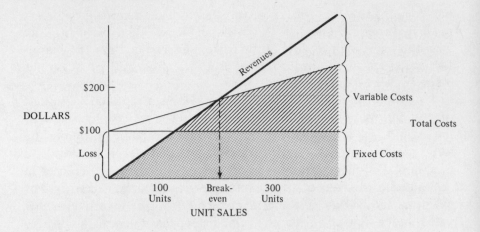

point at which the total-cost line and the revenue line cross. That is, at a volume of 200 units, the total costs [$100 + (200 × $.05)] equal the total revenues (200 × $1.00).

With unit sales below the 200-unit level, total costs exceed revenues, resulting in a loss; and with unit sales above the 200-unit level, each additional unit sold generates profit for the company. The relationship between the four factors can be expressed as an equation:

$$\text{Break-even units} = \frac{\text{fixed costs}}{\text{price} - \text{variable cost}}$$

In the preceding example, costs and price were assumed to be fixed, and the equation was solved to determine the number of units. As the following examples show, given values for any three of the variables, the fourth variable's value can be determined. Suppose, for example, management was quite certain that 100 units could be sold and wanted to know what price would have to be charged at least to break even. That price would have to cover the $100 in FIXED COSTS and $50 in VARIABLE COSTS. Dividing the total costs by the number of units ($150/100 units) gives a price of at least $1.50. Or suppose that management knew it could sell 300 units at $.50 each and that the FIXED COSTS would be $100, how much could it spend on VARIABLE COSTS and still break even? The total sales would be 300 units × $.50, which equals $150. Total sales of $150 minus $100 in FIXED COSTS leaves $50 to spend in VARIABLE COSTS for 300 units, which equals $.16 per unit.

Although the algebra of BREAK-EVEN ANALYSIS is not very complex, determining what the relevant costs are can be difficult. In general, the FIXED COSTS include outlays for plant and equipment, research and development, advertising committees, and sales force personnel. The variable costs include labor, materials, maintenance, energy, and sales force bonuses. Given management's estimates of fixed and variable costs, different combinations of units and prices will yield a set of break evens.

When one is assessing the probability of achieving a break-even sales level, comparing the sales level to the market size and computing the implied MARKET SHARE are key steps. That MARKET SHARE can also be compared with the MARKET SHARE of competitors. The resulting implied RELATIVE MARKET SHARE can prove a helpful indicator of how realistic the break-even level is as a sales goal. Further analysis might involve estimating the MARKET GROWTH to see how much of the business's sale gain would come from an increase in the size of the market and how much would have to come from its competitors.

If management feels that there is a low probability that sales will exceed the break-even level, then this analysis indicates that the investment decision is quite risky. The RISK can be lowered by changing the investment proposal to reduce the break-even sales level or to enhance the probability of reaching it. If management feels that there is a high probability that sales will exceed the break-even level, then the investment decision is not very risky. In that case, management should proceed to estimate how high the returns will be at different sales levels and to compare this estimate with the REQUIRED RETURN on incremental investments in that business.

Bubble Chart: a matrix with businesses displayed as circles, resembling a picture of bubbles. A circle is drawn for each business in a company or an industry in proportion to a characteristic such as sales, assets, or MARKET SHARE. These characteristics usually provide an indication of competitive strength based on resources or market position. A standard matrix allows the strategist to compare businesses along two dimensions; displaying the businesses as circles incorporates a third. Two bubble charts encountered often are the GROWTH/SHARE MATRIX and the COMPETITOR MAP.

Build Plan: a scheme for increasing the sales of a business faster than its market is growing. A BUILD PLAN is one of three types of plans distinguished by the underlying MARKET SHARE target. The OB-

JECTIVE of a BUILD PLAN is to increase market share, the objective
of a HOLD PLAN is to maintain it, and the objective of a HARVEST
PLAN is to reduce it.

A BUILD PLAN identifies the sources of the increased sales, specifies the TACTICS for generating those sales, and quantifies the expected
costs and returns involved.

There are three basic sources of increased sales: (1) current buyers seeking new uses, (2) new buyers seeking new uses, and (3) new
buyers seeking current uses. A BUILD PLAN may specify TACTICS that
are designed to stimulate sales from one or more of the three sources.
In many industries, the BUYER GROUP in each cell is different, and
so are the TACTICS required to reach that BUYER GROUP. For this reason, many strategists believe that a BUILD PLAN should identify, for
each cell, the size of the market, the sales increase sought, and the
tactics to be employed.

In order to gain share in a BUYER GROUP, a business must improve its ability to satisfy DEMAND relative to its competitors or—as
some strategists put it—"give the customer either more product or
more information." In this instance, the term "customer" refers to
intermediate users as well as to END USERS. Examples of tactics that
would give them "more product" include offering the same product
at a lower price or offering a product with more UTILITY at the same
price. One measure of the relative attractiveness and utility of a
product to customers is its PRICE-TO-PERFORMANCE RATIO. Calculation of this ratio can be helpful in assessing and devising tactics for
offering the customer "more product." Tactics for giving the customer "more information" include both inducements to the end user
such as advertising, branding, or improving service to "PULL (the
product) THROUGH" the distribution channels, and incentives for the
distributors or intermediate buyers such as increasing channel margins or sales support to "PUSH (the product) THROUGH."

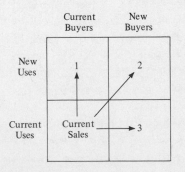

The costs of the increased investment, additional expenditures, or reduced short-term margins implicit in a BUILD PLAN must be calculated and compared to the anticipated returns to determine the impact of a BUILD PLAN on the business's long-term profitability.

The costs of a BUILD PLAN are going to depend on the INDUSTRY STRUCTURE in which the business competes. The expected return will be affected by any changes in the INDUSTRY STRUCTURE resulting from the BUILD PLAN and competitors' reactions. Each STRUCTURAL FACTOR in an industry must be considered to determine its effect on costs and expected returns. The outlook for MARKET GROWTH is a key determinant of the costs, expected returns, and likely competitive responses to a BUILD PLAN. For example, in a high-growth market, increasing share will often require increasing the CAPACITY of the business to meet DEMAND faster than competitors. This increase in CAPACITY may require additional FIXED CAPITAL and will surely require more WORKING CAPITAL. This is especially true in periods of high INFLATION. The plan may also require an increase in advertising and selling expenses. The ratio of marketing expenses to sales may increase, too, at least in the short term. Fast-growing markets tend to involve new buyers. To the extent that these buyers are either using the product differently or are experimenting with the product, there can be a significant amount of uncertainty about how the product will evolve. Changes in the product's design and the processes involved in making it can be very expensive for the competitor who has invested in having a large RELATIVE MARKET SHARE.

A BUILD PLAN in a slow-growth market may also be expensive but for different reasons. Consider, for example, a business with a 25 percent MARKET SHARE that is trying to gain a 35 percent share of a market that is expected to continue growing at 5 percent. All its competitors appear to be committed to maintaining current market share. Therefore, the business can increase share only if one or more of its competitors fails to execute an effective HOLD PLAN. The business will have to spend to overcome its competitors' efforts to hold their share. If another competitor adopts a BUILD PLAN, it could be all the more expensive. For this reason, analyzing competitors is especially important in formulating a BUILD PLAN in a low-growth market. PENETRATION CHARTS for competitors are often useful and can help a business to determine which competitors would be least able to defend their share. On the basis of that analysis, the business could direct its BUILD PLAN to take share from its most vulnerable competitors.

A plan to build share in a stagnant or declining market can be even more expensive because any increase in sales means an absolute decrease in competitor's sales. RIVALRY can be expected to be high as competitors attempt to defend their positions. However, it is possible that other competitors may be formulating HARVEST PLANS that would reduce the cost of gaining share.

A BUILD PLAN can carry with it RISKS and rewards regardless of the expected growth rate of a market. Some strategists advocate BUILD PLANS in high-growth industries. They believe that it is worth absorbing the cost of UNCERTAINTY REDUCTION and building ahead of sales in order to be able to establish their commitment early and discourage ENTRY. Other strategists, especially those with the funds to buy the effects of any pioneers' CUMULATIVE EXPERIENCE, prefer to wait for a significant amount of UNCERTAINTY REDUCTION and then usurp the leadership position. Other strategists will point out that BUILD PLANS in low- or no-growth markets offer good opportunities to push competitors to HARVEST or EXIT and then to build share at their expense. These strategists often use MARKET SIGNALS to tell their competitors that they intend to be the DOMINANT FIRM in the industry from here on in order to discourage competitors from investing in their businesses and in the hope of encouraging them to HARVEST. In any case, a successful BUILD PLAN must be consistent with the goals and capabilities of the business behind it and based on a realistic assessment of competitors.

Bundling: the practice of joining two or more products in such a way that they are sold to buyers only as a package at a PACKAGE PRICE. Products may be bundled because they are COMPLEMENTARY PRODUCTS, because additional services may make an unfamiliar product more attractive to a buyer, and because the seller may be able to command a higher price for the "bundle" than for the products sold separately. All buyers do not have the same needs, so there is a tendency to unbundle products over time in response to buyer pressure and the emergence of competitors who supply the bundled products separately. Bundling is a pervasive and, at times, unquestioned practice in many industries with a strong influence on INDUSTRY STRUCTURE.

Business Cycle: alternating periods of expansion and contraction in overall economic activity. The term is misleading because it refers to business when, in fact, the aggregate economic activity of government, businesses, and individual consumers is involved. It is also misleading because the word "cycle" implies regularity when, in fact, BUSINESS CYCLES tend to vary in duration and intensity. The term "economic fluctuation" is often used as a more descriptive alternative.

The level of aggregate economic activity changes for a number of reasons. These include the effects of seasonal variations in DEMAND and production; political events, such as war; long-term trends, such as increases in employment or production that may be tied to population growth; and "long-wave" changes that run for about 50 years and may be caused by new technologies.

In a developed industrial society, the major stream of buying that precedes and usually sets off changes in overall economic activity is the spending for durable CONSUMER GOODS or durable INDUSTRIAL GOODS. Although to some degree their purchase is discretionary and postponable, durable goods have a fairly definite "lifespan." As a result, the DEMAND for durable goods tends to occur in successive spurts at almost the same levels of aggregate economic activity. When a point of recurring DEMAND is reached, business activity in general starts an upswing. During the interim periods when DEMAND for durable goods is low, general business activity drops off.

Although no two BUSINESS CYCLES are exactly alike, they follow a pattern of moving through phases of prosperity, recession, and recovery. (A depression is an extended, deep recession.) These phases have meaning only when considered in relation to one another. The determination of which phase the economy is in depends on relative measurements such as the number of unemployed, amount of production, volume of consumption, and price levels. These, in turn, are interdependent and depend on the spending decisions of one or more of the four primary types of spenders: consumers, business, government, and foreign buyers. In general, if the spenders buy less, business activity declines; if they buy more, business activity rises.

The prosperity phase of a BUSINESS CYCLE is characterized by conditions that prevail when most production facilities are in use and when employment, output, wages, and profits are at correspondingly high levels. Prosperity will continue until the DEMAND for both INDUSTRIAL GOODS and CONSUMER GOODS begins to slow down because of a decrease in spending by any of the four major types of spenders.

In a recessionary phase, businesses cut down on their orders to produce as DEMAND for INDUSTRIAL GOODS and CONSUMER GOODS falls off. As a result, production is curtailed, and unemployment rises. As unemployment increases, incomes become smaller, the DE-MAND for all types of goods decreases, and a contraction of business activity spreads through the economy. Furthermore, pessimism induced by the slowdown may dampen investment in new ventures and lead to cutbacks in inventories.

The recovery phase is the upswing of a BUSINESS CYCLE. Once the progress of a recession has been slowed and finally stopped by the need to replace outworn durable goods, government intervention, or other influences, the momentum that was generated in the recession reverses to spur recovery. As activity increases, optimism, instead of pessimism, begins to sway business decisions. Orders run ahead of sales, and installment buying increases. Idle capacity is put into use, employment increases, and wages rise. Recovery may continue to the point of reaching a period of general prosperity, or it may revert to a recession.

Industries are affected in varying degrees and in different ways by the business cycle. For example, sales of replacement parts are likely to rise during a recessionary phase in contrast to those of machine tools. When formulating a CORPORATE STRATEGY, a strategist may try to balance the effect of the BUSINESS CYCLE on the businesses in the company's portfolio. In some companies, the CONCEPT OF FIT rests on this balance.

Business/Industry Attractiveness Matrix: one of a number of charts used to analyze the businesses in a company's portfolio in order to facilitate RESOURCE ALLOCATION. Businesses are arranged on the matrix based on the businesses' strengths and the attractiveness of their industry. One composite of factors is used to access each business's strength, and another composite of factors is used to measure the attractiveness of each business's industry. The businesses are then plotted on the matrix based on whether they have low, medium, or high strength and on the basis of whether they are in industries with a low, medium, or high degree of attractiveness.

The matrix recommends a BUILD PLAN, a HOLD PLAN, or a HARVEST PLAN on the basis of the cells in which a given business falls. The recommendations reflect a balance between the two assumptions underlying the BUSINESS/INDUSTRY ATTRACTIVENESS MATRIX. The first is that a company should compete in an attractive industry and withdraw from an unattractive one. The second is that a company should invest in a business with a strong competitive position and harvest a business with a weak competitive position. The process of assessing

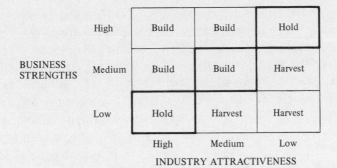

	High	Build	Build	Hold
BUSINESS STRENGTHS	Medium	Build	Build	Harvest
	Low	Hold	Harvest	Harvest
		High	Medium	Low

INDUSTRY ATTRACTIVENESS

business strengths and industry attractiveness is basic to the matrix. The factors used to determine each business's strength vary, but they usually include MARKET SHARE, RELATIVE MARKET SHARE, MARKET GROWTH, buyer group growth rate, RETURN ON INVESTMENT, COST STRUCTURE, RELATIVE COSTS, PRODUCT DIFFERENTIATION, process technology, and management skills. The factors used to determine the attractiveness of the industry usually include the size and growth of industry sales volume, the degree of PRICE COMPETITION, industry CONCENTRATION and SHARE BALANCE, industry profitability, the role of technology in the industry, and the effect of possible changes in sociopolitical factors that impact the industry. Usually, these two sets of factors are weighed subjectively to produce two rankings for each business. However, sometimes numerical scoring systems are used to weight each factor, and quantitative indexes of strength and attractiveness are computed.

In addition to specific recommendations for the individual businesses, the matrix highlights the need to balance the cash-flow needs of the businesses in a company's portfolio. A BUILD PLAY is expected to absorb cash, and a HARVEST PLAY is expected to generate it. Balancing BUILD PLANS with HARVEST PLANS reduces the need to look to outside sources to finance growth.

The BUSINESS/INDUSTRY ATTRACTIVENESS MATRIX is very similar to the GROWTH/SHARE MATRIX and the LIFE CYCLE PORTFOLIO MATRIX except that it tends to be less quantifiable than the former and more inclusive than the latter.

Business Interrelationships: complementary aspects of the activities, management, or competitive environment among BUSINESS UNITS within a company. INTERRELATIONSHIPS fall into three categories: tangible, intangible, and competitor INTERRELATIONSHIPS. Tangible

INTERRELATIONSHIPS arise largely from LINKAGES in the areas of production, marketing, procurement, technology, and infrastructure that lead to FUNCTIONAL FIT. Intangible INTERRELATIONSHIPS are related to skills, KNOW-HOW, or experience in implementing a particular GENERIC STRATEGY that leads to FORMULA FIT. Competitor INTERRELATIONSHIPS arise when the competitive activities of one BUSINESS UNIT allow for a BLOCKING POSITION or otherwise affect a MULTI-POINT COMPETITOR. This situation can make it more complicated to carry out the COMPETITIVE STRATEGY of that business but also creates more levers that can be used to influence the behavior of a competitor.

Identifying INTERRELATIONSHIPS and setting coordinated GOALS and policies joining BUSINESS UNITS is the essence of devising a HORIZONTAL STRATEGY. The VALUE CHAIN is the basic tool used to identify the underlying INTERRELATIONSHIPS.

Exploiting interrelationships can lead to COMPETITIVE ADVANTAGES not otherwise available to the businesses involved. However, those advantages must outweigh the POLICY COSTS of coordination, compromise, and inflexibility.

Business Plan: a STRATEGIC PLAN for a BUSINESS UNIT. Such a plan is usually derived from the COMPETITIVE STRATEGY for that BUSINESS UNIT and details the TACTICS, RESOURCE ALLOCATION, programs, and projects necessary to carry out the strategy. A BUSINESS PLAN is often described as a BUILD PLAN, a HOLD PLAN, or a HARVEST PLAN depending on its GOALS for growth and RELATIVE MARKET SHARE.

Business Policy: the field of study and endeavor that deals with the functions and responsibilities of top management, especially as they relate to determining the purpose of the organization. As it has evolved, the field has dealt with the pivotal role of setting corporate GOALS and associated POLICY VARIABLES such as CORPORATE CULTURE, RESOURCE ALLOCATION, and the assessment of corporate STRENGTHS AND WEAKNESSES.

Some strategists see STRATEGIC MANAGEMENT as one aspect of BUSINESS POLICY. Other strategists see BUSINESS POLICY as being limited to the formulation of policy vis-à-vis administrative processes and problems and see STRATEGIC MANAGEMENT as the much broader field encompassing the former.

Business Profiling: the process of gathering data about a business, its INDUSTRY STRUCTURE, and its competitors. Most strategists believe that BUSINESS PROFILING should be a continuous process in which a company adds to its base of information about its businesses and industries each year. Other strategists prefer to do zero-based profiling that involves almost starting from scratch in order to gain a fresh perspective on a business.

BUSINESS PROFILING is often the first step in a PLANNING PROCESS. A business profile includes an analysis of the COMPETITIVE FORCES which shape the industry. The analysis is updated to reflect the emergence of new entrants to the industry, the development of new SUBSTITUTE PRODUCTS, and changes in the buyer and supplier groups. Competitors are monitored for signs of new strategies, of enhanced capabilities, and of changes in the ASSUMPTIONS and GOALS underlying their strategies. The data necessary to compile such a picture is not easily obtained. The strategist must comb published sources for industry and competitor information and develop a system for collecting field data from sources such as the company's sales force, distributors, suppliers, and security analysts.

STRATEGIC INTELLIGENCE GRIDS are sometimes used for BUSINESS PROFILING.

Business Segment: a subdivision of an industry which has some unique characteristics that are meaningful for strategic purposes. The characteristics are usually significant because they influence the strength of one of the five COMPETITIVE FORCES that shape the industry. For example, a business segment may represent a part of the industry which services a particular group of customers, which supplies a particular type of product, or which uses common technology. Some companies are subdivided organizationally or for planning purposes into BUSINESS UNITS which coincide with BUSINESS SEGMENTS.

Business Systems Analysis: the process of identifying the VALUE ADDED CHAIN of a business and comparing it with those of its competitors. The term "business system" refers to the combination of value added stages and cost elements that are the basis of COST ANALYSIS.

Strategists who use BUSINESS SYSTEMS ANALYSIS feel that it provides a framework for comparing one business's strategy with those of its competitors. This comparison is intended to reveal the business's COMPETITIVE ADVANTAGES or weaknesses by indicating if and where each competitor is achieving an opportunity or investment cost advantage.

Some strategists use BUSINESS SYSTEMS ANALYSIS as a basis for formulating a COMPETITIVE STRATEGY. Having identified the VALUE ADDED CHAINS of a business and of its competitors, the strategist can assess their competitive positions by asking a series of questions such as, How is this business adding value at this stage? How are its competitors doing it? How will EVOLUTIONARY PROCESSES in the industry affect the way value is added at this stage? How is the way value is added at this stage linked to other value added stages for both this business and its competitors? What other ways are there to add value at this stage? Are any of those alternative ways better?

BUSINESS SYSTEMS ANALYSIS is often used in developing a GAME GRID for an industry.

Business Unit: the basic entity for which a COMPETITIVE STRATEGY is developed. A BUSINESS UNIT is a PLANNING HIERARCHY entity that may or may not correspond to an entity in the ORGANIZATIONAL HIERARCHY. In some companies BUSINESS UNITS correspond directly with divisions or departments or product lines while in other companies BUSINESS UNITS may be made up of pieces of divisions, departments, or groups of product lines. Although there may not be an operating manager in charge of a BUSINESS UNIT, there is usually a manager with planning responsibility for the unit.

BUSINESS UNITS usually comprise the lowest level in the strategic PLANNING HIERARCHY. The SEGMENTATION of the company into BUSINESS UNITS is a key step in the PLANNING PROCESS. A BUSINESS UNIT should be defined to include as many activities as possible that affect the business's COMPETITIVE ADVANTAGE.

A BUSINESS UNIT usually includes the R&D, manufacturing, marketing, and other functions for one or more related products. The products can be related in terms of BUYER GROUPS; for example, a company may put all its hospital supply products in one BUSINESS UNIT. Or the products could be related in terms of their use; for example, a company might want to put all its dermatological products in one BUSINESS UNIT. Or the products could be related in terms of how they are made; for example, a company might want to put all its bent metal products in one BUSINESS UNIT. Any combination of the preceding or other dimensions has been used to distinguish BUSINESS UNITS. However, since the purpose of the BUSINESS UNIT is to act as an entity for which a strategy can be developed, the key to determining BUSINESS UNITS is to make sure that the COMPETITIVE FORCES for that entity can be identified. That is, a BUSINESS UNIT should have meaningfully identifiable competitors, suppliers, buyers, and substitutes.

A BUSINESS UNIT is often referred to as a STRATEGIC BUSINESS UNIT or SBU.

Buyer Concentration: the number and size of buyers that purchase an industry's products. High BUYER CONCENTRATION occurs when there are relatively few buyers for an industry's products. In theory, if all other factors are held constant, the higher the BUYER CONCENTRATION, the higher the BUYER POWER. If each seller must sell most of its output to a few buyers, each buyer's volume is very important to the seller and increases the BUYER'S POWER. If one of a few buyers puts pressure on the seller, the seller has few, if any, other places to sell its products. In addition, if there are few buyers, they can easily keep an eye on each other to deter anyone from paying a higher price. An industry with a single buyer is called a MONOPSONY. BUYER VOLUME is a related term which refers to the concentration of an individual business's customers.

In many industries, buyers try to preserve their concentration by multiple sourcing and otherwise maintaining a large number of suppliers. In general, strategists try to reduce BUYER CONCENTRATION or at least try to prevent their buyers from becoming more concentrated. BUYER SELECTION is an important approach to the problem. In addition, strategists usually attempt to offset BUYER POWER due to BUYER CONCENTRATION by building PRODUCT DIFFERENCES, BRAND IDENTITIES, or SWITCHING COSTS.

Buyer Group: a set of potential customers with similar needs which uses or perceives the value of a product in the same way. The unfilled needs of each BUYER GROUP can be served in a number of ways. For example, the need for shelter can be served with houses, apartments, mobile homes, or condominiums. A business can contribute to satisfying that need by acting as a builder, architect, engineer, plumber, electrician, supplier of heating and air conditioning equipment, producer of building materials, or industrial distributor. The unfilled needs of the BUYER GROUPS that comprise a market may be widely recognized or latent, in which case buyers may need to be educated to recognize the UTILITY of the product and its value.

The process of MARKET SEGMENTATION is often used to isolate specific BUYER GROUPS for a given product. The characteristics of the group affect product design and distribution, as well as marketing and sales tactics. For example, the buyer's need for BUYER INFORMATION about the product, as well as the relative importance of PRODUCT DIFFERENCES and brand identity, will vary greatly by BUYER GROUP. Customers in a BUYER GROUP may often be alike in the purchasing DECISION-MAKING PROCESS that characterizes the way they buy.

BUYER CONCENTRATION is a key determinant of BUYER POWER, one of the five COMPETITIVE FORCES which determine the attractiveness and profitability of an industry. Differences among the BUYER GROUPS served by an industry also influence the dynamics of other COMPETITIVE FORCES. The degree of RIVALRY will almost always vary as different competitors push harder for some BUYER GROUPS and not for others. In the market for computers, for example, some companies specialize in selling to financial organizations such as banks and insurance companies; others, to scientific laboratories; and still others cover the full range of applications. The threat of SUBSTITUTE PRODUCTS will also differ from one group to another. An aluminum producer, for instance, faces competition from tin plate, glass, and plastic in the container market and faces competition from lumber, asphalt shingles, brick, corrugated steel sheet, and reinforced plastic in the construction market. The likelihood of facing new entrants can differ for each BUYER GROUP as well.

The types of characteristics which distinguish BUYER GROUPS for CONSUMER GOODS tend to be different from those which distinguish BUYER GROUPS for INDUSTRIAL GOODS. As a result, the factors considered in the course of a BUYER GROUP ANALYSIS differ as well. The needs of BUYER GROUPS of CONSUMER GOODS typically differ along demographic lines. That is, consumers may have different needs depending on their age, income level, level of education, marital status, or place of residence. They may also have psychographically determined needs based on their life-styles and their attitudes toward their homes, their families, their work, and the societies in which they live. For example, buyers of new cars are likely to have different income levels from those of buyers of used cars. Buyers of Cadillacs and the buyers of expensive sports cars are likely to have psychographic differences.

BUYER GROUPS of INDUSTRIAL GOODS tend to differ in four ways: the physical characteristics of the product and the technology required to meet the needs of the BUYER GROUP, the geographic location of the BUYER GROUP, the way the BUYER GROUP uses the product, and the BUYER GROUP'S DECISION-MAKING PROCESS.

The first discriminant of BUYER GROUPS, product technology, is important because, within any broad market, segments exist for specific kinds of products manufactured with different technologies. The market for containers, for example, includes BUYER GROUPS interested in plastic containers, both bags and rigid; glass containers, both disposable and reusable; metal containers, both cans and drums; cardboard containers, both corrugated and single ply; wooden containers; and many other products designed to hold, transport, and store goods.

The second discriminant, geographic location, accounts for differences among BUYER GROUPS to the extent that geography tends to be a surrogate for such things as the government regulatory environment, cultural biases, value systems, and transportation problems. These combine to affect competition in a geographic area. For example, in the case of trucks, different national governments have widely ranging standards relating to safety requirements, import and export restrictions, fuel economy, and pollution. Other products can be shipped economically only a limited distance from their point of manufacture because of their weight or size relative to their value. In such cases, the choice of a plant site restricts the business to those BUYER GROUPS that are located nearby.

For many INDUSTRIAL GOODS, there is a great deal of variation in the way each BUYER GROUP uses the product. The range of use is typically much broader for INDUSTRIAL GOODS than CONSUMER GOODS. Potential BUYER GROUPS for nylon fiber, for example, include manufacturers of such products as stockings, tires, rope, fishing rods, and carpets. The manufacturing processes for these products are completely different from one another as are the channels through which they are sold.

The last discriminant is purchasing behavior. Purchasing behavior can depend on a number of factors. For example, large companies typically have more formal DECISION-MAKING PROCESSES than smaller ones. Also, differences in the DECISION-MAKING PROCESS may exist within a single organization depending on the nature of the purchase. Some companies make important distinctions among materials that go into the products they make, supplies consumed in the manufacturing process, capital equipment, and such services as advertising and security. DECISION-MAKING UNITS may also be different. Different individuals may be responsible for buying different types of products; and concerns about PRODUCT QUALITY, delivery, and price may vary widely within an organization as a result.

BUYER GROUPS in an industry will be different at different stages in the product's VALUE ADDED CHAIN, ranging from raw materials to finished product. For example, a business could participate in the market for corrugated cardboard boxes by selling timber, wood pulp, rolls of corrugated materials, or finished boxes printed with the customer's label. There are buyers at each stage in the chain whose function is to purchase materials at different stages of completion and carry the process forward one or more stages in the chain. The choice of where to sell in the VALUE ADDED CHAIN is an important aspect of BUYER SELECTION, and many strategists elect to participate in more than one stage in a given industry.

Buyer Group Analysis: the process of identifying and comparing current and potential customers in order to find sets of buyers with similar needs and uses for a product. BUYER GROUP ANALYSIS helps a strategist to assess BUYER POWER in an industry and to discern what type of product can be expected to satisfy each portion of a market.

A typical approach to buyer analysis is presented as follows. The first step is to segregate BUYER GROUPS on the basis of one key variable such as the customer's concern with price or quality, physical specifications for the product, or distribution channels.

Then BUYER GROUPS are arrayed across the top of a chart in order of their size. In the example that follows, buyer group 1 is the largest, accounting for 50 percent of potential sales. The strategist then assesses each on the basis of additional STRUCTURAL FACTORS.

Some strategists develop indices for each relevant factor on the basis of the factor's influence on BUYER POWER and then calculate a weighted index for the whole market. If, in the previous example, the values of 1, 2, 3 were assigned to low, medium, and high ratings for price sensitivity, then an index weighted by BUYER GROUP size would be calculated like this: $(.50 \times 2) + (.25 \times 1) + (.15 \times 3) + (.10 \times 1) = 1.80$. Similar indices could be calculated for all relevant factors. A rank ordering of the factors by their weighted index

RATING BY BUYER GROUP

RELEVANT FACTOR	Buyer Group 1 50%	Buyer Group 2 25%	Buyer Group 3 15%	Buyer Group 4 10%
Buyer's Purchasing Incentives	Utility	Image	Price	Quality
Buyer Concentration	M	M	H	L
Buyer Volume	L	H	M	M
Buyer Information	M	M	H	M
Potential to Backward Integrate	L	H	L	L
Buyer Utility Sensitivity	H	M	L	M
Buyer Image Sensitivity	M	H	L	M
Buyer Price Sensitivity	M	L	H	L
Buyer Risk Aversion	M	H	M	M
Buyer Switching Costs	H	M	L	M
Price Relative to Buyer's Cost Structure	H	L	H	L
Buyer's Profitability	M	H	M	H

would give a profile of the overall market. BUYER GROUP GRIDS are visual presentations of specific combinations of relevant factors.

BUYER GROUP ANALYSIS is important for both CONSUMER GOODS and INDUSTRIAL GOODS. Some strategists feel the analysis is especially important for INDUSTRIAL GOODS managers who frequently deal with multiple BUYER GROUPS, often involving multiple distribution channels. For example, an electrical equipment business could sell to as many as fifty BUYER GROUPS through a number of channels. BUYER GROUP ANALYSIS is often the foundation for BUYER SELECTION because a business's profitability can depend significantly on which BUYER GROUP it serves.

A less typical, but increasingly popular approach to BUYER GROUP ANALYSIS is to build VALUE CHAINS for either a BUYER GROUP or, in the case of INDUSTRIAL GOODS with few END USERS, for specific buyers. The value chains are then analyzed to understand how BUYER VALUE can be achieved.

Buyer Group Grid: a BUBBLE CHART that is used to compare sets of current and potential customers called BUYER GROUPS. A circle for each BUYER GROUP is positioned on a grid on the basis of two factors such as SWITCHING COSTS and buyer profitability. As in the example

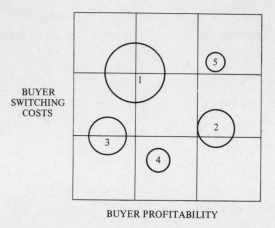

BUYER
SWITCHING
COSTS

BUYER PROFITABILITY

above, the circles are often drawn in proportion to sales made by the industry to each group.

Arrows are sometimes added to indicate how BUYER GROUPS may be moving. Also, strategists often indicate on the grid which BUYER GROUPS they and their competitors are targeting.

Sometimes BUYER GROUP GRIDS are raised to a higher level of abstraction by combining relevant factors to develop a measure of BUYER POWER, using indicators of a BUYER GROUP's intrinsic power, its ability to play one seller off against another, and its inclination to exercise its power. BUYER GROUP GRIDS can be visual supplements for BUYER GROUP ANALYSIS.

Buyer Information: the knowledge a BUYER GROUP has of a supplier's product in terms of the way it is made and used, the DEMAND and INDUSTRY CAPACITY for it, the supplier's UNIT COSTS, actual MARKET PRICES, and the VALUE being offered buyers in other MARKET SEGMENTS. Strategists are concerned with BUYER INFORMATION because of its impact on the intrinsic BUYER POWER of the group. Buyers that have high levels of information tend to have greater bargaining leverage than buyers with little information. Information places the buyer in a better position to evaluate and counter the manufacturer's claims and to demand the most favorable price.

Over time, buyers tend to gain information about a product through repeat purchasing and other means and to become more powerful. In many industries, strategists face the choice of thwarting this tendency or taking advantage of it. For example, for some products, it makes sense to try to maintain either the sense of mystique, technological complexity, or product risk in order to keep the buyer ill-informed and dependent on the manufacturer. For other products, UNCERTAINTY REDUCTION makes sense. For example, in do-it-yourself repair-type products, it makes sense to inform the user so that greater numbers of consumers will feel they can buy and use the products without RISK.

An increase in BUYER INFORMATION is sometimes called buyer learning and can lead to SEGMENT SPILLOVER.

Buyer Learning: *see* BUYER INFORMATION.

Buyer Needs: *see* BUYER GROUP.

Buyer Power: the ability of a given BUYER GROUP to reduce the returns that can be earned in selling to that BUYER GROUP. BUYER POWER is one of the COMPETITIVE FORCES that determine the level and variance of RETURN ON INVESTMENT in an industry. Powerful buyers can affect ROI both by reducing return on sales in an industry and by increasing the amount of investment required by an industry to generate those sales. Buyers do this by bargaining down prices, by requiring high levels of service, by holding ready inventory, and so on. The power of buyers in an industry is a function of three phenomena. The phenomena are the intrinsic clout of the buyers, the opportunity to play off sellers against one another, and the PRICE SENSITIVITY of the buyers. Therefore, BUYER POWER in an industry can be determined by analyzing the STRUCTURAL FACTORS in the industry in terms of their effect on each of the three phenomena.

The STRUCTURAL FACTORS that affect intrinsic buyer clout are BUYER CONCENTRATION, BUYER VOLUME, BUYER INFORMATION, and the threat of backward integration. For example, if buyers are more concentrated than sellers, each buyer is more important to each seller than vice versa. Many buyers deliberately maintain this relationship by multiple sourcing and by balancing their purchasing among sellers. Also, a buyer that purchases a large percentage of a seller's volume has potential bargaining power over the seller. In addition, the more the buyer knows about a product, the more potential intrinsic clout the buyer has. For example, a buyer that knows exactly what the DEMAND for a product is, what the COST STRUCTURE of the product is, and exactly what UTILITY is required to satisfy its needs is in a good position to bargain. Such buyers can calculate exactly what they should be paying for the product and are not likely to pay for extra features. For this reason, many sellers have TACTICS for minimizing BUYER INFORMATION. However, no matter how much intrinsic clout a buyer may have, its effect on industry profitability will be less if there is no opportunity to play off sellers against one another or if the buyer is not price sensitive.

The STRUCTURAL FACTORS that affect a buyer's opportunity to play off sellers against one another are BUYER CONCENTRATION, the availability of SUBSTITUTE PRODUCTS, PRODUCT DIFFERENCES, BRAND IDENTIFICATION, SWITCHING COSTS, and the potential for PULL THROUGH. As in the case of intrinsic clout, if there are more sellers than there are buyers, the buyers have a greater opportunity to play off sellers against one another than if there were fewer sellers. If there are SUBSTITUTE PRODUCTS available, then buyers can play the sellers off against the substitute. In some industries, buyers are continually looking for substitutes as part of such programs as VALUE ANALYSIS. However, if the seller is able to build PRODUCT DIFFERENCES, BRAND IDENTIFICATION, or SWITCHING COSTS and to increase buyer loyalty, it is more difficult for the buyer to move to another seller. Even if the seller is unable to build buyer loyalty with those tactics, it may use PULL THROUGH to tie the buyer to it by reaching the END USER. Nevertheless, even buyers with a lot of clout and many sellers they can play off against one another may not affect industry profitability if they are not price-sensitive enough to exercise their power.

PRICE SENSITIVITY depends on such STRUCTURAL FACTORS as price relative to COST STRUCTURE, product impact on quality or performance, buyer profits, and the decision makers' incentives. For example, if the price of the product is one of the largest elements in the buyer's COST STRUCTURE, then the buyer is likely to be price-sensitive. In INDUSTRIAL GOODS, buyers very often have a list of products about which they are very price-sensitive and for which their purchasing policy encourages a tough stance. In CONSUMER GOODS, individuals are obviously more price-sensitive about purchases that are significant elements in their cost of living. However, if the buyer expects the UTILITY or BRAND IDENTITY of the product to have a significant effect on the buyer's business or life style, the buyer is less likely to be price-sensitive. In the case of INDUSTRIAL GOODS, for example, buyers will be less price-sensitive about a product that could hold up entire assembly lines if it failed. In the case of CONSUMER GOODS, an individual will be less price-sensitive about a product that could negatively affect them, such as a perfume that could smell wrong. Also, in general, the wealthier the buyer, the less price-sensitive he is likely to be. This seems to be true both of wealthy individuals and profitable companies despite the adage about how they got that way. No matter how price-sensitive the buyer should be if the individual decision maker's incentives do not involve prices, that buyer may not be price-sensitive. However, if the DECISION-MAKING UNIT's incentives are such that the individuals involved are encouraged to keep prices down, the buyer will be price-sensitive. For this reason, many sellers develop tactics to change either the DECISION-MAKING UNIT or the incentives to reduce the buyer's PRICE SENSITIVITY.

The degree of BUYER POWER in an industry depends on the interaction between these three phenomena. The STRUCTURAL FACTORS change over time, and businesses can both adapt their strategies to offset the current level of BUYER POWER in an industry and work to reduce it over time.

Buyer Preference Chart: a chart used to display market research data by arraying the UTILITY preferences of the BUYER GROUPS for a particular product. In the illustration that follows, buyer preferences for beer are analyzed along two dimensions, taste and color.

The percentages in the cells indicate the proportion of buyers that prefer that particular combination of taste and color over the others. The chart can also be used as the basis for a BUBBLE CHART on which circles are positioned for competing brands with each circle drawn in proportion to MARKET SHARE.

Strategists often compare changes in BUYER PREFERENCE CHARTS over time. If, for example, the lower right-hand cell had shown only 5 percent three years ago, this might indicate that buyers are increas-

ingly interested in the dark color. Strategists also compare charts over time to note changes in competing products.

Buyer Segmentation: the process of dividing the buyers for a product into BUYER GROUPS which share common characteristics and needs. For any product there exists a hierarchy of markets ranging from a macro market, including all buyers who might ever be able to purchase the product, to a selected group of buyers who have specified characteristics.

For example, a brewer's macro market might include every man, woman, and child in the world. A first pass at segmentation might be to take out those buyers who are below drinking age and a second might be to take out those who do not live in the United States. At this point, the market could be further segmented into a number of different BUYER GROUPS on the basis of sex, age, and income.

Market research departments often specialize in segmenting markets along a comprehensive range of specifications in order to isolate specific BUYER GROUPS. The VALUE CHAIN and the DECISION-MAKING PROCESS of each BUYER GROUP is studied in order to understand the group's level of PRICE SENSITIVITY, interest in PRODUCT DIFFERENTIATION, reaction to BRAND IDENTIFICATION, and potential for SWITCHING COSTS, as well as how much of the product the BUYER GROUP purchases. The strategist is interested in BUYER SEGMENTATION because BUYER SELECTION is an important element of COMPETITIVE STRATEGY. For example, in the brewing industry, market re-

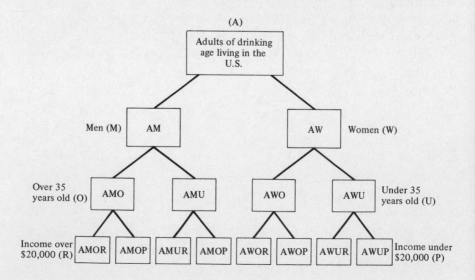

search has shown that 10 percent of the total population drinks 60 percent of the beer consumed in the United States. Some brewers have developed a strategy of appealing to as wide a group of beer drinkers as possible; others have developed a TARGETED STRATEGY directed at very specific BUYER GROUPS.

Buyer Selection: the choice of which BUYER GROUPS in an industry a business should target. Criteria for BUYER SELECTION may be determined by the company's CONCEPT OF FIT, or each business may select its buyers as part of its COMPETITIVE STRATEGY.

All other things being equal, target BUYER GROUPS are selected on the basis of the return that can be earned in selling to them. Aside from selecting on the basis of the size and growth rate of potential sales to a given BUYER GROUP, return will be maximized by selling to BUYER GROUPS with the least BUYER POWER. Minimizing the amount of BUYER POWER a business faces can make it less expensive to build MARKET SHARE and can increase the business's margins or lower its required investment. Although some businesses begin the BUYER SELECTION process with an assessment of the business's STRENGTHS AND WEAKNESSES, it is often more creative to start with the process of BUYER SEGMENTATION and buyer VALUE CHAINS.

Once the strategist has segmented the market into BUYER GROUPS and rank-ordered the groups in terms of BUYER POWER, the next step is to assess the cost of serving each group. The cost of serving BUYER GROUPS can vary because of such factors as the order size, required lead time, stability of order flow and size, and the degree of customization or modification required. Also affecting the cost of serving buyers are such distribution and marketing factors as direct-versus-distributor sales, shipping costs, and sales-force costs. Therefore, the questions regarding how much it costs to serve a BUYER GROUP can be quite specific. For example, how much capital is needed to build plants and warehouses? What types and amounts of technical support are needed? What are the requirements for establishing and maintaining an after-sales product service system? How important is advertising, and how much of it will be needed? The important task for the strategist is to determine what it would cost for a given business to serve members of a given BUYER GROUP and to compare that with an estimate of what it would cost for competitors to serve them. This analysis can then be expanded to include the potential for building in PRODUCT DIFFERENCES and SWITCHING COSTS. When selecting buyers, the strategist wants to pick ones that promise high profitability and that can be protected by MOBILITY BARRIERS from competitors.

Some strategists feel that BUYER GROUPS are inherently good or bad based on the criteria of sales volume and BUYER POWER. Other strategists feel that good buyers can be made by tactics such as building SWITCHING COSTS, controlling BUYER INFORMATION, and changing the DECISION-MAKING UNIT.

Buyer Transaction Cycle: a theory describing changes over time in the way a product is sold and in the way the buyer perceives the purchase. Accordingly, a product can be sold in four basic ways: as a stand-alone COMMODITY, as a stand-alone differentiated product, or as a COMMODITY or differentiated product that is BUNDLED as part of a system. In some industries, there are BUYER GROUPS for all four types of transactions. In other industries, where there is a transaction shift going on, either buyer groups are experiencing changes in preference or a competitor is encouraging change. Transaction shifts can result in a predominance of one transaction type over the others. Transaction shifts are often followed by periods of stability until a buyer or competitor initiates change again.

Proponents of the BUYER TRANSACTION CYCLE see it as a useful way to think about BUYER VALUE and to avoid the CONVENTIONAL WISDOM that the current transaction figure is the only way. These strategists often use a matrix of the four transaction types to illustrate the transition shifts over time and the implications for SEGMENT SCOPE.

SEGMENT SPILLOVER can often result in transaction shifts.

Buyer Value: the extent to which a product lowers the buyer's costs or increases the buyer's performance relative to competitive products. In the case of an INDUSTRIAL GOOD, a buyer will value a product that lowers its costs either directly with a lower price or indirectly by allowing the buyer to be otherwise more efficient. A buyer of an INDUSTRIAL GOOD will also value a product that increases its performance by increasing the value of that INDUSTRIAL GOOD to its customer. This may be true even if the product is sold at a high relative price. For example, the purchase of an enclosure that is well-designed may allow the buyer to sell the INDUSTRIAL GOOD at a price that more than offsets the price differential.

In the case of the buyer of a CONSUMER GOOD, the value of a lower price is obvious, as may be the value of saving time and, therefore, lowering costs. The value of increasing the performance of the CONSUMER GOOD can be explained in terms of increasing the buyer's satisfaction or enjoyment.

Some strategists say that only a differentiated product can provide BUYER VALUE. Other strategists say that a COST LEADERSHIP STRATEGY often provides BUYER VALUE through lower costs, and a DIFFERENTIATION STRATEGY usually provides BUYER VALUE through increased performance.

BUYER VALUE is sometimes called ECONOMIC VALUE to the customer, and it is abbreviated as EVC.

Buyer Volume: refers to the percentage of a given business's sales made to a specific customer or group of customers. The percentage of a business's immediate customers which accounts for 50 percent of its sales is a frequently used benchmark for comparing and analyzing businesses.

BUYER VOLUME is important to strategists because of its effect on BUYER POWER. A business which is dependent on a small number of customers is likely to have little leverage in its dealings with them. The term BUYER CONCENTRATION refers to the relationship between buyers and suppliers for an industry as a whole. Strategists usually look for changes in BUYER VOLUME over time for a given business when developing COMPETITIVE STRATEGIES and look for trends in BUYER VOLUME across businesses in their portfolios when developing a CORPORATE STRATEGY. A comparison across businesses might show that most of the company's sales are coming from businesses with high BUYER VOLUME whereas most of its profits are coming from businesses with low BUYER VOLUME. This type of analysis is often a good place to start in developing a FIX PLAN or a HARVEST PLAN. Many strategists find that the 80:20 rule seems to apply to BUYER VOLUME. That is, for many businesses, 80 percent of the sales are made to 20 percent of the buyers.

By-Product: *see* JOINT PRODUCT.

C

Cannibalization: occurs when one of a company's products draws sales away from another of its products. For example, the introduction of an instant coffee might cannibalize the sales of the company's regular coffee, and the introduction of a freeze-dried coffee might cannibalize the sales of both the company's instant and regular coffee. In analyzing the impact of CANNIBALIZATION, strategists must weigh how much their own sales will be cannibalized against how many additional sales will be taken from their competitor's businesses. Depending on the incremental sales and the profitability of the products involved, CANNIBALIZATION may be acceptable and even desirable.

The ability of a business to respond in kind to a competitor's new product introduction may be compromised by its fear of cannibalizing existing products. Faced with MIXED MOTIVES of defending existing products and parrying a competitor's moves, the business may respond slowly or tentatively. This situation can be exploited by a competitor. ENHANCEMENT is the opposite of CANNIBALIZATION and a welcome side effect when introducing and positioning a new product.

Capacity: the total output that a business can produce with a given configuration of plant and equipment during a particular period of time. Different industries have different conventions for measuring CAPACITY, based on the units in which CAPACITY is measured and the time frame to which it refers. For example, in one industry, CAPACITY may be measured in bushels per day; in another, it may be measured in 12-ounce equivalent bottles per year; and in a third, it may be measured in dollars per month. A dollar capacity figure is usually equal to the sales dollar value of the physical capacity of the business under the business's standard cost assumptions and is called standard capacity. Capacity measurements also differ in the ASSUMPTIONS made about the rate at which equipment is used, the number of shifts working, or the amount of overtime incorporated. Capacity measurements can be very complicated when a plant makes a wide range of products.

CAPACITY may be increased by scheduling workers to work more hours, by building more plants, or by buying more equipment. In those cases, CAPACITY is sometimes measured as greater than 100 percent. CAPACITY can also be increased by becoming more efficient. For example, as businesses gain CUMULATIVE EXPERIENCE, they may be able to increase their output without necessarily increasing the amount of labor or plant or equipment required. Industry capacity is the sum of the capacities of the businesses competing in the industry. Reliable measures of industry capacity can be hard to construct because of variations in how each business calculates its CAPACITY.

The decision to expand CAPACITY is a critical strategic decision. This is especially true in industries in which capacity additions are made in large increments and involve major investments in plant and equipment. An analysis of a business's CAPACITY UTILIZATION, as well as industry capacity utilization, is a common starting point when making an investment decision. In addition, strategists will compare a competitor's CAPACITY SHARE to its MARKET SHARE in order to anticipate its moves and reactions.

Capacity Share: the proportion of total industry capacity attributable to a given business. This is usually calculated by taking the ratio of that business's standard capacity to total industry capacity. In a simplified example, if Business A is capable of producing $200 million worth of roofing shingles and the entire industry is capable of producing $800 million worth, then Business A has a capacity share of 25 percent. Although the arithmetic involved in calculating CAPACITY SHARE is very simple, the difficulty (just as with calculating MARKET SHARE) is in deciding what to use for a numerator and what to use as a denominator. The capacity figures used for each business in the industry must be stated in the same units and measured over the same time period. They must be based on similar assumptions about the rate at which equipment is used, the number of shifts working, and the amount of overtime included.

Capacity Utilization: the percentage of its productive potential being employed by a business. A business's CAPACITY UTILIZATION is usually expressed as its total output in a given period divided by its total CAPACITY during the same period. For example, a business that only produces $800,000 worth of widgets even though it has the CAPACITY to produce $1 million worth is said to be running at 80 percent CAPACITY or to have CAPACITY UTILIZATION of 80 percent.

CAPACITY UTILIZATION can be calculated for a single plant, a business, or an entire industry. In the latter case, INDUSTRY CAPACITY UTILIZATION would equal the total sales of all the competitors in an industry divided by the total CAPACITY of all the competitors in the industry. Strategists often consider an industry's COMPETITOR CONFIGURATION to be unstable when any one competitor's CAPACITY UTILIZATION is out of line with total industry's CAPACITY UTILIZATION. Differences in the relationship between MARKET SHARE and CAPACITY SHARE among competitors is another indicator of instability.

Capital Asset Pricing Model (CAPM):   a theory which explains how investors value a company's securities and which provides a basis for determining the expected return required for individual securities. The theory is based on ASSUMPTIONS about investors' attitudes toward risk, about the nature of the RISK associated with individual securities, and about the impact of portfolio DIVERSIFICATION.

The difference between CAPM and other models of portfolio DIVERSIFICATION is that CAPM uses stock market prices to value a security's RISK versus its return instead of using subjective measures of the investor's attitudes toward RISK. CAPM assumes that investors are RISK-AVERSE and that investors can and will reduce risk by holding a diversified portfolio. Therefore, they need to be compensated for the riskiness of a given security only to the extent that that security adds to the riskiness of their whole portfolio.

CAPM identifies two types of risk borne by the holder of a security. RISK that is associated with events unique to a firm and independent of other firms is called UNSYSTEMATIC RISK and can be eliminated through DIVERSIFICATION. The RISK that is associated with the movement of other securities and related to the market as a whole is called SYSTEMATIC RISK and cannot be eliminated by DIVERSIFICATION. Because UNSYSTEMATIC RISK can be eliminated simply by holding a large portfolio, investors are rewarded with higher returns only for bearing systematic or market-related risk according to the CAPM model. This implies that investors who put all their money in one stock are exposed to both SYSTEMATIC and UNSYSTEMATIC RISK but are only rewarded for exposure to the systematic risk.

The model provides a method for determining the REQUIRED RETURN for a particular security using BETA, an indicator of the correlation of the security's return with that of the market as a whole, as a measure of its SYSTEMATIC RISK. According to CAPM:

$$\text{Expected return on risky security} = \text{assured return on a risk-free security} + \text{risk premium}$$

The risk premium is a function of BETA and can be calculated using the following formula.

$$\text{Risk premium} = \text{beta} \left(\text{market return} - \text{assured return on risk-free investment} \right)$$

Estimates of the assured return on a risk-free investment are based on current yields of U.S. government securities. Estimates of the market return are developed by using current yields on corporate fixed income securities and adjusting for the historical spread between returns in the bond market and returns in the stock market. BETA, CAPM's measure of the relative degree of SYSTEMATIC RISK, is derived by REGRESSION ANALYSIS of past variation in the returns on the individual security relative to the movement of the stock market as a whole or to the movement of an index such as the Standard & Poor's 500. An investment with a BETA of greater than 1.0 has more SYSTEMATIC RISK than the market, and an investment with a BETA of less than 1.0 has less SYSTEMATIC RISK than the market. Using these inputs, the return required by investors on a particular common stock can be determined. This return required by investors is equivalent to the COST OF EQUITY capital to the firm.

Using CAPM's estimate of the COST OF EQUITY, a manager can calculate the overall COST OF CAPITAL for the firm, which provides an important benchmark for evaluating investment alternatives. The manager of a diversified firm can use CAPM to estimate the COST OF EQUITY associated with each line of business by looking at the COST OF EQUITY for other businesses in the same industries. These estimates can then be used to set individual investment criteria and performance measures for each line of business.

Also, the CAPM can be extended to isolate that portion of the risk premium which is attributable to FINANCIAL LEVERAGE and allows the financial manager to evaluate the impact of a change in financial structure on the firm's COST OF EQUITY and overall COST OF CAPITAL.

Capital Intensity: generally refers to the amount of plant and equipment or other fixed assets required in a business relative to the amount of labor or relative to the business's total output. Businesses which must maintain large investments in research and development, in raw materials, or in work in process inventory are sometimes considered capital intensive, too. Some strategists find the ratio of investment in a business to that business's sales to be a good indicator of CAPITAL INTENSITY. Others prefer to use the ratio of FIXED TO VALUE ADDED because of the relationship between that ratio and RIVALRY in an industry. CAPITAL INTENSITY can act as an ENTRY BARRIER because would-be competitors are blocked by large initial investment requirements. On the other hand, competitors in the industry are likely to be very tenacious in defense of their large investments in plant and equipment, research programs, or raw material stocks.

Capital Market: a financial market for securities. Financial markets serve two related functions. First, they provide a marketplace for bringing together those who wish to invest their money with those who are looking for money. Second, financial markets provide a pricing mechanism for valuing different types of investments in different types of assets. Therefore, the CAPITAL MARKETS determine a company's COST OF CAPITAL.

Strategists address the CAPITAL MARKETS in developing a CORPORATE STRATEGY. On the one hand, the COST OF CAPITAL by the CAPITAL MARKETS is both a constraint and a benchmark for strategists faced with generating and selecting investment alternatives. The CAPITAL ASSET PRICING MODEL (CAPM) is one method of deducing the COST OF CAPITAL for a firm using information from the CAPITAL MARKETS. On the other hand, because a CORPORATE STRATEGY aims at maximizing the ECONOMIC VALUE of the company to its shareholders, the impact of a strategy on the share price of a firm is one indicator of that strategy's success.

Capital Structure: refers to the mix of securities that is used to finance a company. The securities are usually segregated into long-term debt and equities, the two most significant components of a company's CAPITAL STRUCTURE. The balance between the two is most often described in terms of the ratio of DEBT TO EQUITY. The CAPITAL STRUCTURE can be further analyzed in terms of the classes and associated characteristics of the stocks that make up the company's equity, the various bond issues that make up the company's debt, and the nature of the company's earned surplus.

In theory, in setting its CAPITAL STRUCTURE, a company can choose from countless combinations of securities. In practice, the choice is more narrow than the theory implies, but it is still a challenging problem to determine an optimal CAPITAL STRUCTURE for a given company. An optimal CAPITAL STRUCTURE is one that provides the company with the funds to create real and increasing ECONOMIC VALUE without exposing the company to too much financial risk or dilution of control.

A company's CAPITAL STRUCTURE can affect a company's returns through FINANCIAL LEVERAGE. The following simplified example (page 46) shows four CAPITAL STRUCTURES for a company that can borrow at 10 percent and must pay a 10 percent dividend.

Notice that in this first example the company's EBIT remains constant no matter what the CAPITAL STRUCTURE but that the returns available after paying dividends for reinvesting in the company change. That is, the higher the company's DEBT-TO-EQUITY RATIO, the lower the company's COST OF CAPITAL and the higher the company's returns. This happens because in this example, as is often true in practice, the after-tax cost of debt is less than the after-tax COST OF EQUITY. Therefore, the more debt relative to equity, the lower the COST OF CAPITAL, and the higher the return.

The example implies that a company can continue to increase its returns and lower its COST OF CAPITAL by adding more debt. In fact, the example implies that the optimal CAPITAL STRUCTURE is one with 100 percent debt. In practice, this is not the case because as a company adds more debt, it increases its financial risk. The financial risk rises because of the fixed charges associated with the debt. These charges amplify the effects of fluctuations in EBIT, and the company unable to meet these charges may be faced with bankruptcy or financial reorganization. The CAPITAL MARKET responds to this increased RISK by raising both the cost of debt and the COST OF EQUITY. The less simplified example (page 47) assumes that as the company adds more debt, the company becomes riskier and that both the debt holders require a higher interest rate and the shareholders require a higher return. (In this example, as in the previous example, the shareholders are taking their return in dividends.)

Notice that in this second example the COST OF CAPITAL decreases and the returns increase as more debt is added to the CAPITAL STRUCTURE until the percent of debt reaches 60 percent of the total capital. At some point between 40 percent and 60 percent debt, the COST OF CAPITAL reaches its lowest point, and the returns reach their

	Capital Structure A	Capital Structure B	Capital Structure C	Capital Structure D
	ASSUMPTIONS			
Total capital	$10,000	$10,000	$10,000	$10,000
Debt (10% interest)	0	2,000	4,000	6,000
Equity (10% dividends)	10,000	8,000	6,000	4,000
Earnings before interest and taxes	3,000	3,000	3,000	3,000
Tax rate	50%	50%	50%	50%
	CALCULATIONS			
Debt-to-equity ratio	.00	.25	.67	1.50
Earnings before interest and taxes (EBIT)	$ 3,000	$ 3,000	$ 3,000	$ 3,000
− Interest expenses	− 0	− 200	− 400	− 600
	$ 3,000	$ 2,800	$ 2,600	$ 2,400
− Taxes	($ 1,500)	($ 1,400)	($ 1,300)	($ 1,200)
After-tax earnings	$ 1,500	$ 1,400	$ 1,300	$ 1,200
− Dividends	($ 1,000)	($ 800)	($ 600)	($ 400)
"RETURNS"	$ 500	$ 600	$ 700	$ 400
After-tax cost of debt (interest)	5%	5%	5%	5%
After-tax cost of equity (dividends)	10%	10%	10%	10%
COST OF CAPITAL	10%	9%	8%	7%

	Structure A	Structure B	Structure C	Structure D
	ASSUMPTIONS			
Total capital	$10,000	$10,000	$10,000	$10,000
Debt	0	2,000	4,000	6,000
Equity	10,000	8,000	6,000	4,000
Interest expenses	0	200	480	960
Dividends	1,000	880	720	560
Earnings before interest and taxes	3,000	3,000	3,000	3,000
Tax rate	50%	50%	50%	50%
	CALCULATIONS			
Debt-to-equity ratio	.00	.25	.67	1.50
EBIT	$ 3,000	$ 3,000	$ 3,000	$ 3,000
− Interest expenses	− 0	− 200	− 480	− 960
	$ 3,000	$ 2,800	$ 2,520	$ 2,040
− Taxes	($ 2,500)	($ 2,400)	($ 1,260)	($ 1,020)
− Dividends	($ 1,000)	($ 880)	($ 720)	($ 560)
"RETURNS"	$ 500	$ 520	$ 540	$ 460
After-tax cost of debt (interest)	0	5%	6%	8%
After-tax cost of equity (dividends)	10%	11%	12%	14%
COST OF CAPITAL	10.0%	9.8%	9.6%	10.4%

highest point. That point is the optimal CAPITAL STRUCTURE under the given assumptions. When the percent of debt is increased beyond the optimal point, the capital costs go up, and returns go down.

By optimizing its CAPITAL STRUCTURE, a company can minimize its COST OF CAPITAL or increase its returns, thereby creating ECONOMIC VALUE. However, some theorists maintain that this is not possible. They would say that in the second example the COST OF EQUITY and debt would change with changes in the CAPITAL STRUCTURE so that the relationship between the company's returns and its COST OF CAPITAL remained constant. However, in practice, many strategists find that FINANCIAL LEVERAGE is an effective way to create ECONOMIC VALUE.

Carrying Costs: *see* ECONOMIC ORDER QUANTITY (EOQ).

Cash Cow: a business in a company's portfolio that contributes a significant positive CASH FLOW to the company. A CASH COW provides a company with excess cash that can be invested in other businesses, paid to the shareholders, or used to acquire new businesses. The term CASH COW was popularized as the label for a business appearing in one quadrant of the GROWTH/SHARE MATRIX.

Cash Flow: the difference between a company's or business's cash inflow and cash outflow over some period of time. CASH FLOW is not the same as net income or profits because all inflows or revenues on accounting statements are not cash, and all outflows or costs on accounting statements are not cash.

An income statement shows net income to be equal to sales (inflows) minus expenses (outflows). However, some sales could be credit, not cash; and some expenses may not require current cash outflows from the company. A common example of the latter is depreciation, which is a deduction from income but not a cash outflow. Therefore, income statements must be modified to reflect actual cash transactions in order to understand the operation's CASH FLOW.

Comparing one year's balance sheet to a previous year's gives an indication of balance sheet-related cash inflows and outflows. For example, if the balance sheet shows that debt has gone up, then this indicates a cash inflow. If the balance sheet shows that the company now owns more gross plant and equipment, this probably indicates a cash outflow. CASH FLOWS are calculated by combining the income statement and balance sheet-related inflows and outflows.

Because a company cannot survive very long without cash, it is important to understand the effects of carrying out a strategy on the CASH FLOW of a company. Some strategists use a PORTFOLIO AP-PROACH to balance the CASH FLOW requirements of their businesses. It is also important to understand the CASH FLOWS of competitors in order to estimate what kind of strategies they can afford to sustain.

Cash Flow Estimate: a calculation of the likely balance of cash inflow and outflow of a company or business over a period of time. There are a number of ways to estimate CASH FLOWS; but they all involve estimating cash inflows, estimating cash outflows, and subtracting the cash outflows from the cash inflows to get the estimated net CASH FLOW. It can be helpful to group inflows and outflows related to ongoing operations, which are obtained by modifying the income statement, separately from those related to investment and financing decisions, which are likely to be reflected on the balance sheet.

Take, for example, a company that over the past five years has had sales of $1,000, profits after taxes of $100, a capital structure that is one-third debt, and a 40 percent dividend payout policy throughout its history. Assume that the company wants to estimate its future five-year net CASH FLOWS, taking into consideration its plan to make a onetime investment of $200 next year in order to increase its sales to $1,100 for that year and each year thereafter. Assume that annual depreciation will be $20.

The first step is to estimate the flows related to operations. In this example, it simplifies the calculation to assume that the ratio of profit after taxes to sales will stay constant even after changes in interest expense or depreciation. In that case, the company can expect a profit after tax of $110 per year for a total of $550 over five years. The profit after tax is then adjusted for any noncash expenses such as depreciation, which are added back to the profit after-tax total. The resulting CASH FLOWS from operation are shown in the following chart.

The next step is to identify the cash inflows and outflows resulting from financing and investment activities. If the company continues to pay out 40 percent in dividends, it leads to an outflow of $44 per year, leaving $60 in incremental retained earnings per year. In order to maintain its DEBT-TO-EQUITY RATIO, the company can borrow $33 per year against the incremental retained earnings. The final item to be included in the estimate is the $200 investment to be made in the first year.

The final step is to combine the inflows and outflows for each

CASH FLOWS	YEAR				
	1	2	3	4	5
From operations					
Profit after tax	$110	$110	$110	$110	$110
Depreciation	20	20	20	20	20
	$130	$130	$130	$130	$130
Financing and investment					
Dividends	($ 44)	($ 44)	($ 44)	($ 44)	($ 44)
New debt	33	33	33	33	33
Investment	($200)				
	($211)	($ 11)	($ 11)	($ 11)	($ 11)
Net cash flow	($ 81)	$119	$119	$119	$119
Aggregate					$395

year and then to add the annual totals for a five-year estimate. In this example, the company has a positive estimated CASH FLOW of $395 over the five-year period.

Most strategists begin with a very simple CASH FLOW analysis like the previous example and then increase the amount of detail and accuracy to meet the requirements of the decision at hand. Often the first additional step is to look at the timing of inflows and outflows. For example, in the preceding example, though the net CASH FLOW over the five years was positive, the CASH FLOW in the first year would be negative unless the company could spread payment for its new investment over time. Further sophistication could involve calculating the PRESENT VALUE of the CASH FLOWS as well.

Regardless of the level of sophistication, to develop a meaningful CASH FLOW estimate, a strategist should use a consistent approach to INFLATION and taxes; consider WORKING CAPITAL requirements, OPPORTUNITY COSTS, and other related effects such as might be shown in a DECISION TREE; ignore SUNK COSTS; and beware of allocated overhead costs because they are very likely to represent accounting phenomena and not INCREMENTAL COSTS.

Cash Generator: a business that generates more cash from its operations than it can profitably reinvest in those operations. The positive CASH FLOW provides the parent company with funds to invest in other lines of business. An extreme example of a cash generator is a business that is LIQUIDATING its assets. Such a business generates an even greater CASH FLOW to the company than it is generating from its operations.

Strategists often try to balance their portfolios of businesses between CASH USERS and CASH GENERATORS. Some strategists use a PORTFOLIO APPROACH to analyze this balance.

CASH GENERATORS are often called CASH COWS.

Cash Trap: a business which requires a significant investment in cash to grow or, in extreme cases, to remain viable and yet offers a very low probability of ever becoming a CASH GENERATOR. Inasmuch as ECONOMIC VALUE cannot be created unless a business eventually earns a positive CASH FLOW, CASH TRAPS can have a long-term negative effect on a company's portfolio. Sometimes the term CASH TRAP is also used to describe a business that earns a positive CASH FLOW on its investment but has a very low probability of ever earning its REQUIRED RETURN. Further cash injections in such businesses are sometimes justified by the payout in prolonging or enlarging the remaining CASH FLOW. CASH TRAPS are often low–market share businesses competing in industries that have little or no MARKET GROWTH. These businesses are sometimes called DOGS.

The problem most strategists have with CASH TRAPS is that they can be hard to identify. It is often difficult to prove that a business will never be sufficiently profitable to make further investment worthwhile, and it is often emotionally difficult to reach that conclusion.

Cash User: a business that consumes more cash in its operations than it is currently generating. CASH USERS may or may not be profitable. A growing business with large inventory and working capital requirements is often a profitable cash user. Unprofitable cash users include businesses with good future prospects, such as one introducing a new product with an expensive marketing effort, as well as CASH TRAPS, businesses with little hope of generating positive cash flows or high returns in the future. Depending on the company's CORPORATE STRATEGY, the company may satisfy the cash requirements of these businesses with funds from CASH GENERATORS or with funds obtained from the CAPITAL MARKETS.

Catch-up Plan: *see* FIX PLAN.

Causes of Profitability: the combination of factors that determine a business's profitability. Some strategists identify two components of a business's profitability, POSITIONAL PROFITS and PERFORMANCE PROFITS. POSITIONAL PROFITS are attributed to the STRUCTURAL FACTORS that favor profitability in an industry or within a STRATEGIC GROUP of that industry. PERFORMANCE PROFITS are attributed to the effectiveness of the COMPETITIVE STRATEGY devised and carried out by a business.

Centralized Organization: an ORGANIZATIONAL STRUCTURE in which the power and authority to make decisions are heavily concentrated in a few individuals at the top of the ORGANIZATIONAL HIERARCHY. Centralization can allow for tight coordination and consistency in decision making because those few individuals are always involved. For a CENTRALIZED ORGANIZATION to grow and diversify, it must develop more and more effective MANAGEMENT SYSTEMS to enable the few at the top to continue to make decisions. At some point, the proliferation of systems and staff necessary to coordinate such an organization may lead to DISECONOMIES OF SCALE.

A DECENTRALIZED ORGANIZATION is the opposite of a CENTRALIZED ORGANIZATION.

Cherry Picking: selecting the best among a number of alternatives. CHERRY PICKING usually refers to the COMPETITIVE SCOPE of businesses that only compete in very attractive MARKET SEGMENTS. It can also refer to buyers that pick individual products from the lines of competing suppliers. Opportunities for CHERRY PICKING arise from PRICE UMBRELLAS, BLOCKING POSITIONS, and CROSS SUBSIDIES. BUNDLING, PACKAGE PRICE, and SWITCHING COSTS are ways to minimize CHERRY PICKING.

Coalition: A long-term cooperative undertaking among companies. COALITIONS may involve technology, licenses, supply or marketing agreements, and joint ventures. They can provide a means of attacking an industry leader or play a part in DEFENSIVE STRATEGY. Frequently, coalitions bring unequal benefits to the partners involved, so a strategist must consider carefully the impact of such cooperative activities on the COMPETITIVE POSITION of a business, especially if control of proprietary information, market position, or image is compromised.

Strategists who favor the use of coalitions indicate that they cost less than integration and are more flexible. Other strategists point out the difficulty in coordinating the responsibilities and in dividing the benefits.

Using coalitions to build SHARED EXPERIENCE is sometimes called cooperative competition. For example, competitors might form a CO-ALITION for combined production in order to reduce costs and allow the concentration of RESOURCES on aspects of the VALUE CHAIN that are central to COMPETITIVE ADVANTAGE. There is often potential for cooperative competition in markets that are small relative to MINIMUM EFFICIENT SCALE or that allow high STRATEGIC DIVERSITY.

Commodity Imperative: *see* COMMODITY/SPECIALTY MATRIX.

Commodity Product: a product sold to buyers who perceive the offerings of all competitors to be essentially the same. An industry in which competitors offered no PRODUCT DIFFERENTIATION would be an industry offering a commodity. In such an industry, participants tend to compete on the basis of price or reliability of supply. However, if one or more competitors have developed BRAND IDENTIFICATION or SWITCHING COSTS, even if there are no physical differences among the competitors' products, they are not considered commodities.

Some strategists feel that certain products are inherently commodities, and other strategists feel that a product is only a commodity until someone figures out a way to differentiate it.

Commodity/Specialty Matrix: one of a number of charts used to analyze the businesses in a company's portfolio. This matrix is often used to relate each business's COMPETITIVE STRATEGY to the importance its buyers place on PRICE and PRODUCT DIFFERENTIATION.

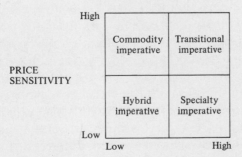

Each business can be located in one of the four cells depending on whether the buyers for that business's products are price-sensitive or not and whether or not the buyers perceive differences among the products of competitors. The position on the matrix indicates a strategic imperative that should guide the business in formulating its COMPETITIVE STRATEGY.

Businesses that are located in the upper left-hand cell are selling to price-sensitive buyers who do not perceive differences among competing products. The commodity imperative indicates that these businesses should follow a COST LEADERSHIP STRATEGY or a FOCUS STRATEGY that allows the business to be the low-cost producer in its TARGET MARKET, a particular region perhaps.

Businesses that are located in the lower right-hand cell are selling their products to buyers who are not price-sensitive and are very aware of differences among competing products. The specialty imperative indicates that those businesses should follow a DIFFERENTIATION STRATEGY or a FOCUS STRATEGY that allows the business to be the differentiated producer in its TARGET MARKET.

Businesses that are located in the upper right-hand cell are selling their products to price-sensitive buyers who are also aware of differences among competing products. The transitional imperative indicates that those businesses should follow a COST LEADERSHIP or FOCUS STRATEGY emphasizing low costs but should be very wary of new ways of differentiating that a competitor could use to induce buyers away despite a higher price.

Businesses in the lower left-hand cell are selling their products to buyers that are neither price-sensitive nor aware of differences among competing products. The hybrid imperative indicates that the business should follow a COST LEADERSHIP STRATEGY or a FOCUS STRATEGY emphasizing low costs but should be very careful to avoid PRICE COMPETITION. PRICE COMPETITION can only lower profitability for the industry and is unlikely to lead to increased profits for any one competitor unless another EXITS.

Strategists who are comfortable with using the COMMODITY/SPECIALTY MATRIX feel that it focuses attention on buyers as a key determinant of what the business's COMPETITIVE STRATEGY should be and also that the matrix gives them a picture of the different strategic imperatives for businesses in their portfolios. Strategists who are uncomfortable with the matrix feel that the imperatives obscure the process of developing a GENERIC STRATEGY. Some strategists feel that the matrix is best used without the imperatives as a simple BUBBLE

CHART to show the mix of buyers a company's businesses are selling to.

Comparative Advantage: a theory which states that on the basis of variations in the relative efficiency of countries in producing different goods, countries will benefit from specializing in the production of particular goods and trading for others. The implications of the theory are not always intuitively obvious. It implies, for example, that even a country which is absolutely more efficient in the production of two goods should specialize in the production of one and trade for the other. However, consider the parallel situation of a strategist who is also the world's fastest typist. Just as the strategist can earn more money by paying a typist and plotting strategy, so can a country benefit by concentrating its efforts and resources where it is relatively more efficient.

The goods in which a country enjoys a COMPARATIVE ADVANTAGE are determined by the fit between the production requirements of the industry and the factor endowment of the country. That fit is judged relative to other countries. Common sources of COMPARATIVE ADVANTAGE are low labor costs, low energy costs, abundant raw materials, and favorable climate and soil conditions.

Comparative Factors Profile: a chart that can be used to compare the attributes of a business with those of a competitor. Key OPERATING POLICIES or capabilities are listed along the vertical axis of the

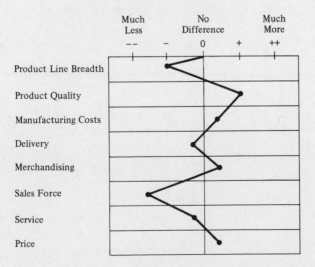

chart, and the difference from the competitor is measured along the horizontal axis. The analyst plots the nature and extent of the difference between the business and its competitor. Usually, a business is compared with its major competitor, but it can also be compared with the industry average. In the sample COMPARATIVE FACTORS PROFILE that follows, the business has similar manufacturing costs to its major competitor but has a narrower product line and higher product quality.

Strategists often analyze a set of these charts for each business in a company to identify patterns in capabilities and performance that cut across the company's portfolio. They also compare portfolios representing different time periods to determine trends in COMPETITIVE POSITION.

Competence Profile: a chart which compares the COST STRUCTURE of one business with that of another, usually a competitor. It also highlights areas in which one business enjoys ECONOMIES OF SCALE or benefits from SHARED EXPERIENCE or costs. In the simplified example that follows, a COMPETENCE PROFILE for Business A is shown next to one for its competitor, Competitor A. Business A has higher sales, but Competitor A is part of a larger company which produces and sells several related products.

Each bar represents a stage in the business's VALUE ADDED CHAIN. The width of each bar is proportional to the percentage of total costs incurred during each value added stage. The height of each bar is determined by the total expenditures of the entire company, not just the business itself, in related activities.

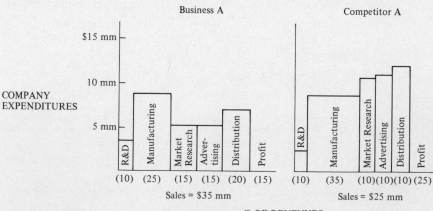

In this example, the width of the bars indicates that manufacturing costs for Business A are equal to 25 percent of revenues and the distribution costs total 20 percent. For Competitor A, manufacturing costs are equal to 35 percent of revenues and distribution costs only 10 percent. Notice that although Competitor A has lower sales and higher manufacturing costs, it still enjoys a higher profit margin than Business A. Competitor A more than compensates for its higher manufacturing costs by spending less on market research, advertising, and distribution.

The height of the bars provides some clues to explain Competitor A's apparent advantage. Business A is not part of a larger company, and all expenditures are related to the production and sale of its single product and included in the costs. Therefore, the height of each bar is proportional to its width. Because Competitor A's company has other businesses in its portfolio that use the same marketing research and advertising skills as well as the same distribution channels, corporate expenditures in these related activities are included in determining the height of the bars even though they are not allocated as costs for the particular product. The height of the bar is an indicator of Competitor A's overall corporate experience, of likely ECONOMIES OF SCALE, and of likely SHARED COSTS or experience. In the example given, most of the advantages enjoyed by Competitor A are due to shared costs and experience with other products. However, even a competitor which is a single product company but much larger can benefit from important ECONOMIES OF SCALE. Consider the case of two beverage companies mounting a national advertising campaign. The cost of a national campaign will be very similar for both companies but will represent a much smaller expenditure in proportion to the sales of the larger company. The advertising bars of the COMPETENCE PROFILES of the two will be roughly the same height, but the bar of the larger company will be much narrower.

Strategists who employ COMPETENCE PROFILES contend that they provide insight into variations in margins by highlighting areas of STRATEGIC LEVERAGE and into differences in CORPORATE STRATEGIES.

Competing Brand: a different brand of a particular product produced by the same company. For example, Procter & Gamble's brand of detergent, Tide, competes with Procter & Gamble's other detergent brands such as Cheer. Individual brands are usually used as COMPETING BRANDS, but the product can be marketed under a family/corporate name or a private label as well.

Generally, strategists use COMPETING BRANDS to satisfy buyer interest in trying new brands and to appeal to different BUYER GROUPS. COMPETING BRANDS can also be used to fill up a distribution channel in order to build an ENTRY or MOBILITY BARRIER.

Competitive Advantage: a factor that allows one business to be more profitable than its competitors. Many factors can give one business a COMPETITIVE ADVANTAGE over its competitors including such diverse phenomena as a more efficient plant, valuable patents, a clever advertising message, favorable government relationships, a smart president, and easy access to credit. If no competitor in a given industry has any advantage over another, it follows that all competitors should be equally profitable.

A COMPETITIVE ADVANTAGE works to make a business more profitable than another in the following fundamental way. It allows a business to have lower costs and to enjoy higher margins, or it allows a business to differentiate itself vis-à-vis its competitors and to charge a higher price or gain loyalty at the same RELATIVE PRICE.

Strategists have found it useful to distinguish between a short-term and a long-term COMPETITIVE ADVANTAGE for a particular competitor, but a long-term sustainable COMPETITIVE ADVANTAGE is the basis for building a profitable protected competitive position. The factor favoring a competitor becomes the foundation for a COMPETITIVE STRATEGY which either gives a business an enduring COST ADVANTAGE over its competitors or gives it a solid basis for PRODUCT DIFFERENTIATION. In order to sustain that advantage, a COMPETITIVE STRATEGY must develop ENTRY and MOBILITY BARRIERS and position the business to influence or adapt to the COMPETITIVE FORCES in its industry better than its competitors. Some strategists adamantly maintain that any successful COMPETITIVE STRATEGY must correspond to one of the three GENERIC STRATEGIES.

COMPETITIVE ADVANTAGE is sometimes called distinctive competence.

Competitive Advantage Matrix: *see* POTENTIAL ADVANTAGE MATRIX.

Competitive Force: one of the five basic features that determine the profitability of an industry. These five forces are RIVALRY, BUYER POWER, SUPPLIER POWER, the THREAT OF ENTRY, and the threat of SUBSTITUTE PRODUCTS. The strength of each COMPETITIVE FORCE is determined by the mix and type of STRUCTURAL FACTORS in that industry.

STRUCTURAL ANALYSIS is the process of understanding the COMPETITIVE FORCES in a given industry.

Competitive Position: the situation of a participant in an industry based on its current performance and on the strengths and advantages it enjoys over its competitors. A business with a strong COMPETITIVE POSITION is one with a COMPETITIVE ADVANTAGE that is protected by high MOBILITY BARRIERS. Such a business will enjoy above-average returns that are sustainable against its competitors' strategies. Some strategists focus on MARKET SHARE or RELATIVE MARKET SHARE as a measure of the strength of a competitor. They encourage a business to develop a COMPETITIVE POSITION that can be described as either dominant, leading, or important relative to its competitors as defined in the following table.

	DOMINANT	LEADING	IMPORTANT
Relative market share	$1.5x$	$1x$ to $1.5x$	$1x$
Cost position	Low-cost factor	Some cost advantage	Second lowest costs
Influence on industry prices	High	Moderate	Follower

Those strategists feel that a business that has not or is not likely to attain one of those three positions is a business that cannot be expected to provide positive ECONOMIC VALUE to the company and therefore the company should EXIT.

Other strategists do not think that a business's MARKET SHARE is a good indicator of COMPETITIVE POSITION. Rather, they feel that COMPETITIVE POSITION can only be evaluated within the context of the INDUSTRY STRUCTURE in which the business competes. They argue that a good COMPETITIVE POSITION is based on a GENERIC STRATEGY that gives the business a sustainable COMPETITIVE ADVANTAGE.

Competitive Scope: the extent of a company's or business's activities in terms of the range of products produced, BUYER GROUPS served, geographic markets served, the range of industries in which it competes, and the degree of VERTICAL INTEGRATION. The range of products produced and BUYER GROUPS served is called segment scope. The range of regions and countries in which it competes is called its geographic scope, and the range in which it competes is called its industry scope.

A company's COMPETITIVE SCOPE is the sum of the scopes of its businesses, but a business in a company that effectively uses BUSINESS INTERRELATIONSHIPS will accrue COMPETITIVE ADVANTAGES beyond those allowed by its own scope.

The breadth or narrowness of COMPETITIVE SCOPE can be judged only with respect to its competitors. The extent and variation in COMPETITIVE SCOPE among competitors are important aspects of INDUSTRY STRUCTURE. They can influence the height of ENTRY BARRIERS and the boundaries of STRATEGIC GROUPINGS within the industry.

COMPETITIVE SCOPE is also a determinant of the range of possibilities for building STRATEGIC LEVERAGE within a company's portfolio. Broad scope may allow for effective BUSINESS INTERRELATIONSHIPS. Too broad a scope may result in an organization with overwhelming INTEGRATING SYSTEMS. Narrow scope may allow FOCUS STRATEGIES that outperform the broader competition. Too narrow a scope may increase the threat of ENTRY and may mean missed opportunities. Some strategists see COALITIONS as a way to expand COMPETITIVE SCOPE without having major alterations to ORGANIZATION STRUCTURE or CAPITAL STRUCTURE.

A number of techniques such as HERFINDAHL INDICES, VALUE CHAINS, and MULTIPOINT COMPETITION MATRICES are used to analyze COMPETITIVE SCOPE.

A company with a broad geographic scope is said to have a GLOBAL PERSPECTIVE.

The four dimensions of COMPETITIVE SCOPE are analyzed with SCOPE GRIDS.

Competitive Strategy: a business's approach to taking part in its industry. A COMPETITIVE STRATEGY consists of a statement of what the business's GOALS are in terms such as REQUIRED RETURN, REAL GROWTH, and MARKET SHARE; a statement of how the business is going to compete or position itself; and a series of OPERATING POLICIES to guide the business's FUNCTIONAL AREAS. For purposes of illustration, a COMPETITIVE STRATEGY can be represented as a wheel with the business's GOALS in the center and its OPERATING POLICIES radiating around it.

Key operating policies to carry out the goals

A successful COMPETITIVE STRATEGY provides a business with a consistent approach to building a profitable and protected COMPETITIVE POSITION in its industry.

Many strategists begin the formulation of a COMPETITIVE STRATEGY by filling in a wheel that identifies the business's current GOALS and its implicit or explicit OPERATING POLICIES. This rough sketch is then refined and analyzed to determine what ASSUMPTIONS are being made about INDUSTRY and INTRA-INDUSTRY STRUCTURE to justify the OPERATING POLICIES now guiding each FUNCTIONAL area.

The strategist's attention then turns to the structure of the industry and an analysis of the five underlying COMPETITIVE FORCES. The results of the industry and COMPETITOR ANALYSIS are then compared with the ASSUMPTIONS about the dynamics of the industry identified earlier to see if they are consistent. If the current strategy and ASSUMPTIONS are not consistent with the STRUCTURAL ANALYSIS, then modifications are made to the logic of the current strategy where possible and the remaining inconsistencies are noted.

The strategist then considers whether the current strategy takes full advantage of industry OPPORTUNITIES and protects against industry THREATS. This step usually requires further competitor and INTRA-INDUSTRY ANALYSIS and leads to the formulation of alternative strategies. The alternatives can then be compared with the current strategy to see which one is most attractive, given the GOALS for the business and the business's capabilities.

In addition to the tests of external consistency described earlier, there are questions of internal consistency within the strategy, such as these.

- Are the business's goals mutually achievable? For example, a goal of a high sales growth may be inconsistent with a goal of short-term margin increases.
- Do the operating policies reinforce the goals? For example, a ME-TOO PRODUCT R&D policy may be inconsistent with the goal of high product quality.
- Do the operating policies reinforce each other? For example, a high-speed streamlined approach to manufacturing may be inconsistent with a sales force promising customization.

In order to be successful in the long run, a COMPETITIVE STRATEGY must not only be internally and externally consistent but must also provide a sustainable COMPETITIVE ADVANTAGE. Many strategists feel that a business cannot do that without pursuing one of the three GENERIC STRATEGIES. Also, many strategists feel that a business should influence industry changes in its favor as much as possible and that a COMPETITIVE STRATEGY must be adapted in anticipation of uncontrollable changes in the industry.

A COMPETITIVE STRATEGY is the basis for the STRATEGIC PLAN or BUSINESS PLAN which details specific OBJECTIVES, TACTICS, budgets, and schedules to be followed in order to implement the strategy. Although the term COMPETITIVE STRATEGY refers to the approach taken by a single business to competing in its particular industry, the term CORPORATE STRATEGY refers to a company's approach to optimizing the ECONOMIC VALUE of its portfolio of businesses.

Competitor Analysis: a systematic study of the capabilities, current STRATEGY, GOALS, and ASSUMPTIONS of a competing business. Analysis of a competitor's actions and the factors governing its behavior helps the strategist to anticipate the competitor's strategic moves and responses to changes in the industry. COMPETITOR ANALYSIS coupled with STRUCTURAL ANALYSIS of the industry provides the foundation for devising a COMPETITIVE STRATEGY.

Drawing COMPETITOR MAPS, identifying VALUE CHAINS, and applying DELPHI METHODS are a few of many techniques which strategists use to sort out the interactions among an array of competitors. At the corporate level, MULTIPOINT COMPETITORS may be analyzed and complex VALUE SYSTEMS illustrated to show COMPETITIVE SCOPE and SHARED EXPERIENCE.

COMPETITOR ANALYSIS should lead to COMPETITOR SELECTION as well as to INSIGHTS into new strategies.

Competitor Configuration: the combination of CONCENTRATION and SHARE BALANCE among participants in an industry. COMPETITOR CONFIGURATION is usually expressed in terms of a CONCENTRATION RATIO, a HERFINDAHL INDEX, MARKET SHARES, RELATIVE MARKET SHARES, CAPACITY SHARES, and other summary statistics. COMPETITOR CONFIGURATION is an important determinant of the intensity of RIVALRY in an industry. An industry with numerous balanced competitors is likely to be unstable because competitors may feel that their strategic moves will go unnoticed. Even a smaller group made up of balanced competitors may continually jockey for position. Companies in an industry with few and unequal competitors are more likely to be receptive to the leadership of the dominant firm in matters such as pricing and product design.

Because of the effect that COMPETITOR CONFIGURATION can have on RIVALRY in an industry, many strategists feel that there is an optimal configuration for a given business. A MONOPOLY position at first look is attractive but brings with it problems such as antitrust, exposure to public opinion, strict regulation, and the potential for nationalization. If one concedes, then, that a business is better off with some competitors, the question becomes how to determine an optimal configuration for those competitors. Some theorists have proposed that, regardless of the industry involved, the ideal is to be the leader in an industry with three major competitors having MARKET SHARES in the proportion of 4:2:1. Other theorists propose that the ideal configuration will vary from industry to industry depending on the COST STRUCTURES of the competitors and the STRUCTURAL FACTORS shaping the industry. Still others point to the pattern and diversity of COMPETITIVE STRATEGIES being pursued by industry participants as important elements of COMPETITOR CONFIGURATION.

Some strategists feel that COMPETITOR CONFIGURATION is something that they can and should influence as part of formulating an effective COMPETITIVE STRATEGY. Other strategists see COMPETITOR CONFIGURATION as a given within which they have to formulate strategies.

COMPETITOR CONFIGURATION is sometimes called market configuration.

Competitor Interrelations: *see* BUSINESS INTERRELATIONSHIPS.

Competitor Map: a BUBBLE CHART on which industry participants are displayed in order to highlight differences in two key elements of their strategies, such as pricing, quality, or distribution policies. COMPETITOR MAPS are often drawn to illustrate the basis for the differences in profitability among competitors in an industry and to identify STRATEGIC GROUPS among competitors. The following is a simplified COMPETITOR MAP of an industry.

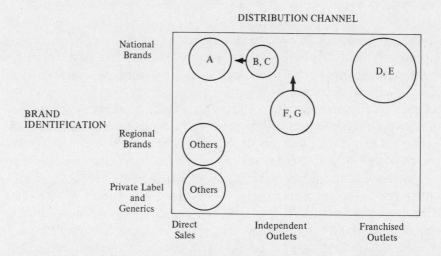

Circles are drawn for each competitor or STRATEGIC GROUP in proportion to sales or MARKET SHARE. The circles are positioned along the x-axis on the basis of the competitors' selection of distribution channels and on the y-axis on the basis of BRAND IDENTIFICATION. Footnotes to the chart often indicate the profitability of the competitors in each group and point out other aspects of their COMPETITIVE STRATEGIES, such as advertising ratios and breadth of product line. Also, arrows are often used to indicate trends in the evolution of competitors' strategies and the formation of new STRATEGIC GROUPS.

Many strategists look for OPPORTUNITIES in the positions on the map which are unoccupied and look for THREATS in the actual and potential movement of competitors around the map.

Competitor Selection: the identification and encouragement of particular competitors in an effort to increase COMPETITIVE ADVAN-

TAGE, improve current INDUSTRY STRUCTURE, aid market development, or deter the ENTRY of more threatening rivals. The two premises underlying COMPETITOR SELECTION are that some competitors are better than none, given the visibility or likelihood of political interference in a MONOPOLY, and that some competitors are better than others. Moreover, even if desired EXITS and ENTRIES can not be controlled, COMPETITOR SELECTION can involve encouraging beneficial behavior and discouraging harmful behavior so as to increase the number of GOOD COMPETITORS.

MARKET SIGNALING is very often used in COMPETITOR SELECTION.

Complementary Product: a product which is used or consumed jointly with another and for which DEMAND rises when the price of the other falls. For example, the DEMAND for popcorn is expected to increase when the price of movies falls. However, when one product is a complement of another, the reverse is not necessarily true. For example, the demand for movies is probably independent of the price for popcorn.

Strategists are interested in COMPLEMENTARY PRODUCTS in FORECASTING and ENVIRONMENTAL SCANNING because the price of complements can affect an industry's DEMAND. Also, PRICE POLICY should take COMPLEMENTARY PRODUCTS into consideration.

SUBSTITUTE PRODUCTS are the opposite of COMPLEMENTARY PRODUCTS. If one product is a substitute for another, the demand for the first will decrease when there is a fall in the price of the other.

Concentration: the degree to which the largest sellers in the market account for a large proportion of sales. If all sellers hold identical shares, the lower the number of sellers present, the more concentrated the market. In markets with identical numbers of sellers, the more concentrated market is the one in which the largest sellers account for the greater proportion of sales. The most concentrated industry is one with one competitor, called a MONOPOLY. OLIGOPOLIES are industries with more than one competitor but not so many as to make them unaware of their mutual dependence. An atomistic industry is one with a very large number of competitors. Industry concentration is often measured in terms of a CONCENTRATION RATIO or a HERFINDAHL INDEX.

An industry's buyers can also be concentrated; a market with one buyer is called a MONOPSONY. However, BUYER CONCENTRATION is usually discussed separately from industry concentration, which is sometimes called seller concentration.

Because of the effect of concentration on RIVALRY, many strategists consider it important to predict and influence it.

Concentration Ratio: a measure of the degree to which a few large sellers in the industry account for a large proportion of the sales. The first step in calculating an industry's CONCENTRATION RATIO is to rank the competitors on the basis of MARKET SHARE, starting with the highest. Then the MARKET SHARES of groups of the largest competitors are added to get a CONCENTRATION RATIO. A C_4 ratio is the sum of the MARKET SHARES of the four largest competitors. A C_8 ratio is the sum of the MARKET SHARES of the eight largest competitors. Take, for example, an industry with ten competitors having market shares of 25 percent, 20 percent, 15 percent, 10 percent, 5 percent, 5 percent, 5 percent, 5 percent, 5 percent, and 5 percent. The C_4 ratio would be 70 percent, and the C_8 ratio would be 90 percent.

In general, the closer the CONCENTRATION RATIO is to 100 percent, the more concentrated the industry. However, the CONCENTRATION RATIO can be misleading because it does not take into consideration SHARE BALANCE. For example, if the MARKET SHARES of the ten competitors in the example just given had been 55 percent, 5 percent, 5 percent, 5 percent, 5 percent, 5 percent, 5 percent, 5 percent, and 5 percent, the C_4 and C_8 ratios would also be 70 percent and 90 percent even though this industry appears to be much more concentrated than the previous one. To capture the presence or absence of SHARE BALANCE, many strategists prefer to use the HERFINDAHL INDEX.

The use of C_4 and C_8 ratios is somewhat arbitrary and reflects the data available in SIC CODE statistics. Recent research seems to show that a C_2 ratio is also useful.

Concept of Assembly: a statement of a company's approach to adding new businesses to its portfolio. It is one of the four components of a company's CORPORATE STRATEGY. When formulating a company's CONCEPT OF ASSEMBLY, corporate strategists must maintain consistency with the other three elements: the GOALS of the company, its CONCEPT OF FIT, and its CONCEPT OF MANAGEMENT. The CONCEPT OF ASSEMBLY determines whether the company will develop new businesses internally or whether it will look outside. Depending on the outcome of this decision, a company may establish either a venture capital subsidiary, a new business R&D department, or an acquisition study group or search for JOINT VENTURE partners. If the company chooses to depend on internal development, then its managers must be encouraged to seek out and create new products and to explore new businesses. This message must be reinforced by the company's CONCEPT OF MANAGEMENT.

If the company's portfolio is to be developed predominantly through ACQUISITION, then the CONCEPT OF ASSEMBLY will need to specify the types of ACQUISITION CANDIDATES the company would be interested in and the company's approach to ACQUISITION SCREENING. For example, companies that rely on FORMULA FIT for STRATEGIC LEVERAGE are likely to be constrained by management's ability to run a large group of companies and may consider only ACQUISITION CANDIDATES with the potential to represent at least 10 percent of the company. Other companies, especially those that are relying on FINANCIAL FIT for STRATEGIC LEVERAGE, may not want any one business to represent more than 5 percent of the company's portfolio.

The company that relies on acquisitions to enter new businesses will need to make itself attractive to the type of businesses it wishes to acquire. For example, a company that favors privately held companies whose founders take pride in their businesses might do well to develop a reputation for building acquired companies into major, high-quality competitors.

Concept of Fit: a statement of how the businesses in a company's portfolio will be linked and will relate to each other. It is one of the four components of a company's CORPORATE STRATEGY. Fit refers to the way and the extent to which a business is worth more as part of a company's portfolio than it would be as a stand-alone entity. Three categories are sometimes used to describe the synergies that can result when businesses are joined in one corporate portfolio. FINANCIAL FIT refers to a better use of the companies' financial resources. FUNCTIONAL FIT refers to the ability to capitalize on shared technical and operating competence. FORMULA FIT refers to a consistency in strategy which clarifies and strengthens the strategic focus for the company as a whole.

Basically, a company's CONCEPT OF FIT defines which businesses are and are not suitable for the company's portfolio and why. A company defines a CONCEPT OF FIT as a framework for building

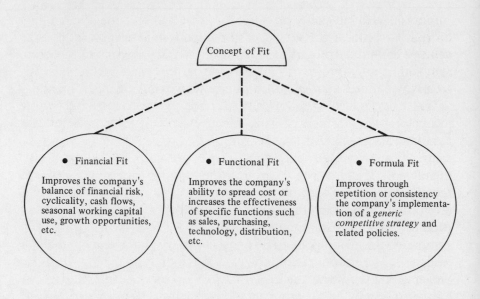

STRATEGIC LEVERAGE and creating the ECONOMIC VALUE required by its goals.

Some strategists are uncomfortable with a CONCEPT OF FIT. They feel that a good company is built by recognizing businesses that are or have the potential to be good OPPORTUNITIES, and then by acquiring or developing those businesses. Other strategists feel that formulating a CONCEPT OF FIT is the most important task of the corporate strategist. They argue that putting businesses together to take advantage of the three different forms of fit is the greatest source of STRATEGIC LEVERAGE for many companies. Furthermore, they argue that STRATEGIC LEVERAGE can be maximized if the company formulates a CONCEPT OF MANAGEMENT that supports the implementation of its CONCEPT OF FIT and a CONCEPT OF ASSEMBLY that allows it to grow. Theorists who agree with the importance of a CONCEPT OF FIT argue that the STRATEGIC LEVERAGE that is built with BUSINESS INTERRELATIONSHIPS is leverage that shareholders are unable to build for themselves simply by diversifying their holdings.

Concept of Management: a statement of how a company will organize and control the businesses in its portfolio. It is one of the four components of a company's CORPORATE STRATEGY. In formulating a company's CONCEPT OF MANAGEMENT, corporate strategists must keep in mind the GOALS of the company, the company's CONCEPT OF ASSEMBLY, and especially the company's CONCEPT OF FIT.

Important elements of a CONCEPT OF MANAGEMENT include the OR-
GANIZATIONAL STRUCTURE, the ORGANIZATIONAL HIERARCHY, the
MEASUREMENT SYSTEMS, the INCENTIVE SYSTEMS, the INTEGRATING
SYSTEMS, the strategic PLANNING PROCESS, the PLANNING HIER-
ARCHY, and the RESOURCE ALLOCATION process.

A CONCEPT OF MANAGEMENT defines the relationship between
the company and its businesses as well as BUSINESS INTERRELA-
TIONSHIPS. It specifies the roles that the managers must play in carrying out the company's strategies and the incentives for managers
to fulfill those roles. A company's CONCEPT OF FIT is a major determinant of its CONCEPT OF MANAGEMENT. For example, the autonomy
given to managers and the controls centralized at the corporate level
should reflect how the businesses are expected to fit together in the
company's portfolio. The CONCEPT OF MANAGEMENT should also include the company's approach to identifying businesses that no
longer fit within the portfolio and its approach to EXITING from those
businesses.

Some strategists are uncomfortable with including "how to
manage the company" as part of its CORPORATE STRATEGY. Other
strategists feel that, in a diversified company, how the businesses are
organized, funded, and evaluated are key determinants of how business units will behave. Therefore, they argue, a CORPORATE STRAT-
EGY cannot exist without a CONCEPT OF MANAGEMENT designed such
that STRATEGY AND STRUCTURE are consistent with each other. They
also point to the tight link between the success of any GENERIC STRAT-
EGY and the daily operating decisions and management of a business
as further support of their argument.

Conformance: a measure of the degree to which a product consistently meets the buyer's specifications. Some strategists define this
as dependable UTILITY.

Conglomerate: a diversified company that provides ECONOMIC
VALUE by investing in a portfolio of business so as to take advantage
of FINANCIAL FIT and build FINANCIAL LEVERAGE. A CONGLOMERATE
usually expands through ACQUISITION, and its CONCEPT OF MANAGE-
MENT involves autonomous multifunctional divisions required to
meet top management's financial performance goals. Top management rarely has any functional responsibilities, and its legal and financial staffs are usually hard at work evaluating current perfor-
mances and formulating investment strategies.

Consistency Tests: *see* COMPETITIVE STRATEGY.

Constant Dollar: a nominal dollar value adjusted to eliminate the effect of INFLATION or price changes from financial comparisons. The nominal dollar amount is multiplied by an index which reflects either some change in prices or costs or a change in the general level of the purchasing power of the dollar. Data expressed in CONSTANT DOLLARS is also called REAL DOLLARS and can be used to calculate REAL GROWTH.

Take the example of a business with 1982 sales of $600 and 1980 sales of $500. In order to compare the 1982 sales with 1980 sales, one can adjust the 1982 dollar figure to reflect price changes since 1980. If industry prices were known to have increased by 20 percent during that period, 1982 sales expressed in constant 1980 dollars would be $600 divided by 1.2, or $500. The comparison of 1980 sales of $500 with 1982 sales of $500 in CONSTANT DOLLARS indicates no change. On the other hand, if the 1982 sales of $600 were adjusted for an 8 percent INFLATION rate per year, then 1982 sales would be about $518 in 1980 CONSTANT DOLLARS, indicating REAL GROWTH of 1.78 percent per year. A series of dollar values adjusted to reflect current price levels is said to be stated in CURRENT DOLLARS.

Constructive Conflict: a theory dealing with the control of the potential conflicts between the business and its employees and the business and its competitors. In trying to achieve its GOALS, management faces two forces of potential conflict—its employees and its competitors. Therefore, success depends on understanding the different interests and demands of both groups, anticipating their response to any action management might make, as well as anticipating management's own reaction and so on. This circular response leads to the realization that if conflict is allowed to ensue, the business will find itself in conflict with its own actions and reactions as well as those of its employees and competitors. Therefore, successful management depends on the integration of the best interests of a business with those of its employees and competitors.

CONSTRUCTIVE CONFLICT is often seen as the precursor of INTEGRATION SYSTEMS, COMPETITOR SELECTION, and DEFENSIVE STRATEGY.

Consumer Good: a product whose END USERS are primarily individuals or families. CONSUMER GOODS are often categorized on the basis of durability and on the basis of PRODUCT DIFFERENTIATION. Products that are expected to last three years or more are called consumer durables. Products that are expected to last much less than three years are called consumer nondurables. For example, a refrigerator would be a consumer durable and a toothbrush would be a consumer nondurable.

CONSUMER GOODS that are not differentiated are often called COMMODITIES. CONSUMER GOODS that are differentiated are often called SPECIALTY PRODUCTS. Differentiated consumer durables are sometimes called "shopping goods" because they are considered to be significant purchases that the buyer is willing to shop around for. Differentiated consumer nondurables are sometimes called "convenience goods" although the term "convenience good" can also be used for any nondurable regardless of whether it is differentiated or not. Such items are called convenience goods because they are insignificant purchases and the buyer is expected to choose among immediately available brands rather than spend time shopping for a particular brand.

Convenience Good: *see* CONSUMER GOOD.

Conventional Wisdom: widely held ASSUMPTIONS about how to compete in an industry. Managers often rely on CONVENTIONAL WISDOM about all five of the COMPETITIVE FORCES in an industry. For example, managers in a given industry might believe that buyers always trade up, that suppliers must have fixed contracts, that makers of SUBSTITUTES will never innovate, that competitors cannot afford to advertise, that Company X would never enter, and so on.

Strategists are often frustrated by the reliance on CONVENTIONAL WISDOM in their own companies. They may learn early in their careers that the past behavior of managers is based on comfortable ASSUMPTIONS and CONVENTIONAL WISDOM. In order to get managers to look at their businesses and their industries differently, the strategist has to invest a considerable amount of effort in understanding those ASSUMPTIONS and in collecting the data to change them.

However, strategists often appreciate CONVENTIONAL WISDOM in their competitors because this can provide OPPORTUNITIES to take advantage of BLIND SPOTS.

Cooperative Competition: *see* COALITION.

Corporate Brand: *see* BRAND IDENTIFICATION.

Corporate Culture: the underlying norms that influence the behavior of a company's employees. CORPORATE CULTURE is a set of interrelated beliefs, shared by most of the employees of a company, about how one should behave at work and what activities are more important than others.

A company's CORPORATE CULTURE can be obvious or amorphous depending on the circumstances involved. For example, a company that has been established for many years, that is located in one geographic area, that is involved in only a few similar businesses, that has hired a homogenous group of employees, and that has experienced low management turnover would be expected to have a strong definable CORPORATE CULTURE. On the other hand, a new company, a company with very high management turnover, a company that has been growing very fast, a company that is made up of a number of diverse businesses, or a company that has made a number of recent ACQUISITIONS would be expected to have an amorphous CORPORATE CULTURE.

CORPORATE CULTURE can be deliberately determined or simply allowed to evolve. For example, top management may decide to develop a CORPORATE CULTURE that emphasizes high levels of attention and service when dealing with customers, moderation and cost control when spending, a familylike cooperative atmosphere, a hard day's work in return for an unwritten no-fire agreement, or an up-or-out attitude. Although the examples imply that some CORPORATE CULTURES are desirable and others are not, this is a debatable point. For example, some strategists feel that an inherently good CORPORATE CULTURE emphasizes fairness, honesty, pride, the excellence of one's work, and a commitment to the company. Other strategists feel that the ideal CORPORATE CULTURE for a given company depends upon the strategy of the company and the kinds of COMPETITIVE FORCES its businesses are dealing with. However, most strategists agree that a company is better off trying to determine CORPORATE CULTURE rather than letting it evolve and that a company is better off with a good CORPORATE CULTURE, however defined, than with a bad CORPORATE CULTURE.

Most strategists consider the key determinant of CORPORATE CULTURE to be the leadership and example given by top management. Some strategists believe that the appropriate culture should be iden-

tified during the formulation of a company's CONCEPT OF MANAGE-
MENT as part of its CORPORATE STRATEGY.

Corporate Goals: *see* CORPORATE STRATEGY.

Corporate Stakes: refers to the importance a company places on
having a business with a strong COMPETITIVE POSITION in a particular
industry. An industry in which many of the competitors place high
stakes can be expected to exhibit a high level of RIVALRY even if all
other STRUCTURAL FACTORS would seem to indicate the opposite. For
example, one can see that an industry in which most of the competitors wanted to be the DOMINANT FIRM would have a high level of
RIVALRY no matter what the other STRUCTURAL FACTORS indicated.

Strategists use a number of COMPETITOR ANALYSIS techniques to
assess their competitor's CORPORATE STAKES. Usually, this involves
charts of each competitor's portfolio of businesses and their changes
over time. A PENETRATION CHART is often used in that analysis along
with an INDUSTRY IMPORTANCE GRAPH.

Corporate Strategy: a company's approach to optimizing the social
and ECONOMIC VALUE of its portfolio of businesses to its shareholders. A CORPORATE STRATEGY is a framework within which a company
can make decisions about its GOALS, the kinds of businesses it wants
to be in, the ways in which it will add new business to its portfolio,
and the ways in which it will manage its businesses. These four types
of decisions lead to a corporate strategy framework that has four
components. That is, just as a COMPETITIVE STRATEGY for an individual business involves a statement of GOALS and a series of OP-
ERATING POLICIES to carry them out, a framework for a CORPORATE
STRATEGY involves a statement of GOALS for a group of businesses
and three concepts for achieving these goals.

The first component of a CORPORATE STRATEGY is the company's corporate GOALS. These GOALS should reflect the social and
economic requirements of the company's shareholders.

The second component is the company's CONCEPT OF FIT. This
should address how the company plans to link the business within
its portfolio in order to create ECONOMIC VALUE through STRATEGIC
LEVERAGE. This concept also provides the basis for determining
which new industries a company should enter.

The third component of CORPORATE STRATEGY is the company's

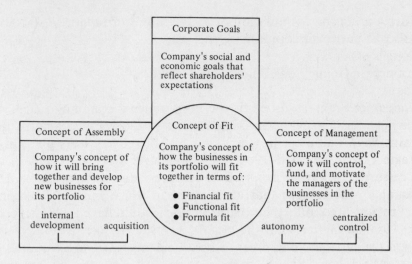

CONCEPT OF ASSEMBLY. This addresses how the company will add new businesses to the portfolio that meet the criteria of the company's CONCEPT OF FIT. For example, this will determine whether the company will ENTER new industries by developing new businesses internally or whether it will look outside to JOINT VENTURES or ACQUISITIONS.

The fourth component of CORPORATE STRATEGY is the company's CONCEPT OF MANAGEMENT. This specifies how the company will control and motivate the managers of each business in order to gain the benefits of its CONCEPT OF FIT and its CONCEPT OF ASSEMBLY.

The success of a company's CORPORATE STRATEGY depends on consistency among the four components. That is, the company may have set clear GOALS reflecting the OBJECTIVES of its shareholders but may not be able to achieve those GOALS because its CONCEPT OF FIT does not allow the company to develop sufficient STRATEGIC LEVERAGE. Or even if the company has a viable CONCEPT OF FIT, it may be unable to create increasing ECONOMIC VALUE without a CONCEPT OF ASSEMBLY that allows it to continue to add to its portfolio. Finally, even if the other three components are insightful and consistent, the company can only be as effective as its CONCEPT OF MANAGEMENT allows it to be. That is, the company may be unable to carry out the best CORPORATE STRATEGY without an appropriate CONCEPT OF MANAGEMENT that provides its managers with motivations that are consistent with its CONCEPT OF FIT, its CONCEPT OF ASSEMBLY, and its corporate GOALS.

Cost Advantage: a favorable difference in the amount that a business spends to produce and sell its product relative to its competitors. COST ADVANTAGES can occur at any stage of a business's VALUE ADDED CHAIN, and, as a result, competitors may have very different COST STRUCTURES. COST ADVANTAGES may be due to a business's strategy, its company's CORPORATE STRATEGY, or a combination of the two. Two widely recognized COST DRIVERS are ECONOMIES OF SCALE and CUMULATIVE EXPERIENCE. Other sources are patents that create proprietary products and proprietary technology, favorable access to raw materials, or favorable locations. Government policy can also provide cost advantages by giving subsidies or preference to specific competitors.

Identifying the sources of current COST ADVANTAGES through COST ANALYSIS as well as the potential sources of future COST ADVANTAGES is important in developing a COMPETITIVE STRATEGY. Essentially, strategists are looking for ways of developing a sustainable COMPETITIVE ADVANTAGE from one or more COST ADVANTAGES.

Cost Analysis: a technique for studying the pattern and behavior of the expenditures a business makes to produce and sell its products. The strategist lays the groundwork for the analysis by constructing a VALUE ADDED CHAIN for the product, business, or industry being studied. Depending on the reason for doing the COST ANALYSIS, the VALUE ADDED CHAIN can be based on the specific costs for an individual product, the average costs for all the products in a given business, or the average costs for all the businesses in a given industry; and it can involve historical costs, current costs, or forecasted costs. Therefore, the first step in COST ANALYSIS is to decide at what level of aggregation the VALUE ADDED CHAIN should be developed.

The second step in COST ANALYSIS is to determine the general stages of VALUE ADDED to be analyzed. Usually, this is best done by drawing a VALUE ADDED CHAIN that includes PURCHASED VALUE, the steps by which additional value is added to the PURCHASED VALUE, and the margin. Once the general stages have been identified, they can be broken down into more specific stages depending on the needs of the particular COST ANALYSIS. For example, marketing could be broken down into advertising, promotion, and sales force stages. Step two should result in a reasonably detailed VALUE ADDED CHAIN with the stages ordered in a way that makes the most sense, given the reason for the COST ANALYSIS. Usually, the stages are ordered as in a traditional chain with the stages moving from left to right as they get further away from raw materials and closer to the END USER. However, strategists should feel free, for example, to locate R&D closer to manufacturing if it involves mostly process development or closer to marketing if it involves mostly customer applications.

The third step in COST ANALYSIS is to calculate for each stage in the VALUE ADDED CHAIN the percentage of total selling price that it represents and the percentage of total FIXED CAPITAL and WORKING CAPITAL that are employed in connection with that stage. The value stages should then be ranked according to those percentages. The rankings of different stages will differ from industry to industry and will differ among competitors within an industry. The rankings will also usually differ among products within the product line of a given business. Therefore, the ranking of the value stages can be used to indicate for a specific COST ANALYSIS which stages are likely to be the most important.

The fourth step in COST ANALYSIS is to break down each stage, with particular emphasis on the high-ranking stages, into specific activities and operations that are the cost elements of that stage. For example, a sales force stage might be broken down into sales force salaries and bonuses, the cost of making the sale, the cost of processing the order, etc. Segregating the cost elements of each stage is often one of the more difficult steps in COST ANALYSIS. That is because the breakdown of activities and operations of the value stage may be quite different from the business's traditional cost accounting classifications. Therefore, accounting data often has to be recast in order to arrive at the values for the cost elements called for in strategic COST ANALYSIS. Also, the number of cost elements to be identified is often difficult to decide. For example, production can be considered a single cost element, or it can be broken down into such cost elements as the cost of component fabrication, subassembly, buffer inventory, and final assembly. The appropriate number of cost elements in any one stage depends on the judgment of the strategist. A common consideration is the size of the cost element. If an item is a small percentage of the cost of the value stage and especially if that value stage is, in turn, a small percentage of the selling price, then the cost element may not have to be separately identified. However, some strategists feel that at a minimum all cost elements in a given stage that are affected by a different COST DRIVER must be identified separately.

The fifth step is to determine the factors that influence the behavior of each cost element, both in terms of operating costs and in terms of asset utilization. The behavior of costs is usually analyzed in six ways. The first is to determine to what extent each cost element involves FIXED or VARIABLE COSTS. The second is to determine to what extent the cost element is subject to ECONOMIES OF SCALE. Whereas FIXED COSTS almost always imply ECONOMIES OF SCALE, it can be important to distinguish between economies that can be realized by filling existing CAPACITY and economies that could be realized by operating on a larger scale. The MINIMUM EFFICIENT SCALE that is relevant for a given cost element should probably be identified as well. Third, the extent to which each cost element is subject to cost declines with CUMULATIVE EXPERIENCE should also be determined. Fourth, the cost elements should be analyzed to determine to what extent they are or could benefit from SHARED COSTS. Fifth, the COST DRIVERS for each cost element should be identified and analyzed in order to determine current levels and expected changes. Finally, the links between cost elements should be identified. For example, an increase in the cost of PRODUCT QUALITY control may allow for a more than compensating decrease in the cost of repair service.

Once the VALUE ADDED CHAIN has been created, the cost elements identified, and the behavior of each cost element understood, the strategist is ready to relate that analysis to the problem at hand. Typical problems that COST ANALYSIS can be used to address are these.

- To what extent is MARKET GROWTH affecting this business's RELATIVE COSTS?
- How will a BUILD PLAN to double MARKET SHARE affect the business's costs?
- To what extent and why are some cost elements becoming more or less important? Because they are becoming a more significant percentage of total costs? Because competitors are matching them, making other cost differentials more important?
- How are technological changes affecting this business's RELATIVE COSTS?
- To what extent are changes in input prices changing the importance of specific cost elements?
- Are this business's RELATIVE COSTS consistent with its GENERIC STRATEGY?

The VALUE CHAIN, rather than the VALUE ADDED CHAIN, is used as the basis for a COST ANALYSIS by some strategists. They argue that the VALUE CHAIN's distinction between primary and support activities and its treatment of purchased inputs lead to a better understanding of a business and the interrelationships among businesses within a company portfolio. Some strategists use COST ANALYSIS as a basis for comparing and analyzing different COMPETITIVE STRATEGIES. If two businesses have a very different set of cost elements in their VALUE ADDED CHAINS, then their COMPETITIVE STRATEGIES are likely to differ. A COST ANALYSIS of those two businesses is likely to reveal what those differences and the sources of COMPETITIVE ADVANTAGE are.

Some strategists also use COST ANALYSIS as a basis for formulating a new COMPETITIVE STRATEGY or as a basis for thinking of ways to change an existing COMPETITIVE STRATEGY. Creating a new combination of cost elements and VALUE ADDED stages can change the COMPETITIVE FORCES in an industry. For example, if a business has a competitor with the same VALUE ADDED CHAIN but one with cost elements that are being driven by COMPETITIVE ADVANTAGES in scale and experience, it may well be difficult for the first business to improve its returns as long as it continues to have the same VALUE ADDED CHAIN. However, if the business can change its VALUE ADDED CHAINS such that its new COST DRIVERS give it a COMPETITIVE ADVANTAGE, it may be able to overcome existing MOBILITY BARRIERS or create a new STRATEGIC GROUP. Examples of these kinds of changes include moving from indirect to direct sales, providing service directly rather than through independents, developing new distribution channels, using a new raw material, or becoming more VERTICALLY INTEGRATED. The use of COST ANALYSIS to develop COMPETITIVE STRATEGY is sometimes called BUSINESS SYSTEMS ANALYSIS.

Some strategists use VALUE CHAINS instead of VALUE ADDED CHAINS to give them a clearer picture of how costs interrelate and what the effect of change is.

Cost Center: an entity in a company's ORGANIZATIONAL HIERARCHY for which the company's MEASUREMENT SYSTEM measures the cost of producing a unit of output. Managers in charge of COST CENTERS are usually responsible for controlling the costs incurred by their entities. The production department in a plant would be an example of a COST CENTER. The manager of that department is generally responsible for minimizing the variance between the department's actual costs and its budgeted costs.

COST CENTERS are usually part of a PROFIT CENTER or an IN-VESTMENT CENTER.

Cost Curve: a graph showing the relationship between the UNIT COST of a product and a COST DRIVER. COST CURVES are drawn for individual products, for specific companies, and for industries as a whole. Economists frequently use COST CURVES showing the relationship between production costs and level of output. In these graphs production costs may be stated in terms of aggregate output or on a per unit basis. Total costs for aggregate output are usually broken down to show FIXED COSTS and VARIABLE COSTS. MARGINAL COSTS and AVERAGE COSTS are usually presented on a per unit basis.

Strategists more often use EXPERIENCE CURVES and curves that compare the costs of different products, different processes and different competitors. An EXPERIENCE CURVE is a COST CURVE showing the relationship between UNIT COSTS and CUMULATIVE EXPERIENCE. COST CURVES of JOINT PRODUCTS will be related, and different COST DRIVERS will affect costs differently. Depending on the COMPETITIVE STRATEGIES involved, the COST CURVES of competitors will differ.

TECHNOLOGICAL CHANGE will often cause a drop in costs resulting in a "knee" in the COST CURVE.

Cost Driver: a factor that affects the cost of an end product. The cost of an end product is built up by the VALUE SYSTEMS of activities that incorporate that end product. The cost of one or more activities can be expected to change when the level of its COST DRIVERS changes. For example, the national advertising cost per unit for a given product will go down as the business sells more units of that product. In an industry where all competitors spend an equal amount on national advertising, the business with the highest national MARKET SHARE should have the lowest advertising costs per unit. Therefore, scale economies through MARKET SHARE is likely to be the COST DRIVER for advertising costs per unit and will affect total costs.

Research has shown that there are ten major cost drivers: ECONOMIES OF SCALE, pattern of CAPACITY UTILIZATION, LINKAGES, BUSINESS INTERRELATIONSHIPS, VERTICAL INTEGRATION, timing, DISCRETIONARY POLICIES, location, and institutional factors. Therefore, a business's overall costs will be driven by the interaction of those ten drivers, and that interaction may be very different for its competitors. Furthermore, the COST DRIVERS may arise from an activity in a business's VALUE CHAIN as well as from interrelationships with the VALUE CHAINS of other businesses in the company. For example, if the nationally advertised product in the example just given had a family BRAND IDENTIFICATION, advertising for individual products would reinforce brand awareness for the family as a whole, further lowering advertising costs per unit.

ECONOMIES OF SCALE drive costs by allowing activities to be performed more effectively at high volume or by spreading the cost over that volume. Increasing the utilization of capacity will also spread costs; however, expanding capacity may increase the SCALE OF OPERATIONS without ECONOMIES OF SCALE. The cost of an activity may also decline over time with KNOW-HOW and the effects of the LEARNING CURVE. The cost of one activity may also be driven by the performance of a linked activity. Such LINKAGES can be within the business, with buyers or suppliers, or with other businesses in the company. VERTICAL INTEGRATION or DEINTEGRATION may drive costs by changing the transaction between activities. Timing can drive costs because of its effect on technology choices, UNCERTAINTY REDUCTION, LEARNING CURVES, etc. Costs can also be driven by discretionary OPERATING POLICIES such as delivery times, relative compensation, scheduling procedures, etc. Physical location can drive cost because of proximity to other VALUE CHAIN activities, geography, climate, culture, politics, etc. Institutional factors, which are often largely outside the business's control, also drive costs through labor unions, public utilities, government regulation, subsidies, etc.

Identifying COST DRIVERS in a VALUE CHAIN is a critical task of a strategist when completing a COST ANALYSIS. Managing COST DRIVERS is essential to carrying out a COST LEADERSHIP STRATEGY and cannot be ignored in carrying out any strategy.

A UNIQUENESS DRIVER is an analogous factor that yields differentiation.

Cost Dynamics: changes in the absolute and relative costs of a business's activities over time due to the interplay of COST DRIVERS, to the growth of the business, or to industry change. The term COST DYNAMICS refers to changes which do not stem directly from a business's STRATEGY but from factors such as INDUSTRY EVOLUTION, differences among activities in scale sensitivity or learning rates, and TECHNOLOGICAL CHANGE. Although COST DYNAMICS are independent of strategy, they are not unrelated. The strategist must have a firm grasp of the underlying COST DYNAMICS of a business because they can either enhance or impede efforts to implement a particular strategy.

Differentiation dynamics are comparable changes in a business's degree of differentiation caused by nonPOLICY VARIABLES, like changing consumer demographics.

Cost Leadership Strategy: a GENERIC STRATEGY with which a business seeks to become the low-cost producer in its industry. Achieving a successful COST LEADERSHIP STRATEGY allows a business to earn returns that are above its industry average even if there are strong COMPETITIVE FORCES in its industry. The business's low-cost position protects against RIVALRY because the business can still make a profit even if its competitors cut prices as low as they can. In the same way, it protects the business against BUYER POWER because buyers can push prices down only to the costs of the next–most efficient competitor in the industry. If buyers push any harder, they will eliminate all the business's competition and thereby eliminate their own BUYER POWER. That is, they will no longer have at least two businesses to play off against one another. A COST LEADERSHIP STRATEGY also protects against SUPPLIER POWER because the business has more room in its COST STRUCTURE to absorb increases in PURCHASED VALUE than its competitors. To the extent that a business's low-cost position would either be expensive for an entrant to duplicate or can be kept proprietary, such a position provides good ENTRY BARRIERS and MOBILITY BARRIERS. Finally, being in a low-cost position is likely to protect the businesses against most SUBSTITUTES except those that offer a better PRICE-TO-PERFORMANCE RATIO due to even lower costs.

Achieving a sustainable low-cost position usually requires efficient operations that take advantage of ECONOMIES OF SCALE or of declining costs due to CUMULATIVE EXPERIENCE. To the extent that ECONOMIES OF SCALE and CUMULATIVE EXPERIENCE are the basis of low costs in an industry, an effective COST LEADERSHIP STRATEGY may require a high MARKET SHARE—and, in fact, a high RELATIVE MARKET SHARE. To achieve that high RELATIVE MARKET SHARE, the business will have to design its products to appeal to the greatest number of buyers, as well as design its products to be the most efficient to manufacture. However, it is possible for a business to have the lowest costs without having the highest MARKET SHARE if it enjoys a strong FUNCTIONAL FIT with other businesses in its company's portfolio and benefits from SHARED COSTS or experience. COST ANALYSIS is often used to identify such OPPORTUNITIES. A COST LEADERSHIP STRATEGY may rest on other cost advantages beyond scale and CUMULATIVE EXPERIENCE, such as favorable access to raw materials, favorable government policy, and favorable location. Finally, it can also require that the management focus on any number of related cost-reducing and controlling activities such as VALUE ANALYSIS and BUYER SELECTION.

Successful implementation of a COST LEADERSHIP STRATEGY demands specific types of management skills and ORGANIZATIONAL STRUCTURES. For example, such a strategy is likely to require managers with strong process engineering skills and a strong orientation toward efficiency and control. It may also dictate that the business improve its cost position through SHARED EXPERIENCE or other forms of FUNCTIONAL FIT as part of its parent's CORPORATE STRATEGY. Cost leadership may also require an ORGANIZATIONAL STRUCTURE that allows for close supervision, specifies clearly defined areas of responsibility, provides MEASUREMENT SYSTEMS to maintain tight cost control, and employs INCENTIVE SYSTEMS which reward the achievement of strict qualitative OBJECTIVES. In addition, corporate management has to be willing to allocate resources for the kinds of significant expenditures that COST LEADERSHIP demands. The most important of these expenditures is usually the investment required to maintain state-of-the-art, low-cost technology. Others include continuous investment in plant and equipment, and in process research and development. Businesses pursuing cost leadership are likely to have high FIXED COSTS. Most strategists do not recommend cost leadership to managers who are uncomfortable with that kind of COST STRUCTURE.

As with any strategy, there are two major risks involved in attempting to carry out a COST LEADERSHIP STRATEGY. The first risk is that the business will fail to become the low-cost producer in its industry, and the second is that the business will fail to maintain its low-cost position as competitors respond and the INDUSTRY STRUCTURE changes. If it is assumed that a business can achieve COST LEADERSHIP at the outset, there are four threats to its ability to sustain that strategy in the long term. First—and most obvious—the business's costs can increase so that they are no longer sufficiently lower than its competitor's to make a difference. Second, a competitor can copy the business's methods or buy the business's experience and match or even improve on the business's costs. This can occur even if the business is doing everything right but simply cannot keep its activities proprietary. For example, a competitor can wait until the business has worked with suppliers to develop the right component and then order that component itself or wait until the business has worked out its plant layout and then hire the plant supervisor. The third threat is a competitor's development of new lower-cost technology that makes the business's approach to production out-of-date. If the business harbors MIXED MOTIVES which make it difficult for the business to invest in the new technology, its response to the threat may be too slow and tentative. Finally, the business can be so involved in keeping its costs low that it misses product-related changes in the industry. Two types of changes seem to be the most significant. First, characteristics of the product that the business produces with its SPECIALIZED ASSETS may no longer be the ones that most of the buyers in the industry want even at the business's low price. Take, for example, a business that has the most cost-effective way of making a given product out of wood. That business would be in trouble if most of the buyers in the market decided they wanted a plastic version of the product instead. Second, competitors who are making a differentiated version of the product may have lowered their costs and prices enough to offer buyers a differentiated product for which they are willing to pay a slight premium.

Many strategists feel that the difficulty involved in carrying out an effective COST LEADERSHIP STRATEGY is significant. Therefore, they feel that once a company is comfortable with the formula for a low-cost strategy, it can build STRATEGIC LEVERAGE by making FORMULA FIT part of its CORPORATE STRATEGY. For cost leadership, that formula has three elements. First, the company must be willing to build the kind of ORGANIZATIONAL STRUCTURE that supports cost leadership. Second, the company must be willing to spend to invest in state-of-the-art, low-cost technology. Third, the company must provide the business with managers who are capable of monitoring their RELATIVE COSTS and the degree of PRODUCT DIFFERENTIATION vis-à-vis their competitors and who are capable of keeping the sources of their low-costs proprietary.

Cost of Capital: the rate of return required by suppliers of funds. A company's COST OF CAPITAL is usually calculated as the weighted average of its cost of debt and COST OF EQUITY.

Take, for example, a company that has raised $5 million in capital by acquiring $1 million in debt and by issuing one million shares of common stock at $40 per share for total equity of $4 million. If the company has to pay 5 percent after taxes on the debt and the REQUIRED RETURN of its shareholders is such that its after-tax COST

OF EQUITY is 10 percent, then the cost to the company of having raised the \$5 million in capital is the sum of the weighted average.

$$\left(\frac{\$1\text{mm}}{\$5\text{mm}} \times 5\%\right) + \left(\frac{\$4\text{mm}}{\$5\text{mm}} \times 10\%\right) = 9\% \text{ COST OF} \atop \text{CAPITAL}$$

The mix of debt and equity in a company's CAPITAL STRUCTURE affects the company's COST OF CAPITAL to an important degree. Balancing the benefits of FINANCIAL LEVERAGE with the financial risks associated with different levels of debt in a company's CAPITAL STRUCTURE is the primary task of the chief financial officer. The CAPITAL ASSET PRICING MODEL is one tool available to help determine the underlying COST OF EQUITY and to evaluate the impact of changes in CAPITAL STRUCTURE on the overall COST OF CAPITAL.

The strategist's key task is to develop a framework for investing a company's capital at a return higher than the company's COST OF CAPITAL in order to create ECONOMIC VALUE. Therefore, the COST OF CAPITAL is an important benchmark for evaluating investment alternatives. In a diversified company, the strategist's framework for investing capital is the company's CORPORATE STRATEGY.

Cost of Equity: the return required or expected by shareholders of a company's common stock. This REQUIRED RETURN at any given time is reflected in the price the investor is willing to pay for the company's stock. The CAPITAL ASSET PRICING MODEL is one theory which uses the past behavior of a company's stock price relative to movements of the stock market as a whole to calculate the required return for individual stocks. According to the theory, expected return is a function of the return the investor would expect from a risk-free investment adjusted for some additional return to compensate for the risk involved in owning the company's stock. The formula used to calculate the COST OF EQUITY capital for a company is the following.

$$K_e = R_f + \beta(K_m - R_f)$$

Where:

K_e is the COST OF EQUITY capital for the company.

R_f is the rate of return an investor requires on a risk-free investment. The rate on 90-day U.S. treasury bills is generally used as an approximation of the rate.

K_m is the investor's REQUIRED RETURN on an investment exposed to an average level of systematic or market risk. Various measures of how much investors have earned from common equities in the past are used to approximate this return.

β is the BETA for this company, which measures the tendency of the return on a stock to change with the return on the market as a whole.

In a simplified example, the preceding equation can easily be used to calculate the COST OF EQUITY for a given company. If 90-day treasury bills are returning 10 percent, the average return on common equities has been 14 percent, and the given company has a BETA of 1.25, that company's COST OF EQUITY would be 15 percent. The overall COST OF CAPITAL for the company can be calculated by taking the weighted average of the company's COST OF EQUITY and cost of debt.

Given that the price an investor is willing to pay for a share of stock in a company is related to the return that investor expects, a company must continue to, or promise to, return enough to meet investors' expectations, or the price of the company's stock will fall. Theoretically, then, in order to maintain its stock price, a company should be careful to invest in businesses that can provide a RETURN ON INVESTMENT high enough to maintain its RETURN ON EQUITY. That is, a company should invest only when it expects to earn at least its COST OF EQUITY on the equity financed portion of its investment. If no such investments are available, the company should pay dividends instead.

A minimum RETURN ON EQUITY is usually one of the economic GOALS in a company's CORPORATE STRATEGY.

Cost-Plus Pricing: a method of determining price by estimating cost and then adding a percentage markup. One advantage of COST-PLUS PRICING is its simplicity. However, the method tends to allow costs to get out of control because prices are always set after the fact and there are no decreasing margins to warn management.

Strategists tend to oppose COST-PLUS PRICING because they feel that the method ignores the COMPETITIVE FORCES in the industry in which a business competes. That is, they feel that COST-PLUS PRICING exposes the business to THREATS and masks OPPORTUNITIES. For example, there is the THREAT that COST-PLUS PRICING can create a PRICE UMBRELLA that a competitor can take advantage of. Conversely, COST-PLUS PRICING may cause the business to miss opportunities for higher prices that could result in increased profitability.

Cost-Push Inflation: an increase in the general price level that re-sults from an increase in the costs of inputs such as labor or raw materials. An individual business experiences COST-PUSH INFLATION as an increase in one or more of its costs without a corresponding increase in productivity, so that the business must raise its prices in order to maintain profitability. A business simply participates in COST-PUSH INFLATION to the extent to which it passes on its cost in-creases as price increases in order to protect its profitability. A busi-ness is squeezed by COST-PUSH INFLATION to the extent to which it is unable to raise prices and must settle for lower margins or reduced volume.

Cost Structure: a breakdown of the expenditures made to produce and sell a product or to operate a business. Costs are usually clas-sified according to either activity or value added stage and the mix of FIXED and VARIABLE COSTS identified for the particular product, business, or industry. The COST STRUCTURE of a product is often il-lustrated by a bar chart.

The following example shows the simplified COST STRUCTURE of a product when manufactured by Company A and the same product when manufactured by Company B, in terms of dollars per unit and percent of total sales. Both companies pay the same material cost per unit, but Company B's lower manufacturing costs and marketing

COMPANY A		
$5	Profits	10%
$10	Marketing	20%
$2	Overhead	4%
$3	R&D	6%
$20	Manufacturing	40%
$10	Materials	20%

$50 SELLING PRICE 100%

COMPANY B		
$10	Profits	20%
$8	Marketing	16%
$2	Overhead	4%
$5	R&D	10%
$15	Manufacturing	30%
$10	Materials	20%

$50 SELLING PRICE 100%

costs allow it to spend more on R&D and still earn a higher profit margin. It may be that Company B is able to take advantage of ECONOMIES OF SCALE that Company A cannot. Note that the costs have been broken down by general areas of VALUE ADDED but have not been broken down into FIXED COSTS and VARIABLE COSTS as would be done in a more complex COST ANALYSIS.

Comparisons of differences in COST STRUCTURES between industries and among competitors help the strategist to understand the economics of a business and the competitive dynamics of an industry. The identification of FIXED COSTS and VARIABLE COSTS helps the strategist to anticipate the impact of growth or volume changes. In addition, many strategists develop hypothetical COST STRUCTURES to analyze alternative VALUE ADDED CHAINS in order to explore new ways of getting the product to the buyer. Other strategists illustrate a complete VALUE SYSTEM in order to understand how costs affect upstream and DOWNSTREAM VALUE.

Cost Umbrella: *see* PRICE UMBRELLA.

Critical Path Method (CPM): a technique for scheduling and analyzing programs and projects. The technique is used to identify the activities which are "critical" in their impact on the overall completion time of a project. The individual activities are presented on a diagram which highlights the sequence in which each activity takes place and the time necessary to complete each one.

Consider the introduction of a new product for which production facilities must be built and a marketing plan developed and implemented. The individual activities for the project are listed as follows. Each activity is identified by a letter, and those which must precede it are listed along with the completion time for the activity.

	ACTIVITY	PREDECESSOR	TIME (DAYS)
a	Start		0
b	Production plan	a	20
c	Marketing plan	a	15
d	Prototype	b,c	10
e	Pilot plant built	b	35
f	Plant to full production	e	10
g	Distribution channels filled	f	5
h	Advertising program	d	30
i	Finish	g,h	0

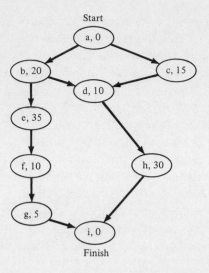

Each activity is then represented on a diagram by a circle, which is identified by the letter and completion time of the activity. The circles are connected by arrows which indicate the sequence in which the activities must take place.

The result is a number of different paths leading from start to finish of varying total times. The preceding graph has three paths. Path one goes via circles a, b, e, f, g, and i; and the total of the completion time is seventy days. Path two consists of a, b, d, h, and i and is sixty days long. Path three consists of a, c, d, h, and i and is forty-five days long. The critical path is path one because it is the longest and governs the completion time of the project overall. Shortening the completion time of any of the activities along the critical path will affect the completion time of the project. For example, reducing the construction time for the pilot plant by five days shortens the critical path and overall completion time to sixty-five days. Cutting the time devoted to the advertising program by even twenty days has no impact on the time necessary to complete the project because it is not on the critical path. However, cutting the completion time of an activity can shift the critical path. For example, if construction time for the pilot plant is reduced to twenty days, then path two becomes the new critical path. In that case, the completion time for the advertising program takes on new importance. Although the CPM is used most frequently by managers of large production or construction projects, strategists also use rough CPM diagrams to estimate implementation time for major programs and to identify bottlenecks.

A S Q C
LIBRARY

Cross Parry: occurs when a company responds to a competitor's aggression in one area by making an aggressive move in a second area. A CROSS PARRY is often a MARKET SIGNAL intended to warn the competitor against continuing its aggressive actions. The company may respond in a different area, i.e., product line or market, for two reasons. The first is to signal that its response is not interpreted as a willingness to fight in the original area. The second is that the company may be able to send a stronger threat in the second area. A FIGHTING BRAND is often used as a CROSS PARRY. Other such market signals include pricing changes, sales promotions, and advertising pushes.

Cross Subsidy: occurs when the profits from one or more products in a business are covering the lower profits or losses incurred by other products in that business. Take, for example, a business that sells two kinds of meters that are both priced at $100. If Meter A's real UNIT COST is $80 and Meter B's is $105, then Meter A is providing a CROSS SUBSIDY for Meter B. CROSS SUBSIDIES can be deliberate, or they can happen unintentionally because the business's MANAGEMENT SYSTEMS obscure the differences in the two products' COST STRUCTURES.

CROSS SUBSIDIES can be advantageous. For example, if the fact that the business can offer both meters is what allows it to get the $100 price for the less costly Meter A, then the CROSS SUBSIDY is likely to be to the business's benefit. This might occur because the full line helps the business differentiate itself or makes it more attractive to the distributors.

However, CROSS SUBSIDIES can be dangerous if they cause a product to be priced above the ENTRY DETERRING PRICE. For example, if sales of Meter B do not enhance sales of Meter A, a competitor who realizes that may cut prices on Meter A in order to gain MARKET SHARE. By doing so, the competitor may be able to put the business in a MIXED MOTIVE position. That is, the business does not want to lose MARKET SHARE, but it also does not want to cut prices for both of its products. This may be the case if it would be difficult for the business to redeploy its investment in the subsidized product toward making more profitable products.

CROSS SUBSIDIES can also occur among businesses and are likely to involve JOINT PRODUCTS.

Cumulative Experience: the proficiency and competency gained through repetition by a business in producing a product or performing a particular function. The impact of cumulative experience is difficult to quantify although in some businesses there is an observed tendency for REAL UNIT costs to decline as the business increases its CUMULATIVE EXPERIENCE. The phenomenon, called the EXPERIENCE CURVE, occurs because the business learns ways to become more efficient as it gets more experience. Total aggregate production is the measure used as a proxy for cumulative experience. For example, the cumulative experience of a business which produced 50 units of a product per year for three years would be 150 units.

Although it is common to analyze a business's CUMULATIVE EXPERIENCE in making a specific product, CUMULATIVE EXPERIENCE can cut across products as well. This is called SHARED EXPERIENCE. Take, for example, a business that has made 1,000 central air conditioning units and 2,000 central heating units per year for ten years, using the same kind of motor for both types of units. The firm's CUMULATIVE EXPERIENCE in making motors is 33,000 units.

For simplicity, the example assumes that the business has the same level of output each year. In reality, this is rarely the case, and getting accurate counts of how many units are made each year can be quite difficult. Also, in many cases, units of production are not available, and annual sales have to be used to estimate them.

Because it is hard to find out about a competitor's production, strategists often use MARKET SHARE or RELATIVE MARKET SHARE as an indicator of CUMULATIVE EXPERIENCE. The assumption that the competitor with the highest RELATIVE MARKET SHARE also has the most CUMULATIVE EXPERIENCE is an underlying concept of the GROWTH/ SHARE MATRIX. A business's CUMULATIVE EXPERIENCE relative to its competitors is often the foundation of a COST LEADERSHIP STRATEGY. ASSUMPTIONS about the impact of CUMULATIVE EXPERIENCE are also the basis for EXPERIENCED-BASED PRICING.

Cumulative Production: *see* EXPERIENCE CURVE.

Current Dollar: a nominal dollar value adjusted to reflect today's purchasing power.

Cyclicality: refers to the degree to which demand in a given industry is affected by BUSINESS CYCLES. Businesses in cyclical industries are sometimes called cyclical businesses.

Strategists consider the CYCLICALITY of the businesses in their portfolios when formulating a CORPORATE STRATEGY. Many try to avoid having too many businesses in the portfolio that either all go up or all go down at the same time in the BUSINESS CYCLE. Cash management is often a serious problem in a portfolio with a high degree of CYCLICALITY. To avoid this, a strategist may either look for businesses that are not cyclical to provide a stable base for the portfolio or look for businesses that are countercyclical to balance the portfolio.

Strategists are also concerned with the CYCLICALITY of an individual business as part of formulating its COMPETITIVE STRATEGY. For example, businesses that are very sensitive to BUSINESS CYCLES often require plans for compensating for, or at least for coping with, fluctuating demand. INTERMITTENT OVERCAPACITY and inventory management can be problems for such businesses.

D

Debt-to-Equity Ratio: a company's debt divided by the company's equity. For example, a company with $1 million in debt and $5 million in equity has a D-TO-E RATIO of .2. A company with a CAPITAL STRUCTURE of equal portions of debt and equity has a D-TO-E RATIO of 1. Sometimes the numerator includes total debt and sometimes just long-term debt. This ratio is one of many that is used to assess a company's exposure to financial RISK based on the balance of debt and equity in the company's CAPITAL STRUCTURE. Businesses in the same industry tend to have standard D-to-E ratios, and the optimal capital structure for a business is usually described in terms of a particular D-TO-E RATIO. Variances among competitors can explain differences in financing costs and profitability.

Strategists use an assumed D-TO-E RATIO as the basis for estimates of future borrowings when making CASH-FLOW ESTIMATES. The D-TO-E RATIO is also one of the elements of the formula used to estimate the SUSTAINABLE GROWTH RATE for a company. In addition, varying D-TO-E RATIOS were used to quantify the impact of changes in LEVERAGE on the COST OF EQUITY in the CAPITAL ASSET PRICING MODEL.

Decentralized Organization: an ORGANIZATIONAL STRUCTURE in which the authority to make decisions is delegated to lower levels in the ORGANIZATIONAL HIERARCHY. The more authority is dispersed to lower levels of management, the more decentralized the structure. The purpose of decentralization is to give decision-making responsibility to people who are close to the sources of information and who are responsible for implementing the decisions. Advocates of decentralization say that it results in better decisions, in faster responses to changes in the business environment, and in greater commitment to carrying out decisions. However, in order for a DECENTRALIZED ORGANIZATION to carry out the kind of coordination and communication required to formulate and implement strategies, the organization must develop effective MANAGEMENT SYSTEMS, especially INTEGRATING SYSTEMS.

A CENTRALIZED ORGANIZATION is the opposite of a DECENTRALIZED ORGANIZATION.

Decision-Making Process: a marketing term describing the steps taken by an individual or business making a purchase. The purchasing process involves four stages: a need is recognized, alternative ways or products available to satisfy the need are identified, the purchase is made, and the choice is evaluated. A strategist studies the DECISION-MAKING PROCESS of a buyer in order to develop ways of influencing the process, such as creating or calling attention to specific needs, supplying appropriate information about a product, setting attractive financing terms, and reinforcing a buyer's decision by providing continuing service.

A DECISION-MAKING PROCESS can range in the degree of formality and in the level and number of people involved from routine orders placed by a purchasing department clerk to selections by senior managers based on detailed studies of alternative purchases. The nature of the DECISION-MAKING PROCESS often depends on a combination of the significance of the purchase and the type of purchasing decision. The matrix that follows shows the impact of the two factors.

A purchase is significant if it is large relative to the buyer's total purchases or if it is important to the buyer's image or performance. In general, the greater the significance of the purchase, the more management attention it receives. In addition, the significance of the purchase influences the price consciousness of the buyer. The larger the purchase, the greater the PRICE SENSITIVITY. However, the greater

PURCHASE SIGNIFICANCE

	Low	High
TYPE OF PURCHASE		
New Purchase	Informal comparisons of alternatives at low levels of organization	Exhaustive study preceding decision by senior management
Modified Rebuy	Cursory reevaluation of alternatives at same level	Systematic review of alternatives
Straight Rebuy	Routine reordering at low levels	Highly formalized approval process

the impact of the purchase on image or performance, the lower the PRICE SENSITIVITY tends to be.

The type of purchase ranges from new or onetime purchases to frequently repeated purchases called straight rebuys. Modified rebuys fall somewhere in between. A new purchase is made to meet a need that has not arisen before. The DECISION-MAKING UNITS have little buying experience to draw on. When making a first-time purchase, the buyer has the highest need for information, and the buyer's confidence based on past experience is the lowest. As the significance of the purchase increases, the level of management involvement and the effort expended to identify and evaluate alternatives are likely to increase.

A straight rebuy involves a continuing or recurring requirement. Usually, the decision is made in the purchasing department on a routine basis from a list of acceptable suppliers. Buyers feel they have sufficient BUYER INFORMATION, and hence little new information is sought to make the decision. If the repeat purchase is a significant one, the process is likely to be more formal. The purchasing department may be given more explicit criteria for price and quality, and its decisions are likely to be reviewed more carefully.

A modified rebuy may develop from either straight rebuy or new purchase situations. It occurs when the need for the product or its significance changes. The buyer may feel more or less confident of his or her knowledge of the alternatives, but the criteria for the choice changes. The changes may be triggered internally owing to new emphasis on cost reductions, quality improvements, or service benefits or externally by changes in government policy.

A marketing strategy for relatively insignificant, repeated purchases generally aims to reinforce the routine buying patterns of existing customers and to introduce incentives for a competitor's loyal buyers to modify their buying patterns. A marketing strategy for significant purchases is likely to require a more customized approach to each customer and continuing reinforcement to generate repeat purchases.

The purchasing decision includes considerations of SUBSTITUTE PRODUCTS, product quality, and price, as well as where to purchase the product, how much to purchase, when to purchase, and how to pay. These considerations do not take place in a prescribed order. For example, a buyer may decide first where to buy the product and then consider only the alternatives offered by that vendor. A strategist should understand how and when and by whom these factors are considered and what importance is attached to each one. This analysis is especially useful in determining why a buyer is purchasing a competitor's product. The analysis should reveal which of these considerations is swinging the decision. The analysis is also useful in determining if a new set of buyers will buy a current product or if a new product will appeal to a current set of buyers. BUYER GROUP ANALYSIS uses this concept.

Decision-Making Unit (DMU):   a marketing designation for the individual or group which influences and controls the purchasing process. The roles played by individuals within the DMU include identifying the need, influencing the choice, giving final approval, making the purchase, and using the product.

The DMUs within an organization often vary according to the nature of the purchase. These different DMUs can be isolated by looking for groups of individuals who have a common goal and share a common risk in making the purchase. Strategists are most often interested in identifying and analyzing the behavior of the different DMUs involved in purchasing their products. That usually involves identifying the relevant DMUs within the buyer's organization, analyzing the perceived goals and risks of each DMU, selecting the DMU whose goals and risks best fit with the business's GOALS, and making sure that the business's MARKETING POLICY influences the selected DMU in a direction consistent with the business's COMPETITIVE STRATEGY.

It is also important to recognize that, in addition to selecting a DMU, MARKETING POLICIES can include programs for changing the GOALS, perceived RISKS, or even roles of the individuals within the DMU.

Decision Tree: a graphic representation of the RISKS and payoffs of each alternative in a decision. A DECISION TREE outlines the sequence of choices, uncertainties, and outcomes associated with alternative courses of action. Choices or decisions are represented by squares or boxes; uncertainties are represented by circles. Probabilities are estimated for each uncertainty, and the financial outcome associated with each sequence of choices and uncertainties is then calculated. The alternative courses of action can then be compared by "folding back the tree" or calculating the product of the probabilities and outcomes along each branch. The product of the two is the expected monetary value or EMV, a weighted average of the outcomes which can be used to evaluate alternatives.

Take, for example, Company A's decision whether or not to produce a new product. Company A really faces two decisions. The first is whether to produce the product. The second is whether to build a new plant or convert an existing plant to make it if the company does choose to produce the product. The outcome of each decision depends on whether a market for the product materializes and whether the market is large or small. Company A estimates that there is a 50 percent chance that any market for the product exists and that if it does, then the probability of its being a large market is 20 percent, and the probability of its being a small one is 80 percent. The DECISION TREE for Company A is shown as follows. The prob-

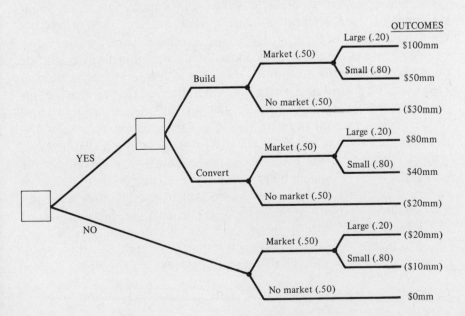

abilities are given in parentheses, and the outcomes are shown at the end of each branch.

To calculate outcomes for the build or convert branches, the company considered three factors: the CASH FLOW expected from a large or small market; the costs of building or converting; and, in the case of conversion, the reduction in CASH FLOW from the products currently produced at the plant. The outcomes associated with not producing the new product at first appeared to be zero. However, the company figured that current sales would be adversely affected if even a small market materialized and was tapped by competitors who could then offer a fuller line of products. In order to compare the three alternatives—build, convert, or don't produce the product—the probable payoff or EMV of each branch is calculated by multiplying each outcome by the probabilities which precede it and adding the products for each branch. For example, the expected payoff for the build branch is equal to the sum of $100mm × .2 × .5 (the large market case) plus $50mm × .8 × .5 (the small market case) and $30mm × .5 (the no market case) for a total of $15mm. Using the same method, the probable payoff for the conversion option is $14mm, and the probable payoff for the no-production option is a loss of $6mm.

On the basis of these calculations, the build option looks the most attractive. However, because the probable payoffs of build and convert options are so close, it would be prudent to test different estimates of the probabilities and outcomes to see how sensitive the choice is to these ASSUMPTIONS before making a final decision.

When drawing a DECISION TREE, it is very important to include all choices and decisions and to draw them in their proper sequence. Decisions are placed at the point at which the decision maker is committed to the choice, and uncertainties are included at the point and in the order in which they are resolved for the decision maker. Estimating realistic probabilities for each uncertainty is a difficult but critical aspect of using a DECISION TREE. The final decision can be very sensitive to the probability estimates. Sometimes DECISION TREES are most helpful simply in indicating which uncertainties have the greatest influence on the decision so that effort can be allocated to collecting the information necessary to refine the crucial estimates.

Strategists often use DECISION TREES to rough out the consequences of various STRATEGIES under different SCENARIOS.

Decline: *see* PRODUCT LIFE CYCLE.

Declining Industry: an industry with falling DEMAND due to technological obsolescence, sociological or demographic changes, or changes in fashion. Research has shown that industries decline differently depending on a number of factors. For example, some industries, like slide rules, decline very quickly whereas others decline slowly, and still others decline in steps supported by isolated BUYER GROUPS and replacement demand. Research has also shown that some combinations of factors lead to industries that are more favorable to end game strategies than others. Those factors include the rapidity of demand decline, the uncertainty of demand forecasts, the presence of MARKET SEGMENTS with continuing DEMAND, price stability, reinvestment requirements, DISECONOMIES OF SCALE, excess CAPACITY, age and market for assets, PRODUCT DIFFERENTIATION, buyer profitability, SWITCHING COSTS, EXIT BARRIERS, BUSINESS INTERRELATIONSHIPS, and MOBILITY BARRIERS.

END GAME BOARDS are used to assess STRATEGIES for competitors in DECLINING INDUSTRIES.

Defensive Intelligence: *see* STRATEGIC INTELLIGENCE GRID.

Defensive Strategy: components of a COMPETITIVE STRATEGY intended to deter or respond to competitors' moves in order to make a COMPETITIVE ADVANTAGE more sustainable. A DEFENSIVE STRATEGY is designed to lower the probability of attack by a competitor, to divert any attacks to less vulnerable targets, or to lessen their intensity. Defensive TACTICS available to a business to ward off or influence a competitor's ENTRY or repositioning in an industry include raising STRUCTURAL BARRIERS, increasing EXPECTED RETALIATION, and reducing incentives for attack.

The elements of a DEFENSIVE STRATEGY must be carefully chosen because BUYERS, SUPPLIERS, and nonthreatening competitors can all be affected by any actions taken. The strategist must be aware of any unintended negative impact on these groups and the possibility that a defensive move could start a chain reaction which destabilizes the entire industry.

BLOCKING POSITIONS and COMPETITOR SELECTION are often elements of DEFENSIVE STRATEGIES.

Strategists who like DEFENSIVE STRATEGIES say that such deterrence is often less expensive than a comparable offensive.

Deintegration: occurs when a business decreases its level of VER-
TICAL INTEGRATION. DEINTEGRATION may increase profitability by
eliminating low-return activities from the business's VALUE ADDED
CHAIN.

Delphi Method: a qualitative method of forecasting that employs
a panel of experts. The panel of experts are kept apart so that they
do not influence each other and are asked to make FORECASTS in
response to specific questions, such as when a new process will gain
broad acceptance or what new development will take place in a given
industry.

A study of future innovations, conducted in four phases, illustrates the technique. In phase one, the experts on the panel are asked
to list inventions and scientific breakthroughs that they think are
both urgently needed and can be achieved in the next fifty years.
From these lists a master list of fifty innovations are compiled. In
phase two, the master list of fifty innovations is sent to the experts
who are asked to indicate when in the next fifty years they think the
innovations are most likely to take place.

Based on an analysis of those responses, a list of those innovations on which there is general consensus is made, and those experts who do not agree with the majority are asked to state their
reasons. On those innovations on which there is no general agreement, the experts are also asked to state their analysis of the widely
divergent estimates. Often as a result, several of the experts reeval-
uate their time estimates, and a narrower range for each innovation
is determined. This becomes the panel's FORECAST.

The DELPHI METHOD, unlike many forecasting methods, does
not necessarily produce a single FORECAST as its output. This is because the DELPHI approach can result in a spread of opinions rather
than in consensus. The objective is to narrow down the range of
estimates as much as possible without pressuring the experts.

The reliability of the DELPHI METHOD is limited by its sensitivity
to ambiguous questions and the difficulties involved in picking experts. Despite these concerns, the DELPHI METHOD offers certain advantages to the strategist. First, panel experts can be selected from
within the company for their specific knowledge and from outside a
company for their objectivity. In addition, people at all different
levels of the organization can be involved, as well as people from
different FUNCTIONAL AREAS. This is because the experts need not be
equally qualified or qualified in the same area in order to participate.

In fact, a diversity of perspectives is often a benefit because a problem or a concern in a company that requires the attention of a strategist usually involves complex issues with uncertainty in many areas.

The DELPHI METHOD is often used to analyze and predict the behavior of a business's competitors.

Demand: the quantity of a product that one or a combination of BUYER GROUPS will purchase at any given price. A demand curve represents the different quantities of a particular product that buyers will purchase at different price levels. An example of a demand curve is shown as follows.

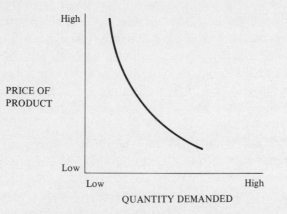

The curve, like most, though not all, demand curves, is DOWNWARD sloping. That is, as the price rises, a BUYER GROUP purchases less of the product. The DEMAND for some products is more responsive to changes in prices than is the DEMAND for other products. The responsiveness of the DEMAND for a product to changes in price is called ELASTICITY OF DEMAND.

The shape and position of the demand curve for a product is affected by such factors as the buyer group's tastes or needs, income, and the price and availability of SUBSTITUTE and COMPLEMENTARY PRODUCTS. DEMAND shifts as any of these factors changes. For example, a buyer group's income determines the amount it has available to purchase all products and therefore affects the DEMAND for a particular product. The responsiveness of DEMAND for a product to changes in the buyer group's income is called the income elasticity of demand.

Changes in the price of SUBSTITUTE products and COMPLEMENTARY PRODUCTS affect a product's demand curve in opposite ways.

An increase in the price of a SUBSTITUTE increases DEMAND for the product whereas a decrease in the price of a SUBSTITUTE decreases DEMAND for the product. For example, an increase in the price of frozen peas will increase DEMAND for canned peas and vice versa. On the other hand, an increase in the price of a COMPLEMENTARY PRODUCT results in a decrease in DEMAND for the product. For example, an increase in the price of bread may reduce the DEMAND for jam.

A final important point is that both the position and the shape of the demand curve often change over time. In the short run, an increase in the price of a product may have little effect on DEMAND because SUBSTITUTES are not instantly developed or accepted. In the long run, however, SUBSTITUTES can be found. Similarly, when the price of a product comes down, it may take a while for buyers to learn about it and for buyers to learn to use more of the product. Thus, it is usually true that DEMAND is more elastic in the long run than in the short run. Short run and long run are relative terms and depend on the particular situation and product.

Demand-Pull Inflation: occurs when final buyers increase demand for the current flow of products, enabling suppliers to increase their prices. Under DEMAND-PULL INFLATION an individual business enjoys increasing margins at least until the rising DEMAND for inputs increases its costs as well. DEMAND-PULL INFLATION can also result from a constriction of SUPPLY, such as an embargo.

Most economists feel that generally INFLATION cannot be accurately labeled as either DEMAND-PULL or as COST-PUSH although occasionally a specific source can be identified.

Dematurity: occurs when a mature industry or one on the verge of maturing returns to either a growth stage or a stage of unpredictable fluctuation in sales. This may occur as a result of PRODUCT INNOVATION, PROCESS INNOVATION, and TECHNOLOGICAL CHANGE either in one or more of the industry's competitors or on the part of its buyers or suppliers.

DEMATURITY may result in a new PRODUCT LIFE CYCLE.

Demographic Trends: *see* ENVIRONMENTAL SCANNING.

Depression: *see* BUSINESS CYCLE.

Derived Demand: occurs when the DEMAND for one product is a function of the DEMAND for another product. For example, a large amount of the DEMAND for rubber is derived from the DEMAND for automobiles.

DERIVED DEMAND can be an important consideration in PRICE POLICY because DERIVED DEMANDS tend to be inelastic. That is, a 1 percent increase in the price of the product will lead to a decline of less than 1 percent in the quantity demanded, raising total revenues. For example, say that the price of rubber went up 10 percent but that all the other costs of making tires stayed the same, resulting in a 5 percent increase in the cost of making a tire. Suppose as well that tire manufacturers raised the price of tires 5 percent and that the DEMAND for tires, which was elastic, went down 5 percent. The result would be a 5 percent decrease in the DEMAND for the rubber. So, in this simplified example, a 10 percent increase in the price of rubber resulted in a decrease of only 5 percent DEMAND for rubber. Note that the more easily other inputs could be substituted for rubber, the more elastic the derived demand would be. Therefore, the pricing and availability of SUBSTITUTE products are key factors to be considered by the strategist setting pricing policy for products with DE-RIVED DEMAND.

Deterrence: *see* DEFENSIVE STRATEGY.

Differentiation Dynamics: *see* COST DYNAMICS.

Differentiation Strategy: a COMPETITIVE STRATEGY that seeks to set the product or service of a business apart from those of its competitors, distinguishing it on the basis of a characteristic other than price. One or several attributes can provide the basis for PRODUCT DIFFERENTIATION. For example, it can be based on BRAND IDENTIFICATION, PRODUCT QUALITY, or some other characteristic leading to UTILITY such as distribution or service. A DIFFERENTIATION STRATEGY is one of the three GENERIC STRATEGIES.

Achieving a successful DIFFERENTIATION STRATEGY can allow a business to earn returns that are above its industry average even if there are strong COMPETITIVE FORCES in the industry. Differentiation provides protection against RIVALRY because it builds buyer loyalty to the business's products. This loyalty also makes it difficult for buyers to exercise BUYER POWER even if they are otherwise inclined to do so. In the same way, it protects the business against SUBSTITUTE PRODUCTS. Differentiation also provides ENTRY and MOBILITY BARRIERS because entrants incur the cost of inducing the loyal buyers away. In the case of SUPPLIER POWER, differentiation per se doesn't seem to protect the business; however, the strategy is likely to allow the business high enough margins to absorb the cost of supplies as well as any other competitor in the industry.

Achieving an effective DIFFERENTIATION STRATEGY usually requires specific types of management skills and ORGANIZATIONAL STRUCTURES. For example, such a strategy may require managers with strong marketing skills and with creative approaches to process and product research and development. It also may require a CORPORATE STRATEGY that enhances the business's ability to build an image of PRODUCT QUALITY, to maintain state-of-the-art technology or to develop LEVERAGE over its distribution channels. The success of the strategy is also likely to depend on an ORGANIZATIONAL STRUCTURE that ensures coordination among the FUNCTIONAL AREAS and provides MEASUREMENT and INCENTIVE SYSTEMS that are subjective enough to encourage creativity. The CORPORATE CULTURE must support and attract creative individuals as well. Finally, corporate management has to be willing to allocate resources for the large advertising, market research, and R&D budgets that a DIFFERENTIATION STRATEGY is likely to require.

As with any strategy, there are two major RISKS involved in attempting to carry out a DIFFERENTIATION STRATEGY. The first risk is that the business will fail to become appropriately differentiated, and the second is that the business will fail to maintain that differentiation as competitors respond and the INDUSTRY STRUCTURE changes. If the business can identify a unique position for itself within the industry initially and devotes the resources necessary to carry out a DIFFERENTIATION STRATEGY, then the challenge is to maintain that position.

Strategists have found four threats to sustaining a DIFFERENTIATION STRATEGY. First, the cost of differentiating the product can get so high that too few buyers can afford the product to make the business profitable enough. Even if the business controls its costs, this can occur if the prices of competitors' products get so low that buyers are unwilling to pay the higher RELATIVE PRICE for the differentiated product. Second, a competitor can come out with a ME-TOO PRODUCT, so that the business's product is no longer effectively differentiated. Third, a competitor can outdifferentiate the business's product so that the business's buyers turn to the competitor instead. Finally, the buyers may lose their need for the differentiating factor that the business has been relying on.

Many strategists feel that the difficulty involved in carrying out an effective DIFFERENTIATION STRATEGY is significant. Therefore, they feel that once a company is comfortable with the formula for a DIFFERENTIATION STRATEGY, it can build STRATEGIC LEVERAGE by making FORMULA FIT part of its CORPORATE STRATEGY. For a DIFFERENTIATION STRATEGY, that formula involves three aspects. First, the company must be willing to build the kind of ORGANIZATION STRUCTURE that supports the creativity and coordination a DIFFERENTIATION STRATEGY requires. Second, the company must be willing to spend to understand the buyer well enough to differentiate the product and to carry out that differentiation. Third, the company must provide the business with managers who are capable of monitoring the degree of differentiation and the relative price of their products vis-à-vis their competitors.

Diffusion of Proprietary Experience: the process by which exclusive expertise and KNOW-HOW are spread to other companies. Proprietary experience is usually diffused when suppliers, channels, or end users inspect the products or even processes of a business. This information may then be haphazardly or deliberately passed among them and to competitors. Even with deliberate diffusion, the process may be slowed by the complexity of the technology involved, the specialized backgrounds of employees, excellent wages and benefits, ECONOMIES OF SCALE, or patents. Most strategists point to the importance of preventing diffusion to competitors in order to preserve MOBILITY BARRIERS. Other strategists add that a company should prevent diffusion to suppliers, channels, and END USERS in order to protect against VERTICAL INTEGRATION and to preserve ENTRY BARRIERS.

Businesses that rely on proprietary experience to protect the relative VALUE they offer their buyers need to set policies and security measures to slow down diffusion, need to develop new levels or types of proprietary experience continually, and may need to build other MOBILITY BARRIERS.

Diffusion Theory: a theory derived from sociology that explains the processes by which innovations are adopted by the END USER. END USERS have been found to go through five stages from awareness to interest, to evaluation, to trial, to adoption. And research has shown that BUYER GROUPS can be classified into five categories based on how quickly they go through these steps relative to others. Accordingly, approximately 30 percent of the eventual buyers for a given product will be innovators and the fastest adopters, 16 percent of the buyers will follow as early adopters, and 34 percent will be next as early majority, putting the sales over 50 percent. Then come the 34 percent late majority and finally the 16 percent laggards.

The combined stages of adoption tend to lead to substitution and adoption forecast models showing an S-shaped curve.

Strategists introducing a new product often attempt to compress the time it takes to reach the desired volume. They do this by targeting the innovators and early adopters, by lowering SWITCHING COSTS, and by UNCERTAINTY REDUCTION. Strategists protecting a product from substitution will want to raise switching costs, distract innovators and early adopters, and maintain or increase uncertainty about the substitute.

Discounted Cash Flow (DCF):   a method for taking the time value of money into consideration when evaluating cash-flow streams. Investment decisions of all types are often evaluated in terms of DCFs.

The value of a dollar received a year from now is less than that of one received today because of the foregone reinvestment opportunity. For the same reason, even nominally equal streams of cash can be of different value depending on the pattern and timing of the cash inflows and outflows. The DISCOUNTED CASH FLOW method incorporates the time value of money into comparisons of the CASH FLOWS by discounting future flows by a rate which represents the returns available on alternative investment opportunities. Cash flow streams can then be compared on the basis of their PRESENT VALUE. The selection of the appropriate discount rate is very important and can determine the relative attractiveness of different cash-flow streams. The higher the discount rate, the more attractive the alternatives which generate a quick return appear to be.

Discretionary Policies: *see* POLICY VARIABLE.

Diseconomies of Scale: increases in the cost per unit of an activity as the number of units produced or handled increases. DISECONOMIES OF SCALE occur when the cost reductions gained by increasing efficiency or spreading costs over larger numbers of units are more than offset by the cost increases involved in managing or otherwise coping with the increased scale. For example, a business might find that although a plant with high capacity allows it low costs once it gets running, those cost savings are offset by the cost of modifying the plant to make the annual style changes that its buyers want. In another example, a plant can get so big that it costs more to move work-in-progress from one area to another than is saved by concentrating the work areas. In another case, transportation costs to the buyer may get too high to make a single large plant worthwhile.

A common example of DISECONOMIES OF SCALE involves management: As the company grows, the executive is confronted with more and more decisions. At the same time, the executive gets further and further away from what is actually going on in the FUNCTIONAL AREAS of the business. The combination of these two makes it increasingly difficult to make sound, profitable decisions; and the result is an increase in costs. Put the company in a rapidly changing or an uncertain environment, and the problem becomes even worse.

Another related example illustrates DISECONOMIES OF SCALE in communication. That is, as the company increases in size, it becomes more difficult and more expensive to coordinate the activities of the organization. Increasing numbers of middle managers, coordinators, expediters, and integrators must communicate with one another in order to coordinate all the functions. In addition to the increasing salaries and benefits of the expanding bureaucracy, there are two other costs. The first is the cost associated with the increasing time it takes for decisions to be made in a bureaucracy, and the second is the increasing cost of the mistakes that are made. As the example goes, a platoon leader's mistake may be corrected with an "As you were!" but a general's mistake may cost a lot to set right.

However, it is important to remember that the ability of managers to deal with large complex organizations varies from company to company. Some executives have developed effective INTEGRATING SYSTEMS which provide decision-making information for managers, have designed effective MEASUREMENT SYSTEMS to monitor those decisions, and have instituted new types of ORGANIZATIONAL HIERARCHIES. In addition, advances in technology, especially in telecommunication and computer information systems, have facilitated communications on an increasing scale.

DISECONOMIES OF SCALE are also called diminishing returns to scale.

Distinctive Competence: *see* COMPETITIVE ADVANTAGE.

Diverse Competitors: competitors in an industry with very different histories or relationships with their parent company and, therefore, with different perspectives on how to compete. This STRUCTURAL FACTOR usually works to affect the intensity of RIVALRY in an industry. Industries with competitors from different countries, with both privately held and publicly traded competitors, or with both large national competitors and small regional competitors are industries with DIVERSE COMPETITORS.

The usual effect of DIVERSE COMPETITORS in an industry is to make it difficult for the competitors to understand and predict one another's behavior because they have different GOALS, time horizons, and degrees of RISK AVERSION. For example, the presence of DIVERSE COMPETITORS can make it difficult for a PRICE LEADER to understand its competitors well enough to carry out its role.

Strategists are especially concerned with understanding the diversity of their competitors when predicting what competitors are likely to do as part of developing a COMPETITIVE STRATEGY.

Diversification: the inclusion of several different financial assets in the portfolio of an investor or the incorporation of several different businesses within a company. The incentive for the individual investor to diversify is to avoid the RISK of failure in a single investment. Although any one company may be a good investment and yield excellent profits, investing everything in that company exposes the investor to the RISK that the worst possible might happen and to catastrophic losses. Therefore, in buying the stock of several companies, an investor reduces the probability that they will all yield excellent profits but also reduces the probability of catastrophic losses.

Corporations diversify by participating in several industries. Corporate DIVERSIFICATION increases with the number and heterogeneity of the products a company produces and the number and heterogeneity of the markets a company serves. Companies can be classified into four categories on the basis of the company's degree of DIVERSIFICATION.

1. SINGLE BUSINESS, a company that generates 95 percent or more of its revenues from a single business.
2. DOMINANT BUSINESS, a company that obtains more than three-quarters of its revenues from a single business. Most

diversification may arise from forward or backward integration. Examples include General Motors and U.S. Steel.

3. RELATED BUSINESS, a company that consists of businesses which produce similar products, compete in the same markets, use the same technology, or share other activities. Examples include Du Pont and Eastman Kodak.

4. UNRELATED BUSINESS, a firm that has diversified without regard to functional relationships between new businesses and current activities. Examples include conglomerate companies like Textron.

Corporations diversify in order to spread their RISK. Some companies base their CORPORATE STRATEGY on providing their shareholders with the ECONOMIC VALUE created by diversifying RISK in their portfolio of businesses. In the case of unrelated diversification, some would argue that the individual shareholder could diversify his or her own portfolio of holdings and that there is no reason for the company to do this for its shareholders. Furthermore, those strategists argue that companies incur overhead and POLICY COSTS when they diversify and that, therefore, companies pursuing related diversification need to follow a CORPORATE STRATEGY that uses a clear CONCEPT OF FIT to enhance the performance of each business by sharing skills, information, and resources.

Strategists tend to approach the issue of DIVERSIFICATION by asking practical questions like, How many businesses are we in? How many businesses should we be in? How do they relate to each other? These questions are key to developing a CORPORATE STRATEGY and are basic to a company's CONCEPT OF FIT.

Divestment: refers to the sale of all or part of a company. Divestment of a business is one of the options that a company considers when the company determines that the business is no longer making a positive contribution to its performance. Usually, however, EXIT BARRIERS lead a company to try a number of other plans before DIVESTMENT, including a FIX PLAN or a HARVEST PLAN to improve the business. DIVESTMENT, therefore, tends to be the option of last resort.

Some strategists do not believe that companies should wait so long to divest. They assert that, if a given business is providing a minimal or negative contribution to the company's ECONOMIC VALUE, the company should immediately consider DIVESTMENT. In that case, the first step for the company would be to make a quick assessment of whether there is anything that can be done to improve the business, the expected costs of doing so, and the PRESENT VALUE of the investment and the expected returns. At the same time, it is necessary to make a quick assessment of the sale value of the business "as is" and after any improvement. Sale value is affected by the possibility that a business that has NEGATIVE ECONOMIC VALUE within the context of one company's CORPORATE STRATEGY may have very positive value within the context of another company's portfolio of businesses. One should, therefore, estimate the value of the business to companies who could be expected to get the most out of it.

Divisional Structure: an ORGANIZATIONAL STRUCTURE in which the ORGANIZATIONAL HIERARCHY is divided into units consisting of a more or less full range of FUNCTIONAL AREAS. Companies usually adopt DIVISIONAL STRUCTURES when they expand into different markets or into different products.

For example, a company might have an East Coast division and a West Coast division, each with its own manufacturing function, marketing function, sales function, etc. Another company might have a consumer products division and an industrial products division, each with its own FUNCTIONAL AREAS. Divisions tend to be managed as INVESTMENT CENTERS.

The more fully a structure is organized into divisions rather than into FUNCTIONAL AREAS, the more fitting it is to call the hierarchy a DIVISIONAL STRUCTURE.

Dog: a business in a company's portfolio that is currently making a low or even a negative contribution to ECONOMIC VALUE. Usually, DOGS are businesses that have weak COMPETITIVE POSITIONS or compete in unattractive industries, and they are often CASH TRAPS. The GROWTH/SHARE MATRIX specifically defines a DOG as a business with a low RELATIVE MARKET SHARE in a slow-growth industry.

Dominant Design: the product among those supplied by the industry that provides the UTILITY that most buyers prefer and whose physical characteristics set the standard for the industry. The product may also be made by the process that most manufacturers use.

Dominant Firm: the competitor with the largest MARKET SHARE in an industry. Some strategists feel that, to be a DOMINANT FIRM, a business should have a RELATIVE MARKET SHARE of at least $1.5x$. In industries where a DOMINANT FIRM exists, other competitors tend not to take actions without the implied permission of the DOMINANT FIRM, which stabilizes RIVALRY.

DOMINANT FIRMS are often also PRICE LEADERS, but not necessarily. Occasionally, a competitor that does not have the highest MARKET SHARE, but has some other valued distinction such as the technological leadership, is called the DOMINANT FIRM.

DOMINANT FIRMS are sometimes called market leaders.

Downstream Value: the value that is added to its product by a business's IMMEDIATE CUSTOMER and others as it moves toward the END USER. DOWNSTREAM VALUE may include further processing, repackaging, END USER marketing and also the markups of importers, wholesalers, and retailers.

Strategists analyze DOWNSTREAM VALUE as part of a strategic COST ANALYSIS, as part of BUYER GROUP ANALYSIS, and to evaluate the potential for VERTICAL INTEGRATION.

A given industry, its upstream value, and its DOWNSTREAM VALUE constitute a VALUE STREAM for that industry.

Durable Good: *see* CONSUMER GOOD.

E

EBIT: an acronym for earnings before interest and taxes. EBIT is often used as the numerator in calculating measures of a business's profitability in order to isolate the operating performance of the business from the impact of its CAPITAL STRUCTURE and TAXATION. Sometimes EBIT is further adjusted to remove allocations of corporate overhead as well.

Econometric Model: a set of relationships among economic variables usually expressed as an algebraic equation. Theorists often use REGRESSION ANALYSIS to build models that explain the differences in performance among different businesses. The PIMS PROGRAM has developed the best-known of these models.

Economic Fluctuation: *see* BUSINESS CYCLE.

Economic Order Quantity (EOQ):   an equation used to determine the optimal number of units a business should order or produce given the expected DEMAND for the product, the cost of placing the order or of setting up a product run, and the cost of carrying inventory. The EOQ formula identifies the order size at which the sum of the setup or order costs, which decrease with order size, and the carrying costs, which increase with order size, is the lowest. The equation for the EOQ is this.

$$\text{EOQ} = \sqrt{\frac{2 \times \text{demand} \times \text{order cost}}{\text{carrying cost}}}$$

For example, if a business expects to use 1,000 units every year and it cost $200 every time an order is placed for the components and it cost $10 to store a single component for a year, the EOQ is 200 components.

The EOQ formula can be used only when DEMAND is known with certainty and when it is not subject to seasonal variations. Setup costs, variable manufacturing costs, and carrying costs must also be known with certainty and not be subject to change with order or lot size.

To adjust for some of the uncertainty most businesses face, particularly in view of the fact that the formula does not take into consideration the strategic cost of not being able to fulfill DEMAND for a product or a component promptly, some strategists add an estimated strategic cost to the order cost. EOQ is often used in inventory control and can be a consideration in MANUFACTURING POLICY.

Economic Trends: *see* ENVIRONMENTAL SCANNING.

Economic Value: the excess in the rate of return earned by an investment over the cost of financing the investment. For example, an investment that returned 20 percent and had a COST OF CAPITAL of 10 percent would have ECONOMIC VALUE to its investors. On the other hand, an investment that returned just its COST OF CAPITAL would have no ECONOMIC VALUE, and an investment that returned less than its COST OF CAPITAL would have NEGATIVE ECONOMIC VALUE. Corporations create ECONOMIC VALUE for their shareholders when they allocate the corporation's RESOURCES to investments that return more than the corporation's COST OF CAPITAL. The shareholder benefits when that ECONOMIC VALUE is reflected in increased MARKET VALUE of the company's shares.

Take, for example, a company that has a thousand dollars in equity and no debt. Assume that the company's ten shareholders each paid $100 for their stock and that they will keep their money in as long as the company pays them a dividend of $10 per year. Imagine first that the company is able to generate only $10 in cash for every $100 invested for five years, at which point the assets are liquidated at BOOK VALUE and the proceeds returned to the shareholders.

YEAR	TOTAL INVESTED	CASH GENERATED	DIVIDENDS PAID
1	$1,000	$100	$100
2	1,000	100	100
3	1,000	100	100
4	1,000	100	100
5	1,000	100	100
BOOK VALUE after five years: $1,000			

Then imagine instead that the company is able to generate $20 in cash for every dollar invested.

YEAR	TOTAL INVESTED	CASH GENERATED	DIVIDENDS PAID	CASH REINVESTED
1	$1,000	$100	$100	$100
2	1,100	220	100	120
3	1,220	244	100	144
4	1,364	273	100	173
5	1,537	307	100	207
BOOK VALUE after 5 years: $1,744				

In the first case, the ten shareholders each get $10 per year in dividends for five years and their $100 back at the end of the fifth year. In the second case, the shareholders each get $10 per year in dividends for five years and their $100 back at the end of the fifth year, but they also get an extra $74.20 in ECONOMIC VALUE created because the company returned 20 percent instead of 10 percent. (In the second case, the shareholders might have been better off if the company had not paid them any dividends and had instead reinvested all the cash in the company.)

A company can create ECONOMIC VALUE by earning returns that exceed its capital costs either by lowering its cost of capital or by raising its returns. There are two broad approaches to doing this: FINANCIAL LEVERAGE and STRATEGIC LEVERAGE. Effective financing involves optimizing the company's CAPITAL STRUCTURE or designing equity and debt securities that are more attractive to the CAPITAL MARKETS than the company's RISK would otherwise dictate. Therefore, companies can use FINANCIAL LEVERAGE to lower a company's COST OF CAPITAL or to raise its returns.

A strategist uses STRATEGIC LEVERAGE in its CORPORATE STRATEGY to make each business worth more as part of the company's portfolio than it would be worth on its own or as part of a competitor. STRATEGIC LEVERAGE in each of the business's COMPETITIVE STRATEGIES helps to build protected profitable positions in the industries in which the businesses compete. To the extent that the company increases its returns and lowers its RISK by protecting those profits, its COST OF CAPITAL will be lowered. Therefore, STRATEGIC LEVERAGE, like FINANCIAL LEVERAGE, can also allow a company to create ECONOMIC VALUE by lowering CAPITAL COSTS or by raising its returns.

Economies of Scale: reductions in the cost of an activity as the number of units of product involved in a given time period increases. ECONOMIES OF SCALE result from being able to spread a FIXED COST over a larger number of units or being able to carry out the activity in a different and more effective way. ECONOMIES OF SCALE can be present at any stage of the VALUE ADDED CHAIN and in nearly every function of a business, including manufacturing, purchasing, research and development, marketing, service network, sales force utilization, and distribution. However, manufacturing may be the easiest function in which to measure ECONOMIES OF SCALE. Take, for example, three companies in the bent-metal plate industry. The manufacturing function consists of cutting a plate with a stamping press and then bending the plate with hand tools. Assume that a stamping press with a capital cost of $100 a day can cut out a maximum of

100 units per day. If a plant produces an average of 100 units a day, the capital cost per unit will be $1.00. If a plant produces less than 100 units a day, the capital cost per unit will increase as the number of units produced goes down. Therefore, ECONOMIES OF SCALE arise from the ability to spread the capital cost over a greater number of units. It can be seen from the exhibit that Company B, producing 100 units, has a COST ADVANTAGE per unit of $1.00 over Company A, with similar facilities, operating at a rate of only 50 units a day.

Intraplant Manufacturing Scale (units per period in a given plant)

MANUFACTURING COSTS	COMPANY A 50 UNITS	COMPANY B 100 UNITS	COMPANY C 300 UNITS
Fixed capital costs	$100.00	$100.00	$ 300.00
Total variable bending cost ($4 per unit)	200.00	400.00	1,200.00
Total manufacturing cost	$300.00	$500.00	$1,500.00
Manufacturing cost per unit	$ 6.00	$ 5.00	$ 5.00

In this example, 100 units a day is also the MINIMUM EFFICIENT SCALE for this type of manufacturing. Notice that a company can get the same capital cost of $1.00 per unit if it has two stamping presses and processes 200 units or three presses and processes 300 units like Company C as long as the amount produced is a multiple of the MINIMUM EFFICIENT SCALE.

The example can be made more complex by introducing a change in process technology. Imagine that a new laborsaving machine for bending metal has been developed with a maximum operating capacity of 75 units and a capital cost of $150 per day.

Intraplant Manufacturing Scale

MANUFACTURING COSTS	COMPANY A 50 UNITS	COMPANY B 100 UNITS	COMPANY C 300 UNITS
Fixed capital costs:			
Stamping	$100.00	$100.00	$300.00
Bending	150.00	300.00	600.00
Total variable bending costs	-------	--------	--------
Total manufacturing cost	$250.00	$400.00	$900.00
Manufacturing costs per unit	$ 5.00	$ 4.00	$ 3.00

Notice that the industry ECONOMIES OF SCALE in manufacturing have changed. Company C is now at a significant COST ADVANTAGE. Company B can reduce its costs by adding two bending machines at a cost of $300 instead of spending the $400 it costs to bend manually; however, it is able to spread the cost over only 100 units, so total manufacturing costs per unit decline only to $4.00. Company C now has the lowest manufacturing cost per unit. This is because the company that is able to operate at a scale of 300 units (3 stamp presses and 4 bending machines) will keep its machines fully utilized and have the lowest manufacturing costs under these ASSUMPTIONS. MINIMUM EFFICIENT SCALE is now 300 units per day.

Another simple example of ECONOMIES OF SCALE would be purchasing. Because Company C produces more units than any other competitor, it probably purchases more raw materials than all others. If each company has one purchasing agent to do all its buying, Company C would be able to spread the cost of that purchasing agent over more units than Companies A and B. However, if an individual purchasing agent could manage without additional help only at a scale of 100 units, then Company B would have the same ECONOMIES OF SCALE in its purchasing function. Although an economist would not label them as ECONOMIES OF SCALE, strategists would point out the benefits of large-scale bargaining power in purchasing as well as being able to afford efficient computer systems, etc.

The manufacturing and purchasing examples illustrate what economists call intraplant economies of scale, that is, economies that occur within a single plant or facility. For example, Company C would not have gotten the same manufacturing ECONOMIES OF SCALE if it had two plants each producing 150 units instead of one plant producing 300 units. But what about purchasing? In the example, purchasing took place within the plant, but what if purchasing could be centralized so that one agent did all the purchasing for all the plants and a single purchasing agent could buy for 600 units as easily as 300 units? In that case, a company with two plants each producing 300 units would have higher purchasing ECONOMIES OF SCALE than Company C with one plant producing 300 units even though both companies would have the same manufacturing costs. ECONOMIES OF SCALE that occur across more than one plant (or facility) are called interplant ECONOMIES OF SCALE.

The most obvious examples of interplant ECONOMIES OF SCALE are in marketing. Say, for example, that each of the companies decided to take out a single-page advertisement in a trade magazine.

The price of the page would be the same for each company, but the company with the highest total production would be able to spread that cost over the most number of units for the lowest advertising per unit. This would be true regardless of how many plants the units were made in.

The existence of ECONOMIES OF SCALE may seem to indicate that UNIT COSTS will continue to decline as long as production increases. However, at some point the effort involved in raising production or the cost of managing production at higher levels equals or exceeds the reduction in UNIT COSTS expected from the effort.

Many strategists feel that ECONOMIES OF SCALE are an important strategic consideration at both the business and corporate levels. They argue that at the business level the decision to invest in achieving ECONOMIES OF SCALE should be based on the business's COMPETITIVE STRATEGY and on an understanding of EVOLUTIONARY PROCESSES in its industry. This is because building scale economies may commit a business to purchasing long-lived SPECIALIZED ASSETS and sustaining very high sales volumes. This lack of flexibility may be risky to the extent that DEMAND or technologies change. A CORPORATE STRATEGY that calls for building scale economies across businesses by way of FUNCTIONAL FIT can compound both the STRATEGIC LEVERAGE that can be gained and the RISK of the inflexibility.

Efficient Market: a market in which buyers have perfect and costless information about the availability, price, and UTILITY of products. Because buyers have instantaneous, perfect information, all suppliers must charge the same price, and the MARKET PRICE for the product instantly adjusts to any changes, eliminating any excess SUPPLY or DEMAND.

Although EFFICIENT MARKETS may exist only under theoretical conditions of perfect information, it can be important for strategists to consider which inefficiencies in the market for their products benefit them and which do not and also to recognize both the value of information to the buyer and the cost of controlling it. For example, almost all COMPETITIVE STRATEGIES benefit from controlling BUYER INFORMATION.

Although there is considerable debate about how efficient the CAPITAL MARKETS are, there are a number of theories explaining the behavior of the CAPITAL MARKETS which are based on the ASSUMPTION that they are totally efficient.

80:20 Rule: *see* BUYER VOLUME.

Elasticity of Demand: a measure of the responsiveness of the quantity demanded to changes in the price of a product. ELASTICITY OF DEMAND or, more precisely, the price elasticity of demand is defined thus.

$$\frac{\text{Percentage change in quantity demanded}}{\text{Percentage change in price}}$$

It is always expressed as a positive number. When the percentage change in the quantity demanded is less than the percentage change in price, elasticity is less than one, and DEMAND is said to be inelastic. If the percentage change in quantity is greater than the percentage change in price, then the elasticity is greater than one, and DEMAND is said to be inelastic. A demand curve does not usually have the same elasticity at every point along the curve. The graph that follows illustrates how the elasticity differs at two points on a demand curve.

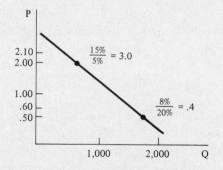

The elasticity of demand is an important consideration in PRICING POLICY because price times quantity determines total expenditure for a product and hence sellers' revenues. If demand is elastic, a decrease in price raises total expenditures, and an increase in price reduces it. Conversely, if DEMAND is inelastic, an increase in price raises expenditures, and a decrease reduces it.

The responsiveness of DEMAND to changes in factors that affect it other than price can also be measured. The responsiveness of DEMAND to changes in income is called income elasticity and is defined thus.

$$\frac{\text{Percentage change in quantity demanded}}{\text{Percentage change in income}}$$

DEMAND for most goods increases with income. These goods have positive elasticity and are called normal goods. DEMAND for some goods falls with increases in income. Such goods have negative elasticity and are called inferior goods.

The responsiveness of demand to changes in the price of other goods is called cross elasticity of demand. Cross elasticity of demand is defined thus.

Percentage change in the quantity of product A demanded

Percentage change in the price of product B

COMPLEMENTARY GOODS have negative cross elasticities because the quantity demanded of product A falls when the price of product B increases. SUBSTITUTES have positive elasticities because the quantity of product A rises when the price of product B increases.

Elasticity of Supply: the responsiveness of supply to changes in price. Elasticity of supply is defined thus.

Percentage change in quantity supplied

Percentage change in price

The behavior of costs as output is varied is a key determinant of the ELASTICITY OF SUPPLY. If costs increase quickly as output is raised, then rising prices are unlikely to stimulate production greatly, and supply is said to be inelastic. When costs are unaffected by a rising level of output or decreasing, then supply is likely to rise in response to increasing prices. In this case supply is said to be elastic.

Emerging Industry: an industry that is newly formed or one that has recently been transformed owing to a major increase in DEMAND or TECHNOLOGICAL CHANGE. In terms of the PRODUCT LIFE CYCLE, the concept of an EMERGING INDUSTRY can cover the introduction stage through the early growth stage. Industries that have been transformed are considered EMERGING INDUSTRIES because the problems of newness and uncertainty are analytically similar to those in recently formed industries. The distinguishing characteristics of both are that the INDUSTRY STRUCTURE is ill-defined and that the INTRA-INDUSTRY STRUCTURE is in a state of change.

Although EMERGING INDUSTRIES can differ greatly, some characteristics are commonly found. Usually, the industry is far from having a DOMINANT DESIGN, which means that there is likely to be both product and process technological uncertainty. In addition, because buyers are likely to be buying the product for the first time, their purchasing DECISION-MAKING PROCESSES are likely to be varied and poorly understood. The level of BUYER INFORMATION may be so low as to leave them confounded and unable to make a decision to buy. Even if buyers feel well enough informed to buy, they often mistake product changes for PLANNED OBSOLESCENCE and are, therefore, slow to buy.

Suppliers may also be uncertain. They will either be new suppliers that are themselves an EMERGING INDUSTRY or competitors in an existing industry faced with a new set of customers. They are likely to have to modify their product or expand their output, and they have to learn to sell to a new industry. Very often producers of a SUBSTITUTE PRODUCT are threatened, and their reactions must be anticipated. Competitors in EMERGING INDUSTRIES are likely to be DIVERSE and difficult to understand. Many of them will be START-UP BUSINESSES.

The INTRA-INDUSTRY STRUCTURE will be equally ill-defined. There will be no proved OPERATING POLICIES to be followed, and competitors will be experimenting with different COMPETITIVE STRATEGIES, inventing CONVENTIONAL WISDOM as they go. Also, the fact that one can expect the COST STRUCTURE to change rapidly as high initial costs fall off quickly with CUMULATIVE EXPERIENCE puts many competitors under pressure to try something and get going.

Most strategists find the uncertainty in EMERGING INDUSTRIES very frustrating. Therefore, some strategists are comfortable ENTERING such an industry only after there has been a significant amount of UNCERTAINTY REDUCTION.

EMV: *see* DECISION TREE.

End Game Board: a technique for choosing strategies in declining industries. Research has identified five major types of end game strategies: investing to become the DOMINANT FIRM, holding the investment constant, selectively shrinking the level of investment while changing its mix from the less attractive MARKET SEGMENT to the more attractive segments, harvesting to recover cash, or DIVESTING. Research has also shown that the appropriate strategy for a given business in a given DECLINING INDUSTRY depends on the combination of the business's competitive position and the attractiveness of the industry. The END GAME BOARD that follows shows these relationships.

BUSINESS'S COMPETITIVE POSITION

		Strong	Average	Weak
ATTRACTIVENESS OF DECLINING INDUSTRY	Favorable	Increase investment or Hold investment	Hold investment or Shrink selectively	Shrink investment or Harvest
	Intermediate	Hold investment or Shrink selectively	Shrink selectively or Harvest	Harvest or Divest
	Unfavorable	Shrink selectively or Harvest	Harvest or Divest	Divest

Strategists who use the end game board appreciate the range of alternatives and the emphasis on INDUSTRY STRUCTURE.

End User: the buyer who ultimately uses the finished product. Any buyer who purchases a product and then, in turn, sells that product to another buyer is an intermediary buyer and not an END USER. The first intermediary buyer of the product from a seller's perspective is called the IMMEDIATE CUSTOMER. For example, a manufacturer of cigarettes might sell to a cigarette wholesaler. That cigarette wholesaler might sell to a jobber, who, in turn, might sell to a newsstand, which, in turn, sells to an individual who smokes the cigarettes. From the cigarette manufacturer's perspective, the immediate customer is the wholesaler, the jobber and newsstand are the intermediary buyers, and the smoker is the END USER.

The END USER may or may not be the buyer with the most influence in the purchasing chain or over product specifications. For example, for a brand name cigarette manufacturer, the most important buyer is the END USER. The manufacturer will use PULL THROUGH advertising directed to its END USER to move its products through its intermediary buyers. On the other hand, to the producers of electrical fixtures, the electricians who supply and install their product may have greater strategic importance than the END USER. In this case, the intermediary buyer is the target of the manufacturers' marketing and selling efforts. Understanding the END USER may also be important if the product is subject to DERIVED DEMAND.

Enhancement: occurs when the fact or process of selling one product leads to higher sales of another product. For example, bars find the enhancing effect of salty snacks on the sales of drinks is so strong that it is worth giving the snacks away.

Strategists look for opportunities for ENHANCEMENT at the business level when building product lines and at the corporate level when building a portfolio of businesses. Strong FUNCTIONAL FIT in distribution or marketing with a newly acquired business may enhance sales of businesses already in the portfolio.

CANNIBALIZATION is the opposite of ENHANCEMENT.

Entry: the arrival of a new competitor in an industry. A new competitor can affect dramatically the profitability as well as the dynamics and intensity of competition of the industry. The likelihood or threat of ENTRY is one of the five competitive forces determining the structure of an industry. Additional CAPACITY can change industry supply-and-demand relationships, and a new competitor is most likely to increase the RIVALRY by affecting such STRUCTURAL FACTORS as DIVERSE COMPETITORS and CORPORATE STAKES. The threat of ENTRY or conversely the attractiveness of an industry to potential competitors is a function of the structural characteristics of the industry, which act as ENTRY BARRIERS by raising the cost of establishing a viable competitive position, and the anticipated reactions of incumbent competitors to a new entrant.

Six common and formidable barriers to entry are ECONOMIES OF SCALE, PRODUCT DIFFERENTIATION, high capital requirements, SWITCHING COSTS, lack of access to distribution channels, and other cost disadvantages independent of scale such as proprietary technology. Businesses competing behind high ENTRY BARRIERS tend to enjoy higher-than-average returns if it is assumed that high EXIT BARRIERS do not prevent competitors who are earning low returns from leaving the industry. For this reason, strategists are interested in developing ENTRY BARRIERS and MOBILITY BARRIERS.

From the perspective of a company entering a new business, there are three approaches to entering: internal development, COALITIONS, and ACQUISITION. From the entrant's perspective, acquisition is often considered less risky. From the incumbent's perspective, ACQUISITION may not be considered to be ENTRY. Usually, the incumbent considers ACQUISITION to be an ENTRY if the new company makes significant changes in the old competitor's COMPETITIVE STRATEGY. This is especially true if the changes involve a BUILD PLAN. The entrant usually considers such an ACQUISITION to be an ENTRY unless the company has absolutely no plans to change the business in any way and is, at the most, only looking for FINANCIAL FIT in adding the ACQUISITION to its portfolio.

New entrants frequently build their strategy for establishing a strong COMPETITIVE POSITION on one of six concepts. The entrant attempts to reduce product costs, to cut price to build MARKET SHARE, to offer a superior product, to serve a new market niche, to use an innovative marketing approach, or to capitalize on existing distribution systems.

Entrants' approaches to an industry can vary a great deal. One way of classifying these approaches is on the basis of whether the company enters with a new product or with a ME-TOO PRODUCT. In general, a new product is considered more risky and expensive than a ME-TOO PRODUCT. However, research has shown that in industries where competitors are pursuing a number of different COMPETITIVE STRATEGIES involving very different products with very different UTILITIES or BRAND IDENTIFICATIONS, a new product may be the less risky way to enter.

A company's approach to ENTRY and strategic objective can also be analyzed in terms of the timing and the scale of the ENTRY.

Some strategists prefer to enter industries early in their evolution before much UNCERTAINTY REDUCTION has occurred in order to affect how the industry will evolve. The more conservative are likely to enter on a small scale as the beachhead from which to expand if the industry meets their expectations. Others feel that the business is not being given a chance to meet their expectations unless the company is willing to make a large-scale ENTRY or at least one consistent with the COMPETITIVE POSITION the company expects for the business in the future. These strategists feel that if the business intends to be a major competitive force in the industry, then it should make that very clear up front. Furthermore, these strategists feel that this commitment to a large-scale ENTRY will act as an ENTRY BARRIER to discourage others by raising the threat of retaliation.

STRATEGIC OBJECTIVE

	Small Scale	Large Scale
EARLY	Pioneer a strategic group	Pioneer a dominant firm
LATER	Improve a specific strategic group	Become a long-term dominant firm

Other strategists prefer to enter industries at a later stage in their evolution when there is still REAL GROWTH, but there has been significant UNCERTAINTY REDUCTION. Usually, these companies have ample resources and like to use those resources to adapt and implement more effectively the successful COMPETITIVE STRATEGIES of the incumbents. Some of these strategists prefer to enter on a small scale. Usually, this is done by entering the STRATEGIC GROUP with the lowest MOBILITY BARRIERS and then moving to a more profitable STRATEGIC GROUP as the entrant gains the familiarity required to surmount those barriers. Others prefer to enter on a large scale either by entering the most significant STRATEGIC GROUP or by making an entry that covers more than one STRATEGIC GROUP. Usually, these strategists intend to become the DOMINANT FIRM in the industry for the long term.

Entry Barrier: a characteristic of an industry which raises the cost of establishing a viable COMPETITIVE POSITION for new competitors. ENTRY BARRIERS discourage ENTRY to the extent that they cost so much to overcome that they make the expected returns after ENTRY seem insufficient even though the incumbent competitors may earn adequate returns. In addition to raising costs, ENTRY BARRIERS can raise the perceived RISK of ENTRY with the same discouraging effect.

ENTRY BARRIERS can be classified as either structural or nonstructural barriers. A structural barrier is inherent in established features of the industry. Structural barriers can be grouped into two categories: those costs or RISKS related to the physical or financial requirements of producing and selling the product and those related to inducing buyers. Nonstructural barriers include the anticipated reactions of incumbent competitors to ENTRY and government policy. The differences between these types of barriers can be subtle and sometimes not meaningful at all in that they all translate into costs and RISKS of entering an industry.

ECONOMIES OF SCALE present ENTRY BARRIERS because they force the entrant either to invest enough to enter with a minimum efficient operation or to enter with higher costs than the incumbents who are operating at that scale. If the entrant does decide to enter at MINIMUM EFFICIENT SCALE, it has to make a large investment and capture a sufficient amount of MARKET SHARE in order to earn acceptable returns on that investment. The larger the MARKET SHARE implied by MINIMUM EFFICIENT SCALE in an industry, the higher the ENTRY BARRIER presented by ECONOMIES OF SCALE.

TYPE OF BARRIER	COST/RISK OF COMPETING
STRUCTURAL BARRIERS	Economies of Scale Capital Requirements Absolute Cost Advantages Access to Distribution
	COST/RISK OF INDUCING BUYERS
	Product Differences Brand Identity Switching Costs
NON-STRUCTURAL BARRIERS	GOVERNMENT POLICY
	EXPECTED RETALIATION

Industries which require large up-front investments in capital for whatever reason are likely to have capital requirement ENTRY BARRIERS. They arise when the size of the up-front investment is large enough to drive up the COST OF CAPITAL for most or all potential entrants, and substantial components of the up-front investment would have limited salvage value in the event of failure.

An absolute COST ADVANTAGE enjoyed by an incumbent that cannot be replicated is an ENTRY BARRIER. Usually, these absolute COST ADVANTAGES rest on patented or otherwise proprietary products or processes, favorable access to raw materials, preferred locations, and cost declines gained through proprietary CUMULATIVE EXPERIENCE.

If the incumbents have tied up the current distribution channels in the industry, the entrant may have to spend to supersede the incumbent's relationship with the distribution channel or invest to develop a new way to distribute. The stronger the incumbent's hold on the channels, the more of an ENTRY BARRIER access to distribution is likely to be.

PRODUCT DIFFERENCES, BRAND IDENTIFICATION, and SWITCHING COSTS all tend to make buyers loyal to the incumbents. They serve as ENTRY BARRIERS to the extent that the entrant has to spend to overcome loyalty and induce buyers to purchase the entrant's products instead. Also, the presence of these differentiating factors usually means that there are meaningful STRATEGIC GROUPS in the industry. This can have pluses and minuses for the entrant. On the positive side, it may be possible for the entrant to enter one STRATEGIC GROUP with a SEQUENCED STRATEGY and then move out from that beachhead position. On the other hand, the presence of strong MOBILITY BARRIERS complicate the ENTRY and make it difficult to establish a strong COMPETITIVE POSITION.

Government policy can build and destroy ENTRY BARRIERS both in the United States and around the world. Government policies can regulate ENTRY directly or set standards and requirements that increase the cost of ENTRY.

The last type of ENTRY BARRIER is EXPECTED RETALIATION. Even if all other conditions seem favorable, if the entrant expects the incumbents to retaliate forcefully with pricing changes and marketing programs or to respond quickly to product changes, the anticipated costs and RISK of ENTRY may rise sufficiently to discourage the entrant. Some strategists feel that raising the threat of EXPECTED RETALIATION is one of the least expensive ENTRY BARRIERS for an incumbent to build. It also has the advantage of not contributing to EXIT BARRIERS.

Strategists in incumbent businesses are interested in building ENTRY BARRIERS in order to discourage new entrants who are likely to decrease industry profitability. New entrants can do that by bringing in new CAPACITY, new resources, new ways of competing, new processes, new products, and new technology. They can reduce the incumbents' profitability by bidding down prices and by forcing incumbents to increase expenses and investment. Strategists have also found it important to understand how ENTRY BARRIERS are changing over time. Changes in the industry that appear to lower ENTRY BARRIERS should be perceived as a THREAT to the industry's profitability, and changes that allow for higher ENTRY BARRIERS may be OPPORTUNITIES to increase profitability. Another important consideration is the relationship between the ENTRY BARRIERS and the EXIT BARRIERS in an industry. ENTRY BARRIERS are often the key STRUCTURAL FACTORS that allow the industry to be profitable, and EXIT BARRIERS can have a significant effect on the stability of that profitability.

Finally, ENTRY BARRIERS should be evaluated vis-à-vis the most likely or well-positioned group of potential entrants. This group may be large and ill-defined, or it may be a small and specific group which the incumbent can monitor closely.

Entry Deterring Price: the highest price the incumbent competitors in an industry can charge without attracting new competitors. The highest price any one competitor in an industry can charge without causing its competitors to copy its COMPETITIVE STRATEGY is also called an ENTRY DETERRING PRICE or a mobility deterring price.

The ENTRY DETERRING PRICE varies for potential entrants because the cost of ENTRY is relative depending on the resources of the company considering the ENTRY. For example, in a given industry, if the products were sold at two dollars instead of at one dollar, the industry still might not be profitable enough for most companies to consider entering. However, a company with the right combination of resources might find the industry attractive enough to ENTER at that price. From the perspective of the incumbent competitors, the ENTRY DETERRING PRICE of the most favored or likely entrant is the price to be considered when formulating a PRICING POLICY.

Environmental Scanning: analyzing trends in those external factors that affect a company's performance in order to make ASSUMPTIONS and FORECASTS about the future. Because a company can at best influence and not control its environment, it must make FORECASTS, not decisions, about what trends there are in its environment and how they will affect the company.

Most strategists categorize different aspects of the environment into five categories. Economic trends include changes in gross national product, interest rates, employment rates, energy costs, and INFLATION. Demographic trends include changes in population growth rates by region, family size, and age group distribution. Social trends include changes in people's values, life-styles, and education levels. Political and legal trends include changing political climates and regulatory pressures. Technological trends include all aspects of new technologies and changes in old ones.

A major problem in ENVIRONMENTAL SCANNING is knowing which of the huge number of trends are important to forecast. In many cases, the most serious and likely error is overlooking a trend rather than forecasting it inaccurately. Corporate strategists often try to focus on trends that will affect the CAPITAL MARKETS and shareholders' expectations, both social and financial. Business level strategists focus on analyzing trends in terms of their effect on the EVOLUTIONARY PROCESSES relevant to a given business's INDUSTRY STRUCTURE.

Another problem in ENVIRONMENTAL SCANNING is the increasing rate of change. This increasing rate of change means that there is less time to recognize and compensate for an error or oversight. In order to give continuous attention to ENVIRONMENTAL SCANNING, some companies have specific individuals responsible for the analysis on an ongoing basis. These individuals often generate broad environmental SCENARIOS by varying sets of ASSUMPTIONS. Three typical SCENARIOS might be a pessimistic, a likely, and an optimistic SCE-

NARIO based on three inflation rate ASSUMPTIONS. These SCENARIOS would address each of five categories of trends. Strategists would then decide which aspects of each SCENARIO are likely to have the most significant effect on performance and where more information or certainty is needed.

UNCERTAINTY CHARTS are often used to index the impact of environmental trends.

EOQ: *see* ECONOMIC ORDER QUANTITY.

Equilibrium Price: the price at which the quantity supplied is equal to the quantity demanded. In the short run, price rations DEMAND to the fixed supply that is in existence. In the long run, the EQUILIBRIUM PRICE adjusts until no seller desires to change his or her output given that price.

EVC: *see* BUYER VALUE.

Evolutionary Process: a catalyst that creates incentive and pressure for change in INDUSTRY STRUCTURE and INTRA-INDUSTRY STRUCTURE. EVOLUTIONARY PROCESSES are the drivers of INDUSTRY EVOLUTION. Some obvious EVOLUTIONARY PROCESSES are changes in demographics, changes in buyer needs, changes in the PRICE-TO-PERFORMANCE RATIO of SUBSTITUTE PRODUCTS, changes in the price or performance of COMPLEMENTARY PRODUCTS, changes in product UTILITY, and market SATURATION. These developments can affect the anticipated future growth and profitability of an industry. They can also either undermine or reinforce the competitive strengths of businesses in the industry or those contemplating ENTRY.

The following is a list of other EVOLUTIONARY PROCESSES that may be at work in an industry.

- Emergence of new BUYER GROUPS.
- Increasing BUYER INFORMATION.
- UNCERTAINTY REDUCTION.
- Diffusion of proprietary knowledge.
- Increasing CUMULATIVE EXPERIENCE.
- Increasing or decreasing SCALE OF OPERATIONS.
- Innovative product UTILITY.
- Innovative MARKETING POLICIES.
- PROCESS INNOVATION.

- Increases or decreases in the cost of inputs such as labor, energy, and materials.
- Changes in currency exchange rates.
- Evolution in supplier, buyer, or SUBSTITUTE PRODUCT industries.
- Changes in government policy.

Most strategists feel that it is very important to monitor change in the EVOLUTIONARY PROCESSES that are relevant to their industries. They feel that this monitoring is necessary in order to be able to anticipate THREATS and OPPORTUNITIES as their industries evolve.

Exit: the departure of a competitor from an industry. In general, a company EXITS an industry with some combination of LIQUIDATION, redeployment, and DIVESTMENT. Each of the three routes has a different effect on the remaining competitors. Only redeployment completely removes a competitor from the industry by placing the assets in another use. DIVESTMENT turns the business over to a new company, and LIQUIDATION leaves open the possibility that some or all of the business's equipment and other assets will remain in use in the industry under the control of another company. For this reason, many strategists consider it important to anticipate how a competitor is likely to EXIT before pushing that competitor to the point of EXIT.

The ease with which competitors can EXIT from an industry is an important determinant of the level and stability of profitability for the industry as a whole. The existence of EXIT BARRIERS which raise the cost of departing from an industry can hold down returns for all competitors. Competitors earning low or even negative returns may continue to compete, holding down prices and returns for all rather than bear the cost or RISK of withdrawing.

Exit Barrier: a STRUCTURAL FACTOR or aspect of COMPETITIVE STRATEGY that makes it expensive or risky for a business to depart from an industry. EXIT BARRIERS keep a business in an industry even when it is earning a low or even negative RETURN ON INVESTMENT. EXIT BARRIERS can be classified as economic, sociopolitical, or emotional.

Economic barriers can be due to specialized assets, FIXED COSTS of exiting, or strategic BUSINESS INTERRELATIONSHIPS with other businesses in the company's portfolio. For example, the assets used in the business may be too specialized to be of much value to a potential buyer. There may be onetime fixed costs, such as fulfilling a labor agreement. Finally, the business may supply other businesses in the portfolio or share a distribution channel. Exiting from such a business may be sufficiently disruptive to the strategies of the other businesses to make EXIT economically unattractive again.

Sociopolitical EXIT BARRIERS are found more commonly outside the United States. They are likely to involve other government restrictions or social discouragement from EXIT. The underlying issue is often the loss of jobs or the loss of a politically important industry.

Emotional barriers to EXIT involve an emotional attachment to a business either on the part of the business's or the company's management. The basis of this attachment can be loyalty to employees, identification with the industry, pride in past achievement, and original involvement in entering the business.

Strategists avoid building EXIT BARRIERS in their own businesses where possible because the barriers cut down flexibility. They also do not like to see EXIT BARRIERS being built around their competitors' businesses because those barriers may prevent competitors from exiting. Understanding the EXIT BARRIERS faced by competitors is also very important in evaluating the RISK of making an aggressive move in an industry.

It can be useful to know when competitors have EXIT BARRIERS in other businesses in their portfolios. Those EXIT BARRIERS may weaken the competitors' portfolios and prevent them from increasing their LEVERAGE in the strategist's industry.

Expected Monetary Value: *see* DECISION TREE.

Expected Retaliation: the reactions of incumbents anticipated by potential entrants to an industry. If potential entrants do not expect much reaction from the incumbents, then EXPECTED RETALIATION is low. On the other hand, if potential entrants expect that the incumbents will fight very hard to keep a new entrant out and will continue to retaliate long after entry, then EXPECTED RETALIATION is high.

Strategists considering ENTRY look for a number of indicators of EXPECTED RETALIATION. The most obvious indicator is past behavior. If incumbents have a history of retaliation, this is likely to indicate vigorous retaliation in the future. A second indicator is the degree of commitment incumbents have to the industry, measured by the extent of CORPORATE STAKES or emotional EXIT BARRIERS. A third indicator is the level of financial resources incumbents have available for retaliation, including unused debt capacity and excess CASH FLOW. A fourth indicator is the likelihood that the incumbents will suffer a significant financial impact because of the ENTRY. Usually, the STRUCTURAL FACTORS that lead to RIVALRY are good indicators of that financial impact. For example, in an industry with slow growth, retaliation is likely because the entrant's success will have to come at the incumbent's loss.

Some strategists consider industries where there is a high degree of RIVALRY to be attractive for ENTRY. They see the RIVALRY as absorbing the incumbents, making retaliation unlikely. Other strategists look for industries in which RIVALRY is low and especially for industries where it is being kept low by a DOMINANT FIRM or by a PRICE LEADER. They consider those industries to be unfamiliar with retaliatory tactics and likely to be slow to respond to the ENTRY.

Some strategists in incumbent businesses have recognized that EXPECTED RETALIATION can be a very inexpensive and often a most effective ENTRY BARRIER. Therefore, those strategists add tactics to their COMPETITIVE STRATEGIES that build that expectation. A history of successful retaliation is an obvious way of enhancing the threat. However, action is not really necessary unless the industry is tested. Instead, a business can increase the perceived threat by making its commitment known. That is, the business can publicize its interest in the industry by such TACTICS as announcing its intention to build CAPACITY ahead of DEMAND. It can also publicize its high R&D expenditures and its ambitious plans for the future. Furthermore, it can make known its financial strength and its corporate commitment to the business. MARKET SIGNALING is often used to build a sense of EXPECTED RETALIATION.

Experience-Based Pricing: PRICING POLICIES based on an analysis of the EXPERIENCE CURVES of the business and its competitors.

EXPERIENCE-BASED PRICING makes the assumption that the competitor with the most experience has the lowest costs. Given this assumption, the low-cost competitor has three basic choices as to PRICE POLICY, illustrated in the following example of Business A's choices in competing with Business B and Business C.

The EXPERIENCE CURVE in the example shows that Business A has the most CUMULATIVE EXPERIENCE, having produced 500 units. Because of this experience, Business A's costs have declined to $30 per unit. Business B and Business C, having only produced sixty and

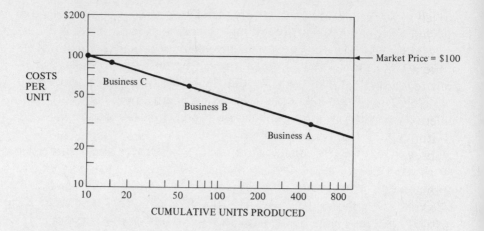

fifteen units respectively, have much higher per unit costs of $60 and $90. The current MARKET PRICE in the industry is $100 per unit. This means that Business A is making $70 on each unit it sells whereas Business B and Business C are making $40 and $10 respectively. As the cost leader, Business A has pricing policy options that range from setting an UMBRELLA PRICE above the costs of all its competitors to dropping prices below current costs in anticipation of future cost declines. On middle ground it can drop prices roughly in line with costs, maintaining more or less generous margins. Each of these choices has benefits and RISKS. (All prices and costs in this example are in CONSTANT DOLLARS.)

If Business A chooses to hold prices up, it benefits from high profits on each unit. These profits can be reinvested in further lowering costs in this business or, in the case of a DIVERSIFIED company, invested in other businesses in the portfolio. However, one RISK is that Business B, which is earning lower but still attractive margins, may use those profits to gain share or even surpass Business A. One way for Business B to do this is to invest in new technology that puts it on an even faster EXPERIENCE CURVE. Another way is for Business B to purchase Business A's experience. Say, for example, that over the last four years Business A has developed an excellent cost-reducing inventory management system. Business B can probably "buy" the experience that took Business A years to develop by hiring away Business A's inventory manager. Another risk involves Business C. Business C will not make as much money as either A or B, but it will still be profitable. Depending on how many units it produces each year, Business C's costs are probably coming down relatively quickly. Depending on other ENTRY BARRIERS, the fact that the price is high enough to allow a small company to make money may attract additional entrants. The more profitable competitors there are in the industry, the more likely one of them will develop a new technology and be able to surpass Business A's cost position.

Some strategists recommend this pricing strategy in situations where Business C and possibly Business B as well are marginal competitors and unlikely to make effective use of whatever profits an umbrella MARKET PRICE allows them. In these situations, Business A, as the low-cost producer, can make a great deal of money while minimizing RISK. This type of umbrella for weaklings is especially effective when buyers are price-sensitive but want alternative sources of SUPPLY. This means the buyers are forced to accept the price of Business C, the high-cost producer. The only way the buyers can get around the problem is to try to bring experience in line by attempting to redistribute the shares. However, an attempt on the buyers' part to affect SHARE BALANCE can be met with price cuts by Business A that Business C cannot follow and that Business B will be reluctant to follow. If Business A chooses to hold prices up, it must carefully monitor competitors' costs to make sure its COST ADVANTAGE is not lost.

If Business A chooses to drop prices as costs decline, it faces another set of benefits and RISKS. Although Business A won't make as much on each unit as it would if it held prices up, it will still earn higher margins than the competition, and total industry demand may rise. For example, assume that Business A decides to lower its price to $70. Not only are some of the buyers of Business B and Business C now likely to buy from Business A, but new buyers are also likely to be attracted by the lower price. To the extent that Business B matches Business A's price, Business A may not take buyers away, but the industry is likely to sell even more units than when everyone's price was $100. Depending on the EXIT BARRIERS, Business C may go out of business. This would increase both Business A's and B's sales volume.

One RISK of choosing to drop prices is that the prices may get too low to generate enough CASH FLOW to finance growth. Another RISK is that to the extent that the lower prices have generated expanded DEMAND in the industry, this DEMAND may attract ENTRY. If the lower prices are also constraining the ability of the industry to finance capacity expansion to meet demand, this offers potential entrants even more encouragement. However, the threat of new entrants is minimized if Company A can protect its experience and COST ADVANTAGE.

If Business A chooses to lower prices below its costs, it is engaged in an extreme form of PENETRATION PRICING. This implies both a commitment to gain MARKET SHARE, forcing as many competitors as possible out of the industry, and a presumption that Business A can protect a high share position with a COST LEADERSHIP strategy. The risk is that another competitor or new entrant will either buy or invent its way to a lower-cost position.

The last type of policy could be considered to be PREDATORY PRICING.

Experience Curve: the observed tendency for the UNIT COST of a product to decline as cumulative production increases. The EXPERIENCE CURVE is an expansion of the learning curve phenomenon. A famous study of the effect of "learning by doing" was done of World War II aircraft production. The study showed that labor costs per unit declined as more and more aircraft were assembled. Research by the Boston Consulting Group and many academic researchers led to the observation that it was not just labor costs that declined with learning but many other categories of costs as well. Empirical studies showed that doubling a company's CUMULATIVE EXPERIENCE caused the UNIT COST of a plane to decline by 20 percent. That is, the 200th unit produced can be expected to cost 20 percent less than the 100th unit produced. This expanded concept is called the EXPERIENCE CURVE. As the concept has evolved, researchers have noted that a particular EXPERIENCE CURVE applies to a given technology for making a given product or component of a product. The products of one industry may show a 20 percent EXPERIENCE CURVE whereas the products of another may show a 30 percent EXPERIENCE CURVE. In addition, it is possible for one competitor in an industry to be on a 20 percent EXPERIENCE CURVE and for another competitor with a different technology to be on a 30 percent EXPERIENCE CURVE.

There appear to be three reasons why unit costs decline with experience. The first is labor efficiency, as demonstrated in the aircraft assembly study. As individuals repeat an activity, they become more efficient through familiarity with the activity as well as by thinking of better ways of doing it. This is especially true of assembly operations but can also be true in any function at any level of management, including, for example, such diverse functions as purchasing, maintenance, or labor relations.

The second reason for cost declines with experience is process improvements. These can range from modifications of existing methods to extensive changes in equipment and plant layout. Experience may allow other FUNCTIONAL AREAS such as the accounting department to develop better control systems and the marketing department to learn what mix of advertising media produces the best results.

The third reason for cost declines with experience is product improvements. To be effective, these improvements usually lead to a more standardized product. For example, as the R&D and sales departments become familiar with exactly what type of product meets their performance and sales goals, they may settle on a standard product design. At the same time, manufacturing begins to think of design changes that make it easier and cheaper to manufacture by substituting a less expensive material for a certain component or cutting back on material waste. All these contribute to declining UNIT COSTS.

An EXPERIENCE CURVE can be graphed by plotting data on the number of units produced and UNIT COSTS in CONSTANT DOLLARS over time. In the following simplified example, Business A produced fifty units a year for five years in a single plant.

OUTPUT AND COST DATA

Year	Units Produced	Cumulative Units	Unit Costs (Constant $)	$ Cost Savings	% Cost Decline
1	50	50	$60		
2	50	100	$48	$12	20%
3	50	150	$41	$7	15%
4	50	200	$38	$3	8%
5	50	250	$36	$2	6%

EXPERIENCE CURVE FOR BUSINESS A

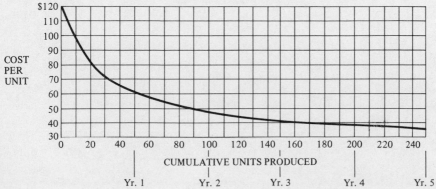

Notice that the business's SCALE OF OPERATIONS has remained constant at fifty units per year, but that every year it gained experience. By Year 2 the business had doubled its CUMULATIVE EXPERIENCE and UNIT COSTS declined by 20 percent. However, at fifty units a year, it took until Year 4 before experience doubled again and costs declined another 20 percent, and it will not be until Year 8 that experience will double again. Because at a constant SCALE OF OPERATIONS it takes longer and longer to double CUMULATIVE EXPERIENCE, annual cost declines become less and less dramatic. (Of course, if the business increased its production to more than fifty units per year, it would gain experience faster.)

Experience curves are often drawn on log paper as follows. This is done to make the relationship between unit costs and cumulative production more obvious and to provide a simplified straight-line estimate of future costs.

But regardless of how the EXPERIENCE CURVE is drawn, the difficult task is collecting the necessary data. In the example just given, data on production and per UNIT COSTS in CONSTANT DOLLARS were given. In practice, there are a number of problems in collecting data. The first involves defining the product to be studied. Should, for example, all models of a given product be plotted on the same curve, or should each model be plotted separately, or should specific components of each model be plotted? The answers depend on the question the analysis is expected to answer and the COMPETITIVE STRAT-

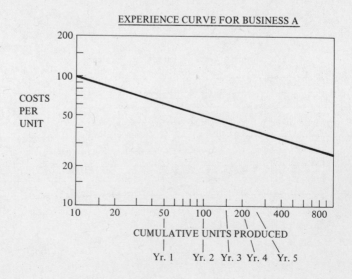

EXPERIENCE CURVE FOR BUSINESS A

EGY of the business being studied. The second problem involves collecting cost data that is relevant to the units being plotted and comparable over time. Obviously, CURRENT DOLLAR costs must be deflated to represent CONSTANT DOLLAR costs, but there can be a number of other problems as well. For example, cost data may be collected by department rather than by product, or there may be discontinuities in the data because of organizational changes or changes in accounting methods.

Sometimes strategists seek to estimate the EXPERIENCE CURVE of a business about which they have no cost information. This is often the case in assessing the ENTRY BARRIERS as part of the process of making an ENTRY decision. In such cases, prices in CONSTANT DOL-LARS can be used as a proxy for costs. In using price, one is assuming that the MARKET PRICE of the product has had a constant relationship to the cost of the product.

Note that measures of costs declining with experience will cap-ture some ECONOMIES OF SCALE to the extent that, in addition to gain-ing experience over time, many businesses also increase their SCALE OF OPERATIONS. Even though the effects of experience and scale economies are both reflected in declining costs, they are quite dif-ferent in two important ways. First, they are different because the source of the EXPERIENCE CURVE cost declines is not how many units are produced in a given time period but rather the total number of units the company produced over time, that is CUMULATIVE EXPE-RIENCE. Second, the two phenomena differ in the way costs decline. With ECONOMIES OF SCALE, costs most often decline as a result of production increases that allow FIXED COSTS to be spread over more units. With experience, it takes conscious effort on the part of man-agement to cut costs. In fact, without control, costs tend to increase, so the effort involved in reversing the tendency should not be under-estimated. Of course, cost declines in some products, like those pro-duced on an assembly line, may be easier to control than others. But even on an assembly line, where workers may become more efficient at performing a repeated task, it requires effort on management's part to maintain motivation and minimize employee turnover in or-der to stay on the EXPERIENCE CURVE. VALUE ANALYSIS is an example of the kind of management effort that is required to take advantage of cost declines through CUMULATIVE EXPERIENCE.

Many strategists feel that effective COST ANALYSIS is the key to taking advantage of experience at the business level. Those strategists argue that building CUMULATIVE EXPERIENCE and monitoring com-

petitors' experience are very important in implementing a COST LEAD-
ERSHIP STRATEGY or in developing EXPERIENCE-BASED PRICING policies. They also point out that, in COMPETITOR ANALYSIS, understanding the EXPERIENCE CURVE of each business in a company's
portfolio can be the key to that company's CORPORATE STRATEGY,
especially if the strategy is based on the GROWTH/SHARE MATRIX.

Some strategists also feel that opportunities for SHARED EXPE-
RIENCE can be a key to building an effective CONCEPT OF FIT in a
company's CORPORATE STRATEGY.

Most strategists recognize that experience can give a business a
sustainable COST ADVANTAGE only if the experience can be kept proprietary. That is, experience can be used to build MOBILITY and EN-
TRY BARRIERS but only to the extent that competitors can be pre-
vented from buying or duplicating the experience of the business or
from inventing a new technology with a steeper curve.

Expertise: *see* FORMULA FIT.

Externality: the impact on third parties of the actions of those directly involved in the production of a COMMODITY or the use of a
resource. The impact can be beneficial or detrimental. Pollution is
the most frequently cited example of an EXTERNALITY. Wastes generated by one company can pollute a water supply, making the area
less attractive. Both individuals living in the area and companies
trying to attract new employees suffer. The impact of the product
failures of one business, which can make it difficult for competitors
to sell their products, is another example of EXTERNALITY.

Governments often point to EXTERNALITIES as a reason for their
intervention into business activities. Strategists should be aware of
such EXTERNALITIES in order to protect their company from EXTER-
NALITIES that can reduce the ECONOMIC VALUE of the company and
to help the company take advantage of EXTERNALITIES that can benefit it.

F

Fair Market Value: the theoretical price of something in an idealized marketplace. That is, a FAIR MARKET VALUE of a product would be the price that the seller and buyer would agree to under conditions of PERFECT COMPETITION. Under such ideal circumstances, the seller would be willing to sell, but under no compulsion to do so, and the buyer would be willing to buy, but under no compulsion to do so. Also, both the seller and the buyer would have perfect or near-perfect knowledge of all relevant facts about the product. Because of imperfections in the marketplaces for most products, the MARKET PRICE rarely equals the FAIR MARKET VALUE.

Family Brand: *see* BRAND IDENTIFICATION.

Field Theory: an approach to corporate resource evaluation that defines a company's businesses as linked networks of products or markets (or both) and the relevant value added steps.

The emphasis in FIELD THEORY is on how a company can best allocate its resources to create COMPETITIVE ADVANTAGES in its businesses as opposed to how it can weed out the bad from the good businesses.

Strategists who use FIELD THEORY develop STRATEGIC FIELD MAPS to analyze the relevant relationships.

FIFO: an accounting method for valuing inventory that assumes that the business's oldest inventory is sold first. FIFO is an acronym for "first in, first out." The essential issues for the strategist in working with FIFO can be illustrated in the simplified example of Business A. During the past year, Business A produced one hand-made sailboat per quarter. All the boats were identical except that, as the year went on, the cost of making each boat increased such that the first boat cost $60,000 to build and the last boat cost $90,000 to build. Business A made its first sale in January of the current year for $100,000. The question of which boat to send the customer was settled by selecting the boat which was the easiest to move out. But how much did the boat cost? Under FIFO, the accounting department would assume that the boat built first was sold first and that, therefore, the cost was $60,000 and the gross margin was $40,000.

However, under the LIFO method, which stands for "last in, first out," the accounting department would assume that the last boat built was the one sold so that the cost would be $90,000 and the gross margin would be only $10,000.

As the preceding example shows, the choice of FIFO or LIFO can affect reported income. It can also affect reported investment because of the impact on the value of inventory. In the example just given, the first boat cost $60,000 to build, and the fourth cost $90,000. Assume that the second boat cost $70,000 and that the third cost $80,000. Before any sales were made, the value of finished goods inventory was the sum of the costs of the four boats, which was $300,000. Under FIFO, after the first sale was made, the three remaining boats would add up to an investment in inventory worth $240,000. After the first sale under LIFO, the three boats would add up to an investment of only $210,000 in inventory. Therefore, FIFO often results in a more meaningful balance sheet but a less realistic income statement, and LIFO often results in a more meaningful income statement but a less realistic balance sheet.

Most strategists recognize four implications in the preceding analysis: (1) The returns of a business are going to be affected by the choice of inventory valuation method, both in terms of income and investment. (2) It may be difficult to compare returns of competitors with different valuation methods. (3) INFLATION makes the differences more dramatic. For example, FIFO undervalues inventory when costs are rising and overvalues it when costs are falling. (4) Inventory valuation methods may affect management behavior. For example, under LIFO, management would be much quicker to raise prices to protect margins than under FIFO. For this reason, LIFO accounting is often called a contributor to COST-PUSH INFLATION. Also, because FIFO makes taxable income higher during inflation, many companies switch to LIFO during highly inflationary periods.

Fighting Brand: a brand that a business introduces to punish or threaten a competitor. FIGHTING BRANDS are most often introduced as a warning to a competitor either to stop making a move or to give up a planned move. FIGHTING BRANDS may or may not be successful in their own right; but to fit the definition, they have to have MARKET SIGNALING as their intention.

FIGHTING BRANDS can be used defensively to block a competitor's planned ENTRY into a business's industry. For example, a business might produce small quantities of a few private-label products to prevent a competitor from doing so even though the business's main products have strong brand identities. The business is signaling its competitors that it is prepared to defend its brand name business from a private label ME-TOO PRODUCT by expanding its own private label.

FIGHTING BRANDS can also be used offensively. For example, a business may introduce a small FIGHTING BRAND to signal its intention to ENTER a market in a big way and to prepare the incumbents for a major new entrant. Acquisitions of small brands have been used in this way.

A FIGHTING BRAND is often used as a CROSS PARRY.

Financial Fit: complementary financial characteristics of the businesses in a company's portfolio which lower the company's overall COST OF CAPITAL. The FINANCIAL FIT of a given business is measured in terms of that business's contribution to the company's balance of financial risk, CYCLICALITY, CASH FLOWS, seasonality, WORKING CAPITAL USE, and growth opportunities, etc. Selecting the financial characteristics on which to build FINANCIAL FIT is the responsibility of corporate strategists. FINANCIAL FIT builds STRATEGIC LEVERAGE by allowing the business to have less expensive and more effective funding as part of the company's portfolio than it could have on its own.

Some CORPORATE STRATEGIES build ECONOMIC VALUE solely on the basis of FINANCIAL FIT. Others use FORMULA FIT and FUNCTIONAL FIT as well.

Financial Leverage: the use of effective financing to increase the ECONOMIC VALUE of a company by lowering the COST OF CAPITAL. Although strategists are most concerned with using STRATEGIC LEVERAGE to create ECONOMIC VALUE, there is no denying that FINANCIAL LEVERAGE can also create VALUE.

VALUE is created through FINANCIAL LEVERAGE in a number of ways. The most significant way is to optimize the company's CAPITAL STRUCTURE by giving the company the ideal mix of debt and equity financing. Another is to design equity and debt securities that are more attractive to the CAPITAL MARKETS than others. A third is to structure acquisition deals so as to minimize the cost of the ACQUISITION. Others include optimizing the choice between buying and leasing, effective tax planning, etc.

Sometimes balancing characteristics, such as WORKING CAPITAL needs and CASH-FLOW requirements among the businesses in a company's portfolio, are called FINANCIAL LEVERAGE. However, strategists usually think of this as part of STRATEGIC LEVERAGE because determining the degree of FINANCIAL FIT in the company's portfolio is part of the strategic choice of which businesses to be in. That choice will be determined by the company's CORPORATE STRATEGY.

Some theorists feel that FINANCIAL LEVERAGE is impossible under EFFICIENT MARKET assumptions.

First Mover: *see* PREEMPTIVE TACTIC.

Fixed Capital: a company's investment in fixed assets and other noncurrent assets. Fixed assets include assets that can be expected to exist forever, such as land, as well as assets that depreciate over time, such as buildings, machinery, and fixtures, usually referred to as plant and equipment. Fixed assets can also include other tangible assets, such as dies and patterns, and such intangible assets as trademarks or patents. In general, fixed assets are assets of a relatively permanent nature that cannot be disposed of without interfering with the company's current operation.

Noncurrent assets are assets that also have a relatively permanent nature, but they are not inherently necessary to the continuing operation of the company. Such assets are not classified as current because they are not to be converted into cash within the year. Noncurrent assets include such things as investments in the company's own stock, investments in other companies, and investments in affiliated companies.

The BOOK VALUE of the FIXED CAPITAL of a business is not necessarily indicative of the current MARKET VALUE of the assets or the importance of the assets to the business. REPLACEMENT VALUE or current MARKET VALUE is often the relevant consideration for the strategist dealing with DIVESTMENT, ACQUISITIONS, and RESOURCE ALLOCATION.

Fixed Costs: costs that do not vary with short-term changes in the volume of business activity. They are the opposite of VARIABLE COSTS. FIXED COSTS for a plant include such things as depreciation, property taxes, storage, and top management's salaries. These costs may increase or decrease over time, but for the most part they do not change with increases or decreases in the output of the plant. For example, the warehouse's overhead may not go up with increases in the output of the plant. However, many FIXED COSTS are only partially fixed. For example, management's salaries tend to increase when production goes up. FIXED COSTS that vary somewhat with changes in volume are often called semifixed or semivariable costs.

FIXED COSTS are only fixed with respect to a particular time period and way of operating the business. For example, with changes in technology and changes in COMPETITIVE STRATEGY, a business can change its FIXED COSTS. Over the long term, no costs can be considered fixed. In the short term, a contract may make any cost fixed. For example, a contract to buy a certain amount of raw material may make material costs fixed even if the plant produces nothing at all.

A high FIXED COST component in the UNIT COST of a product can increase price-cutting pressure and intensify RIVALRY in an industry. This is because FIXED COSTS have to be paid regardless of output, and any price above VARIABLE COST makes a contribution toward covering those FIXED COSTS. The FIXED-TO-VALUE ADDED RATIO is often used to compare this pressure for price-cutting between competitors and across industries.

Fixed–to–Value Added Ratio: a business's ratio of annual FIXED COSTS to its dollar of VALUE ADDED. This ratio is used as an indicator of the amount of pressure that a business is under to indulge in PRICE COMPETITION. The ratio is computed by adding up all the business's FIXED COSTS involved in competing in its industry and dividing it by the total sales minus PURCHASED VALUE.

Take, for example, a business that purchases $40 worth of materials for every unit it makes, sells those units for $60, and therefore has $20 in VALUE ADDED per unit. Also, assume that the business has annual FIXED COSTS of $10,000, including financing and warehousing; that its CAPACITY is 1,000 units per year; and that annual sales are 650 units. Its total VALUE ADDED is equal to its VALUE ADDED per unit times the number of units. That would be 650 units times $20, which equals $13,000. Dividing the business's FIXED COSTS of $10,000 by $13,000 in VALUE ADDED gives a ratio of .77. That means that 77 percent of the business's VALUE ADDED is being used to recover annual FIXED COSTS, leaving only 23 percent to cover VARIABLE COSTS and profit. As the ratio approaches 1.0, the business's profits turn negative at a point which depends on the VARIABLE COSTS the business incurs. A business with a high ratio has the incentive to cut price to gain share or increase sales as long as total VALUE ADDED increases and FIXED COSTS remain unchanged. For example, if marketing research indicated that the business could sell 1,000 units if it cut the price to $55, this might prove tempting. At $55, the total VALUE ADDED would be $15,000. With FIXED COSTS still at $10,000, the business's FIXED-TO-VALUE ADDED RATIO would be .67, and its contribution to VARIABLE COSTS and profits would be $5,000.

Note that it is not necessary for a business to be capital-intensive to have a high FIXED-TO-VALUE ADDED RATIO. For example, it can have a high ratio simply because it has high storage costs. Some strategists, who feel that their company has a general problem with PRICE COMPETITION in many of its businesses, find that a good way to begin to understand the problem is to start by computing FIXED-TO-VALUE ADDED RATIOS for each of its businesses and competitors.

Other strategists feel that a better indicator of the incentives for price-cutting is the ratio of FIXED COSTS to total costs. This indicator does not fluctuate with the level of prices in the industry, and so it is affected less by current industry conditions and more by the underlying COST STRUCTURE which creates the incentive. The strategists point out that a business with a high FIXED-TO-VALUE ADDED RATIO has no incentive to cut price to below VARIABLE COST and that, unlike the fixed–to–total cost ratio, the FIXED-TO-VALUE ADDED RATIO gives no indication of what that price is.

Fix Plan: a plan for increasing the profitability of a business that management feels is not currently as profitable as it was in the past or is otherwise not as profitable as its INDUSTRY STRUCTURE indicates it should be. A FIX PLAN is often a modified HOLD PLAN. That is, the plan usually calls for holding MARKET SHARE but includes programs to increase profitability. In identifying the problem, strategists often ask questions like these: Is this the wrong MARKET SEGMENT? Can it be changed? Are these the wrong products? Can they be changed? Has the technology fallen behind the industry? Can it catch up? Are there problems in manufacturing? Can they be fixed? Are these the right MANAGEMENT SYSTEMS? Is this the right ORGANIZATIONAL STRUCTURE with the right people in charge? Given the answers to such questions, the strategist does a cost-benefit analysis of investments to improve the business. Depending on the analysis, the best option may turn out to be a HARVEST PLAN.

The most simple approach to formulating a FIX PLAN involves breaking the business down into its FUNCTIONAL AREAS or into its VALUE ADDED components and then assessing the problems in each

area. A more sophisticated approach is to analyze the COST STRUC-
TURE of the business in detail, including a comparison of this business's costs with those of its competitors to isolate the problems.
Additional sophistication would involve an analysis of the business's INDUSTRY STRUCTURE, its EVOLUTIONARY PROCESSES, and a detailed COMPETITOR ANALYSIS to determine what it takes to build a
profitable and protected position in the business's industry.

In the absence of a reasonable FIX PLAN for a low- or no-profit
business, many companies consider DIVESTMENT.

A FIX PLAN is also called a recovery plan or a turnaround plan.

Focal Point: an indicator of outcome on which competitors center
their expectations. The term is derived from GAME THEORY to indicate the importance of the expectations of businesses competing in
an OLIGOPOLY. If expectations do converge on a FOCAL POINT, this
will stabilize competition. For example, an industry with DIVERSE
COMPETITORS may exhibit a high degree of RIVALRY because those
competitors are making moves with very different outcomes in mind.
If, on the other hand, the competitors converge on a given COM-
PETITOR CONFIGURATION, RIVALRY may well be stabilized; and overall
industry profitability, increased. Although MARKET SHARE is a very
common FOCAL POINT, other indicators such as RELATIVE PRICES can
also be used.

Many strategists favor the use of MARKET SIGNALS to build stabilizing FOCAL POINTS. Other strategists consider FOCAL POINTS as
BLIND SPOTS to be taken advantage of for increased profitability.

Focused Factory: a plant which deals with a limited, specified, and
manageable set of demands for products, technologies, volumes, and
markets. The MANUFACTURING POLICY of such a plant focuses attention on the key MANUFACTURING TASK that must be done well so that
the business can compete effectively. Research has shown that a business's profitability can be significantly increased by having an explicit MANUFACTURING POLICY that addresses one explicit MANUFAC-
TURING TASK rather than many conflicting implicit tasks. In choosing
what task to focus on, the business gains an advantage over a competitor who requires its manufacturing function to do everything well
without regard to which task may be the most important.

Implementing a FOCUSED FACTORY concept involves making sure
that on a plant-by-plant basis, specific choices are being made in four
general areas. The first area is PRODUCT DIFFERENTIATION, especially

related to quality and features. A FOCUSED FACTORY should make only products with similar levels of PRODUCT QUALITY and features and options. This will allow a consistent approach to quality control and product modifications. It will also allow a consistent approach to such issues as equipment type, tooling, inspections, training, supervision, job content, materials, handling, etc.

Second, a FOCUSED FACTORY should be required to deal only with one unproved technology at a time. Furthermore, the number of proved technologies the factory should be required to contain is limited to what management can handle. Usually, this is three technologies. For example, a single FOCUSED FACTORY might be required to do metal founding, metalworking, and metal finishing.

Third, a FOCUSED FACTORY should be required to make only products that have comparable expected levels of volume. This allows the factory to have a consistent approach to ECONOMIC ORDER QUANTITIES, run lengths and setups, inventories and plant layouts, etc. Strategists who use the FOCUSED FACTORY concept believe that short runs, customer specials, and one-of-a-kind orders should be done in separate plants or in separate parts of a plant.

Fourth, a FOCUSED FACTORY should be required to make products only for BUYER GROUPS with comparable demands for reliability, price, lead timing, delivery, packaging, etc. That is, a FOCUSED FACTORY can be expected to fulfill only one or at most two types of buyer demands.

It is not necessary to build a number of small plants to implement the FOCUSED FACTORY concept. The same benefits can be achieved by creating smaller areas within plants that physically isolate operations with different focuses. For example, in the same plant, one area might produce high-volume, high-quality products with a continuous flow operation having long-order lead times; and another area might produce the same product in short runs to meet orders for custom packaging of quick delivery. MANAGEMENT SYSTEMS and controls would have to be different for each area.

The arguments against the FOCUSED FACTORY concept usually involve issues of ECONOMIES OF SCALE and spreading overhead over large volumes. The arguments for the concept usually point out that loading more and more products with different requirements as to quality, volumes, technologies, and buyer expectations can only lead to increased overhead; complex systems that cannot be integrated; and problems between manufacturing, marketing, the controller, and buyers.

A FOCUSED FACTORY concept is easier to implement given a strong GENERIC STRATEGY or a CORPORATE STRATEGY with a well-defined concept of FUNCTIONAL FIT. Also, the implementation of a FOCUSED FACTORY concept may influence the company's approach to DIVERSIFICATION.

Focus Strategy: a GENERIC STRATEGY that aims to serve a particular TARGET MARKET in the industry. Achieving a FOCUS STRATEGY usually requires that a business have that combination of low costs and differentiation that best serves the TARGET MARKET. Implementing a successful FOCUS STRATEGY can allow a business to earn returns higher than its industry average even if there are strong COMPETITIVE FORCES. This is because as long as there exists a viable TARGET MARKET, that business enjoys the same position vis-a-vis the COMPETITIVE FORCES in its TARGET MARKET that a COST LEADERSHIP or DIFFERENTIATION STRATEGY allows the broad market competitor.

The objective of a FOCUS STRATEGY is to enable the business to serve its TARGET MARKET better than any other competitor, especially those who are competing more broadly. Although the FOCUS STRATEGY will not make the business either the low-cost producer or the differentiated producer for the industry, it will make it one or both of those for its TARGET MARKET. In most industries an effective FOCUS STRATEGY will not result in a high MARKET SHARE although if the industry is very FRAGMENTED, it may result in a high RELATIVE MARKET SHARE.

Successful implementation of a FOCUS STRATEGY requires management skills and an ORGANIZATIONAL STRUCTURE that supports the requirements of serving the TARGET MARKET. In addition, management has to be comfortable with the TARGET MARKET and not tempted by a broader approach.

As with any STRATEGY, there are two major RISKS involved in attempting to carry out a FOCUS STRATEGY. The first risk is that the business will fail to achieve an advantage in serving its particular TARGET MARKET, and the second risk is that the business will fail to maintain its advantage as competitors respond and the INDUSTRY STRUCTURE changes.

Most strategists feel that there are three aspects to successfully carrying out a FOCUS STRATEGY. First, the company must be able to identify a TARGET MARKET that is different enough to make it profitable to serve separately from a broad market. Second, the company must be willing to make the required investment to serve that TARGET MARKET and must not be tempted to go beyond it. Third, the company must provide the business with managers who are capable of monitoring that TARGET MARKET and the business's competitors to make sure that the market remains distinct and the business is not outfocused.

If the company is able to provide the business with what it requires in order to achieve an advantage in serving a particular TARGET MARKET, then the second type of risk becomes the main concern. That is, if it is assumed that a business can achieve a FOCUS STRATEGY at the outset, what can happen to make it unable to sustain that strategy in the long term? Strategists have found that three things can happen. First, the differences between what the TARGET MARKET wants in terms of UTILITY, price, and information and what the market as a whole wants may narrow in such a way that the TARGET MARKET is no longer meaningfully distinct. This means that, in effect, there no longer is a different-enough MARKET SEGMENT for the business to target. Second, a competitor can outfocus the business by developing a successful FOCUS STRATEGY to serve a submarket within the business's market. This has the effect of eroding the business's MARKET SHARE. Third, the cost differential between the broad market competitors and the business can get so wide that the business can no longer serve the TARGET MARKET profitably at an attractive price. A FOCUS STRATEGY is also called a targeted strategy.

Forecast: a prediction about future events or conditions. Forecasts can usually be categorized along three dimensions: content, time horizon, and forecasting approach. Forecasts are made about any conceivable topic, but those of greatest interest to strategists include social and political trends, general economic conditions, specific economic performance indicators, industry conditions, competitor's actions, factory output, or product sales.

Time horizons in forecasting are usually classified as being either short-term, medium-term, or long-term. Short-term forecasts generally extend three to eighteen months ahead (one to six quarters). Medium-term FORECASTS predict two to three years ahead, and long-term FORECASTS predict five to fifteen years ahead.

There are two general types of forecasting approaches, quantitative and qualitative. REGRESSION ANALYSIS is an example of a quantitative approach, and the DELPHI METHOD is an example of a qualitative approach. FORECASTS about the evolution of an industry and predictions about the behavior of buyers, suppliers, and competitors are the basis on which the strategist builds a COMPETITIVE STRATEGY. Virtually every strategic decision involves identifying uncertainties and the range and likelihood of possible outcomes. FORECASTS become the ASSUMPTIONS on which SCENARIOS are built.

Foreign Competition: *see* GLOBAL INDUSTRY.

Formula Fit: a consistency in strategy among the businesses in a portfolio which clarifies and strengthens the strategic focus for the company as a whole. The FORMULA FIT of a given business is measured in terms of that business's contribution to the company's understanding of how to formulate and implement a specific GENERIC STRATEGY.

Take, for example, a company with four businesses in its portfolio, all of which are carrying out a COST LEADERSHIP STRATEGY. A fifth business that also competes with a COST LEADERSHIP STRATEGY would benefit from the company's current ability to manage such a strategy and could further enhance the company's overall experience in doing so. FORMULA FIT builds STRATEGIC LEVERAGE because the business benefits from the experience of the others in the portfolio and is then able to carry out its COMPETITIVE STRATEGY more effectively as part of the company's portfolio.

Deciding what mix of GENERIC STRATEGIES the company is willing to undertake and, therefore, what the basis is of FORMULA FIT is the responsibility of corporate strategists. In some companies, all the businesses follow the same GENERIC STRATEGY. In other companies with portfolios of businesses pursuing diverse strategies, businesses with the same GENERIC STRATEGY are grouped together. For example, such a company might manage all its businesses following a COST LEADERSHIP STRATEGY as one group and its businesses following a DIFFERENTIATION STRATEGY as another group.

Few corporate strategies can build ECONOMIC VALUE solely on the basis of FORMULA FIT. Most companies use FINANCIAL FIT and especially FUNCTIONAL FIT as well.

FORMULA FIT is sometimes called expertise or KNOW-HOW.

Forward Integration: *see* VERTICAL INTEGRATION.

Fragmented Industry: an industry in which many businesses compete. A FRAGMENTED INDUSTRY generally has a low CONCENTRATION RATIO and lacks a DOMINANT FIRM. Most strategists feel that industries are fragmented because the COST STRUCTURES of the businesses in the industry do not allow for the development of COST ADVANTAGES. For example, if MINIMUM EFFICIENT SCALE in an industry is equal to less than 5 percent of industry sales, then it is possible that no one competitor will have more than a 5 percent MARKET SHARE. Other characteristics which are common in FRAGMENTED INDUSTRIES include low ENTRY BARRIERS, high transportation costs, high inventory costs, erratic sales fluctuations, diverse market needs, high EXIT BARRIERS, and government regulation.

Some strategists feel that industries evolve from FRAGMENTED to concentrated. Other strategists feel that industries become more concentrated over time but that it can only happen when it becomes possible to build strong MOBILITY BARRIERS.

Free Money: obligations for future payments that can be postponed without having to pay interest. Usually, the term FREE MONEY refers to accounts payable. Sometimes the term is used to refer to such deferred expenses as taxes and accounting phenomena related to pension funds, etc. Because these involve noncash expenses, they can be important in calculating CASH FLOW.

Functional Area: the personnel and assets devoted to performing a specific activity. Typical FUNCTIONAL AREAS are manufacturing, marketing, planning, accounting, finance, R&D, personnel, sales, and purchasing. Depending on the ORGANIZATIONAL HIERARCHY, a business may also have functional areas such as order taking, fulfillment, and customer services.

FUNCTIONAL AREAS are sometimes called functional departments.

Functional Fit: LINKAGES in the activities of the businesses in a company's portfolio which allow them to cooperate or combine to lower the cost or increase the performance of one or more activities. The FUNCTIONAL FIT of a given business is measured in terms of that business's contribution toward the company's ability to spread the cost and increase the effectiveness of a specific function such as sales, purchasing, distribution, or advertising. Developing FUNCTIONAL FIT involves having businesses in a portfolio that can share functions and then managing those businesses so as to take advantage of ECON-OMIES OF SCALE and CUMULATIVE EXPERIENCE. This results in SHARED COSTS and SHARED EXPERIENCE. FUNCTIONAL FIT can also result from having businesses that build BLOCKING POSITIONS or otherwise deter MULTIPOINT COMPETITORS. This type of FUNCTIONAL FIT usually results in more effective selling.

Selecting the basis of FUNCTIONAL FIT is the responsibility of corporate strategists. Capitalizing on FUNCTIONAL FIT often depends on the company's CONCEPT OF MANAGEMENT, especially regarding such issues as TRANSFER PRICES.

FUNCTIONAL FIT builds STRATEGIC LEVERAGE because it allows the business to lower costs and to be more effective in one or more FUNCTIONAL AREAS as part of the company's portfolio than it would be on its own. Some companies build ECONOMIC VALUE solely on the basis of FUNCTIONAL FIT. Others use FINANCIAL FIT and FORMULA FIT as well.

G

Game Changer: an industry event that changes the competitive rules of the game. GAME CHANGERS are usually EVOLUTIONARY PROCESSES that change the COMPETITIVE FORCES in an industry and its INTRA-INDUSTRY STRUCTURE or indications that the COMPETITIVE FORCES could be changed by an innovative competitor. The eight GAME CHANGERS most commonly referred to are these.

1. Development of a new manufacturing technology.
2. Changes in type or availability of raw materials.
3. Development of a new SUBSTITUTE PRODUCT.
4. Changes in government regulations or trade restrictions.
5. Lack of a DOMINANT DESIGN.
6. Reversal of the trend toward UNCERTAINTY REDUCTION.
7. Change in the degree of VERTICAL INTEGRATION.
8. Outbreak of competition or cooperation between the MAR-KET SHARE leaders.

Game Grid: a technique for comparing different COMPETITIVE STRATEGIES on the basis of game plan and market focus. The technique presumes that strategies can be compared on the basis of whether they involve a standard or innovative approach to competing, and whether they involve focusing on the standard MARKET SEGMENTS in the industry or on different MARKET SEGMENTS.

		MARKET FOCUS	
		Conventional Segments	Different Segments
GAME PLAN	Conventional Approach	Doing more of the same, hopefully better	Doing more of the same, but for different buyers
	Innovative Approach	Doing something different	Doing something different for different buyers

Businesses in the upper left-hand cell are following a conventional approach and are focusing on the same MARKET SEGMENTS as most of their competitors. These businesses are making no attempt to change their INDUSTRY STRUCTURE. They may be trying to build MARKET SHARE by implementing the conventional approach more effectively than others in the industry. Unless a business in this cell has the highest MARKET SHARE in the industry, it is presumed to be just following the leader. That is, it is using the same market definition as the leader, and it has similar GOALS and OPERATING POLICIES. Such a business can surpass the leader only to the extent that the leader becomes ineffective at carrying out its own strategy. Strategists who support the law of MUTUAL EXCLUSION would be very uncomfortable with a business in this cell. Such COMPETITIVE STRATEGIES are likely to be low RISK but unlikely to yield above-average returns.

Businesses in the upper right-hand cell are following a conventional approach but are focusing on different MARKET SEGMENTS than most of the competitors in their industries. These businesses are making no attempt to change their INDUSTRY STRUCTURE. However, they are trying to resegment the market to serve some new or redefined BUYER GROUPS. These businesses may be trying to find BUYER GROUPS that are less price-sensitive and have less BUYER POWER or trying to avoid the level of RIVALRY in the conventional MARKET SEGMENTS. However, because these businesses are following the conventional industry approach, they are unlikely to be building any distinctive MOBILITY BARRIERS. Therefore, whatever profitability they may be able to achieve may well be unprotected. Some strategists feel that businesses in this cell can be expected to earn reasonable returns only if the MARKET SEGMENT is too small to attract the business's larger competitors or because those competitors are deterred by legal and regulatory considerations. In the absence of either of these phenomena, some strategists try to develop in competitors a sense of EXPECTED RETALIATION to discourage mobility. Usually, strategists try to move businesses in this cell into the bottom right-hand cell.

Businesses in the bottom right-hand cell are not only focusing on different MARKET SEGMENTS from those of the rest of the industry, but they are also attempting to change the COMPETITIVE FORCES in their industries as well as INTRA-INDUSTRY STRUCTURE. These businesses are going against CONVENTIONAL WISDOM. To the extent that they are successful in carrying out their GENERIC STRATEGY and can thereby build a sustainable COMPETITIVE ADVANTAGE, these businesses can be expected to earn above-average returns for their industries.

Businesses in the lower left-hand cell of the grid are trying to implement an innovative approach toward serving the conventional MARKET SEGMENTS in the industry. This usually implies that these businesses are trying to make fundamental changes in the COMPETITIVE FORCES for their industry as well as in their INTRA-INDUSTRY STRUCTURE. Their innovative approach also means defying CONVENTIONAL WISDOM in the belief that their new game is a better way of doing business. Businesses in this cell that are successful in implementing their innovative approaches can be expected to earn average returns for their industries.

The GAME GRID can be used to compare the COMPETITIVE STRATEGIES of competing businesses in a given industry, or the grid can be used to compare the COMPETITIVE STRATEGIES of businesses in a company's portfolio with one another. A company that finds most of its businesses in the upper left-hand cell or the upper right-hand cell should think about its CONCEPT OF MANAGEMENT and its manner of motivating its managers.

An underlying assumption of the GAME GRID is that a business that does not have the dominant MARKET SHARE position in its industry can be expected to earn above-average returns only by serving different MARKET SEGMENTS or by taking an innovative approach. The implication is that a business following the leader can rarely be more profitable than the leader and that a business following the leader but serving a different segment can expect to earn above-average returns only if there are MOBILITY BARRIERS protecting its segment. INSIGHT into how to take an innovative approach is considered to be the way out of the two old-game situations.

Implementing an innovative approach can be expensive and risky. Some strategists feel that the RISK can be minimized by trying an innovative approach with a different MARKET SEGMENT first and then rolling the approach out to the conventional segments as the approach proves successful and the business becomes profitable. They feel that by starting with segments for which the innovative approach is most likely to work, the business can reduce its risk. Other strategists feel that if the plan is to appeal eventually to the conventional segments, then the business is best off doing that as soon as possible to discourage competition rather than waiting and risking imitation.

Some strategists feel that INDUSTRY EVOLUTION can be analyzed in terms of the pattern of changes that businesses in an industry have made in moving around the GAME GRID. Strategists who use the GAME GRID often use BUSINESS SYSTEMS ANALYSIS as a way of determining whether a business is taking a conventional approach or an innovative approach.

Game Theory: the study of games as models of real-world competition. GAME THEORY is often applied to business situations in order to consider the indefinite outcome of interactions among individuals and groups of individuals who are making choices. What makes GAME THEORY relevant is that those choices and outcomes are interdependent. That is, the choices facing one competitor in an industry are often dependent on what one or more of its competitors choose. The outcome for any one competitor is very likely to be determined by the combination of what all competitors did. For example, there is a lot of interdependency involved in the decision whether or not to build new CAPACITY. A given competitor's decision is likely to be influenced by the knowledge that another competitor is committed to greatly expanding CAPACITY SHARE. In addition, the return on any one competitor's new CAPACITY is going to depend on how much CAPACITY the other competitors build.

Competitive situations can be described and simplified in terms of the moves or strategies open to competitors and the outcomes resulting from those choices. In fact, diverse business situations can often be described in terms of similar models. GAME THEORY can highlight key aspects of the situation. For example, there may be advantages to making the first move or making a move that commits the individual so that he or she cannot back off. In addition, the outcome of a game may differ depending on whether the individual plays repeatedly or one time. The PRISONER'S DILEMMA is a game that is often used to characterize oligopolistic competition.

Gaming: a process for evaluating plans that generates SCENARIOS combining "what if" analysis with SENSITIVITY ANALYSIS. Essentially, it involves taking a plan and asking, "What if this happened?" "What if that happened?" "How sensitive is my plan to this change?" "How sensitive is my plan to changes in that?" The process of GAMING can range from back-of-the-envelope estimates to highly complex computer simulations involving infinite combinations and permutations.

Gap-Based Planning: an approach to planning in which OBJECTIVES are set and then compared with the current plans in order to focus the planning effort on analyzing and closing the gap between the two. For example, a company may decide that over the next five years it should have 10 percent REAL GROWTH. If the current and anticipated REAL GROWTH of all its businesses adds up to only 5 percent, then the company has to devise a STRATEGY to generate the additional growth.

Some strategists think that GAP-BASED PLANNING is simplistic and that OPPORTUNITY-BASED PLANNING yields better results. They argue that GAP-BASED PLANNING usually forces a planner to devote too much effort negotiating between corporate managers and the business managers about how much will be required of them. Other strategists feel that GAP-BASED PLANNING can be effective if the objectives are sound. For example, some strategists assess the company's shareholder's REQUIRED RETURN to arrive at a sophisticated set of OBJECTIVES. They then use OPPORTUNITY-BASED PLANNING to generate BUSINESS PLANS and attempt to reconcile the two.

Gap Map: a chart that shows different approaches to increasing the consumption of a product. A typical GAP MAP shows the current sales level as a base point to which additional sales could be added by filling in the gaps. For example:

Source of Sales	Options
Usage gap	• Find new uses • Find new users • Increase variety of uses • Increase frequency of use
Distribution gap	• Expand distribution intensity • Expand distribution share
Product gap	• Expand product line • Add utility
Competitive gap	• Penetrate other strategic groups • Penetrate current strategic group
Current sales level	• Defend

Some strategists are uncomfortable with a GAP MAP because of its circularity. For example, penetration of a STRATEGIC GROUP is likely to require an expansion of distribution share, additional UTILITY, and a different frequency of use. Other strategists recognize these problems but still use a GAP MAP to generate issues and evaluate BUILD PLANS.

General Electric Matrix: the original nine-box matrix developed by the General Electric Company to display a portfolio of STRATEGIC BUSINESS UNITS. This matrix is more generally known as the BUSINESS/INDUSTRY ATTRACTIVENESS MATRIX.

Generic Imperatives: *see* COMMODITY/SPECIALTY MATRIX.

Generic Strategy: one of three basic COMPETITIVE STRATEGIES that allow a business to build a sustainable COMPETITIVE ADVANTAGE and, therefore, to earn a superior return. The three GENERIC STRATEGIES are described in terms of the source of the business's COMPETITIVE ADVANTAGE and on the business's TARGET MARKET. The matrix that follows indicates the differences between the three strategies.

		TARGET MARKET	
		Broad	Focused
COMPETITIVE ADVANTAGE	Low Cost	1. Cost leadership—a strategy that focuses on being the low-cost producer.	3. Focus—a strategy that serves a target market
	Uniqueness	2. Differentiation—a strategy that focuses on providing a unique product	

A business's COMPETITIVE STRATEGY can be directed toward being the low-cost producer, being the differentiated producer, or focusing on a TARGET MARKET. A business with a COMPETITIVE STRATEGY that cannot be classified as one of the three GENERIC STRATEGIES is considered "STUCK IN THE MIDDLE" without a sustainable COMPETITIVE ADVANTAGE.

A business pursuing the first strategy, COST LEADERSHIP, works on being the overall low-cost producer in its industry. Such a business cannot afford to ignore PRODUCT QUALITY and UTILITY, but the core of its COMPETITIVE STRATEGY must be on having the lowest costs in the industry.

A business pursuing the second strategy, DIFFERENTIATION, works on differentiating the product so as to be perceived industry-wide as being unique. Approaches to differentiating can involve many forms of UTILITY, BRAND IDENTIFICATION, information, etc. The OBJECTIVE is to provide a uniqueness that is desired by a sufficient number of buyer groups who are willing to pay for the DIFFERENTIATION. Note that a business cannot ignore costs when implementing a DIFFERENTIATION STRATEGY but that the central aim of the COMPETITIVE STRATEGY must be on DIFFERENTIATION.

A business pursuing the third GENERIC STRATEGY, a FOCUSED STRATEGY, serves a particular TARGET MARKET better than any other competitor in the industry. This strategy may allow the business to be the low-cost competitor in serving that TARGET MARKET, or it may allow it to be the unique competitor in serving that TARGET MARKET. Or it may allow it to be both. However, once a suitable TARGET MARKET has been identified, the focus of the business's COMPETITIVE STRATEGY is to do whatever it takes to serve that market and not be tempted by a broader market perspective.

Some strategists feel that there are only two GENERIC STRATEGIES, because, they say, a FOCUSED STRATEGY is just a COST LEADERSHIP or DIFFERENTIATION STRATEGY in a different market. Other strategists argue that if a business believes that, it is missing some of the key RISKS involved in carrying out a FOCUSED STRATEGY and doesn't know who its competitors are. For example, they would argue that a company that made paint for professional painters and didn't think it was competing with all other paint companies was kidding itself.

Not all industries have businesses competing with all three strategies. For example, in some industries it seems the only really profitable game is the COST LEADERSHIP STRATEGY. In other industries, it may be that the only STRATEGY that seems to earn good returns is a DIFFERENTIATION STRATEGY. For this reason, many strategists feel that there is a relationship between profitability and MARKET SHARE in a given industry and the viability of a particular COMPETITIVE STRATEGY in that industry. For example, an industry in which the COST LEADERSHIP STRATEGY seemed to be the only viable one might show a relationship like that on the left.

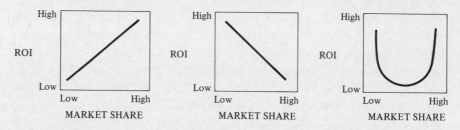

An industry in which DIFFERENTIATION STRATEGY seems to be the most viable is likely to show a relationship like that in the middle. An industry where all three GENERIC STRATEGIES are present might show a relationship like the one on the right. These three charts are simplifications, but they indicate that one should expect a different relationship between profitability and MARKET SHARE in different industries. The relationship depends on the MARKET SHARE implied by the scale required to be the low-cost producer, on the MARKET SHARE required to reach a PROFITABLE BREAK-EVEN with a given cost of differentiation, and on the MARKET SHARE comprising a targetable BUYER GROUP.

Some strategists feel that all industries have the potential of supporting all three GENERIC STRATEGIES. They argue that if that is not currently the case, it is only because no competitor has had the INSIGHT to figure out how to implement the unrepresented strategy. Other strategists feel that as industries evolve, the viable strategies change and that, therefore, the insight is in knowing when a new strategy is possible. Some of those strategists feel that industries are continually cycling through different potential combinations of viable strategies. Those strategists feel that the INSIGHT is in knowing when to change strategies. Finally, there are some strategists who subscribe to the law of MUTUAL EXCLUSION and believe that there can only be one business successfully pursuing a given GENERIC STRATEGY in a given industry.

Gentleman's Game: an industry in which competitors minimize RIVALRY. Such industries are most often characterized by the presence

of a DOMINANT FIRM that perceives stability as being in its best interests. Other industries may arrive at the same point with FOCAL
POINTS. GENTLEMAN'S GAMES are often thought of as providing good
opportunities for ENTRY.

Geographic Scope: *see* COMPETITIVE SCOPE.

Global Industry: an industry in which businesses competing in a
substantial number of major geographic and national markets derive
a COMPETITIVE ADVANTAGE over national and regional competitors.
In many industries, multinational enterprises compete as separate,
autonomous units in a number of national markets and do not base
their COMPETITIVE STRATEGIES on SHARED COSTS, functions, or scale
beyond the size of each national market. These industries are not
global institutions although the distinction is often a matter of
degree.

There are a number of types of advantages to competing on a
global basis that a business might realize. The most obvious stem
from ECONOMIES OF SCALE. When the MINIMUM EFFICIENT SCALE is
larger than any national market, then there can be an advantage to
competing globally. In the same way, global competition may also
lead to cost declines through CUMULATIVE EXPERIENCE that could not
be realized in a national market. Advantages in procuring raw materials and the ability to support larger expenditures for technological research can also work to benefit global competitors.

There are also a number of costs to competing globally which
must either be outweighed by the advantages or circumvented with
TACTICS. The benefits of ECONOMIES OF SCALE must exceed transportation, inventory carrying, and POLICY COSTS. If different national markets have different UTILITY preferences for a given product, it may not be cost-effective to compete with that product on a
global basis. Differences in approaches and sophistication in distribution among national markets may have the same effect. Also, the
lack of opportunity for PULL THROUGH often makes it expensive to
compete globally.

Some strategists are very comfortable with the concept of
GLOBAL INDUSTRIES because their company's CORPORATE STRATEGY
supports a GLOBAL PERSPECTIVE. Other strategists look to compete
in industries that are protected from global competition as a matter
of preference.

Some strategists see the transition from national industries to
GLOBAL INDUSTRIES as being analogous to the transition from re-

gional industries to national industries. They are considered to be analogous in three ways. First, they are considered analogous in that different industries made the transition at different times and that not all industries have become national. Second, they are considered analogous in that businesses that were unable to make the transition with their industry suffered major decreases in profitability. Third, the process of moving the industry through the transition is usually triggered by a fundamental change in COMPETITIVE STRATEGY by one or more competitors. An industry becomes global when one or more competitors see that the benefits of competing on a worldwide basis outweigh the costs and they take advantage of that INSIGHT as part of the industry's COMPETITIVE STRATEGY. If that competitor is right, then the industry becomes global, and other competitors have to follow to maintain profitability.

Global Perspective: the frame of reference of a company which regards the entire world as its potential market. The CORPORATE STRATEGY of a company with a GLOBAL PERSPECTIVE tends to focus attention on international markets on the basis of economic potential regardless of past experience or familiarity. Such a company's ORGANIZATIONAL STRUCTURE is likely to cross national boundaries freely. Many companies do not have a GLOBAL PERSPECTIVE in that they tend to develop products for the home market and perceive other countries as secondary markets for those products, or they manage each country as a business in an unrelated portfolio of businesses.

Companies that have broadened their COMPETITIVE SCOPE to include an effective GLOBAL PERSPECTIVE tend to compete in one of two ways. The broadest is to compete with a global COST LEADERSHIP or DIFFERENTIATION STRATEGY that reaches all or most major country markets with products designed for broadly defined MARKET SEGMENTS. The second is global segmentation, which involves competing on a worldwide basis but to a narrowly defined market segment.

Companies that have a global perspective such that they recognize that they are in a GLOBAL INDUSTRY but do not wish to compete on a worldwide basis also have two approaches. The first involves a strategy based on competing in protected markets where market positions are protected by government policy. The second involves national responsiveness, that is, a strategy focused on the market segments that are relatively unique to the country and can better be served by unique UTILITY and unique marketing than by the standard approach of a global strategy.

Many companies compete with combinations of the preceding, using the most effective approach in a given market.

Goal: a broadly defined, central aim of a business or company. The GOALS can enunciate long-term OBJECTIVES for such performance indicators as profitability, growth, and MARKET SHARE or articulate more general aims of a social or political nature. Specifying and prioritizing the GOALS of a business or company are important steps in setting a COMPETITIVE or CORPORATE STRATEGY.

Good Competitor: an industry participant that helps a business or strategic group to be more profitable than it would be either without that competitor or with another competitor in its place. Depending on the INDUSTRY STRUCTURE, a competitor can be good by positively affecting each COMPETITIVE FORCE. For example, it can reduce RIVALRY by providing excess CAPACITY, by providing a basis for product differentiation, or by being a PRICE LEADER. It can reduce BUYER POWER by serving the more powerful BUYER GROUPS, and it can reduce SUPPLIER POWER by dealing with the more powerful suppliers. It can increase ENTRY BARRIERS by occupying the easier entry position or by increasing the level of EXPECTED RETALIATION. And it can indulge in such collective industry efforts as industry advertising to build the industry's image vis-à-vis that of SUBSTITUTE PRODUCTS. GOOD COMPETITORS can contribute to all the preceding through general good behavior like sharing technology and opening new MARKET SEGMENTS. A GOOD COMPETITOR is likely to have a long time horizon and to be risk-averse. A competitor with realistic ASSUMPTIONS about the industry, with knowledge of its costs, and with similar GOALS for profitability is less likely to make unpredictable or destabilizing competitive moves. A business can encourage these more attractive rivals by means such as technology licensing, selective retaliation, and selective entry deterrence.

A bad competitor is the opposite of a GOOD COMPETITOR. In addition to behavior that depresses the profits of others, it is likely to have incompatible GOALS and ASSUMPTIONS. For example, its CASH FLOW or RETURN ON INVESTMENT expectations may be too low or unrealistically high, or it may have too short a time horizon to see the damage it is doing or such a long time horizon that it is willing to suffer in the short term.

Many strategists feel that building GOOD COMPETITORS through COMPETITOR SELECTION is not only possible but an important factor in increasing profitability. Even strategists who are unimpressed with that concept do acknowledge that at the very least a competitor can be used as protection against an antitrust suit and that even the very worst competitor can be beneficial if used as a motivator.

Group: *see* SECTOR.

Growth/Share Matrix: one of a number of charts that are used to analyze the businesses in a company's portfolio. The GROWTH/SHARE MATRIX is usually used to analyze the CASH FLOW balance between the businesses. A GROWTH/SHARE MATRIX is drawn as below.

Each business in a company's portfolio is located on the matrix on the basis of that business's RELATIVE MARKET SHARE and the rate of sales growth in the industry in which the business competes. Each business is identified as either a CASH COW, a QUESTION MARK, a DOG, or a STAR.

The matrix prescribes that a company should use its CASH COWS to generate cash to finance the growth of QUESTION MARKS and to build them into STARS. When the rate of growth slows in their industries, those STARS will become the CASH COWS of the future that can be used to build future QUESTION MARKS. Problems arise when the company spends the cash on a particular QUESTION MARK but ends up with a DOG instead of a STAR because it was never able to build its MARKET SHARE. When this happens, the company loses the future cash generation that it would have gotten when the STAR be-

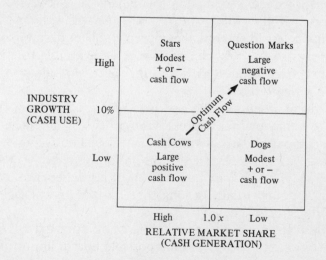

came a CASH COW. Therefore, in order to get some of that cash, the company usually has to DIVEST its DOGS.

The GROWTH/SHARE MATRIX is based on two ASSUMPTIONS. The first ASSUMPTION is that businesses that are competing in high-growth industries tend to use cash and that businesses competing in low-growth industries do not use cash. A business holding or building MARKET SHARE in a fast-growth industry is expected to need cash to finance WORKING CAPITAL as well as to expand CAPACITY.

The second assumption is that businesses that have high RELATIVE MARKET SHARE are capable of generating large amounts of cash and that businesses that have low RELATIVE MARKET SHARES can generate only very small amounts of cash if any at all. The businesses with high RELATIVE MARKET SHARE have more CUMULATIVE EXPERIENCE than their competitors, tend to be further down the EXPERIENCE CURVE, and therefore have lower costs. Because the business has lower costs than its competitors, it must be capable of making the most profits and generating the highest CASH FLOW.

The four combinations of high and low cash use and high and low cash generation yield the four-box GROWTH/SHARE MATRIX. Usually, a company's businesses are plotted on the matrix as circles with the diameter proportional to its sales. Although the dividing line for high and low industry growth and RELATIVE MARKET SHARE is up to the strategist to determine, the convention is to use 10 percent for industry growth and $1.0x$ for RELATIVE MARKET SHARE. RELATIVE MARKET SHARE is calculated by taking the ratio of the sales of a business to the sales of its largest competitor. In this way, a portfolio of businesses can be plotted thus in the simplified example that follows.

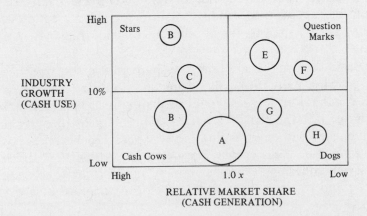

The preceding sample company has eight BUSINESS UNITS. Business A has the highest sales; and Business D, the lowest sales. Business A and Business B are CASH COWS because they are in industries that are growing at less than 10 percent and they are at least as big as, if not bigger than, the largest competitor in their industries. That is, they have RELATIVE MARKET SHARE of 1.0x or greater. As CASH COWS, these businesses should generate more cash than they can use. Therefore, these businesses can be expected to provide the cash to pay interest on corporate debt, pay dividends, cover corporate overhead, and finance R&D and the growth of other businesses.

Business C and Business D also have high MARKET SHARES, but they are in high-growth industries. These businesses are the STARS. All things being equal, these businesses get first call on the resources of the company, including the cash generated by the CASH COWS. In order to make sure that the company will have the cash flow it needs in the future to continue growing, it has to maintain the positions of these businesses so that, as their growth slows down, they can become the new CASH COWS.

Business E and Business F are also in high-growth industries, but they have low-share positions. They tend to need a lot of cash and generate very little cash, meaning that they are net CASH USERS. These businesses are called QUESTION MARKS because the key decision for strategists is to decide which of these businesses they can build into STARS.

Usually, a company cannot afford to build all its QUESTION MARKS into STARS. A company that can afford to do that probably lacks enough QUESTION MARKS from which to select the best. (Making Hobson's choices is not the way to optimize a portfolio.) The best QUESTION MARKS should be built into STARS, and the others should be DIVESTED to produce cash to spend on creating STARS as well as cash to spend on developing or acquiring new QUESTION MARKS.

Business E and F are also low-share businesses, but they are in slow-growing industries. Given the slow industry growth, a BUILD PLAN for these businesses would probably be too expensive, so they can never be expected to provide profitable growth opportunities. Because they will never be in high-share, cash-generating positions, they cannot be CASH COWS. The best option then is to divest these DOGS, remembering that one company's mutt is another's golden retriever, and to use that cash to develop or acquire new QUESTION MARKS.

GROWTH/SHARE MATRICES are often used by companies to test for FINANCIAL FIT as part of monitoring the implementation of a CORPORATE STRATEGY. The most frequently heard criticism of the GROWTH/SHARE MATRIX is of the degree to which it assumes that a company is locked into internally generated CASH FLOW.

Growth/Value Leverage Matrix: one of a number of charts used to analyze the businesses in a company's portfolio. The GROWTH/VALUE LEVERAGE MATRIX arrays the businesses on the basis of the MARKET GROWTH in the industry in which the business competes and on the basis of each business's VALUE LEVERAGE RATIO. The VALUE LEVER-AGE RATIO of a business is equal to the ratio of its RETURN ON EQUITY to its COST OF CAPITAL. The matrix indicates the appropriate plan for businesses in each cell, based on the ASSUMPTION that a business's VALUE LEVERAGE RATIO is a good indication of the business's con-tribution to the company's ECONOMIC VALUE.

The following matrix uses a 10 percent MARKET GROWTH rate and a 1.0 VALUE LEVERAGE RATIO as the relevant cut points. Some strategists prefer to use the company's average sales growth and the company's actual or desired VALUE LEVERAGE RATIO instead.

Businesses in the upper left-hand cell have a low VALUE LEVER-AGE RATIO but are in industries with high MARKET GROWTH. If it is assumed that shareholders will not pay for growth without increasing ECONOMIC VALUE, the matrix indicates that a HARVEST PLAN should be developed for these businesses. Such a plan could be expected to result in a higher VALUE LEVERAGE RATIO for the business.

Businesses in the lower left-hand cell also have a low VALUE LEV-ERAGE RATIO, but they are in low-growth industries. The matrix in-dicates that these businesses should be divested unless the sale value

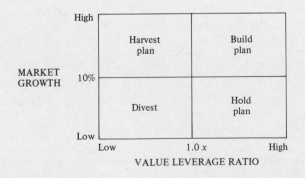

is even less than could be expected from a HOLD PLAN or HARVEST PLAN.

Businesses in the upper right-hand cell have a high VALUE LEVERAGE RATIO and are competing in industries with high MARKET GROWTH. Given the assumption that shareholders will pay a higher price for growing sales with increasing ECONOMIC VALUE, the matrix indicates that a BUILD PLAN is appropriate for these businesses. However, if a BUILD PLAN is likely to reduce the VALUE LEVERAGE RATIO, it may be that the business should have a HOLD PLAN instead. Some strategists feel that additional investment to build a business should be made only until the business's VALUE LEVERAGE RATIO drops to the company's desired VALUE LEVERAGE RATIO. Others feel that no incremental investment should be made that can be expected to reduce a business's VALUE LEVERAGE RATIO significantly.

Businesses in the lower right-hand cell also have a high VALUE LEVERAGE RATIO, but they are competing in low-growth industries. The matrix indicates that a HOLD PLAN is most often appropriate for these businesses. A HOLD PLAN is indicated because in low-growth industries a BUILD PLAN often results in decreased returns in the near term if not indefinitely. The assumption is that it is better to hold onto a high VALUE LEVERAGE RATIO than it is to invest to achieve growth at lower value.

Strategists who are comfortable with the GROWTH/VALUE LEVERAGE MATRIX feel that it gives them a way to analyze their portfolios while focusing on ECONOMIC VALUE and the shareholder perspective.

Strategists who are uncomfortable with the matrix usually point to the difficulty involved in developing a business-level VALUE LEVERAGE RATIO that is really indicative of the contribution that a business is making to the ability of the company to create ECONOMIC VALUE.

H

Harvest Plan: a plan for disinvesting or taking cash out of a business. Harvesting deliberately erodes the COMPETITIVE POSITION of a BUSINESS UNIT in an effort to increase RETURN ON INVESTMENT at the expense of MARKET SHARE. This is usually done by cutting the level of some expense or investment, not increasing them as fast as competitors, or by raising the RELATIVE PRICE of the product without increasing the relative PRODUCT QUALITY. A HARVEST PLAN is often considered when a business is declining, when the returns being generated are insufficient, or when cash is needed elsewhere.

The COMPETITIVE STRATEGY associated with a HARVEST PLAN has a decrease in MARKET SHARE as one of its GOALS. The plan itself should outline where the decrease in share will be, as well as the anticipated savings and the expected effect on returns. The plan should detail how the business will decrease its marketing expenditures, physical plant, sales force, or purchasing functions, etc., as well as the savings involved in doing so. The plan should include an in-depth explanation of which BUYER GROUPS are expected to drop out or reduce their purchases and why.

Most strategists consider MARKET GROWTH to be one of the key STRUCTURAL FACTORS to consider in formulating a HARVEST PLAN. In a growing market, reduced advertising and selling expenditures may indeed reduce MARKET SHARE and increase profits, and yet MARKET GROWTH may still support continued utilization of existing CAPACITY. In a low- or no-growth market, decreasing share will often involve decreasing the CAPACITY of the business. This decrease in CAPACITY may free up FIXED CAPITAL and will certainly free up WORKING CAPITAL. Whereas reducing the ratio of marketing expenses to sales in a growing market may be enough to increase profitability, in a no- or low-growth market an absolute decrease in expenditures is often required. In general, aside from the question of released investment for unused CAPACITY, the higher the growth, the more cash can be saved in making a significant decrease in MARKET SHARE.

Even though it may be easy to harvest a business in a growth market, strategists usually do this only in unusual circumstances. This is because growth markets are usually more attractive ones.

Therefore, strategists usually consider a HARVEST PLAN to be appropriate for a business with a low-to-medium RELATIVE SHARE in a

165

low- to no-growth market. The generated savings and profits are then available to the company to invest in BUILD PLANS for more attractive businesses. This PORTFOLIO APPROACH is often expressed in a GROWTH/SHARE MATRIX or a BUSINESS/INDUSTRY ATTRACTIVENESS MATRIX.

Some strategists consider HARVEST PLANS to be risk-free in that they expect profits to increase when the business cuts back or does nothing. This will be more or less true depending on the RIVALRY in the industry in which the business competes. Moreover, in most industries the kick in profits will probably be short-lived as competitors take advantage of the new situation. For this reason, some strategists use a HARVEST PLAN to give a business a shot of profits in order to make it more attractive for DIVESTMENT. Other strategists consider HARVEST PLANS to be risky because cutting back weakens the business relative to its competitors. For this reason, those strategists feel that a HARVEST PLAN exposes a business to the significant probability of earning no returns and having even less chance of increasing returns.

Hawthorne Effect: the observable increase in PRODUCTIVITY that results from the process of change. The term results from a classic 1920s study on the effect of lighting at Western Electric's Hawthorne plant. The study showed that additional lighting did increase productivity but that dimming the lights also did so. The conclusion was that the attention and group dynamics involved in any change are very likely to increase productivity and that, therefore, the process of change itself is the important consideration.

Herfindahl Index: a measure of industry CONCENTRATION that equals the sum of the squares of the MARKET SHARES of the competitors in the industry. Researchers use the HERFINDAHL INDEX to compare degrees of CONCENTRATION among different industries.

Because the MARKET SHARES are expressed as decimals, the HERFINDAHL INDEX will range from zero to one. It takes a value of one for a MONOPOLY. If an industry has one competitor with a MARKET SHARE of one, the sum of one squared would equal an index of one. If the industry has two competitors, each with market shares of .50, the sum of their shares squared would be .25 + .25, which would be an index of .50. An industry with a large number of very small competitors would have an index of close to zero.

The HERFINDAHL INDEX reflects share balance as well as CONCENTRATION in that the ratio will be higher for an industry with unbalanced shares than for one for balanced shares. For example, the index for an industry with two competitors of equal shares is .50. If the shares were unequal, with one competitor having a much higher share of .80 and the other only .20, then the index would be .68, showing the second industry to be more concentrated.

The HERFINDAHL INDEX contains more information than a CONCENTRATION RATIO but is more difficult to calculate and more difficult to explain.

Hierarchy of Needs: a ranking of the different types of needs of a BUYER GROUP. This concept is based on the motivational model of Abraham Maslow. According to Maslow, there are five levels of needs that can be further grouped into three categories:

Physical (low-level needs)

1. Physiological needs that must be satisfied for survival such as hunger and thirst.
2. Needs for protection that must be satisfied to feel safe.

Social (medium-level needs)

3. Belongingness needs that must be satisfied to feel accepted and loved by relatives and friends.
4. Esteem needs that must be satisfied to feel masterful and prestigious.

Self (high-level needs)

5. Self-actualizing needs that must be satisfied to understand and construct a system of values for oneself.

Maslow's hypothesis is that the low-level needs dominate an individual's behavior until they are met. Once they are satisfied, the higher-level need becomes dominant. Thus, as all the lower-order needs are met, the higher-order needs come into play.

Although Maslow's hierarchy may be somewhat abstract for a strategist to use in determining the UTILITY derived from a given product by different BUYER GROUPS, it can be a useful way of thinking about buyers in that some needs will dominate others and some needs will be perceived as worth paying for only when others have been satisfied. The hierarchy often defines the possibilities for PROD-

UCT DIFFERENTIATION. For example, in industrialized countries, soap is sold on its ability to satisfy belongingness and other higher order needs and not solely on its ability to clean.

High-Cost Position: the situation of the competitor with the highest costs in the industry. The position may reflect high FIXED or high VARIABLE COSTS or both. Costs may be higher because of deficiencies in any function of the business. A high-cost position usually implies below-average profitability. The position may be a risky one, depending on the structure of the industry. To the extent that industry structure allows a business to pursue a DIFFERENTIATION STRATEGY or a FOCUS STRATEGY, a HIGH-COST POSITION may indeed be profitable. In some industries the most profitable competitor may also have the highest costs.

A low-cost position is the opposite.

High Relative Price: *see* RELATIVE PRICE.

Hockey Stick: a type of FORECAST that often results when historical performance has been declining. The graphed effect of the downward line showing actual performance to date and of the sharply angled upward line showing forecasted future performance is said to resemble an ice-hockey stick.

Hold Plan: a plan for maintaining the COMPETITIVE POSITION of a BUSINESS UNIT. A hold plan is one in which a business seeks to grow at the same rate as the market and to maintain its MARKET SHARE.

The HOLD PLAN outlines the actions necessary to maintain share as well as the costs involved. MARKET GROWTH and the level of RIVALRY in an industry are important determinants of the expense and effort required to hold MARKET SHARE. For example, in a growth market, holding share will often involve increasing the CAPACITY of the business to meet DEMAND. This increase in CAPACITY may require additional FIXED CAPITAL and will surely require increased WORKING CAPITAL. This is especially true in periods of high INFLATION. Such a HOLD PLAN should contain the details of how the business will expand its physical plant, sales force, purchasing functions, etc., as well as the costs and benefits involved in doing so.

A plan to hold MARKET SHARE in a low- or no-growth market will probably require an increase in advertising and selling expenses.

However, it is possible that just the absolute level of these marketing expenses and not the ratio of these expenses to sales will have to increase at least in the short term. In general, the slower the MARKET GROWTH, the less it costs to hold MARKET SHARE. However, in both a growth and no-growth market, the cost of holding position depends on what competitors are likely to do.

In developing a HOLD PLAN, the strategist should take note of those competitors who are trying to build share or who are outpacing the business in terms of CUMULATIVE EXPERIENCE or ECONOMIES OF SCALE, etc.

Take, for example, Business A with a 25 percent MARKET SHARE trying to hold share of a market that has been and is expected to continue growing at 10 percent in CURRENT DOLLARS. Any of Business A's competitors that have been increasing share in the past are likely to continue to follow a BUILD PLAN, expecting to grow at greater than 10 percent. Any success the competitors have in increasing their share may well have to come at Business A's expense. Business A's competitors may not be able to make their BUILD PLANS if Business A is to make its HOLD PLAN. Analysis of competition is important in formulating a HOLD PLAN, with PENETRATION CHARTS for competitors being especially useful. Business A must analyze its competitors to determine if it should increase its spending in any area in order to protect against their BUILD PLANS.

Some businesses with very large shares have no choice but a HOLD PLAN in that any meaningful gain in share would be either too expensive or illegal. Still, holding on to a very large share can be expensive.

Many strategists use HOLD PLANS as benchmarks against which they evaluate BUILD PLANS and HARVEST PLANS. That is, they begin by asking what would it cost to hold a business's position and what kind of return can be expected. They then ask how much more it would cost to build the business and what incremental return could be expected or how much could be saved by harvesting the business and what effect that would have on returns. PRESENT VALUE calculations are often used to make those comparisons.

Horizontal Integration: occurs when a company participates in more or less competing businesses. For example, if a chain of stores in one locale built another chain in a different region, it would be integrating horizontally.

Most examples of horizontal integration tend to combine horizontal and VERTICAL INTEGRATION. Take, for example, a chicken processor and marketer that acquires a second brand name frozen chicken company. The chicken processor is making a HORIZONTAL INTEGRATION move in that it already owns a branded frozen chicken company, and it is at the same time becoming more vertically integrated in that it is acquiring some actual or potential IMMEDIATE CUSTOMERS for its processed chickens.

Horizontal Linkage: *see* LINKAGE.

Horizontal Merger: a MERGER in which two or more companies in the same industry are combined. These MERGERS are considered attractive because they often allow for the elimination of duplicate facilities, for the provision of a broader product line, or for greater ECONOMIES OF SCALE. Because a HORIZONTAL MERGER reduces the number of competitors in an industry, such a MERGER is often subject to antitrust restraints.

Horizontal Organization: a set of organizational entities, MANAGEMENT SYSTEMS, and practices cutting across BUSINESS UNITS to exploit INTERRELATIONSHIPS among BUSINESS UNITS and to facilitate collaboration. Although the mechanisms of a HORIZONTAL ORGANIZATION are similar to INTEGRATING SYSTEMS, which cut across functional or geographic divisions within BUSINESS UNITS and link different levels within the corporate hierarchy, the purpose of a HORIZONTAL ORGANIZATION is more wide-ranging. A HORIZONTAL ORGANIZATION is designed to create and channel SYNERGY between BUSINESS UNITS and to overcome impediments to cooperation such as fears about losing autonomy, conflicts over priorities, and asymmetrical benefits resulting from joint activities.

Horizontal Strategy: a coordinated set of GOALS and policies joining distinct but related BUSINESS UNITS and designed to lower costs or enhance the ability to differentiate. HORIZONTAL STRATEGY is based on identifying and exploiting INTERRELATIONSHIPS between BUSINESS UNITS. A HORIZONTAL STRATEGY capitalizes on three types of INTERRELATIONSHIPS between business units: tangible, intangible, and competitor INTERRELATIONSHIPS. Tangible INTERRELATIONSHIPS permit BUSINESS UNITS to share activities and gain from ECONOMIES OF SCALE or learning in areas such as production, distribution, and marketing. Intangible INTERRELATIONSHIPS are harder to realize.

They are based on the exchange of KNOW-HOW and skills between units. Competitor INTERRELATIONSHIPS arise when the competitive moves of one BUSINESS UNIT have implications for another, as is the case when a company faces MULTIPOINT COMPETITORS.

The task of developing a HORIZONTAL STRATEGY falls on the corporate, sector, or group strategist who must weigh the costs of linking the policies or activities of disparate BUSINESS UNITS. Coordinating activities inevitably requires some POLICY COSTS and suboptimization, which managers at the BUSINESS UNIT level are likely to resist. Coordination also carries with it the danger that the business's ability to respond to competitors and its flexibility in the face of industry change will be reduced.

The basic tool for identifying INTERRELATIONSHIPS between business units is the VALUE CHAIN. The VALUE CHAIN provides a basis for comparing the nature of activities and the behavior of the costs of different BUSINESS UNITS.

HORIZONTAL STRATEGY is used to build STRATEGIC LEVERAGE and is articulated in a company's CONCEPT OF FIT.

Hospitable Goal: GOALS held by competitors in an industry that are mutually achievable and, therefore, are not necessarily in conflict with one another. An industry in which competitors all had HOSPITABLE GOALS would be likely to have a low level of RIVALRY. For example, the GOALS of a competitor that wants to optimize short-term profits are likely to be hospitable to the GOALS of a business that would like to build its MARKET SHARE.

Strategists look for HOSPITABLE GOALS as part of analyzing a business's competitors by identifying the GOALS of their own business as well as those of their competitors and comparing them. Some strategists consider the GOALS implied by each of the three GENERIC STRATEGIES to be hospitable to each other because they involve different types of COMPETITIVE ADVANTAGE that appeal to different buyers. That is, they feel that in many industries it is possible for different competitors to pursue different GENERIC STRATEGIES without having a serious conflict of GOALS. Therefore, they see an industry that lacks a competitor following one of the strategies as an OPPORTUNITY.

Hurdle Rate: a rate of return used by a company used as benchmark for evaluating and comparing investment opportunities. A HURDLE RATE can be used to discount future returns in order to compare investment alternatives on the basis of their PRESENT VALUE. In capital budgeting, managers may reject any investment which does not at least meet their HURDLE RATE. A HURDLE RATE is usually set at a level equal to a company's COST OF CAPITAL.

Many strategists are uncomfortable with a single HURDLE RATE for a company that has a diversified portfolio of businesses. Those strategists feel that the HURDLE RATE for any investment should be based on the COST OF CAPITAL prevailing for the particular industry in which the investment is to be made and should take into account the contribution the investment will make to the ECONOMIC VALUE of the portfolio as a whole.

Hybrid Imperative: *see* COMMODITY/SPECIALTY MATRIX.

I

Image: the way in which an industry or a competitor in an industry is popularly perceived or regarded. The IMAGE of an industry is very often a composite of the images of its participants. For example, a GENTLEMAN'S GAME may be made up of stodgy competitors. Many strategists emphasize the importance of controlling the IMAGE of both their businesses and their industries. For example, buyer uncertainty can be reduced by making an industry appear professional and reliable, or the threat of MOBILITY can be reduced with a business image that provides a high level of EXPECTED RETALIATION.

IMAGE is often controlled with MARKET SIGNALS and, specifically, with VALUE SIGNALS.

Immediate Customer: the buyer to whom a business sells its product directly. The immediate customer is the buyer in the next stage forward of the product's VALUE ADDED CHAIN, who may or may not be the END USER of the product. Analysis of the characteristics of the immediate buyers, such as concentration and role, i.e., whether intermediary or END USER, is the basis of an evaluation of the BUYER POWER in an industry. For example, in some cases, the IMMEDIATE CUSTOMER, who is also an intermediate buyer, can effectively control access to the END USER. In other cases, PULL THROUGH can be an effective TACTIC to mitigate the BUYER POWER of such a customer.

Impact/Influence Grid: a technique for analyzing the significance of STRUCTURAL FACTORS in an industry as part of developing a COMPETITIVE STRATEGY for competing in that industry. Strategists use the grid to classify those STRUCTURAL FACTORS on the basis of their impact on industry profitability and the influence the business is able to exert over those factors. The grid is used to focus the attention of the managers and strategists on the factors that have the highest impact on profitability and over which the business has the most influence.

The first step in preparing the grid is to identify the STRUCTURAL FACTORS in the business's industry. Strategists often list the general STRUCTURAL FACTORS and then modify each factor to make it more specific to the industry being analyzed. For example, the general list might include EXIT BARRIERS as a factor, which then is refined to identify specific forms of EXIT BARRIERS such as labor contracts or high emotional barriers on the part of the currently DOMINANT FIRM.

Once a specific list has been developed, the second step is to determine how each factor impacts industry profitability when measured by RETURN ON INVESTMENT. Then the factors are ranked from the most positive to most negative in their impact on ROI. A similar list is then prepared ranking the factors in terms of the degree of influence the business has on each one. Some strategists find that the easiest way to do this is to begin with the ASSUMPTION that the business has no influence and then to think of ways in which it does or could influence the factor.

The two lists are used to position the factors on the grid. For

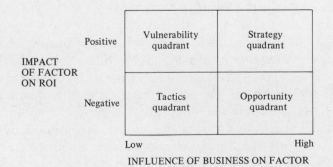

example, if there are twenty factors to be classified, a strategist might divide the horizontal and the vertical axes of the grid into twenty sections such that the grid becomes a twenty-by-twenty matrix with heavy lines at ten and ten. In that way a factor that was ranked fifteenth in impact and fifth in influence would fall in the vulnerability quadrant. A factor that was ranked sixteenth in impact and ninth in influence would be in the same upper left-hand quadrant but would be further to the right on the influence axis. (Note that this procedure assumes the midpoint to be relatively neutral when in fact it may not be.)

Factors that fall in the vulnerability quadrant have a positive impact and are subject to little influence by the business. These factors augment ROI so that the business's profitability is likely to be vulnerable to any change in them. In developing the COMPETITIVE STRATEGY, the strategist should consider what could be done to increase the business's influence over such factors and provide for careful monitoring of changes in those factors.

Factors that fall in the tactics quadrant have a negative impact on ROI and are factors over which the business also has little influence. The business is still vulnerable to the extent that there exists the possibility that the impact could become even more negative, but because of its low level of influence, the best the business may be able to do is to develop TACTICS that either help neutralize the impact or prevent the factor from becoming more negative. If the factor has a significant negative impact, then the strategist should look for ways to increase the business's influence over it.

Factors that fall in the opportunity quadrant have a negative impact on ROI BUT are factors over which the business has some influence. These factors present OPPORTUNITIES for the business to improve its profitability by neutralizing their impact or even by moving the factors into the Strategy Quadrant.

Factors that fall into the strategy quadrant have a high positive impact on ROI and are factors over which the business has some influence. Wielding that influence is likely to be the basis of the business's COMPETITIVE STRATEGY. The strategist's objective can be viewed as moving more and more factors into this quadrant. The more factors there are in that quadrant, the more profitable the business is likely to be. A business can increase its profitability by moving factors up toward the top of the grid and lower its vulnerability by moving factors toward the right of the grid. The more factors the business is able to move into the strategy quadrant, the more its COM-

PETITIVE STRATEGY is doing to build a profitable and protected position for the business in its industry.

Strategists develop variations on the IMPACT/INFLUENCE GRID by using impact on the business's ROI instead of impact on the industry's ROI for the vertical axis and by using potential influence rather than current influence on the horizontal axis.

Some strategists would alter the horizontal axis to reflect the size of the impact of a STRUCTURAL FACTOR on ROI rather than on whether it is negative or positive. They argue that a factor, whether negative or positive, which has a major impact on profitability, should figure prominently in the business's COMPETITIVE STRATEGY.

Imperfect Competition: *see* PERFECT COMPETITION.

Imperfect Information: a situation in which the relevant decision makers do not have full information about their options or the consequences of their choices. Imperfect information is the opposite of PERFECT INFORMATION and is the result of uncertainty or costs in information gathering.

Implementation: *see* STRATEGIC PLANNING.

Importance/Control Grid: a technique for formulating a STRATEGIC PLAN to implement a COMPETITIVE STRATEGY. The grid is used to identify and classify issues that affect the success or failure of the plan, to ensure that the plan gives adequate attention to the issues, and to place control over the related OPERATING POLICIES and decisions with the appropriate people.

To make effective use of the grid, one must identify the business's GOALS and COMPETITIVE STRATEGY, and the business's basic OPERATING POLICIES must be roughed out. The next step is to make an exhaustive list of all the issues that could affect the success or failure of the plan. The list can include issues derived from ENVIRONMENTAL SCANNING, such as a decrease in interest rates and issues derived from possible competitor moves. Some strategists define "issues" very loosely to include issues such as the business's prices, marketing expenditures, sales volume, etc. The next step is to take the issues and independently rank them in terms of importance and control. On the basis of those rankings, the issues can be located on the grid. Once each of the issues has been positioned relative to one another in one of the four quadrants, the strategist can consider ap-

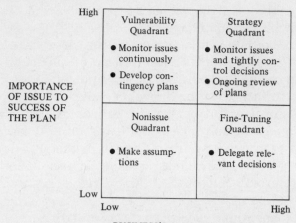

IMPORTANCE
OF ISSUE TO
SUCCESS OF
THE PLAN

High

Vulnerability Quadrant
- Monitor issues continuously
- Develop contingency plans

Strategy Quadrant
- Monitor issues and tightly control decisions
- Ongoing review of plans

Nonissue Quadrant
- Make assumptions

Fine-Tuning Quadrant
- Delegate relevant decisions

Low

Low   High

BUSINESS'S CONTROL OVER ISSUE

propriate actions vis-à-vis each issue given its position. That is, for those events in the Vulnerability Quadrant, the STRATEGIC PLAN should provide for monitoring those issues, for TACTICS to increase the business's control over them, and for developing contingency plans if those issues do not turn out in the business's favor.

For issues that are positioned in the Nonissue Quadrant, the STRATEGIC PLAN should include ASSUMPTIONS as to how those issues are likely to develop and perhaps some provision for further analysis of any issue that is close to being considered important.

The STRATEGIC PLAN should deal very specifically with issues that are in the Strategy Quadrant. Strategists and top management should provide for monitoring the outcome of these issues as well as for an ongoing review of any plan that involves a number of Strategy Quadrant issues. Strategy Quadrant issues are often the key concerns of top management, and decisions relevant to these issues are their responsibility.

Decisions that affect issues in the Fine-Tuning Quadrant are often delegated to the next level of management. Some strategists also recommend using the IMPORTANCE/CONTROL GRID for developing OPERATING POLICY for each FUNCTIONAL AREA and especially for developing PRODUCT POLICY. Decisions concerning issues that fall in the Fine-Tuning Quadrant of an OPERATING POLICY grid might then be further delegated to those managers responsible for developing programs and projects within the relevant FUNCTIONAL AREA.

Some strategists feel that the IMPORTANCE/CONTROL GRID is too wide-ranging in the types of issues included and that the recommendations derived from the grid are redundant if a business has already outlined its COMPETITIVE STRATEGY and identified key OPERATING POLICIES.

Incentive System: a type of MANAGEMENT SYSTEM used to enable and motivate individuals to pursue the company's OBJECTIVES. There are two types of inducements incorporated in most INCENTIVE SYSTEMS. The first is rewards or lack of them. Salary structure, bonus systems, executive prerequisites, profit sharing plans, etc., are all examples of rewards. The second type of incentive is related to the first but worth considering separately. This is the selection and development of individuals as they move through the ORGANIZATIONAL HIERARCHY. Management training, career path development, job rotation programs, etc., are incentives based on the promise of effective selection and development of individuals in the organization.

Together the two types of incentives should attract the appropriate individuals to the organization to carry out its COMPETITIVE STRATEGY and motivate them to carry out the organization's OBJECTIVES. The INCENTIVE SYSTEM of a company influences the balance its managers strike between long-term and short-term OBJECTIVES and whether they take a broad or narrow view of their responsibilities and role in the organization.

Because managers need information to operate the company's INCENTIVE SYSTEMS, INCENTIVE SYSTEMS are limited in effectiveness by the information provided by the company's MEASUREMENT SYSTEMS. A MEASUREMENT SYSTEM must cope with both the objective and subjective factors involved in the evaluation of personnel.

Incremental Cost: the additional cost solely attributable to a change in volume, product line, or other policy variable. INCREMENTAL COSTS are called MARGINAL COSTS in cases in which unit output is changed. INCREMENTAL COSTS are sometimes called differential costs.

Incumbent Competitor: *see* ENTRY BARRIER.

Individual Brand: *see* BRAND IDENTIFICATION.

Industrial Good: a product for which the buyers are primarily businesses and institutions. INDUSTRIAL GOODS are often categorized on the basis of durability. Products that are expected to last a few years or more are commonly called capital goods or producer durables.

Examples include blast furnaces, generators, and company cars. Products that are expected to last less than a few years are called producer nondurables. Examples of these are paper, dies, and components. Often any item that is added to the balance sheet is considered a durable, and any item that is expensed is considered a nondurable. INDUSTRIAL GOODS are sometimes called producer goods.

Industrial Organization: a field of economics that deals with the structure of markets, the behavior of companies, and the social benefits and costs associated with various combinations of market structure and company conduct. The basic Structure-Conduct-Performance paradigm is often illustrated as follows:

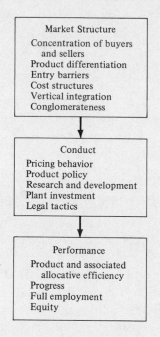

Research in this field has increasingly intersected with the development of STRATEGIC MANAGEMENT.

Industry Capacity: the sum of the capacities of each competitor in an industry. Different industries have different ways of measuring CAPACITY.

Strategists are often interested in industry CAPACITIES and CA-

PACITY UTILIZATION because INTERMITTENT EXCESS CAPACITY in an industry can be a contributing factor to RIVALRY in that industry.

Industry Evolution: the process by which INDUSTRY STRUCTURE changes over time. The initial structure of an industry is determined to a large degree by the approaches that the early competitors, buyers, and suppliers in the industry adopt. Initial structure is bounded by the underlying economics of the product but is often very fluid and dependent on the decisions of pioneers. If the product requires a significant amount of time and material to produce, this will put some constraints on the initial structure that the industry takes. However, one should not underestimate the range of viable approaches that pioneers can choose. For example, there was at one time a thriving business in low-cost mail order assemble-it-yourself houses.

The structure of the industry evolves as the players in the industry make policy choices and invest in implementing them in response to a wide variety of economic, technical, and competitive changes. Those investments change the way different STRUCTURAL FACTORS affect the COMPETITIVE FORCES in the industry. For example, MOBILITY BARRIERS may be erected or a DOMINANT DESIGN may emerge.

The key to understanding how an industry has evolved to its present structure and to forecasting how it is likely to evolve in the future is to understand the underlying factors that cause and motivate change in the structure. These factors are called EVOLUTIONARY PROCESSES.

Industry Importance Graph: a graph used to compare a measure of the relative significance of a business within its parent company's portfolio to that of its competitors. An indicator such as percentage of total company sales or total earnings is used to assess how high the CORPORATE STAKES are for different competitors in the industry. The underlying assumption in comparing businesses in this way is that a competitor's commitment to the industry and responsiveness to competitors' moves rises with the CORPORATE STAKES. The example on page 180 compares the importance of a company's four businesses with the importance of each business to its largest competitor.

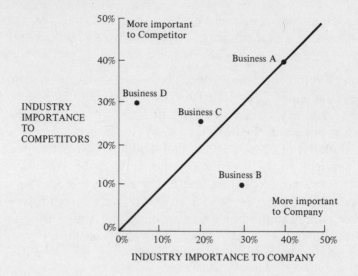

Although there are a number of ways to measure importance, one of the easiest and most commonly used is to calculate the business's sales as a percent of the company's total sales. The first step in the preceding example is to calculate that percentage for each business in the company's portfolio. Business A's sales are 40 percent of the company's total sales; Business B's sales are 5 percent. In the second step, sales data for the largest competitor of each business is collected. Then a similar ratio of each competitor's sales as a percentage of company sales is calculated. Finally, for each business, one point is plotted for each competitor. For example, Business D's biggest competitor accounts for 30 percent of its company's total sales. Business D is only 5 percent of the company's sales. The technique can be easily extended to include more than one competitor for each business. Points that fall above the 45° line indicate situations where the industry is more important to the company than it is to that particular competitor. Notice in the example that most of the company's businesses are competing in industries that are of equal or greater importance to the competitor than they are to the company.

Strategists who use the INDUSTRY IMPORTANCE GRAPH feel that it is a good way to get sense of the different competitive situations that their businesses are facing.

Strategists who are uncomfortable with the graph say that it is confusing because one has to keep remembering that its interpretation depends on the MARKET SHARES involved. For example, Business

D could have 50 percent of the market whereas its largest competitor has only 10 percent of the market and still provides 30 percent of its total company sales. Therefore, say those strategists, the graph can make the importance of Business B's competitor appear much more dramatic than the situation warrants.

Strategists who are comfortable with the graph say that they agree that it is difficult to interpret and that it usually requires a lot of footnotes, especially as to MARKET SHARE. However, they feel that the process of trying to explain each point can bring out a number of interesting issues about each business's competitive situation and that some interesting generalities can often be developed for the portfolio as a whole.

It is important to remember that percentage of total sales is just one way to measure importance and may not be the most meaningful. For example, even if a business accounted for only 10 percent of a company's sales, if it accounted for 50 percent of its earnings, it is likely to be very important to that company. In addition, a business that accounts for a low percentage of both the company's sales and earnings may still be important if it is expected to be a big contributor in the future.

Industry Life Cycle: a series of stages in the development of an industry marked by differences in factors such as the rate of MARKET GROWTH, the speed of product design changes, or the pattern of ENTRY and EXIT. The concept is analogous to that of the PRODUCT LIFE CYCLE, but it encompasses the entire industry product line rather than individual products.

Strategists who are comfortable with the concept see industries as moving through an emerging stage, a growing stage, a maturing stage, and finally a declining stage. Anticipating such an evolution can provide insights for shifting a company's strategy over time.

Other strategists feel that although it makes sense to recognize that differences in industries in terms of MARKET GROWTH and other STRUCTURAL FACTORS can be generalized as stages, it is more important to understand the EVOLUTIONARY PROCESSES involved. They point out that there are frequent deviations from the more predictable path of the product life cycle when the complexities of an entire industry are introduced.

Industry Scope: *see* COMPETITIVE SCOPE.

Industry Segment: an arbitrary subdivision of an industry that is used as a basis for providing line of business information in publicly available reports. The lines of business for which information is published may or may not correspond to organizational or planning entities within a company. A subdivision of an industry which is meaningful for strategic purposes is referred to as a BUSINESS SEGMENT although the distinction is not always maintained.

Industry Segmentation: *see* MARKET SEGMENTATION.

Industry Stability: the condition of having a low level of RIVALRY in an industry. The presence of GOOD COMPETITORS often leads to stability; otherwise, combinations of COMPETITOR CONFIGURATION and MOBILITY BARRIERS are usually analyzed to predict or understand industry stability. Share balance is considered an important indicator of industry stability.

GENTLEMAN'S GAMES often lead to INDUSTRY STABILITY.

Industry Structure: the configuration of fundamental economic and technical characteristics that determine the nature and intensity of industry competition. The individual characteristics are called STRUCTURAL FACTORS. STRUCTURAL FACTORS include technological and economic features of the product, demographic and organizational traits of buyers or suppliers, the number and concentration of competitors, and the availability of SUBSTITUTES. In order to analyze the structure of an industry, the individual STRUCTURAL FACTORS can be grouped on the basis of their impact on one of the five COMPETITIVE FORCES shaping the industry: BUYER POWER, SUPPLIER POWER, COMPETITOR RIVALRY, THREAT OF POTENTIAL ENTRANTS, and SUBSTITUTES.

Variations among industries in the strength of the individual forces and in the way they interact explain differences in the risks and returns available to competitors and, hence, industry profitability.

A STRUCTURAL ANALYSIS is a study of an industry using the framework of the five COMPETITIVE FORCES, and it provides the foundation for building a COMPETITIVE STRATEGY.

Inelastic Demand: *see* ELASTICITY OF DEMAND.

Inelastic Supply: *see* ELASTICITY OF SUPPLY.

Inflation: an increase in the general level of prices in an economy. INFLATION results in a decrease in purchasing power. Deflation refers to a decrease in the general price level. Deflation is very rare. From 1950 to 1980, there was one year, 1955, in which there was a slight decrease in the Consumer Price Index from the previous year.

To some extent, INFLATION is tied to BUSINESS CYCLES because prices tend to rise during periods of prosperity, when industry CAPACITY UTILIZATION is likely to be high. However, recent experience has shown that inflation can persist even with substantial excess CAPACITY in the economy. Many economists believe that the rate of inflation depends mainly on the government's policies toward the money supply and other macroeconomic instruments and that any relation to industrial capacity and its utilization is short-run at best.

Two types of INFLATION are often identified as DEMAND-PULL INFLATION and COST-PUSH INFLATION. DEMAND-PULL and COST-PUSH may have some value for identifying the origins of an inflationary disturbance. However, they do not explain the persistence of INFLATION. Nor do they cover all the possible sources (increases in world prices of primary materials; depreciation of the dollar, etc.).

The strategist is concerned with INFLATION because of its effect on the ECONOMIC VALUE of the company. INFLATION must be taken into account when valuing investment in FIXED CAPITAL and WORKING CAPITAL, as well as when valuing CASH FLOWS. FORECASTING and accounting for INFLATION can be very important in determining REQUIRED RETURNS on investment.

Information system: *see* MANAGEMENT SYSTEM.

Innovation: *see* PRODUCT INNOVATION.

Input-Output Analysis: a technique for analyzing the pattern of industry SUPPLY and DEMAND in the economy as a whole which is used in forecasting DEMAND and economic research. Data collected periodically by the Bureau of Economic Analysis of the U.S. Department of Commerce on the distribution of total sales and purchases made by each industry in the economy is used to construct input-output tables. The tables can be used to predict how a change in the economy will affect DEMAND for the output of an industry. The distinctive feature of the technique is its ability to measure the indirect effects of changes in the output levels of other industries. INPUT-OUTPUT ANALYSIS is valuable for anticipating the effects of large long-run changes in the economy or in economic policy.

Insight: the recognition of either an OPPORTUNITY and the ways to take advantage of it or the recognition of a THREAT and the ways to protect against it. Inasmuch as at the business unit level THREATS and OPPORTUNITIES are a function of INDUSTRY STRUCTURE and INTRA-INDUSTRY STRUCTURE, INSIGHTS are derived from the analysis of the dynamics of those phenomena as well as of the VALUE CHAIN and BUSINESS INTERRELATIONSHIPS.

INSIGHTS can also involve the recognition of an inevitable change in INDUSTRY STRUCTURE or INTRA-INDUSTRY STRUCTURE and the ways to take advantage of that. INSIGHTS can also involve the recognition of the potential for making a desirable change in industry structure by influencing an EVOLUTIONARY PROCESS and the ways to do it.

The value of an INSIGHT declines as more competitors have it; however, a sustainable COMPETITIVE ADVANTAGE can offset that devaluation.

Intangible Interrelationships: *see* BUSINESS INTERRELATIONSHIPS.

Integrating System: the set of policies and methods used by management to facilitate communication and to coordinate the activities of individuals or groups within the company. The methods used frequently fall into five categories: reporting relationships, staff functions, procedures, committees, and location. None of the methods is mutually exclusive, and, because each has its limits, a mix of all five is usually found in any company.

With the first way method, groups are linked to the same individual through reporting relationships, and that individual is responsible for coordinating their activities. This method is limited by the span of attention of the individual involved. A MATRIX ORGANIZATION tends to rely heavily on a complex network of reporting relationships as a way of resolving conflicting OBJECTIVES.

The second method is to build a staff alongside the line functions that have to be coordinated. These staffs are intended to extend the span of attention of the individual responsible for integrating a number of groups. Sometimes companies set up specific integrating roles that are more than staff functions because they have operating responsibility but differ from reporting relationships in that they do not have authority over the interdependent groups. For example, in some consumer package goods companies, a brand manager has no authority over either the manufacturing or the marketing function for the brand but does have the responsibility for coordinating the two. This approach is usually limited by the number of individuals who can handle the role.

A third approach is to establish procedures. For example, a business might set up a book of procedures for integrating its manufacturing and sales functions that includes directives such as the following: manufacturing must be notified immediately of any sale of any more than one thousand units, or orders of less than one hundred must be fulfilled in at least two weeks. However, procedures can be established more easily for routine activities, and there are limits to the amount of procedure any group can tolerate.

A fourth approach is to set up committees. Committees include staff meetings, task forces, planning meetings, etc. Committees tend to offer a flexible approach which can be used to integrate groups under different circumstances from the routine to the one time occurrence. The problem with committee meetings is that they take time and require skilled and effective facilitators and participants.

The last approach relies on physical location. Groups that have to be coordinated are located closely enough to each other to be able to communicate directly with one another. There are definite limits to the number of individuals who can work in close proximity to each other, but audio and visual electronics can be used to simulate proximity.

Three factors that influence the difficulty of coordinating activities and communicating are these: the complexity of the information that has to be communicated, the diversity among the individuals involved, and the physical logistics involved. The complexity of information to be communicated increases with the volume of information to be communicated, the difficulty of standardizing the information, and the number of directions in which the information has to be sent. Individuals are diverse because the interdependent groups to which they belong differ in values, time horizons, manners, etc. In general, the more differences there are between the individuals in one group and the individuals in another, the more difficult it will be to develop effective INTEGRATING SYSTEMS.

Physical separation can also strain INTEGRATING SYSTEMS. It is usually easiest to coordinate and communicate among groups that are located close to one another. Research has shown that just relocating groups to different floors can call for a change in INTEGRATING SYSTEMS. Much stronger systems are needed to integrate among individuals in different buildings and different countries, etc.

INTEGRATING SYSTEMS tend to be very important to strategists because effective implementation of a strategy depends on coordinating the efforts of many individuals in order to achieve a set of related OBJECTIVES. Regardless of the type of hierarchy involved, the most important consideration in developing INTEGRATING SYSTEMS is an analysis of the interdependence of the actions the organization must take to achieve its OBJECTIVES. Different strategies are going to require different degrees of interdependence to implement. For example, a business that sells a high volume of COMMODITY PRODUCTS on a routine basis to the same customers is probably going to require less coordination and communication between its marketing and manufacturing functions than a business that sells a highly customized product with a service contract. The second business is going to require more coordination between the selling and manufacturing areas in order to make the sale and to deliver the product to specification.

An INTEGRATING SYSTEM, along with an INCENTIVE SYSTEM and a MEASUREMENT SYSTEM, comprises a company's MANAGEMENT SYSTEM.

Integration: *see* VERTICAL INTEGRATION.

Inter-Industry Competition: RIVALRY between competitors in different industries. Usually, this occurs when one industry produces products that can be SUBSTITUTED for the products of another. For example, the price and availability of video games may affect the sporting goods industry because they both compete for the consumer's leisure spending. Some strategists address these effects by broadening the boundaries of the industry. Other strategists make a more detailed analysis of the threat of SUBSTITUTE PRODUCTS as part of their analysis of INDUSTRY STRUCTURE.

Intermediary Buyer: *see* END USER.

Intermittent Overcapacity: occurs when industry CAPACITY periodically exceeds DEMAND. INTERMITTENT OVERCAPACITY is likely to happen in an industry that is CYCLICAL and in which DEMAND falls below SUPPLY during periods of low economic activity. The bunching of capacity additions is common in many industries and can also give rise to recurrent episodes of overcapacity. The impact is greater in industries where CAPACITY is hard to shed or has to be added in large increments, especially if the normal increments of CAPACITY tend to be large relative to the average competitor's MARKET SHARE.

Internal Development: *see* CONCEPT OF ASSEMBLY.

Internal Rate of Return (IRR): the discount rate at which an investment has a PRESENT VALUE of zero. Calculating an INTERNAL RATE OF RETURN is one of a number of approaches to evaluating an investment. The discount rate at which an investment has a PRESENT VALUE of zero is calculated, and then that INTERNAL RATE OF RETURN is compared with the INTERNAL RATE OF RETURN of alternative investments to see which is higher. The INTERNAL RATE OF RETURN approach is often contrasted with the PRESENT VALUE approach. With the PRESENT VALUE approach, the future return on one investment is discounted with a rate appropriate to that investment, and then that PRESENT VALUE is compared with the PRESENT VALUE of alternative investments to see which is higher.

Strategists who like using an INTERNAL RATE OF RETURN approach feel that it allows them to compare alternative investments on a common basis. They also point out that the INTERNAL RATE OF RETURN approach does not involve subjective assessments such as the appropriate discount rate used in the PRESENT VALUE approach.

Strategists who are uncomfortable with the INTERNAL RATE OF RETURN approach argue that IRR gives the analyst no idea of the absolute size of the returns and that IRR assumes the returns can be reinvested at the INTERNAL RATE OF RETURN. For example, one investment can have an IRR of 100 percent and, therefore, appear to be superior to another investment having an IRR of 50 percent. However, the first investment may be limited to one dollar and the second may involve hundreds of thousands of dollars. Also, both the 100 percent IRR and the 50 percent IRR assume that as the returns come in, the investor can continue to invest them at the IRR. This may not be possible.

International Competition: *see* GLOBAL INDUSTRY.

Inter-Plant Scale: a business's level of production or CAPACITY aggregated for all its plants and facilities. For example, a business that produces 200 units of a given product per year in one plant, 300 units in another, and 500 units in a third is operating at an INTER-PLANT SCALE of 1,000 units per year even though its INTRA-PLANT SCALE for each individual facility is much lower. Two competitors can have similar INTER-PLANT SCALE and very dissimilar INTRA-PLANT SCALE.

Strategists are interested in INTER-PLANT SCALE because some ECONOMIES OF SCALE transcend the SCALE OF OPERATIONS of a single plant. For example, purchasing ECONOMIES OF SCALE may depend on the purchasing volume of the whole business rather than of the individual plant. CUMULATIVE EXPERIENCE in some elements of a business's COST STRUCTURE may also transcend the SCALE OF OPERATIONS at a single plant.

Intra-Industry Analysis: the process of identifying and interpreting the differences among the competitors in an industry in order to explain the variance in profitability among them.

The first step in the analysis is to identify the different strategies being followed. One way to do this is to fill out a COMPETITIVE STRATEGY wheel for each competitor. Specifically, strategies may differ in the degree to which the competitor has specialized (in terms of product lines or TARGET MARKETS), the approach to BRAND IDEN-TIFICATION (whether some competitors use PULL THROUGH or PUSH THROUGH while others don't), the approach toward manufacturing and distributing the products, and the emphasis on PRODUCT QUAL-ITY. A competitor may be a leader or a follower, which can lead to differences in research and development policies. Different degrees of VERTICAL INTEGRATION; differences in RELATIVE COSTS, RELATIVE PRICES, and UTILITY; and differences in FIXED-TO-VALUE ADDED RA-TIOS should also be noted. Because the analysis aims to identify differing sources of COMPETITIVE ADVANTAGE, it is also important to note differences in the competitors' relationships to their parent company, especially in elements of the company's CORPORATE STRAT-EGY likely to add to the business's STRATEGIC LEVERAGE as well as its FINANCIAL LEVERAGE. To the extent that government policies may be important, one should note differences in both the relevant policy of the countries in which the competitors compete as well as the relevant policies of the home government of an international competitor. These differences can be identified in more or less detail. Some strategists find it convenient to put competitors into STRATEGIC GROUPS rather than to deal with them individually.

Once the differences between the competitors have been identified, the next step is to relate those differences to the competitors' profitability. This is usually done by taking two factors at a time and plotting the competitors on a COMPETITOR MAP. Logically, the first map should record the two factors likely to make the most difference, and the strategist should determine the expected effect on profitability of occupying different positions on the map. The strategist should then plot the actual RETURNS ON INVESTMENT (or whatever measure of profitability is being used) and consider these questions: Does the relationship between profitability and strategic differences make sense? Can the strategist explain the relationship in terms of the effect of those differences on the COMPETITIVE FORCES in the industry?

Mapping combinations of differences should continue until the strategist has found all the combinations that seem to contribute to explaining the difference in profitability. Those differences will be the key MOBILITY BARRIERS that allow competitors in the same industry to earn different returns.

Some strategists feel that this type of analysis is very important in identifying the THREATS and OPPORTUNITIES in an industry as well as in identifying KEY SUCCESS FACTORS. Those strategists consider this type of analysis basic to formulating a COMPETITIVE STRATEGY.

Intra-Industry Structure: the set of differences among competitors in an industry which explains the variations in the returns earned by the competitors. An examination of INTRA-INDUSTRY STRUCTURE can explain why in some industries all the competitors earn about the industry average whereas in other industries some competitors earn much more and some much less than the industry average. An analysis of INTRA-INDUSTRY STRUCTURE explains this variability in returns by helping the strategist identify the relevant differences between the competitors in the industry.

The first difference is that different competitors devise different COMPETITIVE STRATEGIES. However, some competitors are better at formulating a strategy that is appropriate for the industry structure and that creates a protected profitable position for that business. Some strategists feel that certain strategies are more appropriate for specific INDUSTRY STRUCTURES. Other strategists feel that any GENERIC STRATEGY can be implemented in a given industry but that their relative profitability will depend on the INDUSTRY STRUCTURE.

Another obvious difference is that some competitors are better than others at implementing strategies. If all competitors are carrying out the same COMPETITIVE STRATEGY effectively, then logically they should all earn the same return. However, if they vary in effectiveness, the more proficient competitor would be expected to earn a higher return. Differences in the ability to implement a strategy can stem from management ability to articulate and stick to a strategy or from factors such as preferred access to raw materials or favorable government regulations.

The combination of differences in COMPETITIVE STRATEGY and effectiveness in implementation are the basis for MOBILITY BARRIERS which allow one competitor to continue to earn more than another.

Strategists who are comfortable with the concept of INTER-INDUSTRY STRUCTURE feel that INTRA-INDUSTRY ANALYSIS is an important step in formulating COMPETITIVE STRATEGY.

Intra-Plant Scale: the level of production within a single plant or facility. For example, a business that produces half of its total output of 1,000 units per year in each of two plants would be operating at an INTRA-PLANT SCALE of 500 units per year. Another business with the same total output might have an intra-plant scale of 300 units in one facility and 700 units in another.

Strategists are interested in INTRA-PLANT SCALE because many ECONOMIES OF SCALE are relevant only at the plant level. In addition, the CUMULATIVE EXPERIENCE in some elements of a business's COST STRUCTURE may also be relevant only at the plant level.

Investment Center: an entity in a company's ORGANIZATIONAL HIERARCHY for which the company's MEASUREMENT SYSTEMS measure the amount of assets employed, as well as the amount of revenues generated and the amount of costs incurred. Managers of INVESTMENT CENTERS are usually responsible for earning or exceeding a specific RETURN ON INVESTMENT. To achieve their OBJECTIVES, those managers must trade off current profits against incremental investment to generate increased profits in the future.

INVESTMENT CENTERS are sometimes called PROFIT CENTERS.

Invisible Hand: the effect on the general economy of the profit-making motives of the individuals participating in that economy. In the 1930s, Adam Smith wrote that businesses are led by an invisible hand in such a way that in pursuit of their own interests, i.e., profits, they promote the best interests of the society better than when either they intend to promote society or society interferes in order to promote itself. The concept is often used as a rationale for competitive markets.

Issue Management: an approach to STRATEGY that is based on responses to the THREATS or OPPORTUNITIES that are expected to impact the performance of the business. The first step of ISSUE MANAGEMENT is identification of the issues through such techniques as ENVIRONMENTAL SCANNING and COMPETITOR ANALYSIS. The identified issues are then evaluated and categorized on the basis of the expected impact on the business, the timing of the impact, and the probability of the occurrence.

Responses are then developed to deal with the issues that have been evaluated as important. Those responses take the form of strategies for protecting against the THREATS and taking advantage of the OPPORTUNITIES.

UNCERTAINTY CHARTS and STRATEGIC INTELLIGENCE GRIDS are often used in ISSUE MANAGEMENT.

Joint Cost: *see* JOINT PRODUCTS.

Joint Products: two or more dissimilar end products that are produced from the same raw material or value added step. An example of the first would be the meat, frozen meats, pet food, fertilizer, chemicals, and leathers that come from a steer. An example of the second would be the passenger service and air cargo space that result from flying a jet. Joint products are problematic to accountants because the allocation of joint costs to each end product is a matter of judgment. Some companies assign zero costs to by-products.

JOINT PRODUCTS present strategists with both a problem and an OPPORTUNITY. The problem is that joint costs may distort the profitability of any joint product. The OPPORTUNITY results when joint products are managed with a HORIZONTAL STRATEGY to produce a COMPETITIVE ADVANTAGE.

By-products differ from JOINT PRODUCTS only in management intent. A by-product is considered a residual product. This designation does change over time; an example is kerosene, once a crude oil by-product of gasoline, which is now a component of jet fuel.

Joint Venture: a contractual relationship between two or more companies to carry out a specific business or project. Strategists often consider JOINT VENTURES a less risky or a less expensive way to ENTER a new business. Joint ventures are often proposed in order to ENTER an industry for which the company has some, but not all, the critical capabilities. For example, a company might have the required technology but not the cash or the marketing skill. In some industries, a joint venture can construct and utilize facilities of MINIMUM EFFICIENT SCALE when a single company would be unable to absorb all the output.

JOINT VENTURES may work out badly if the partners have different CORPORATE STAKES that lead to inconsistent demands on the managers involved. Some strategists feel that a joint venture is inherently hobbled by having to check with two or more masters. In addition, strategists are often wary of joint ventures when there is a chance of revealing some proprietary experience.

K

Key Success Factor: an attribute or capability of a business which is responsible for its dominance in an industry or the strength of its performance. A key success factor is often closely associated with the basis for carrying out a successful GENERIC STRATEGY. That is, a key success factor can establish a business as the low-cost competitor, the differentiated competitor, or the competitor that best serves a TARGET MARKET. For example, the key success factor in a given industry might be the ability to produce the lowest-cost motor components if that happens to be the most important determinant of COST LEADERSHIP and if COST LEADERSHIP is a viable successful GENERIC STRATEGY in that industry.

KEY SUCCESS FACTORS exist at the functional level as well as at the business level. For example, a high degree of control over PRODUCT QUALITY may be the key to effective manufacturing in a given industry. Some strategists define a FOCUSED FACTORY as one following a MANUFACTURING POLICY that reinforces a business's key success factor.

KEY SUCCESS FACTORS often involve COST DRIVERS and UNIQUE-NESS DRIVERS and lead to COMPETITIVE ADVANTAGE.

Know-How: expertise in any value adding activity. KNOW-HOW usually refers to expertise in procurement, processing, or another VALUE ADDED step; but it can also refer to the ability to pick sites, build plants, or manage advertising budgets. In general, the acquisition of know-how depends on a LEARNING CURVE, and the speed and volume of know-how captured in a company increase with the amount of management attention and policy applied to capturing it.

Strategists point to the importance of building know-how, of keeping it proprietary, and of transferring it from business to business for optimal LEVERAGE.

Know-how can refer to the type of overall strategic management expertise that builds FORMULA FIT.

Knowledge Diffusion: *see* DIFFUSION OF PROPRIETARY EXPERIENCE.

L

Labor Intensity: refers to the amount of labor relative to the amount of capital investment required in a business. A business that has a high ratio of labor expenses relative to the amount of capital investment or an industry with a number of such businesses is often called labor-intensive. A handicraft industry, for example, is very likely to be labor-intensive. Some industries, especially ones involving agricultural products, are becoming less labor-intensive as machines are developed to perform the required functions. Labor-intensive industries usually have lower than average ENTRY BARRIERS and lower than average FIXED-TO-VALUE ADDED RATIOS.

Learning Curve: the ability of individuals to improve their job performance over time as they learn to do it better. The expectation is that as an individual builds experience in a certain task, that individual will be able to do the task faster and better. This, in turn, should increase the individual's output and thereby lower the cost

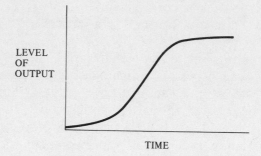

of that output. On a graph with the level of output on the vertical axis and time on the horizontal axis, a typical LEARNING CURVE takes the shape of an S-curve.

Output rises slowly in the beginning and then rises rapidly. The rate of increase eventually falls, and output levels out. Strategists have expanded this concept into the EXPERIENCE CURVE.

Leverage: an enhanced or increased ability or advantage in achieving some GOAL. LEVERAGE often increases RISK in that it can amplify the outcomes. That is, LEVERAGE can often amplify the gain on the upside and the loss on the downside. FINANCIAL LEVERAGE and STRATEGIC LEVERAGE are two types of LEVERAGE sought to increase the ECONOMIC VALUE of a business. FINANCIAL LEVERAGE refers to the use of debt in a company's CAPITAL STRUCTURE in order to affect its returns. STRATEGIC LEVERAGE is a more general concept which refers to the enhanced ability of a business to compete in an industry owing to elements of its strategy, such as market positioning, manufacturing policies, or product development efforts.

Life Cycle Matrix: one of a number of charts used to analyze a portfolio of businesses. The LIFE CYCLE MATRIX is similar to the GROWTH/SHARE MATRIX in that it is used to analyze the CASH-FLOW balance between businesses and to indicate appropriate BUSINESS PLANS.

The first step in using a LIFE CYCLE MATRIX is to classify each business according to the maturity of its industry on the basis of the industry stage in the INDUSTRY LIFE CYCLE. The second step is to classify each business on the basis of the strength of its COMPETITIVE POSITION in its industry. The determination of COMPETITIVE POSITION depends on comparing this company's business with its competitors in its industry. As one would expect, the factors used to assess relative competitive position differ by stage of industry maturity. For

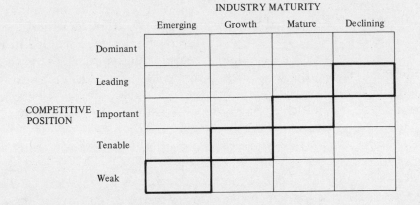

example, RELATIVE MARKET SHARE may be the most important indicator of a dominant competitive position in a mature industry, but not necessarily in an emerging industry. During the emerging stage, a technological edge may be the key to a strong competitive position.

The LIFE CYCLE MATRIX incorporates assumptions about the CASH FLOW and profitability of a competitor during each stage of the INDUSTRY LIFE CYCLE. As a business's industry moves from left to right in the matrix, the business's profits and CASH FLOW are expected to improve. Overlayed on the expected change in profitability as the industry moves through its life cycle is the expected change in profitability as the business improves its COMPETITIVE POSITION.

In the emerging stage, CASH FLOW is expected to be heavily negative because the business is assumed to be spending for growth in such areas as marketing and R&D while simultaneously adding to its capital base in expectation of growth. Businesses in an emerging industry will run at a loss even though individual competitors may for various reasons show a profit. BREAK-EVEN is expected to occur in the late emerging stage. In the growth stage, the capital expenditures and heavy discretionary expenditures for development are expected to consume more cash than the business procedures, resulting in continuing negative CASH FLOWS. Industry profits are expected to be low as a percentage of sales. RETURN ON INVESTMENT is also expected to be low. Both indices are expected to improve through the growth stage as profit growth outpaces sales growth. This is explained by assuming that, during rapid growth, current expenses are made to generate future sales. Thus, spending for growth reduces current profit. Even though capital investment may still be high during the transition to maturity, the industry is expected to be self-financing and to generate a positive CASH FLOW. Absolute profits and rates of profitability are expected to peak in the late mature stage and then decrease in the declining stage. In the declining stage, competitors are expected to withdraw capital for recycling into businesses in other industries. Therefore, a business is expected to be a CASH USER until the end of its industry's growth stage, at which point it becomes a CASH GENERATOR. It is expected to continue to generate cash through its industry's mature and declining stages.

Strategists who use the matrix feel that it is important to consider the stages yet to come in developing a plan for any business. This is because they believe that the economics of improving COMPETITIVE POSITION change as the industry moves from stage to stage. It is considered less expensive to improve COMPETITIVE POSITION in the earlier stages of the life cycle and prohibitively expensive to do so in the later stages.

Some strategists who use the LIFE CYCLE MATRIX feel that a business's position in the matrix defines the appropriate STRATEGIC PLAN for that business. For example, businesses that fall above the diagonal of darkened squares are considered to have a wide range of STRATEGIC PLANS available to them and to be capable of making a significantly positive contribution to the ECONOMIC VALUE of the company. The businesses on the diagonal of darkened squares are considered to have a limited range of STRATEGIC PLANS available to them. The businesses that fall below the diagonal are considered candidates for either a HARVEST PLAN, LIQUIDATION, or DIVESTMENT.

Life Cycle Price: the total cost a buyer incurs in obtaining and using a product during that product's useful life. That price usually includes the prepurchase costs of shopping for the product, the selling price of the product, and the additional costs incurred over the useful life of the product. Additional costs can include the cost of servicing and maintaining the product, the cost of fueling or running the product, the cost of storing the product, etc.

Many strategists feel that it is important to understand what the LIFE CYCLE PRICE of a product actually is as well as what it is perceived to be by the buyer. Those strategists feel that the analysis often reveals ways to attain or demonstrate a superior PRICE-TO-PERFORMANCE RATIO for their product vis-à-vis their competitor's products. Also, they feel that the analysis of LIFE CYCLE PRICES, real and perceived, often reveals ways that the incentives of the purchase DECISION-MAKING UNIT can be changed to benefit their businesses.

LIFO: an accounting method for valuing inventory that assumes that the business's newest inventory is sold first. LIFO, an acronym for last in, first out, is the opposite of FIFO. Changes in production that affect costs are reflected on the income statement more quickly under LIFO than FIFO. During periods of INFLATION, LIFO will tend to lower taxable income while inventories may be undervalued. However, the opposite is true if costs are falling.

Linkage: an interdependency among two or more business activities which affects their costs or performance. For example, the performance of a selling activity may benefit from quality control, which, in turn, may benefit from a number of different activities, including more obvious examples like supplier specifications and less obvious examples like employee relations. LINKAGES exist between the activities of a business and those of its suppliers, its distribution channels, and its buyers as well. These are referred to as vertical linkages. Horizontal linkages exist across businesses within the same company and are sometimes managed as BUSINESS INTERRELATIONSHIPS.

LINKAGES can be used to build COMPETITIVE ADVANTAGE by choosing the configuration of activities to lead to BUYER VALUE and by coordinating those activities.

Main LINKAGES, both actual and potential, are obvious, but many others are not. The latter can be OPPORTUNITIES because they often provide INSIGHT into new ways of building COMPETITIVE ADVANTAGE. They are likely to arise when there are a number of different activities that offer BUYER VALUE and thus offer a wide range of choices from which to optimize or increase the value of coordination. They can also arise when the support activities in a VALUE CHAIN have a significant effect on the primary activities.

TECHNOLOGICAL CHANGE can have a significant effect on LINKAGES.

Strategists who analyze LINKAGES often start with BUYER VALUE and work backward, mapping out actual and potential linkages. They also study competitor VALUE CHAINS, both as a way of understanding their advantages and as a way of generating potential linkages in their own businesses.

Liquidation: to convert an asset to cash, usually by selling it. The amount of cash is called the liquidating value of the asset.

A HARVEST PLAN may call for the LIQUIDATION of some of the

business's assets so that the CASH FLOW can be reinvested in other businesses. The LIQUIDATION of an entire business is often called DIVESTMENT.

Long Wave: *see* BUSINESS CYCLE.

Loss Leader: a product that is sold at a discounted price in order to induce the buyer to buy other nondiscounted products rather than to sell more of that product. Products can serve either as continuous LOSS LEADERS or as occasional loss leaders. Restaurants very often offer continuing loss leaders. For example, in many fast-food outlets, the hamburgers are sold at very low margins to attract buyers. The profits are made by inducing the buyer to purchase additional higher-margin products like sodas, french fries, and onion rings.

Appliances are a good example of an occasional LOSS LEADER. Outlets will advertise discounted prices on selected appliances to induce buyers into the store with the intention of selling the buyer something else and the potential of getting the buyer to trade up. Strategists find that products that are effective occasional loss leaders are usually products that have a high degree of BRAND IDENTIFICATION or products for which the buyer has a good idea of the nondiscounted prices.

Low-Cost Position: *see* HIGH-COST POSITION.

Low-Cost Strategy: *see* COST LEADERSHIP OF STRATEGY.

Low Relative Price: *see* RELATIVE PRICE.

M

Maintenance Strategy: a STRATEGY that calls for a business to preserve its COMPETITIVE POSITION in its industry. Usually, a GOAL of this kind of strategy is to hold the business's current level of MARKET SHARE. In that case, a HOLD PLAN is associated with a MAINTENANCE STRATEGY. The term can also refer to a less ambitious strategy aimed at keeping sales at their current absolute level.

Make or Buy Decision: a business's choice between buying a component from a supplier or making that component itself. Factors which influence the decision include RELATIVE COST, similarities between production of the components and the business's current activities, the significance of a secure supply of the component, and the importance of the component in terms of the final product's cost or performance. These factors are often closely related to SUPPLIER POWER as well. The decision to integrate backward is analogous to the decision to make rather than buy a component, but encompasses a broader range of activities.

Management by Objective (MBO):   a system of management under which managers in a company are given clearly defined responsibilities and requirements for performance. An MBO system combines elements of both a MEASUREMENT SYSTEM and an INCENTIVE SYSTEM. First, OBJECTIVES are set, often as frequently as every six months, telling the manager exactly what that individual is expected to accomplish so that others can meet their objectives and so that ultimately the company can meet its objectives. In this way, the system stresses the interdependence among managers. Then, to make the MBO system work, each manager's compensation and other incentives are tied to the achievement of the objectives.

Management System: a system of policies, programs, and procedures with which a company controls and influences the behavior of its employees. A company's MANAGEMENT SYSTEM links together the individuals and entities which make up the ORGANIZATIONAL HIERARCHY to form a company's ORGANIZATIONAL STRUCTURE. A company's MANAGEMENT SYSTEM is usually comprised of three subsystems. The first, a MEASUREMENT SYSTEM, measures what is being spent and what is being achieved. For example, a cost accounting system is a MEASUREMENT SYSTEM. The second, an INCENTIVE SYSTEM, is used to motivate and develop individuals. An MBO SYSTEM is an INCENTIVE SYSTEM although in many companies it incorporates elements of a MEASUREMENT SYSTEM as well. The third, an INTEGRATING SYSTEM, is used to coordinate the activities of individuals and groups of individuals and to facilitate communication between them. Monday morning staff meetings are a part of an INTEGRATING SYSTEM.

A company's PLANNING PROCESS has to work with and around a company's MANAGEMENT SYSTEMS. The information collected in

MANAGEMENT SYSTEM					
Measurement		Incentive		Integrating	
Expenditures	Achievements	Rewards	Development	Coordinate	Communicate

the company's MEASUREMENT SYSTEMS is used to formulate and monitor the implementation of strategies. In organizations in which the PLANNING HIERARCHY is different from the ORGANIZATIONAL HIERARCHY, the PLANNING PROCESS depends heavily on the company's INTEGRATING SYSTEMS to coordinate all the efforts involved. Finally, the INCENTIVE SYSTEM must reinforce the commitment to a company's strategy.

Manufacturing Policy: the operating policies governing labor and personnel, plant and equipment, product design and engineering, production planning and control, and organization and management style. A business's MANUFACTURING POLICY will determine labor-related issues such as type of labor force, degree of skill and specialization, and job grades. Regarding plant and equipment, policy will determine the SCALE OF OPERATIONS; the location of plants; the degree of SPECIALIZED ASSETS; CAPACITIES, etc. Policy will have to address product design and engineering questions regarding the size of product line, custom vs. standard products, stability of design, technological risk in product and process, etc. Production planning and control issues include size and control of inventory, the timing of breaks for buffer stocks, the level of quality control, and the standards to be used.

A business's MANUFACTURING POLICY must also determine whether the manufacturing function will be organized around products, buyers, or geographic regions; how the managers and personnel will be measured and rewarded; and what information will be collected, how, when, and by whom.

MANUFACTURING POLICY should be derived from the business's COMPETITIVE STRATEGY and should reflect the THREATS and OPPORTUNITIES in the business's INDUSTRY STRUCTURE. This is particularly true regarding choices between alternative processes and technologies. In this area, manufacturing policy has to take into special consideration the rate of technological change in the industry, the current level of technological sophistication, the relationships between costs and ECONOMIES OF SCALE and experience, and the time and resources required to change the manufacturing function in response to changes in the industry. Strategic decisions regarding what products to offer at what price, what markets to target, and what distribution channels to use translate into manufacturing requirements for costs, deliveries, lead times, quality levels, and reliability.

Research has shown that there are clearly defined trade-offs to be made in manufacturing because production facilities cannot satisfy simultaneously demands for high flexibility, low cost, high quality, and high dependability. Within a given industry, the most effective competitors have manufacturing policies reflecting the priorities dictated by the business's COMPETITIVE STRATEGY. A manufacturing facility managed with a specific, manageable set of priorities is often referred to as a FOCUSED FACTORY.

The PRODUCT/PROCESS MATRIX can be used to analyze MANUFACTURING POLICY and highlights the evolution of manufacturing policy as an industry matures. Manufacturing policy is sometimes called manufacturing strategy.

Manufacturing Task: the key requirement or duty of the manufacturing function in carrying out the COMPETITIVE STRATEGY of a business. Sometimes the terms MANUFACTURING TASK and MANUFACTURING POLICY are used interchangeably, but in the strictest sense they are quite different. The first is a specific statement of OBJECTIVES and constraints. The second is a broad philosophy covering the required policy for all aspects of the manufacturing function in order to complete the task. A MANUFACTURING TASK should explicitly state the demands and constraints placed on manufacturing by the company's CORPORATE STRATEGY and the business's COMPETITIVE STRATEGY. Included in that statement should be a list of priorities that ranks the importance of PRODUCT QUALITY, delivery, and cost and defines what each one means to the business. For example, in the case of quality, the particular features and levels of performance required to achieve the desired level of quality should be stated. The definition of the MANUFACTURING TASK is very important to strategists who apply the FOCUSED FACTORY concept.

Marginal Cost: the change in total costs resulting from a one-unit change in output. MARGINAL COST can also be defined as the change in total VARIABLE COSTS resulting from a one-unit change in output. These two definitions hold when considering both the short run and the long run from an economist's point of view. In the short run, it is assumed that the firm cannot vary the inputs which give rise to the firm's FIXED COSTS. There is an upper limit on the amount of output that the firm can produce, but the firm can vary its output up to that point by increasing the quantities of variable resources. In the long run, it is assumed that all resources are variable so that no distinction is made between VARIABLE and FIXED COSTS.

The MARGINAL COST at any output is derived from the total cost curve and is equal to the slope of the total cost curve at that output. A typical margin cost curve is U-shaped. Initially, as total output increases, the cost per unit drops, but eventually the cost per unit turns up again.

According to microeconomic price theory, under conditions of PERFECT COMPETITION, a firm maximizes its profits or minimizes its losses by producing output at which marginal cost is equal to MARGINAL REVENUE or price.

Marginal Revenue: the change in total revenue resulting from the sale of one additional unit of product. According to microeconomic theory, under conditions of PERFECT COMPETITION, MARGINAL REVENUE is equal to price, and a firm maximizes its profits by producing at a level at which MARGINAL REVENUE is equal to MARGINAL COST. For a monopolist or firm operating under conditions of imperfect competition, marginal revenue is less than price because the firm faces a downward sloping demand curve, and price must be lowered to sell an additional unit.

Marginal Utility: the additional satisfaction that a buyer gets from consuming an additional unit of a product. MARGINAL UTILITY tends to fall with each additional unit of a product, and this quality underlies the downward slope of the demand curve for a product. For example, usually the marginal utility of a household's second television is less than the UTILITY of the first, and the third set can be expected to have even lower marginal utility, etc. Therefore, one can see that it usually takes a lower price to get a buyer to purchase more units of a product. Volume discounts are an example of an attempt to lower prices on the additional units to make up for their lower marginal utility.

The term MARGINAL UTILITY is also used more loosely with reference to additional features on a product, as, for example, in the statement that "the marginal utility of making pencils multicolored is

low.'' This type of MARGINAL UTILITY is often analyzed with a PROD-
UCT ATTRIBUTE CURVE.

Market Configuration: *see* COMPETITOR CONFIGURATION.

Market Gap Analysis: a three-step approach to finding a profitable, unserved NICHE or a currently undefined BUYER GROUP for a
given product. The three steps involve testing ASSUMPTIONS, creating
a data base, and testing the buyers. Assumptions are usually tested
by making lists of all assumptions that are being made about each
of the five COMPETITOR FORCES. The process of testing assumptions
should lead to the collection of data needed to answer those tests.
The third step is to test the product with the potential buyers who
have been identified through steps one and two.

Strategists who favor MARKET GAP ANALYSIS do so because of
the emphasis on testing assumptions and data analysis before sur-
veying potential buyers. They feel that the process allows for a better
selection of buyers as well as better-defined market tests.

Market Grid: a chart used to display and compare the BUYER
GROUPS targeted and the buyer needs emphasized by a business or
its competitors. Buyer groups are segmented on the basis of factors
such as demographics or marketing reachability and arrayed across
the top of the grid from smallest to largest. The buyer needs are
arrayed down the left side of the grid and can be ranked on some
measure of UTILITY or importance. Combinations of cells in the grid
can then be identified as being a business's TARGET MARKET. Competitor's TARGET MARKETS can be located as well.

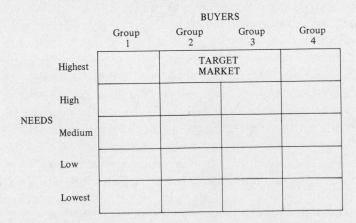

Any overlap in TARGET MARKETS or shared emphasis on particular buyer needs or BUYER GROUPS can point out areas of opportunity or vulnerability for a business.

Some strategists prefer to analyze TARGET MARKETS and competitors by using COMPETITOR MAPS to identify STRATEGIC GROUPS because they provide more insight into the MOBILITY BARRIERS in an industry.

Market Growth: the rate of change in unit sales of an industry. Rising MARKET GROWTH is usually considered to have a positive effect on industry profits because it allows competitors to increase absolute profits by increasing their sales as the industry grows rather than by having to compete with each other for those sales. However, MARKET GROWTH can also attract ENTRY.

Strategists are interested in MARKET GROWTH trends because of the effect on RIVALRY. Also, market growth can allow an industry to operate on a larger scale. Therefore, depending on other STRUCTURAL FACTORS, market growth can allow for such changes in the industry as new technologies, national advertising, ECONOMIES OF SCALE, CUMULATIVE EXPERIENCE, and VERTICAL INTEGRATION.

Marketing Certainty Matrix: a technique which assigns probabilities for the likelihood of success to BUSINESS PLANS based on the newness of the product and the newness of the market involved. The probabilities assigned to the likelihood of realizing a planned level of sales or income are not established empirically but are estimates. The four cells of the matrix are named for the most important or likely source of new sales, and those are shown in parentheses in the sample matrix that follows. The MARKETING CERTAINTY MATRIX is essentially an abbreviated PRODUCT-MARKET UNCERTAINTY MATRIX, although the probabilities assigned in each differ.

Strategists use this matrix to apply probabilities to future plans at the company level, the business level, or the product level. For example, at the company level, all the planned sales in each cell are multiplied by the probability assigned to that cell to get an expected sales level from that particular plan. If the expected sales level is too low, then the plan is analyzed to see what provisions can be made to improve the probabilities or whether more sales can be generated from higher probability cells. Strategists note that part of the uncertainty associated with a plan that calls for a large percentage of its sales growth to come from cells other than the lower left cell is

LIKELIHOOD OF SUCCESS

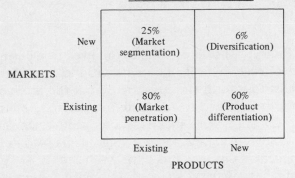

		Existing	New
MARKETS	New	25% (Market segmentation)	6% (Diversification)
	Existing	80% (Market penetration)	60% (Product differentiation)

Existing   New

PRODUCTS

due to the fact that the plan probably incorporates a number of changes in current MARKETING POLICY.

Marketing Innovation: *see* PRODUCT INNOVATION.

Marketing Mix: a business's chosen combination of policies regarding the type of product it will sell, the way it will promote that product, the price it will charge, and the place it will sell that product. These four considerations—product, promotion, price, and place—are often called the four Ps. The MARKETING MIX or the four Ps can serve as a crude checklist for the MARKETING POLICY of a business.

Marketing Myopia: a nearsighted view of a product taken by managers who focus on the product's form rather than on its function. Theodore Levitt, who coined the term, says that these managers tend to see their role as marketing a product rather than as satisfying the needs of its buyers.

Strategists who feel it is important to prevent MARKETING MYOPIA argue that the condition can leave a business vulnerable and can cause it to miss OPPORTUNITIES. For example, they argue that when the calculator arrived, slide rule and adding machine companies were suffering from marketing myopia. This led them to think that there was a decline in the market for their products and that their businesses were no longer any good. In fact, they could have viewed their function as providing quick calculations and seen tremendous opportunity in that business. Even strategists who do not pay so much attention to marketing myopia in their own companies look for opportunities to take advantage of the MARKETING MYOPIA of others.

Marketing Policy: the set of policies followed by a business to identify and select customers, to tailor its products to address its customer's needs, to inform the customer about the product, to entice the customer to buy, and to facilitate the purchase of the product. MARKETING POLICY covers such issues as product choice, distribution systems, advertising, personal selling, media planning, customer credit, technical assistance, BRAND IDENTIFICATION, promotions, merchandising, MARKET SEGMENTATION, and PRICE POLICY. A business's combination of choices vis-à-vis these issues is often called its MARKETING MIX.

A business's MARKETING POLICY must also cover how the marketing function will be organized, whether around products or buyers or geographic regions; how the managers and personnel will be measured and rewarded; and what information will be collected, how, when, and by whom.

MARKETING POLICIES should reflect key elements of the COMPETITIVE STRATEGY of a business. Marketing is an area in which a great deal of competitive activity and maneuvering takes place. Setting positioning, advertising, and promotional tactics, for example, requires a keen awareness of buyer needs as well as competitors' activities. Many strategists feel that an analysis of their buyers' DECISION-MAKING PROCESS is very important in formulating marketing policy. Many elements of marketing policy attempt to influence the incentives of the buyers' DECISION-MAKING UNITS.

Market Leader: *see* DOMINANT FIRM.

Market Price: the price at which a good is bought and sold, free of government administration and controls. In theory, the MARKET PRICE of a product equals the EQUILIBRIUM PRICE, but in practice it rarely does. This is because suppliers never have perfect information about what DEMAND will be, and, therefore, suppliers will often produce more or less than the quantity demanded at a given price. As a result, there is usually some excess SUPPLY or excess DEMAND. However, the strategists should be warned that the market price does tend to adjust continuously toward the equilibrium price. The speed of the adjustment process varies by industry depending on the ELASTICITY OF SUPPLY and DEMAND. The equilibrium price is the point

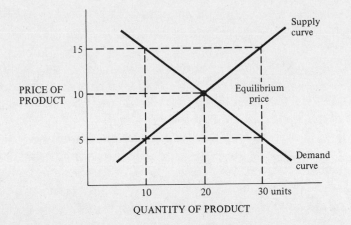

at which the supply curve and the demand curve intersect. In the diagram above, $10.00 is the equilibrium price or the price at which supply equals demand.

At a market price of $15.00, suppliers will produce thirty units but buyers will only demand ten units. Therefore, a market price above an equilibrium price will result in excess supply. However, suppliers will find that they cannot sell all the units they have produced, and inventories will pile up. Suppliers will then do two things. First, they will attempt to sell the excess inventory at reduced prices, and, second, they will cut back in production. This process tends to continue until supply and demand are again in balance at the equilibrium price.

If the market price is $5.00, suppliers will only produce ten units, but buyers will demand thirty units. Therefore, a market price about an equilibrium price will result in excess demand. However, as buyers discover that they cannot purchase all the units they want, they will begin to offer higher prices to bid for the units that are available. Suppliers will notice the upward trend in prices and respond with increased production until supply and demand are again in balance at the equilibrium price.

MARKET PRICES will fluctuate as the SUPPLY or DEMAND curve or both shift for any reason. The volatility of prices in an industry depends on the prevalence of factors in the industry that provoke these shifts. Some industries are very vulnerable to weather, fluctuating consumer tastes, and fluctuating raw material prices and, therefore, can be expected to have volatile prices. In an industry with very inelastic demand and very inelastic supply, industry prices will fluctuate a great deal although the quantities actually sold will change very little. Conversely, an industry where both DEMAND and SUPPLY are elastic, shifting supply and demand curves will have comparatively little impact on the MARKET PRICE but a big impact on the quantity sold. Also, because long-run demand and supply curves are generally more elastic than short-run demand and supply curves, a given change in supply or demand is likely to cause a bigger change in short-run market prices than in long-run prices.

Buyers' inventories add some additional complexities to market price adjustments. In one sense, inventory is stabilizing to market prices because buyers can respond to short-term shortages by drawing down their inventories to avoid the high prices. Conversely, they can take advantage of short-term excess supply by building up inventory at the lower prices. However, the presence of buyer inventories can be destabilizing if buyers' long-term expectations are that prices will go up or down more in the future than they already have. Suppose, for example, that the price of a unit begins to rise. If buyers expect that unit prices will continue to rise, they may decide to buy even more now, before the price gets any higher. This, in turn, pushes the prices even higher, which fulfills the buyers' expectations about price increases, etc. The reverse can happen when prices fall. If buyers expect prices to fall further, they may begin to postpone their purchases, diminishing demand and pushing prices down even further. Therefore, buyers' expectations about prices can be critical to understanding changes in market prices. In forecasting the future conditions in markets, an assessment of these expectations and their implications becomes extremely important. This is especially true of a company that has chosen a PRICE LEADERSHIP role.

Market Return: *see* CAPITAL ASSET PRICING MODEL.

Market Segment: a designation combining BUYER GROUPS and the products for those BUYER GROUPS. A given business's TARGET MARKET is the MARKET SEGMENT in which that business competes. The buyers comprising a MARKET SEGMENT share needs and characteristics which are reflected in similarities in the products offered to and purchased by them. The term MARKET SEGMENT is often used interchangeably with the terms BUYER GROUP, BUSINESS SEGMENT, and INDUSTRY SEGMENT.

Market Segmentation: the process of dividing an industry into MARKET SEGMENTS. Different MARKET SEGMENTS in the same industry may have very different STRUCTURAL FACTORS. This makes the segment aspects of COMPETITIVE SCOPE very important.

MARKET SEGMENTATION may include all possible products, COM-PLEMENTARY PRODUCTS, BUNDLED PRODUCTS, JOINT PRODUCTS, SUB-STITUTE PRODUCTS, and ANCILLARY PRODUCTS with their full range of UTILITY and all current and potential buyers throughout the VALUE SYSTEM.

Some strategists define MARKET SEGMENTATION so broadly as to include the consideration of all four dimensions of COMPETITIVE SCOPE. SCOPE GRIDS are often used in this analysis. MARKET SEG-MENTATION defined this broadly is sometimes called INDUSTRY SEG-MENTATION, and the segments are called BUSINESS SEGMENTS or IN-DUSTRY SEGMENTS.

Market Segment Competition: *see* POTENTIAL ADVANTAGE MATRIX.

Market Share: the sales of a business stated as a percentage of total industry sales. The arithmetic is straightforward, but collecting the data necessary and defining the market in order to calculate the MAR-KET SHARE can be difficult. Industries differ greatly with respect to the ease with which MARKET SHARE data can be obtained. For some products, such as automobiles, published industry sales figures are readily available. For others, information must be purchased from commercial sources or estimated by complicated methods.

There can be many alternatives in defining the appropriate mar-ket. For example, if Business A sells $125 million worth of roofing shingles versus the $5 billion worth of shingles that are sold world-wide, then Business A has a global MARKET SHARE of $125 million divided by $5 billion, which equals 2.5 percent. One could argue that Business A does not compete overseas and that, therefore, the de-nominator should include only the U.S. market, which is half the size of the worldwide market. Business A's domestic market share would then be 5 percent. One could further argue that Business A does not manufacture 225-pound and 300-pound shingles, eliminat-ing the $500 million of those shingles from the denominator and leaving a $2 billion market, for a market share of 6.25 percent.

In the preceding example, the numerator and denominator were expressed in terms of dollars. Instead, they could have been ex-pressed in terms of units. To the extent that Business A sells a higher-than–average priced shingle, its market share in units will be lower than its market share in dollars.

The definition of the business and its market and the ways the market share measure is going to be used determine what to put in the numerator and denominator. There are three general uses for

MARKET SHARE measures: to measure the position and performance of a business in an industry, to forecast future sales, and to set goals. Also, the market shares of competitors are often calculated in order to determine their positions and to forecast their future behavior.

Year-to-year or quarter-to-quarter changes in market shares are often used to appraise current performance. For example, a year-to-year decline in market share, even as little as 1 percent a year, could be considered an ominous sign that the business's position was falling relative to its competitors. The same calculations for competitors could indicate which, if any, of them are changing positions and in what directions. A RELATIVE MARKET SHARE calculation would provide additional information. A sales forecast for a business that assumes no change in COMPETITIVE POSITION can be obtained by assuming that the business will at least maintain its current market share and then multiplying an industry sales forecast by that market share. Finally, Business A might set a sales target of 3 percent of the units sold in the total United States and subtargets by region of 1.5 percent in the South, 3 percent in the West, 2.8 percent in the Northeast, and 2.5 percent in the North Central. Subtargets can also be set by product type. Some businesses first set unit MARKET SHARE targets and then set prices based on what price is required to sell that many units.

Most strategists recognize a number of pros and cons for using market share information. Perhaps the most persuasive argument for using market share as a method of appraising performance is that it helps to avoid holding management accountable for forces over which it has no control. If the economy goes into a recession, the demand for shingles declines. In that case, even though Business A's sales might fall, its management could still be effectively evaluated by looking at the proportion of industry sales it captures. Other so-called uncontrollable forces might be those which affect all competitors equally such as a general shortage of critical materials, an industrywide change in the price structure, a new entrant, or an acquisition that greatly strengthens a competitor's position and injures those of the remaining companies.

Arguments against this reasoning are that a good MARKETING POLICY should protect a business from a new entrant or, for example, that a business that emphasizes a low-priced model may be less adversely affected by recession and less favorably affected by prosperity, etc.

Another problem is that a MARKET SHARE measure does not indicate anything about the cost of gaining that share. For example, a business that shows an increase in MARKET SHARE could be considered to be performing well, but what about profits? What was involved in getting a larger share? Perhaps the increase was achieved by giving bigger dealer discounts, hiring more salespeople, expensive sales contests, more advertising expenditures, or merely loading up dealers with inventory.

In spite of these and other problems, market share measures are often used to help control and measure marketing effectiveness because they are easy to understand and are a convenient way of comparing one company's position with another's. Most companies use market share data in some way. Well-managed companies try to use them in combination with profit standards like RETURN ON INVESTMENT, with expense control mechanisms, and with other information about the INDUSTRY STRUCTURE and COMPETITIVE FORCES.

Market Share Competition: *see* POTENTIAL ADVANTAGE MATRIX.

Market Signal: an action by a competitor that provides an audience with grounds for inferring information about that competitor. The information signaled can be true or false. That is because a MARKET SIGNAL is used to bluff, to warn, and to deceive as well as to communicate facts. MARKET SIGNALS can be classified on the basis of content and audience in addition to intent.

Therefore, MARKET SIGNALS are analyzed by identifying the content of the signal and the audience to which it was directed and then deciphering the message. In addition to the competitor's intended message, there are often ancillary messages that are sent unintentionally. These may be subtle but can prove to be as important as the intended message in discerning a competitor's intentions.

		AUDIENCE					
		Capital Markets	Buyers	Rivals	Suppliers	Potential Entrants	Substitute Products
	Prior Announcements						
	Explanations						
CONTENT	Comments						
	Boasts						
	Actions						

Because of the mix of intended and unintended messages and possible errors of perception and inference, some strategists believe that analyzing MARKET SIGNALS is more confusing than valuable and that their businesses are better off concentrating on their own affairs. Other strategists feel that the analysis of market signals, especially when it builds on a strong base of COMPETITOR ANALYSIS, is very important to the process of recognizing THREATS and OPPORTUNITIES in an industry.

VALUE SIGNALS are a type of MARKET SIGNAL sent to buyers.

Market-to-Book Ratio: the ratio between the MARKET VALUE of a company's equity and the BOOK VALUE of that company's equity. Some strategists feel that a company's MARKET-TO-BOOK RATIO is the best measure of the company's ability to create ECONOMIC VALUE for its shareholders. Simplified, the argument is that shareholders should be willing to pay a million dollars only for something that cost a million dollars, such as a plant. That is, the MARKET VALUE of that plant should equal its BOOK VALUE. However, if the managers of that plant are able to earn very high returns on the shareholders' investments in that plant, then the shareholders will pay more to own a piece of that plant. Because the shareholder will be willing to pay more for the plant than the plant cost, the plant's market-to-book ratio will be more than 1.0. Therefore, the higher a company's market-to-book ratio, the more economic value the company has created for its shareholders. If for the same level of BOOK VALUE the market-to-book ratio increases over time, the company must also be increasing its economic value.

Some strategists consider a MARKET-TO-BOOK RATIO to be invalid unless the BOOK VALUE of the company's assets is adjusted for distortions. For example, they argue that because of INFLATION, REPLACEMENT VALUES should be used instead of book value because otherwise a high market-to-book ratio is just showing how old the plant is. Other strategists feel that the book value of the assets does not have to be adjusted because they feel that a company creates value for its shareholders when it buys plants before their costs are inflated by price increases.

Most strategists find it useful to compare the MARKET-TO-BOOK RATIOS of their own companies to those of their competitors both at current levels and over time. These lists of comparable MARKET-TO-BOOK RATIOS can give strategists a good idea of how the market is valuing their company relative to other companies with businesses in the same or similar industries. That relative value can indicate shareholder expectations vis-à-vis future returns for the company.

Market Value: the value that willing and informed buyers place on an asset. At the corporate level, strategists are interested in the MARKET VALUE of the company to its shareholders. That is, they are interested in the MARKET PRICE investors are willing to pay for securities that are claims on the company's assets. A simple way to calculate the MARKET VALUE of a company is to take the company's current stock price and multiply it by the number of shares of stock outstanding. This MARKET VALUE is often compared to the BOOK VALUE of the company's assets to see if the market is saying that those assets are worth more than the company paid for them or not. This comparison is called a MARKET-TO-BOOK RATIO. Some strategists feel that, for this comparison to be meaningful, the BOOK VALUE of the assets has to be adjusted for INFLATION.

At the business level, strategists are often interested in the MARKET VALUE of the assets tied up in a business when they are considering DIVESTMENT and when they are screening ACQUISITIONS CANDIDATES.

Maslow: *see* HIERARCHY OF NEEDS.

Matrix Organization: an ORGANIZATIONAL STRUCTURE in which areas of responsibility and authority are defined in such a way that the responsibilities of one manager overlap with those of other managers. A MATRIX ORGANIZATION with its complex network of reporting relationships stands in contrast to a pyramid organization with its distinct lines of authority. Typically, a manager's responsibilities are assigned along one of three dimensions: product, function, or market. Meanwhile, another set of managers within the organization is given responsibilities on the basis of one of the remaining two. For example, in one business, there may be an overlap of product managers and manufacturing managers. In another business, there could be a matrix of product managers for each product and market managers for each country in which the business operates. In the latter example, the product managers would be responsible for selling as much of their specific product as possible, and the market managers would be responsible for selling as much of any combination of products as possible in a particular country.

Strategists who do not like MATRIX ORGANIZATIONS feel that the complications involved in having two or more bosses puts too much strain on the company's INTEGRATING SYSTEMS. This, they feel, results in a lack of communication and a lack of decision making and, therefore, a lack of implementation. Strategists who do like MATRIX ORGANIZATIONS feel that it helps managers to think in terms of strategic trade-offs at a lower level in the organization than is usually possible. This, they think, makes for more effective implementation of strategy. Finally, some strategists argue that almost all organizations are MATRIX ORGANIZATIONS to the extent that they involve INTEGRATING SYSTEMS, and so the term is not very meaningful.

Maturity: *see* PRODUCT LIFE CYCLE.

MBO: *see* MANAGEMENT BY OBJECTIVE.

McKinsey Screen: a nine-cell BUBBLE CHART that arrays a portfolio of businesses along two dimensions: the strength of each business's COMPETITIVE POSITION and some composite measures of the attractiveness of its INDUSTRY STRUCTURE. The BUSINESS/INDUSTRY ATTRACTIVENESS MATRIX is a commonly used version of this technique.

Measurement System: data collection and record-keeping procedures designed to provide information to the individuals who must make decisions in an ORGANIZATIONAL HIERARCHY. Usually, two types of information are provided. The first type is information on how the company's human and financial resources are being utilized at various levels of the organization. Cost accounting, personnel scheduling, and capital expenditure reports provide this type of information.

The second type of information MEASUREMENT SYSTEMS can provide is information on the company's progress in achieving its OBJECTIVES, again at various levels of the organization. Sales tracking systems, customer satisfaction reports, and accounts analysis reports provide this type of information.

To be effective, MEASUREMENT SYSTEMS must contribute to the achievement of the company's OBJECTIVES by providing the relevant information when it is needed by the DECISION-MAKING UNIT. Therefore, the design of a MEASUREMENT SYSTEM should take into consideration what actions are needed to achieve the desired objectives and how and when these actions can be measured. This precept may seem obvious, but many strategists find that their ability to formulate and implement STRATEGIES is often hampered by the company's MEASUREMENT SYSTEM. For example, it may be difficult to formulate a BUILD PLAN for a business that has never measured its MARKET SHARE or that of its competitors. Also, it may be difficult for a manager to implement a DIFFERENTIATION STRATEGY on the basis of information provided by a system that emphasizes cost control. Furthermore, implementation of a strategy may be impossible if both MEASUREMENT and INCENTIVE SYSTEMS are ineffective.

Merger: combining the assets and liabilities of one company with the assets and liabilities of another company. Usually, a MERGER is effected by the purchase of one company by another company. MERGERS are classified into three types, based on the degree of similarity between the buying and selling companies' activities. If the two companies are in the same line of business, the merger is called a HORIZONTAL MERGER. If the two companies are in the same business but participating in different stages of the VALUE ADDED CHAIN such that the merger involves VERTICAL INTEGRATION, then the merger is called a vertical merger. If the two companies are in different businesses, the merger is sometimes called a CONGLOMERATE merger.

Strategists evaluate a MERGER on the basis of its contribution to ECONOMIC VALUE. The merger is analyzed to understand why the two companies may be worth more together than they would be apart. One reason is the potential for FINANCIAL LEVERAGE. For example, such factors as potential tax shields, surplus cash, and the way the ACQUISITION is financed may lower the cost of the acquisition below its value. However, for the most part, strategists are interested in STRATEGIC LEVERAGE through FUNCTIONAL FIT, FINANCIAL FIT, or FORMULA FIT.

Me-Too Product: a product that is designed to be a close copy of a competitor's product. Strategists use ME-TOO PRODUCTS to take advantage of the marketing efforts of their competitors without necessarily incurring the cost of that effort. That is, the business attempts to sell its ME-TOO PRODUCT to BUYER GROUPS that are aware of the product because of the competitor's efforts but do not insist on having the competitor's brand or are unable to tell the difference. Strategists also use ME-TOO PRODUCTS to fill out their business's product line.

Minimum Efficient Scale: the lowest SCALE OF OPERATION possible at which relevant ECONOMIES OF SCALE can be fully realized. That is, if a given machine can produce a maximum of 100 units at a capital cost of $100 and if all associated operating costs per unit are constant, then the MINIMUM EFFICIENT SCALE for that operation is 100 units. With the machine operating at that rate, capital costs per unit are $1.00. If, instead, the operation were running at a level below

MINIMUM EFFICIENT SCALE of only 50 units, then the capital cost per unit is $2.00. As long as an operation is running at multiples of its minimum efficient scale, it can take full advantage of related ECONOMIES OF SCALE. For example, a company with three machines running at 100 units each also has capital cost per unit of $1.00.

In most companies, the MINIMUM EFFICIENT SCALE will be different for different operations in different stages of the VALUE ADDED CHAIN. Also minimum efficient scale will change with new technologies and new ways of doing business. For example, minimum efficient scale for the operation just described would change to 200 units if a new machine were invented that could produce a maximum of 200 units at a capital cost of $.50 per unit.

Mission Statement: a statement of what a company's purpose and GOALS are, what businesses it will be in, what markets it will serve, how the businesses will be managed, and how the company will grow. A company's MISSION STATEMENT is usually an abstraction of its CORPORATE STRATEGY.

MISSION STATEMENTS are evolutionary and should be continually reviewed and revised to reflect changes in the environment. For example, a company that sold grass seed may define its mission as providing commercial and residential buyers with the wherewithal to produce beautiful lawns. With the introduction of artificial turf, the company has to consider whether or not the manufacture of artificial turf is a business that falls within its mission. This consideration is especially important because the bulk of its sales is to commercial buyers rather than to residential buyers. Still, the company may well conclude that this is not so and amend its MISSION STATEMENT to specify natural lawns.

Some strategists find that developing a MISSION STATEMENT is a good way to begin to formulate a CORPORATE STRATEGY. Other strategists feel that spending time on a mission statement distracts from the attention that should be placed on the creation of ECONOMIC VALUE. Those strategists would rather proceed directly to analyzing the company's portfolio and their business's relative COST STRUCTURE to look for OPPORTUNITIES for STRATEGIC LEVERAGE.

Mixed Motives: conflicting GOALS which prevent a business from responding directly or forcefully to the moves of a competitor. MIXED MOTIVES put a business in a position where it feels damned if it does respond and damned if it doesn't. The business recognizes what its competitors are doing and wants to react, but, because of its specific situation, the potential responses seem unattractive. MIXED MOTIVES present an OPPORTUNITY for improving COMPETITIVE POSITION while minimizing the RISK of increased RIVALRY by reducing the likelihood that a competitor will retaliate. OPPORTUNITIES can arise from taking advantage of any of a number of strategic commitments a competitor may have made. For example, U.S. auto manufacturers could see the inroads that small, inexpensive foreign cars were making, and yet they were reluctant to develop directly competing products. One reason for this reluctance was the fear that such a response would move the U.S. market away from the more profitable large cars. A prior commitment to certain distribution policies presents another example. A large business may have based its distribution strategy on the principle that all sales will be made through distributors and that these distributors will receive both functional and quantity discounts. If a small competitor should then attempt to sell directly to large accounts at low prices, it becomes difficult for the large firm to defend itself. To do so may mean violating existing policies and commitments.

Realistically, competitors cannot be expected to sit forever and suffer, but taking advantage of MIXED MOTIVES will certainly slow down the response and may lessen its strength.

MNC: *see* MULTINATIONAL CORPORATION.

Mobility Barrier: a STRUCTURAL FACTOR or an element of a business's COMPETITIVE STRATEGY that prevents competitors from moving into the business's STRATEGIC GROUP. MOBILITY BARRIERS raise the costs that have to be incurred in order for a business in an industry to move from one STRATEGIC GROUP to another.

Strategists are concerned with MOBILITY BARRIERS because overcoming them allows a business to increase its profitability by moving into a more profitable strategic group, and building mobility barriers enables a business to protect its profitability by keeping competitors out of its strategic group.

In order for a company to enter an industry, it must overcome both the ENTRY BARRIERS in the industry and the mobility barriers protecting the strategic group it wants to enter.

Monopolistic Competition: a market in which a large number of sellers offer similar but differentiated products. Because of PRODUCT DIFFERENTIATION, the monopolistic competitor has some influence over price; however, each seller is still too small relative to the entire market to influence other competitors. NONPRICE COMPETITION is usually very strong in such a market.

Monopoly: a market situation in which a product with no good substitutes is sold by a single firm from which all buyers must purchase. Because the monopolist controls the entire output of a given product, control over SUPPLY is complete. The position of the monopolist is the opposite of that of a business in an industry with PERFECT COMPETITION.

An individual business operating in a perfectly competitive market is a price taker facing a horizontal DEMAND curve, for changes in its output are too small to influence aggregate SUPPLY. A monopolist faces the downward sloping market DEMAND curve for the product. This allows the monopolist to maximize profitability by choosing the combination of price and output that will accomplish that OBJECTIVE. This combination occurs at a point at which MARGINAL REVENUE is equal to MARGINAL COST. However, unlike the business in a perfectly competitive market, MARGINAL REVENUE for the monopolist is not equal to, but less than, price. This is because the monopolist must lower price to increase sales whereas the competitive business simply offers more output. As a result, the supply of product will be lower, and the price of the product higher in a market controlled by a monopolist.

In practice, many factors limit a firm's ability to occupy a monopolist position. Even poor SUBSTITUTES limit the price a firm can charge without a substantial loss of volume. The monopolist in a regional or local market may have competitors located some distance away, whose prices limit what the firm can charge. These factors—or simply the nature of buyers' preferences—may make DEMAND elastic enough that the advantage of a MONOPOLY is limited. Also, a monopoly may be only marginally profitable if the costs of serving the market are high.

The term "natural monopoly" is applied to certain conditions in which a single seller tends to enjoy efficiency advantages. These advantages might be due to ECONOMIES OF SCALE, as in electric power generation. Or they may be due to fixed facilities that any rival must duplicate, such as the local telephone network or cable TV.

An industry in which there are few competitors is called an OLIGOPOLY.

Monopsony: a market situation in which an industry sells to a single buyer. This type of industry has the highest possible BUYER CONCENTRATION.

Morphological Map: a chart that shows for a given product or product family a matrix of the different forms that a product could take. A simple morphological map might show a product like laundry soap as follows.

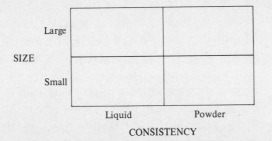

Much more complex maps would break down any two dimensions of product form or UTILITY into a detailed array of the actual and potential range of configurations. The cells might note current competitors, technologies involved, BRAND IDENTIFICATIONS, RELATIVE PRICES, etc.

Multifunctional Divison: *see* ORGANIZATIONAL STRUCTURE.

Multinational Corporation: a company that has an ORGANIZATIONAL STRUCTURE and a strategy for competing in TRANSBORDER SEGMENTS. Some strategists feel that a MNC must have a GLOBAL PERSPECTIVE to be successful.

Multiple Brand Names: *see* BRAND IDENTIFICATION.

Multiple Sourcing: *see* SUPPLIER POWER.

Multipoint Competitor: a competitor with which a company has more than one business in common. MULTIPOINT COMPETITORS are often identified and ranked by developing a MULTIPOINT COMPETITOR MATRIX.

The identification and analysis of multipoint competitors is considered important because competing with a multipoint competitor is likely to be complex and to involve compensating reactions in other businesses to strategic moves in one business. As a result, there are likely to be more sales, investment, or earnings at stake in the contest. Take, for example, the aggressive move of Company 1's Business A toward its counterpart in Company 2. Company

2, like any company under attack, is likely to look for a response. If Company 2 is a MULTIPOINT COMPETITOR with Company 1, the possibility arises that Company 2's compensating reaction will be directed toward another of Company 1's businesses. That is, a MULTIPOINT COMPETITOR may consciously or unconsciously compensate for the loss suffered at the hands of Business A by competing more aggressively with another business of Company 1. A CROSS PARRY is an example of a subtle conscious reaction of a MULTIPOINT COMPETITOR.

Many strategists feel that the analysis of MULTIPOINT COMPETITORS should be a corporate-level responsibility because of the higher stakes involved and the higher probability of confrontation. In addition, many managers tend to see their competitors as being the competing products of the other businesses in their industries rather than as businesses in another company's portfolio. Therefore, they lack the corporate perspective that is necessary to understand MULTIPOINT COMPETITORS.

Multipoint Competitor Matrix: a technique that is used to identify MULTIPOINT COMPETITORS. First, all the company's businesses are listed down the left side of the matrix in order of their sales. Then, names of all the company's competitors are listed across the top in order of each competitor's total sales. The sales of a business listed on the left are entered in the cells of the matrix under the name of each competitor that it faces. In the example that follows, Business D has sales of $25 and competes with Competitors 3 and 5. The sales at stake with each MULTIPOINT COMPETITOR are then calculated by adding up the sales in the column under that competitor's name.

	Competitor 1	Competitor 2	Competitor 3	Competitor 4	Competitor 5
Business A		40			
Business B				0	
Business C		30			
Business D			25		25
Business E	20				20
Business F				20	
Business G	15				
Business H			10		
Business I			5		5
Business J			5		
SALES AT STAKE	$35	$70	$45	$50	$50

Mutual Exclusion: the notion that no two competitors following the same COMPETITIVE STRATEGY can profitably co-exist in the same industry for any length of time.

The first implication of this concept is that, in general, a business should implement a unique COMPETITIVE STRATEGY. That is, it should feel free to imitate strategies from other industries, but the strategy should be unique to its own industry. The second implication of the concept is that a business should attempt a COMPETITIVE STRATEGY similar to that of another competitor in the same industry only when the business is sure it has a sustainable competitive AD-VANTAGE in implementing that strategy. The concept is analogous to a similar law of mutual exclusion in sociobiology. Some argue that the concept has no relevance, particularly in competitive markets. It implies, for example, that two wheat farmers cannot successfully grow and sell wheat the same way.

N

Natural Competition: a mode of competition in which the competitors act without considering either their relative STRENGTHS AND WEAKNESSES or the likely responses to their actions. Change in industries with NATURAL COMPETITION is a result of adaptation through trial and error, and the allocation of RESOURCES is based on survival of the fittest. NATURAL COMPETITION tends to be conservative because it is the result of small tentative experiments rather than deliberate dramatic STRATEGIES. Businesses competing in this mode can be expected to have very short-term perspectives.

STRATEGIC COMPETITION is the opposite of NATURAL COMPETITION.

Negative Economic Value: a reduction in the worth of a company to its shareholders associated with the inclusion of a particular business in its portfolio. That business is considered to have NEGATIVE ECONOMIC VALUE. Although the concept of negative value has intuitive appeal, it is often hard to determine whether a given business in a portfolio has negative value or not. Some strategists find it a difficult determination even when the business has had consistently poor performance. Other strategists feel that any business that earns less than the company's REQUIRED RETURN or any business with a VALUE LEVERAGE RATIO of less than 1.0 has negative value. Those strategists qualify that evaluation only to the extent of withholding judgment on businesses that are experiencing low profitability due to a strike, to the impact of the BUSINESS CYCLE, or to a start-up situation, etc.

However, no matter how they approach the issue, strategists note that although a business may have NEGATIVE ECONOMIC VALUE as part of one company's portfolio, it may have positive ECONOMIC VALUE as part of another's.

New Product Strategy: a business's marketing approach to introducing a new product. A wide range of programs can be generated by varying the elements of a marketing strategy, such as RELATIVE PRICE, promotion, distribution, and PRODUCT QUALITY. The matrix that follows shows four alternatives resulting when just two elements, price and marketing effort, are varied.

A STRATEGY of selective penetration involves introducing the new product with a high price and low marketing effort. The purpose of the high price is to recover as much revenue per unit as possible, and the purpose of the low marketing effort is to keep expenses down. This combination is expected to skim a lot of profit from the market. This STRATEGY makes sense under certain ASSUMPTIONS: that the market is relatively limited in size, that most potential BUYER GROUPS are aware of the product, that buyers who want the product are prepared to pay a high price, and that there is little threat of potential competition. Not all these assumptions have to hold, but the more that do, the more plausible the selective penetration strategy becomes.

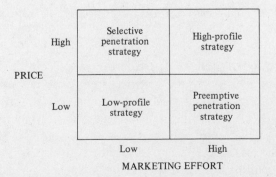

		Low	High
PRICE	High	Selective penetration strategy	High-profile strategy
	Low	Low-profile strategy	Preemptive penetration strategy
		Low	High

MARKETING EFFORT

A low-profile strategy involves introducing the new product with a low price and a low level of marketing effort. The low price will encourage the market's rapid acceptance of the product; at the same time, the company keeps its marketing expenses down in order to realize more net profit. This strategy makes sense if the market is large, the BUYER GROUPS are aware of the product, the buyers are price-sensitive, and there is some potential competition.

A high-profile strategy involves introducing the new product with a high price and high marketing effort. The business charges a high price in order to recover as much revenue per unit as possible; and it spends heavily on marketing to convince the market of the product's merits. The high marketing effort may also accelerate the rate of market penetration. This STRATEGY makes sense if a large number of buyers are unaware of the product, if those buyers who become aware of the product will be eager to have it and pay the asking price, and if potential competitors can be warded off with brand preference in place of price cuts.

A preemptive penetration strategy involves introducing the product with a low price and high marketing effort. This STRATEGY tries to bring about fast market penetration and a large MARKET SHARE for the business. This STRATEGY makes sense if the market is large, if the buyer is relatively unaware of the product, if most informed buyers are price-sensitive, if there is strong potential competition, and if the business's unit manufacturing costs fall with ECONOMIES OF SCALE and CUMULATIVE EXPERIENCE. This type of new product introduction is often associated with EXPERIENCE-BASED PRICING and a COST LEADERSHIP STRATEGY.

Although this analysis of price and marketing effort is a single example of how approaches to new product introductions can be formulated, it does show the important relationship between AS-SUMPTIONS and STRATEGY. A strategist should be aware that different competitors will make different ASSUMPTIONS about the market, and these different ASSUMPTIONS will lead to different STRATEGIES. The diversity of these approaches will affect the RIVALRY in the industry. Therefore, an analysis of each competitor and each likely entrant's approach is important for formulating a STRATEGY for introducing a new product.

Niche: a selected BUYER GROUP. A NICHE strategy for a BUSINESS UNIT is often called a FOCUS STRATEGY.

No-Fit: a business whose COMPETITIVE STRATEGY or policies are inconsistent with the CORPORATE STRATEGY of its parent company. NO-FITS usually have NEGATIVE ECONOMIC VALUE but not necessarily.

Some strategists consider the NO-FITS of other companies to be excellent ACQUISITION CANDIDATES and consider their own NO-FITS to be good candidates for DIVESTMENT.

Nominal Dollar: *see* CONSTANT DOLLAR.

Nonprice Competition: TACTICS for competing in an industry that do not involve varying prices relative to competition. Examples of such tactics include efforts to differentiate a product with branding, advertising, or packaging to increase relative UTILITY and to increase SHARE OF VOICE, etc. TACTICS that take advantage of MIXED MOTIVES or BLIND SPOTS often involve NONPRICE COMPETITION, although not necessarily.

O

Objective: an aim or end to be worked toward. In STRATEGIC PLANNING, the term OBJECTIVE is used in this general sense and also takes on more specific connotations when used in the context of different planning approaches. Some strategists use the term to refer to the aims of particular levels in an organization or to aims that are long-term in nature. Other strategists use the term within a hierarchy of aims and distinguish between a company's MISSION, GOALS, OBJECTIVES, and targets. Typically, GOALS refers to the aims outlined by the company in its CORPORATE STRATEGY. OBJECTIVES are more specific and are associated with OPERATING POLICIES set for each FUNCTIONAL AREA.

Whether the term is used in the general or a specific sense, the appropriateness of an objective can be judged on the basis of five criteria. It must be suitable, measurable, feasible, acceptable, and understandable. A suitable or productive objective is one which reflects a thorough analysis of the INDUSTRY STRUCTURE and which will enhance the COMPETITIVE POSITION of the company when achieved. Such an objective must also be flexible and consistent with other objectives outlined in the company's strategy.

Objectives need to be measurable so that managers can tell if they have been achieved or what progress is being made toward achieving them. Quantitative objectives are usually easily measured. Qualitative objectives should be stated as specifically as possible. Determining whether an objective is feasible or not can be difficult. It involves a great many ASSUMPTIONS about what competitors are likely to do and what is likely to happen to the economic, social, political, and technical aspects of the environment. Feasibility must also be assessed in terms of internal capabilities, such as management know-how and the availability of financial and human resources.

Objectives should also be acceptable to the individuals in the organization who will be responsible for achieving them. This is a condition for making an objective feasible, yet it deserves to be highlighted as a separate criterion. For example, it could be feasible for a business to introduce a given new product but still very difficult to accomplish if the employees involved just did not think it was a good idea. In making objectives acceptable, a manager must develop a commitment to them and provide the incentives necessary for their achievement.

Finally, an appropriate objective should be understandable. If there is one complaint that strategists frequently hear about objectives, it is that an objective cannot be understood or is not being communicated clearly and explicitly. An objective that is either unintelligible or not communicated is not likely to be achieved.

Offensive Intelligence: *see* STRATEGIC INTELLIGENCE.

Offensive Strategy: components of a COMPETITIVE STRATEGY intended to attack a competitor's position. Offensive strategies usually involve increased spending or GAME CHANGERS or both. Strategists who use VALUE CHAINS for analysis use a version of a GAME GRID to consider the options. A sample grid appears on page 226.

As the matrix shows, if the OFFENSIVE STRATEGY is based on having the same COMPETITIVE SCOPE and the same VALUE CHAIN as the competitor or competitors or as it has had in the past, then the strategy is likely to depend on a significant increase in spending. If, however, the strategy allows for a different scope or a different VALUE CHAIN or activities, then the strategy will involve redefinition or reconfiguration, respectively. If it allows for differences in both, it will involve a combination of redefinition and reconfigu-

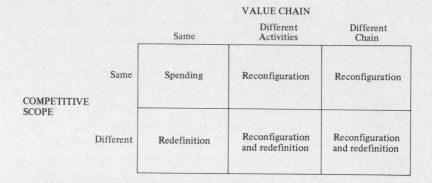

		VALUE CHAIN		
		Same	Different Activities	Different Chain
COMPETITIVE SCOPE	Same	Spending	Reconfiguration	Reconfiguration
	Different	Redefinition	Reconfiguration and redefinition	Reconfiguration and redefinition

ration. Redefinition involves broadening or narrowing a COMPETITIVE SCOPE. Reconfiguration involves removing, adding, or changing the coordination of any activity in a value chain such that BUYER VALUE is changed.

SCOPE GRIDS are used to understand changes in COMPETITIVE SCOPE.

Scope strategists label as an OFFENSIVE STRATEGY a BUILD PLAN in a low-growth market. Other strategists see the concept as referring specifically to an attack on a DOMINANT FIRM.

Oligopoly: an industry in which a few sellers account for almost all the industry's sales. Because there are so few sellers, the activities of one seller affect the activities of the others in the industry, making them interdependent. An oligopolist is not a price taker, facing the horizontal DEMAND curve of a seller in a perfectly competitive market; and, unlike the monopolist, it does not face the market DEMAND curve either. This is because the output that the oligopolist can sell if it changes price depends on the reactions of other sellers to the change.

Because sellers recognize their interdependence, the level of RIVALRY in an oligopolist industry tends to be high. Formulating an effective COMPETITIVE STRATEGY in such an industry requires an evaluation of relative STRENGTHS AND WEAKNESSES and of the probable reactions of competitors to strategic choices.

NONPRICE COMPETITION is more likely in an OLIGOPOLY than in a less CONCENTRATED industry. SIGNALING and playing off MIXED MOTIVES are also more important. It is important to realize that oligopolists do not have to act in illegal collusion in order to have power. For example, just the fact that there are so few ski resorts in a given area gives them the potential to exert SUPPLIER POWER.

Oligopsony: a market situation in which an industry has few buyers. A business that competes in an OLIGOPSONY is selling in an industry with high BUYER CONCENTRATION. The BUYER POWER that is possible in an OLIGOPSONY can have a significant effect on profitability in such an industry.

Operating Leverage: refers to the level of FIXED COSTS in the COST STRUCTURE of a business. The level of FIXED COSTS is an important determinant of the impact of variations in capacity utilization on profitability. A business with high OPERATING LEVERAGE may be more profitable running at a high level of CAPACITY UTILIZATION than a competitor with a low degree of OPERATING LEVERAGE. On the other hand, the competitor with lower OPERATING LEVERAGE may be better off running at low levels of CAPACITY UTILIZATION than the business with high OPERATING LEVERAGE. Taking advantage of ECONOMIES OF SCALE is often associated with high levels of OPERATING LEVERAGE.

Strategists are concerned with OPERATING LEVERAGE because of the effect it can have on accentuating any variation in profits as well as the effect it can have on RIVALRY. Higher OPERATING LEVERAGE provides a competitor with greater incentive to cut price in the hope of generating enough revenue to cover FIXED COSTS. Comparisons of OPERATING LEVERAGE are often made in terms of FIXED-TO-VALUE ADDED RATIO.

Operating Policy: a FUNCTIONAL AREA's statement of purpose or philosophy of operating. OPERATING POLICY for each FUNCTIONAL AREA is usually developed within the framework of the business's COMPETITIVE STRATEGY to indicate the general course of action that that FUNCTIONAL AREA will take toward achieving the business's GOALS. Each FUNCTIONAL AREA then develops programs, procedure, and projects that fit with the function's OPERATING POLICY.

For example, a business may have developed a BUILD PLAN that calls for the business to grow faster than the market as a low-cost producer of standard building supplies. The marketing function's policy might, therefore, emphasize the expansion of sales through major distributors. To that end, marketing management may set up a program to train new sales people, initiate a change in compensation procedures to encourage the development of new distribution outlets, continue a consumer information project, etc. A business's STRATEGY translates into OPERATING POLICIES for each FUNCTIONAL AREA; and each area has a series of programs, procedures, and projects associated with carrying out those policies. The sum of their cost equals the resources required to carry out the business's strategy.

Although strategists are usually not involved in developing functional programs, procedures, and projects, they are very often responsible for reviewing the consistency between these efforts and the OPERATING POLICIES of each function as well as the consistency between all the OPERATING POLICIES and the COMPETITIVE STRATEGY. In addition, during the RESOURCE ALLOCATION process, strategists must often ration the resources to be devoted to each FUNCTIONAL AREA.

Operating Unit: an organizational entity within the corporation that is the responsibility of a general manager. Usually, OPERATING UNITS are identified in the company organization chart and are the basis of a company's ORGANIZATIONAL HIERARCHY. A company's operating units are often different from its STRATEGIC BUSINESS UNITS. For example, the medical products sales division could well be an operating unit in a company, identified on the company's organization chart and headed by a vice president of medical products sales. However, that division may handle the sales for two of the company's strategic business units, which are designated as industrial products and consumer products.

Accounting systems are usually set up to collect data about operating units rather than strategic business units, and this can present problems for planners. In the preceding example of the medical products division, the accounting system may not track industrial products and consumer products separately. When accounting systems, operating units, and BUSINESS UNITS are not congruent, many companies set up strategic information systems to provide data for STRATEGIC PLANNING.

Operations Research (OR):   the use of quantitative techniques to research logistical or business problems and to evaluate alternative solutions. The OR methods used during World War II for military problems were later expanded and refined for use in business activities like inventory control, production scheduling, plant location, and distribution planning. The process of OR involves building teams of interdisciplinary experts to specialize in quantifying each aspect of the problem. Managerial economic techniques like Bayesian decision theory, linear programming, queuing theory, PERT, CRITICAL PATHS, DECISION TREES, regression models, and Monte

Carlo simulations are often combined with computer power to solve the problem.

Many strategists see the application of OR to business problems as the beginning of STRATEGIC PLANNING.

Opportunity: a situation that a business can take advantage of to protect and improve its COMPETITIVE POSITION in its industry. Opportunities arise from changes in the business's INDUSTRY STRUCTURE and INTRA-INDUSTRY STRUCTURE or VALUE SYSTEM that create the potential for increasing the business's COMPETITIVE ADVANTAGE. An opportunity related to INDUSTRY STRUCTURE provides a chance to affect favorably RIVALRY, ENTRY BARRIERS, BUYER POWER, SUPPLIER POWER, or the product's PRICE-TO-PERFORMANCE RATIO vis-à-vis SUBSTITUTE PRODUCTS. An opportunity related to intra-industry structure allows the business to raise the MOBILITY BARRIERS protecting its current STRATEGIC GROUP, to overcome mobility barriers insulating a more profitable STRATEGIC GROUP, or to create a new strategic group.

THREATS are the opposite of opportunities.

Opportunity-Based Planning: an approach to generating CORPORATE STRATEGY that is based on choosing among the most promising projects available to each of the company's businesses. For example, each business is asked to assess the OPPORTUNITIES in its industry and develop its best plan. The company then takes these plans together with the amount of RESOURCES it has to spend and allocates its investments in its businesses to take advantage of the best OPPORTUNITIES.

Some strategists think that OPPORTUNITY-BASED PLANNING is simplistic. They argue that creating ECONOMIC VALUE means meeting or surpassing the shareholder's REQUIRED RETURN, which implies a set of minimum financial OBJECTIVES. These financial OBJECTIVES may not get nearly enough attention in a company that leans toward OPPORTUNITY-BASED PLANNING. They also point out that the approach ignores the possibility of building STRATEGIC LEVERAGE among the businesses in a company's portfolio and does nothing to reinforce management's CONCEPT OF FIT.

Opportunity Cost: the cost of using a RESOURCE, measured by the return available on the best alternative use of that resource.

Take, for example, a business's plan to use a recently emptied plant to manufacture a new product. Although the plant is empty and unproductive, it is not free. If at a minimum the plant could be sold for $10,000, then the OPPORTUNITY COST of using that plant is the $10,000 that would otherwise be realized by selling the plant.

In many companies, the OPPORTUNITY COST of investing in their businesses is considered to be at least the company's COST OF CAPITAL. But OPPORTUNITY COST is not an absolute or invariant number—it depends on what next-best opportunity is being passed up.

An OPPORTUNITY COST is sometimes called an alternative cost.

OR: *see* OPERATIONS RESEARCH.

Organizational Hierarchy: a company's arrangement of individuals in a pattern of authority, responsibility, and reporting relationships. Usually, companies define their hierarchy in organization charts, job descriptions, and job grades. A company's ORGANIZATIONAL HIERARCHY is linked together by a company's MANAGEMENT SYSTEM to form its ORGANIZATIONAL STRUCTURE.

ORGANIZATIONAL HIERARCHIES are often built around OPERATING UNITS with subordinate staff, groups, divisions, departments, functions, etc. An entity within the ORGANIZATIONAL HIERARCHY can often be described as being either a REVENUE CENTER, a COST CENTER, a PROFIT CENTER, or an INVESTMENT CENTER, depending on the OBJECTIVES the manager of the entity is responsible for achieving.

When an ORGANIZATIONAL HIERARCHY is developed, individuals and their roles are ordered and grouped on the basis of specific activities. Over time the roles and activities are likely to change. The ORGANIZATIONAL HIERARCHY often remains locked in to some extent by tradition, MANAGEMENT SYSTEMS, and physical logistics. For example, a company's accounting system often makes it difficult to change the ORGANIZATIONAL HIERARCHY, as does the location of plant and equipment and office space, not to mention the expectations of the individuals involved.

In most companies, the ORGANIZATIONAL HIERARCHY is not the same as its PLANNING HIERARCHY. PLANNING HIERARCHIES tend to be ordered and grouped on the basis of the span of control and information required to formulate and carry out a strategy for competing in a marketplace. PLANNING HIERARCHIES are often described in terms of corporate planning staff, SECTORS, and businesses. At the very least, differences between the ORGANIZATIONAL HIERARCHY and the PLANNING HIERARCHY may make it difficult for the strategist to collect the data necessary to formulate a STRATEGY, as well as the data needed to monitor its implementation. For example, accounting data for divisions may have to be significantly adjusted to develop business by business data. More extreme differences between the two hierarchies may also make it hard to develop consistency between the INCENTIVE SYSTEMS and the OBJECTIVES of the strategies. At some point, the ORGANIZATIONAL HIERARCHY and the PLANNING HIER-ARCHY may get so far apart that no matter how much effort is put into the PLANNING PROCESS and into INTEGRATING SYSTEMS, a company cannot formulate or implement its strategies. Such a situation calls for changes in the ORGANIZATIONAL STRUCTURE of the company.

Organizational Structure: the way in which a company organizes and manages itself in order to carry out its OBJECTIVES. ORGANI-ZATIONAL STRUCTURE consists of two parts: the company's ORGA-NIZATIONAL HIERARCHY and its MANAGEMENT SYSTEM. The ORGA-NIZATIONAL HIERARCHY is the arrangement of individuals and entities on the basis of responsibilities and authority; and the MANAGEMENT SYSTEM consists of the MEASUREMENT, INCENTIVE, and INTEGRATING SYSTEMS which connect them.

The effectiveness of any ORGANIZATIONAL STRUCTURE is measured by the degree to which it achieves its OBJECTIVES. The efficiency of any ORGANIZATIONAL STRUCTURE is measured by the amount of financial and human RESOURCES required to make it effective. Because an organization's OBJECTIVES are derived from its STRATEGY, it follows that, to be effective and efficient, a company's ORGANIZATIONAL STRUCTURE must be consistent with its CORPORATE STRATEGY. In addition, as companies grow and change over time, they tend to be organized and managed differently. Theorists have proposed a number of ways categorizing ORGANIZATIONAL STRUC-TURES, but most of these proposals can be generalized into four stages, as shown in the accompanying exhibit.

A Stage One company offers either a single product or a single line of products. The company tends to have little or no formal OR-GANIZATIONAL STRUCTURE and is run by the owner, who personally performs most of the managerial functions and uses unsystematic control systems and subjective measures of performance. The strat-egy of a Stage One company is whatever the owner wants and can carry out.

A Stage Two company is the Stage One company grown so large that FUNCTIONAL AREAS of expertise have been formalized. A Stage Two company may also have become VERTICALLY INTEGRATED and

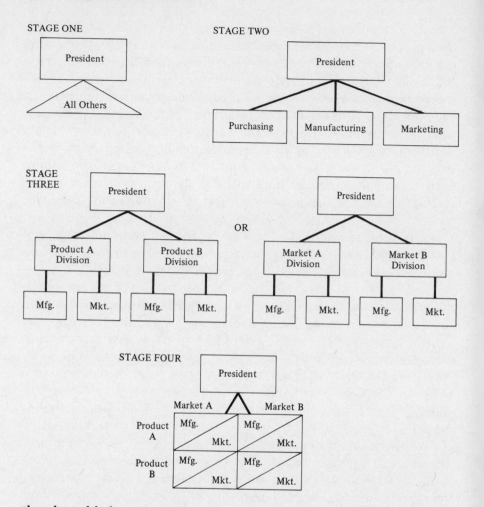

thereby added new FUNCTIONAL AREAS. For coordinating company activities, INTEGRATING SYSTEMS are developed to link such generalized FUNCTIONAL AREAS as purchasing, manufacturing, distribution, and sales. The search for product or process improvement may also have been formalized in a research and development function. A Stage Two company develops MEASUREMENT SYSTEMS and INCENTIVE SYSTEMS to help the owner control its numerous activities. A Stage Two company also formulates OPERATING POLICIES to guide decisions within the FUNCTIONAL AREAS. The strategy of a Stage Two company is constrained by the degree of integration among the FUNCTIONAL AREAS as well as by the lack of DIVERSIFICATION.

A Stage Three company is a Stage Two company that has expanded into either multiple product lines or multiple geographic areas. A Stage Three company is usually organized into multifunctional divisions based on product or market relationships rather than on functions. In some companies, like CONGLOMERATES, each multifunctional division has its own functional areas, and in other companies, functions like R&D and even marketing may remain centralized. Its businesses may or may not be significantly integrated, depending on the degree of DIVERSIFICATION. Its MANAGEMENT SYSTEMS are increasingly systematic and oriented toward results. A greater range of strategies is available to a Stage Three company because its divisions allow it to develop different approaches for different products or markets.

A Stage Four company is a Stage Three company that has diversified to the point where it both competes in several markets and produces several products. A Stage Four company is often a MATRIX ORGANIZATION in which a given functional manager may be responsible to a product division manager as well as to a market division manager. The ORGANIZATIONAL STRUCTURE of a Stage Four company can take many shapes because of the numerous combinations of functional, product, and market activities and responsibilities which can be assigned.

Some strategists are comfortable with the above four-stage approach to classifying ORGANIZATIONAL STRUCTURES. Others favor what they feel is a more simple approach: that companies are either organized around FUNCTIONAL AREAS or products or markets or combinations of the three. The latter combinations would be called MATRIX ORGANIZATIONS.

Regardless of how one classifies ORGANIZATIONAL STRUCTURES, the strategist should recognize that the ORGANIZATIONAL STRUCTURE of a company will define the range of strategies that the company is capable of carrying out. And that a radical change in strategy will often require a radical change in ORGANIZATIONAL STRUCTURE.

STRATEGIC PLANNING is such a central activity for a company that the people involved and the process itself are identified as two separate elements of the ORGANIZATIONAL STRUCTURE by some strategists. They define the PLANNING HIERARCHY as the individuals and entities located throughout the ORGANIZATIONAL HIERARCHY with responsibility for STRATEGIC PLANNING, and the PLANNING PROCESS as the sequence of activities and procedures followed to generate a strategy.

Out-of-Pocket Cost: an avoidable expenditure of current resources. OUT-OF-POCKET COSTS are relevant when considering whether to proceed with a project or investment while SUNK COSTS are not.

P

Package Price: a price that covers the combined purchase of more than one product. The BUNDLING of these products is usually the result of a deliberate TACTIC but may be a BLIND SPOT.

Pareto Optimal: an arrangement or allocation of resources within which one party cannot be made better off without making others worse off. In STRATEGY, a PARETO OPTIMAL point is reached when no competitor can be made more profitable without reducing the profits of another. A PARETO OPTIMAL arrangement is not synonymous with an equal distribution of resources among parties. There is no requirement that the parties be equally well off under a PARETO OPTIMAL arrangement.

Often an arrangement is labeled PARETO OPTIMAL when there are indeed changes or moves to be made which can improve the position of a competitor without diminishing the position of another. For any set of parties and any quantity of RESOURCES, there are an unlimited number of patterns for distributing the resources among the parties which are PARETO OPTIMAL.

Passive Intelligence: *see* STRATEGIC INTELLIGENCE.

Payback Analysis: a technique used to assess an investment decision based on calculation of the length of time before the returns on the investment will equal its cost. For example, a simple PAYBACK ANALYSIS of a new $150,000 machine that will reduce the cost of raw material by $50,000 a year might use a back of the envelope calculation to get a payback period of three years. This means the investment will pay for itself in three years. A more sophisticated PAYBACK ANALYSIS could take into consideration taxes, depreciation, carrying costs, etc., but the answer would still be in terms of how many years it will take to pay back the investment rather than in terms of a RETURN ON INVESTMENT.

Strategists who use PAYBACK ANALYSIS feel that its main virtue is its simplicity. Strategists who do not use it point out that it doesn't take into account OPPORTUNITY COSTS or REQUIRED RETURNS.

Penetration Chart: a technique for displaying the MARKET SHARE dynamics of a portfolio of BUSINESS UNITS. Each business is arrayed on a BUBBLE CHART on the basis of its past sales growth and past growth of its industry. The circle size is usually proportional to the sales of each BUSINESS UNIT, but it can also be based on the size of its asset base or a measure of profitability. Business units above the 45° line, like "F," have sales that are growing more slowly than the industry in which they compete and are, therefore, losing share and not penetrating their markets. Business units on the 45° line, like "E," are holding their position with sales growth equal to MARKET GROWTH. Business units below the 45° line, like "A," are growing faster than their industry and, therefore, penetrating their markets and increasing share.

The chart shows absolute but not relative share trends. For example, it is possible that while business "D" is increasing share, its most important competitor is growing faster and that business "D" is losing RELATIVE MARKET SHARE.

PENETRATION CHARTS can be prepared either for one's own portfolio of BUSINESS UNITS or for competitors' portfolios, often as part of a COMPETITOR ANALYSIS. A PENETRATION CHART which is adapted to reflect the relationship between a company's penetration plans and its SUSTAINABLE GROWTH is called a PLAN PENETRATION CHART.

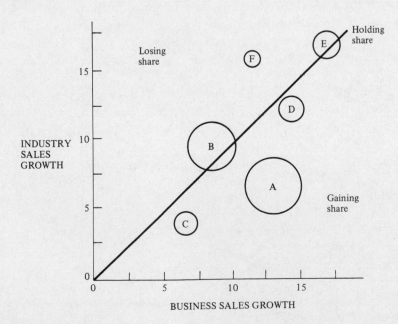

Penetration Pricing: a PRICING POLICY that sets prices as low as is economically feasible in order to capture quickly as large a MARKET SHARE as possible. In addition to the goal of establishing the widest possible distribution and use of the product, PENETRATION PRICING is often used to discourage competitors. Competitors are discouraged in two general ways. First, the low price allows a follower a very small margin. Second, PENETRATION PRICING demonstrates a commitment to being a high MARKET SHARE competitor and raises the level of EXPECTED RETALIATION.

PENETRATION PRICING often involves setting prices initially lower than the expected long-run price level and sometimes lower than current UNIT COSTS. Pricing below costs often occurs when the business is using EXPERIENCE-BASED PRICING. Carried to an extreme, such a PENETRATION PRICING policy runs the risk of being considered illegal PREDATORY PRICING.

A successful PENETRATION PRICING policy can be very profitable when it is consistent with a coherent COMPETITIVE STRATEGY. However, it can be a risky and expensive policy if it isn't well thought out and controlled. For example, when a manufacturer uses PENETRATION PRICING with a PULL THROUGH as part of MARKETING POLICY, the distribution channels will expect at least their usual markups, and the difference will have to be carried by the manufacturer. In addition, the manufacturer may find that, after the desired level of penetration is achieved, the business cannot both raise prices and maintain its MARKET SHARE. This may be because buyers refuse to accept the higher prices or because followers find the market more attractive and start competing again as soon as the manufacturer raises its prices.

Alternative ways for building MARKET SHARE include TACTICS like saturation advertising and taking advantage of BLIND SPOTS or MIXED MOTIVES. An analysis of the RIVALRY in the industry should indicate which tactics would be most effective in a given situation.

SKIM PRICING is the opposite of PENETRATION PRICING.

Perceived Value: the attractiveness or UTILITY of a product as experienced or identified by the buyer. Some strategists separate BUYER VALUE into actual value and PERCEIVED VALUE. They point out that a business may be able to benefit by providing PERCEIVED VALUE without incurring the cost of actual value and that a competitor who is relying on PERCEIVED VALUE may be vulnerable to a business that is willing to incur these costs. Other strategists consider all buyer value to be perceived. For example, they point out that what matters is that the buyer perceives the price to be a bargain, not that it actually is. That is, a buyer will value only what is perceived regardless of what is actual. Furthermore, they argue that what is being called PERCEIVED VALUE is just buyer value created through IMAGE development and value signals, all of which have real costs. However, they acknowledge that when a BUYER GROUP'S perception of the differences between a business's products and those of its competitors is out of line with reality, the business may indeed be vulnerable.

Perfect Competition: a market structure which satisfies the following five conditions:

1. *Each buyer and seller is insignificant in size relative to the market.* No buyer or seller perceives any ability to affect MARKET PRICE by varying the quantity bought or sold.
2. *Products are homogenous.* Buyers have no reason to prefer the output of one seller over another. No seller can profitably attract DEMAND with TACTICS such as inducing buyer loyalty with PRODUCT DIFFERENTIATION.
3. *Artificial restraints are absent.* There is no government or institutional price-fixing. Prices are not administered, and SUPPLY is not restricted or rationed.
4. *Resources, goods, and services are mobile throughout the economy.* They are free to move into the use with the highest return and to the buyer offering the highest price. New producers or companies are free to ENTER the market.
5. *Buyers and sellers have complete, perfect information and are not subject to transaction costs.* As a result, the market adjusts instantaneously to disturbances in conditions of SUPPLY and DEMAND and is always in EQUILIBRIUM.

Competition can be perfect on the buyers' or the sellers' side, independent of the conditions on the other side. PERFECT COMPETITION is distinguished from PURE COMPETITION, which requires that only the first four conditions listed earlier are satisfied. A perfectly competitive market is an idealized construct used by economists to explain behavior. Conditions of imperfect competition, such as ENTRY BARRIERS and MOBILITY BARRIERS, are what allow managers to build COMPETITIVE STRATEGIES to optimize profitability. The strategist tries to take advantage of imperfections in the market and to control the COMPETITIVE FORCES in order to build and protect profitable businesses.

OLIGOPOLIES and MONOPOLIES are industry structures inconsistent with PERFECT COMPETITION.

Performance Measure: a standard used to measure the extent to which managers have achieved their OBJECTIVES and to determine their rewards. PERFORMANCE MEASURES are part of a company's INCENTIVE SYSTEM and used to motivate managers to implement the company's STRATEGIES.

Most strategists evaluate PERFORMANCE MEASURES on the basis of the degree to which they, in fact, measure the manager's effectiveness in carrying out their OBJECTIVES. That can depend on whether the company's CONCEPT OF MANAGEMENT provides the company with appropriate MEASUREMENT SYSTEMS. Also, PERFORMANCE MEASURES can only be effective if the OBJECTIVES themselves relate to the company's GOALS.

Performance Profits: that portion of a business's profits attributable to the COMPETITIVE ADVANTAGES enjoyed and the STRATEGY conceived and implemented by a business, distinct from those available to all industry participants. Those available to industry participants as a group are referred to as POSITIONAL PROFITS, and some strategists define a business's profitability as being the sum of POSITIONAL PROFITS and PERFORMANCE PROFITS. INTRA-INDUSTRY ANALYSIS is often used to understand PERFORMANCE PROFIT.

PERT Network: a technique for charting the implementation of programs and projects. PERT is an acronym for program evaluation and review technique. The technique is also called the CRITICAL PATH METHOD.

PIMS Program: a multicompany project which measures and analyzes the impact of various STRATEGIES on the profitability of a business. The basis of this analysis is a confidential data base of the past experience of the participating companies. PIMS is an acronym for profit impact of market strategy.

Participating companies contribute information to the data base on several of their businesses. Confidentiality is maintained by disguising the data in two ways. First, the data is only identified by a randomly generated business number. The actual products that the business makes, the brand names, or the industry in which it competes are not revealed. Because the products and industries are not identified, it is possible to have two businesses that compete in the same industry in the data base, but it is not possible to tell which two businesses they are. Second, the data is collected in ratios rather than in absolute dollars. Therefore, the size of the business or the size of its industry cannot be discerned. Take, for example, Business A, a $100 million business in a $1 billion industry and Business B, a $1 million business in a $10 million industry. The data base would show them both as being businesses with a 10 percent MARKET SHARE. There would be no way of telling from the data base that one business was one hundred times the size of the other.

The data base is analyzed to determine what the PIMS PROGRAM calls the "general laws" which explain how a given combination of STRATEGY factors and market factors can affect the RETURN ON INVESTMENT of a business. This analysis is based on identifying the strategy factors and market factors in the data base that seem to affect RETURN ON INVESTMENT, calculating the average values for those factors, and then computing how much of an impact on ROI can be expected if a business has a factor that is above or below average. A short list of these factors and a sample set of average values and impacts is shown as follows.

		IMPACT	
	AVERAGE VALUE IN THE DATA BASE	CHANGE IN FACTOR	CHANGE IN ROI
STRATEGY FACTORS			
Market share	20%	+5 pts.	+3 pts.
Relative product quality	25%	+5	+1
Relative price	1.05%	+.01	−1
Capital intensity	50%	+5	−3
Value added-to-sales	60%	+5	+1
Capacity utilization	80%	+5	+1
Marketing-to-sales	10%	+2	−1
MARKETING FACTORS			
Real market growth	8%	+5	+1
Concentration ratio	70%	+10	+1
RETURN ON INVESTMENT	25%		

In the preceding example, the average ROI of all the business in the data base is 25 percent. The strategy factors that seem to impact ROI are MARKET SHARE, relative PRODUCT QUALITY, RELATIVE PRICE RATIO, CAPITAL INTENSITY, value added–to–sales, CAPACITY UTILIZATION, and marketing-to-sales. The two market factors are real MARKET GROWTH and CONCENTRATION RATIO. The average value for each of these factors is shown in the first column. The logic of the program indicates that a business with average values for all the factors should earn an ROI of 25 percent. The impact columns show how values for a factor that are above or below average can be expected to impact ROI. According to the example, a business should expect a three-point increase in ROI for every five-point increase in MARKET SHARE. That is, a business that has a MARKET SHARE of 25 percent and average values for all other factors would be expected to earn an ROI of 28 percent.

In the example, the impacts are shown as linear. In the actual PIMS models, the relationships are much more complex, and different combinations of values for different factors will have a different impact on ROI. The PIMS program uses a number of statistical approaches to modeling these complex interactions. The PIMS models can be used in two general ways: to explain the current performance of a business that uses current actual data and to estimate the level of ROI a business will earn in the future when using pro forma data.

Strategists who are uncomfortable with using the PIMS PROGRAM make three common arguments against it. First, they argue that averages are not relevant to their businesses. They might say that it is all very well to know that the average business spends 10 percent of its sales on marketing and that any higher expenditure will reduce ROI but that in the over-the-counter drug industry, for example, very high ROIs seem to require very high marketing expenditures. Second, they doubt the relevance of the information in the data base. That is, they do not think the data provides the necessary information to explain profitability even for the average business. Third, they argue that information in the data base is not being correctly analyzed. That is, they question the conceptual and statistical approaches that are being used.

Strategists who are comfortable with using the PIMS PROGRAM often acknowledge one or more of the arguments against the program but point out what they feel are two significant virtues. First, they argue that even if the participant is uncomfortable with the models, the experience of filling out the data form itself is often very rewarding. Second, they argue that the generality of the models provides a very understandable first step in the analysis of a BUSINESS PLAN.

Pioneer: *see* ENTRY.

Planned Obsolescence: a TACTIC for increasing the sales of a product by increasing each buyer's frequency of purchase of the product. Specifically, purchase frequency is increased by inducing the buyer to dispose of the product sooner than otherwise and to buy a new one. Usually, periodic changes in styling or product design are used to induce the buyer to stop using the old style and purchase the new. PLANNED OBSOLESCENCE can also be built into a product introduction if the introductory product is deliberately designed with less UTILITY than subsequent product offerings. PLANNED OBSOLESCENCE is very often part of a scheme to induce buyers to TRADE UP.

Planning Cycle: a calendar of events which describes when specific steps in a PLANNING PROCESS will be completed. A simplified typical annual PLANNING CYCLE looks like the following table.

The work involved in most of these steps should be incremental from year to year. That is, each year a company modifies its COR-

STEP	PLANNING ACTIVITY	TIME SCHEDULE
I	Make FORECASTS and ASSUMPTIONS about the environment.	By January 1
II	Set GOALS and CORPORATE STRATEGY.	By February 1
III	Articulate business's ASSUMPTIONS about their industries.	By March 1
IV	Devise tentative business COMPETITIVE STRATEGIES and related STRATEGIC PLANS.	By April 1
V	Review STRATEGIES and plans for each business.	By May 1
VI	Set GOALS for each business.	By May 15
VII	Prepare corporate five-year FORECAST.	By June 7
VIII	Compare current corporate performance with present GOALS and determine how to make up any shortfall.	By June 15
IX	Revise and finalize BUSINESS PLANS and five-year forecasts.	By June 1
X	Review business performance vs. GOALS.	By November 1

PORATE STRATEGY to reflect changes in its environment. In the same way, each year each business adds to the previous year's knowledge of how its industry is evolving and modifies its COMPETITIVE STRATEGY accordingly.

Planning Hierarchy: a company's arrangement of entities and individuals in a hierarchy of responsibility for STRATEGIC PLANNING. Entities and individuals in a PLANNING HIERARCHY are ordered and grouped on the basis of the span of control and information required to formulate and implement a STRATEGY. A company's PLANNING HIERARCHY, together with its PLANNING PROCESS and its ORGANIZATIONAL STRUCTURE, make STRATEGIC PLANNING effective in the company.

Individuals in the PLANNING HIERARCHY have places in the ORGANIZATIONAL HIERARCHY and often have management responsibilities and functional activities in addition to planning. The interface between the PLANNING HIERARCHY and the ORGANIZATIONAL HIERARCHY varies from company to company. For example, in one organization, planning activities may be centralized with a separate staff group reporting to the chief executive officer. In another, general managers may be responsible for planning the activities of subordinates, and they may or may not be supported by individuals or staffs designated as planners. In another company, the ORGANIZATIONAL HIERARCHY may be organized along functional lines, and the PLANNING HIERARCHY is organized along market or geographic lines.

Most PLANNING HIERARCHIES have three levels. Those are the corporate level, the business level, and the functional level. Some companies have added a SECTOR level as shown in the following chart.

At the corporate level, the entity to be planned for is the corporation, and the individuals involved are responsible for formulating and implementing the company's CORPORATE STRATEGY. They are also likely to be responsible for ENVIRONMENTAL SCANNING and for reviewing and evaluating the plans of the other levels.

The use of a SECTOR level in a PLANNING HIERARCHY is relatively new, and strategists differ on the question of appropriate entities and responsibilities. Some strategists feel that a SECTOR should be a group of businesses treated as a smaller portfolio. Other strategists feel that a SECTOR should be a group of businesses with similar industry classifications. Finally, others feel that a SECTOR should be a group of businesses following the same GENERIC STRATEGY in order to build FORMULA FIT.

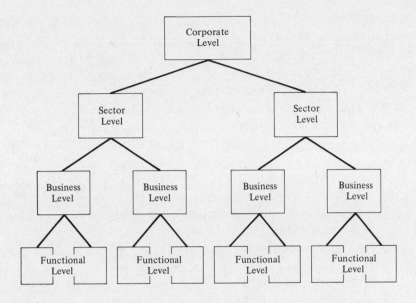

The relevant entity at the business level is the BUSINESS UNIT. The individuals involved are responsible for formulating and implementing a COMPETITIVE STRATEGY for that BUSINESS UNIT based on their analysis of INDUSTRY STRUCTURE and competitors' capabilities.

The relevant entity at the functional level is the FUNCTIONAL AREA, and the individuals involved are responsible for formulating and implementing OPERATING POLICY.

At different levels in the PLANNING HIERARCHY, the information available and the perspective of the individuals involved change, as well as the nature of the trade-offs the individuals are forced to make in carrying out their OBJECTIVES. At the functional level, there is likely to be a great deal of information about manufacturing techniques and specific buyer preferences. At the business level, there is likely to be information about specific markets and other businesses that compete in the business's industry. At the corporate level, there is likely to be more information about the relevant CAPITAL MARKETS, the financial resources of the company, etc. Therefore, one can expect an internal perspective with day-to-day trade-offs at the functional level and an industry perspective with more year-to-year trade-offs at the business level. At the corporate level the focus is likely to be on the shareholders, RESOURCE ALLOCATION, the control of RISK across industries and international markets, and long-term trade-offs.

Planning Process: the series of activities performed within a company to create a STRATEGY, to organize its resources and personnel to execute the STRATEGY, and to monitor the implementation of the strategy. The activities are carried out by the individuals who form the PLANNING HIERARCHY and follow a timetable referred to as the PLANNING CYCLE. The following is a list of the activities usually included in the PLANNING PROCESS of a diversified company.

    A. ENVIRONMENTAL SCANNING
        Social and political trends
        CAPITAL MARKETS analysis
        Macroeconomic trends
        INDUSTRY STRUCTURE studies
        Competitor analyses
    B. Developing and Modifying a CORPORATE STRATEGY
        Corporate GOALS
        CONCEPT OF FIT
        CONCEPT OF ASSEMBLY
        CONCEPT OF MANAGEMENT
    C. Establishing Different GOALS for BUSINESS UNITS
        Identify BUSINESS UNITS (SEGMENTATION)
        Assess Contribution to ECONOMIC VALUE
    D. Developing COMPETITIVE STRATEGIES for BUSINESS UNITS
        Identify current STRATEGY (review implied ASSUMPTIONS)
        Generate alternative STRATEGIES (analyze environment, INDUSTRY STRUCTURE, INTRA-INDUSTRY STRUCTURE)
        Select optimal STRATEGY and determine OPERATING POLICIES to carry out
    E. Reviewing COMPETITIVE STRATEGIES
        Consistency tests
        Contribution to ECONOMIC VALUE
        Ongoing monitoring
    F. RESOURCE ALLOCATION
        Financial resources
        Human resources
    G. Determining Incentives
        Set PERFORMANCE MEASURES
        Evaluate performance
    H. Monitoring Implementation

Plan Penetration Chart: a technique for relating growth plans to a company's SUSTAINABLE GROWTH RATE. The chart plots a company's SUSTAINABLE GROWTH RATE with a combination of a PENETRATION CHART based on plans for a portfolio of businesses and a GROWTH/SHARE MATRIX. First, the businesses in the portfolio are plotted on a GROWTH/SHARE MATRIX to identify them as being STARS, DOGS, CASH COWS, or QUESTION MARKS. Then the growth plan for each business is plotted on a PENETRATION CHART and compared to the ideal positioning of the businesses with respect to the company's sustainable growth.

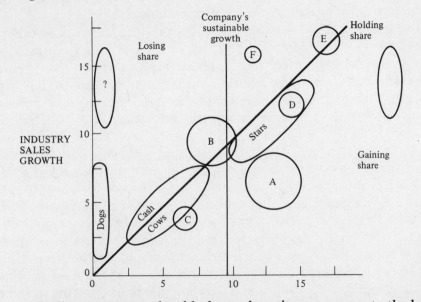

Ideally, a company should plan to have its CASH COWS to the left of its sustainable growth line and on the hold share line. It should plan to have its DOG businesses well to the left of its sustainable growth line and well to the left of the hold share line. Its STAR should be to the right of its sustainable growth line and to the right of the hold share line. Finally, it should plan to have a mix of QUESTION MARKS in the upper left- and upper right-hand corners. Those in the upper right would be the businesses the company plans to push and those in the upper left corner are businesses with HARVEST PLANS in a growth market.

Policy Cost: the negative effect of a company's policies on the performance of one or more of its businesses. POLICY COSTS often occur when company policies (or STRATEGIES) are beneficial to some of its businesses but harmful to others. DIVERSIFICATION usually results in POLICY COSTS. Many strategists feel that it is impossible to eliminate POLICY COSTS in a multidivisional company; however, they say that those costs can be minimized with an effective CORPORATE STRATEGY.

Policy Variable: any occurrence about which a choice can be made. For example, a farmer may not be able to choose the next year's weather, but he or she may be able to choose a location that provides the best weather on average. Therefore, among the many variables that affect a business's profitability, some are given such that no choice is allowed, and others are open to discretionary policy. At different points in an ORGANIZATIONAL STRUCTURE the same occurrences may be considered to be given or to be POLICY VARIABLES.

Some strategists feel that, in determining STRATEGY, they should consider everything to be a POLICY VARIABLE in order to avoid BLIND SPOTS. Other strategists emphasize the importance of controlling POLICY VARIABLES in order to ensure consistency in the implementation of a STRATEGIC PLAN.

Portfolio Approach: the use of portfolio analysis matrices as a basis for evaluating businesses, for setting PERFORMANCE MEASURES, and for balancing and allocating RESOURCES. The GROWTH/SHARE MATRIX, the BUSINESS/INDUSTRY ATTRACTIVENESS MATRIX, and the STRATEGIC CONDITION MATRIX are three of the better-known portfolio analysis matrices. These matrices are intended to help top management understand the relative attractiveness of the industries its businesses are competing in and to relate that understanding to some indication of the business's STRENGTHS AND WEAKNESSES. That understanding can then be used as a basis for deciding which businesses the company should invest in and what OBJECTIVES each business should be given to enable the company to earn its REQUIRED RETURN. Strategists who use a PORTFOLIO APPROACH to RESOURCE ALLOCATION feel that its most important contribution is that it gets top management away from the idea of a single financial GOAL for all businesses regardless of their potential. They feel that a PORTFOLIO APPROACH gives them a technique for evaluating each business within the context of its industry as a basis for determining what the company should expect from that business. Such an approach encourages the company to think in terms of making TRADE-OFFS among investment OPPORTUNITIES in those businesses and in terms of balancing its CASH FLOWS among its CASH USERS and CASH GENERATORS. Also, they argue that a PORTFOLIO APPROACH focuses attention on the industry and the business's competitors in that industry rather than just on the business itself. Finally, they argue that a PORTFOLIO APPROACH helps them apply strategic criteria rather than just financial criteria to DIVESTMENT decisions and in their ACQUISITION ANALYSIS process.

Strategists who are critical of a PORTFOLIO APPROACH to RESOURCE ALLOCATION argue that whereas portfolio matrices should be one technique used in formulating and monitoring a CORPORATE STRATEGY, they should not be the conceptual basis for such a STRATEGY. Specifically, they argue that a PORTFOLIO APPROACH can obscure opportunities for building STRATEGIC LEVERAGE through an effective CONCEPT OF FIT. A related argument is that a PORTFOLIO APPROACH can lead to an underestimation of the importance of INDUSTRY STRUCTURE and EVOLUTIONARY PROCESSES as a basis for determining the potential profitability of existing and new businesses.

Portfolio Cleanup: an approach to increasing the ECONOMIC VALUE of a company by changing its portfolio. The first step in a PORTFOLIO CLEANUP is to isolate businesses that have NEGATIVE ECONOMIC VALUE. Those businesses are then analyzed to determine which have the potential for improvement. FIX PLANS are developed for businesses with potential, and DIVESTMENT plans are carried out for businesses for which there is no way to create positive value. PORTFOLIO CLEANUPS may also lead to the DIVESTMENT of businesses that simply do not fit with the company's CORPORATE STRATEGY.

Some strategists consider companies with portfolios requiring a cleanup to be excellent ACQUISITION CANDIDATES because poor fit among the businesses may obscure the value of the individual units and lower the price asked for the portfolio.

Positional Profit: the portion of a business's profit that is the result of competing in a specific industry rather than the result of the strength of its COMPETITIVE ADVANTAGES or STRATEGY. On average, the POSITIONAL PROFIT of a business competing in an industry with favorable COMPETITIVE FORCES is expected to be higher than the POSITIONAL PROFIT of a business competing in an industry with unfavorable COMPETITIVE FORCES. Industry STRUCTURAL ANALYSIS is often used to understand POSITIONAL PROFITS.

Some strategists define a business's profitability as being the sum of POSITIONAL PROFITS and PERFORMANCE PROFITS.

Potential Advantage Matrix: a technique used to classify industries on the basis of their potential for COMPETITIVE ADVANTAGE. Each industry is classified on the basis of the number of ways to achieve COMPETITIVE ADVANTAGE, which is reflected in the number of successful STRATEGIES available to competitors, and on the basis of the size or variation in the COMPETITIVE ADVANTAGE, which is reflected in the differences in profitability among the STRATEGIES. The industries are arrayed in the four cells of the POTENTIAL ADVANTAGE MATRIX, which follows. Each of the cells is characterized by a different pattern or type of competition.

Industries that fall in the lower left-hand quadrant offer only a few ways to gain a small advantage. The matrix indicates that those industries have stalemated competition. That is, competitors in those industries try variations of the same strategy, and no one competitor is very much more profitable than another. Strategists competing in such an industry with the resources to finance a high RELATIVE MARKET SHARE should look for INSIGHTS into how to increase the size of their advantage or for new ways to achieve a COMPETITIVE ADVANTAGE.

In the lower right-hand quadrant, there are wide differences in profitability among the few strategies available to competitors. Businesses in those industries tend to compete for MARKET SHARE, pursuing similar strategies for increased volume. The industries are sometimes called volume industries. A business with high RELATIVE MARKET SHARE may occupy the position of the DOMINANT FIRM. Strategists with a business that is already the DOMINANT FIRM should compete very aggressively in order to guard that position. Strategists in a business without a high RELATIVE MARKET SHARE or a reasonable

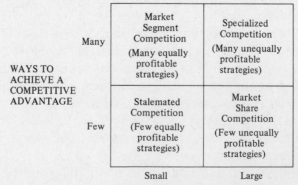

SIZE OF COMPETITIVE ADVANTAGE

chance of gaining it should look for new ways to achieve a COM-PETITIVE ADVANTAGE. This may not make the business the most profitable business in the industry, but profits may improve significantly if the industry moves toward specialized competition. If those strategists do not have the INSIGHT to change the industry, they should EXIT.

Industries that fall into the upper right-hand quadrant offer many ways to gain a large COMPETITIVE ADVANTAGE. The matrix indicates that those industries exhibit specialized competition. Competitors in those industries have a number of different COMPETITIVE STRATEGIES, and some will be much more profitable than others. The industry is likely to have a number of businesses carrying out various DIFFERENTIATION STRATEGIES. Strategists for those businesses should recognize that a DIFFERENTIATION STRATEGY has certain competitive phenomena that must be carefully monitored. Strategists with a business that is not currently the most profitable, who have the resources but not the management ability to carry out a DIFFERENTIATION STRATEGY, may want to try to push the industry into the lower right-hand quadrant. By adapting a COST LEADERSHIP STRATEGY, a business may nullify many of the other ways to achieve a COMPETITIVE ADVANTAGE, but profitability for everyone could be ruined if competition becomes stalemated.

Industries that fall in the upper left-hand quadrant offer many ways to achieve a small advantage. The matrix indicates that those industries are expected to have MARKET SEGMENT COMPETITION. That is, competitors in those industries may use various COMPETITIVE STRATEGIES, but no one will be any more profitable than others. BUYER GROUPS in such industries usually vary in their willingness to pay different prices for different types of product UTILITY and BUYER INFORMATION. The most profitable competitor in this type of industry is probably carrying out a successful FOCUS STRATEGY. Naturally, that competitor has to monitor very carefully the RISKS associated with that GENERIC STRATEGY. Strategists with resources to spend on a business that is not currently the most profitable should look for ways to differentiate their product or consider whether a COST LEADERSHIP STRATEGY would significantly increase the size of their advantage.

Strategists who are comfortable with the ASSUMPTIONS behind the POTENTIAL ADVANTAGE MATRIX find it is useful in three ways. First, they say that at the corporate level it is important to know how much of the company's sales or investment is in each of the four kinds of industries. Second, they find that the matrix is a useful way to relate the COMPETITIVE STRATEGY of a business to its industry environment. Third, they find it helpful to explain INDUSTRY EVOLUTION in terms of the movement of industries around the matrix from one kind of competition to another. For example, they would say that NATURAL COMPETITION results in small moves to the right or to the left whereas STRATEGIC COMPETITION results in moves up and down as well as to the right and left.

Strategists who are uncomfortable with the matrix feel that it obscures the concepts of COMPETITIVE ADVANTAGE and MOBILITY BARRIERS. They feel that an analysis of INTRA-INDUSTRY STRUCTURE will help them to understand their competitor's strategies and that a series of COMPETITOR MAPS is more likely to generate insights into potential THREATS and OPPORTUNITIES. Also, they argue that a key to developing COMPETITIVE STRATEGIES is to understand what the GENERIC STRATEGIES are and what makes them effective. They feel that an analysis of INDUSTRY STRUCTURE is more revealing.

Predatory Pricing: setting prices at a low level in order to weaken or destroy a competitor or to send a MARKET SIGNAL. A business is considered to be using PREDATORY PRICING when it prices its product so low as to forego short-run profits. PREDATORY PRICES set below costs are considered illegal under antitrust laws.

PREDATORY PRICING is often a signal warning the competitor to behave less aggressively or expect strong retaliation.

Prediction: *see* FORECAST.

Preemptive Tactic: a move with which a company seizes an OPPORTUNITY that can be profitable only for the first to take it or a move which forecloses or diminishes an OPPORTUNITY for a competitor. For example, a business may want to discourage a competitor from introducing a new product. A combination of PREEMPTIVE TACTICS could be to introduce a similar product first, to spend a great deal to advertise the new product, and to inform the press of the business's commitment to the product and to being the DOMINANT FIRM in the industry. Another effective but expensive PREEMPTIVE TACTIC is to build CAPACITY well ahead of the industry or at least to announce that the business plans to build a great deal of CAPACITY. Market signaling is often done in conjunction with PREEMPTIVE TACTICS.

Most strategists feel that to be effective in the long term, PREEMPTIVE TACTICS should lead to either ENTRY BARRIERS or MO-BILITY BARRIERS.

The benefits associated with PREEMPTIVE TACTICS are sometimes referred to as first mover advantages.

Present Value: the sum of expected future CASH FLOWS discounted back to the present. The PRESENT VALUE provides a basis for comparing and evaluating investment opportunities. Discounting incorporates the time value of money by adjusting future payments to reflect foregone investment alternatives. The greater the length of time before a payment is to be received, the lower its PRESENT VALUE.

Companies often use a discount rate based on an estimate of their COST OF CAPITAL when calculating the PRESENT VALUE of investment OPPORTUNITIES. Selecting the appropriate rate is a critical aspect of evaluating opportunities. A rate which is too high favors projects which payback quickly. A rate which is too low understates the impact of a long payback period. The table given below shows how the present value is calculated for a onetime payment of $1,000 to be received n years in the future, using a discount rate of r, and illustrates the impact of varying the payment period and discount rate.

Present value calculations can also be performed for complex streams of CASH FLOWS occurring at irregular intervals so that investment opportunities with very different income streams can be compared.

Present value calculations adjust for the time value of money but do not take into account the RISK of not being paid in full and on time. The discount rate is sometimes adjusted upward to compensate for this RISK, which has the effect of lowering the PRESENT VALUE of the investment.

PAYMENT (P)	PAYMENT PERIOD (n)	DISCOUNT RATE (r)	PRESENT VALUE $\dfrac{P}{(1 + r)^n}$
$1,000	5	10	$621
1,000	8	10	467
1,000	5	8	681
1,000	8	8	540

Price Competition: tactics that are based on RELATIVE PRICES. This form of RIVALRY is very destructive to industry profitability because the tactic is easy for competitors to see and to follow. Therefore, it is not likely to benefit any competitor unless some competitors EXIT and MARKET SHARES are reallocated. The PRICE COMPETITION can continue until one or more low-cost producers are left. The presence of EXIT BARRIERS makes an industry even less profitable under conditions of PRICE COMPETITION because it slows down the reallocation of MARKET SHARES. Finally, after the battle, it is often hard to raise prices again if that is the intent.

TACTICS based on service and new product introduction are more likely to expand the industry. Each business may have more time to enjoy successful implementation of such TACTICS before their competitors were able to copy or surpass them.

PRICE COMPETITION can be advantageous to an industry as a whole if industry DEMAND is elastic. In that case, the increase in quantity demanded is greater than the reduction in price. In addition, PRICE COMPETITION may be desirable for low-cost producers, for producers practicing EXPERIENCE-BASED PRICING, or when competitors are caught by MIXED MOTIVES.

Price-Cutting: *see* RIVALRY.

Price Discrimination: charging different buyers a different price for the same product. Ideally, a business would charge each buyer the highest price the buyer was willing to pay. In this way, a business could get the most profit on each sale. However, there are two problems with doing this.

The first problem is classifying buyers and preventing resale of the product from one buyer to another. However, this problem can be overcome by generalizing types of buyers into BUYER GROUPS and pricing for those groups. The most common example of this is to separate industrial buyers and households. For example, industrial carpeting is usually priced differently from carpeting sold to individuals. Also, automobile parts are sold at a lower price to auto manufacturers than they are to individuals through auto supply outlets.

The cost of selling a product to different buyers may be different because of differences in buying patterns and practices. These differences are reflected in prices that vary with different volume purchases, or different prices can be charged for the same products by BUNDLING. For example, a business might charge a different price for a nut and a bolt separately than for the pair. Other examples include charging different prices on different but related products, such as first class and economy airfares. Differences between BUYER GROUPS can be reinforced by selling through different distribution channels to each group.

The second problem with practicing price discrimination is that the U.S. government discourages certain forms of PRICE DISCRIMINATION. Generally, PRICE DISCRIMINATION is illegal if it gives an unfair advantage over a competitor. A general example of such illegal PRICE DISCRIMINATION would be offering buyers who buy one of a business's products the chance to buy another product at a reduced price. It is also generally considered illegal for a company to sell its products at a lower price to one buyer and at a higher price to a competing buyer because it may constrain competition in the buyer's industry.

Price Leader: a business that influences or controls the MARKET PRICE in its industry through its PRICING POLICIES and initiatives.

The ability of a business to exercise price leadership in an industry depends on the INDUSTRY STRUCTURE. Usually, the CONCENTRATION RATIO must be high and the SHARE BALANCE must be uneven. That is, price leadership usually appears in an OLIGOPOLY where the price leader has a much higher RELATIVE MARKET SHARE than any other competitor. It is important to note that price leaders do not always have the largest MARKET SHARE. However, they usually need some COMPETITIVE ADVANTAGE to give them the clout to carry out their leadership role. Take, for example, a price leader whose competitive advantage is the fact that it has the lowest costs in the industry. In that case, competitors know that the price leader can cut prices lower than anyone and still make money; therefore, they recognize that the leader is capable of punishing them for out-of-line behavior. Price leaders do not always have their role by choice. Many price leaders prefer, if they can, to discourage others from following their price changes.

The price leader is not the only factor influencing price levels. Price leaders can enforce market price stability only to a limited extent because the general price level tends strongly to reflect SUPPLY and DEMAND forces. However, the leader tends to be the reference point around which changes in price are noted.

Price leaders are often able to maintain price discipline only at the expense of their own market share when facing price-sensitive BUYER GROUPS and falling industry demand. One way of anticipating the degree to which a price leader will have to give up market share is to compare the market share of each competitor to its CAPACITY SHARE. Competitors usually try to maintain a one-to-one relationship between these two ratios. A competitor with a ratio of less than one can be expected to try to increase its market share. Even if the price leader itself currently has a ratio of less than one, it is still very often expected to release the difference.

In order to be an effective price leader, a business should have a number of capabilities. The price leader should have the best available information on the COMPETITIVE FORCES in the industry and a clearly defined STRATEGY that recognizes its role as a price leader. Traditionally, this role has been statesmanlike; that is, the price leader has been expected to have a broad-ranging concern for the profitability and stability of its industry and not just its own selfish interests. However, with the introduction of such pricing policies as EXPERIENCE-BASED PRICING, price leaders themselves act in many unstatesmanlike ways. Suffice it to say, then, that price leaders should have a good understanding of what they want their industries to be like and should define a role for themselves that will lead the industry in that direction. This strategy should be supported by an INCENTIVE SYSTEM that takes the price leadership role into account by, for example, using PERFORMANCE MEASURES that take a long enough time horizon to allow for the short-term sacrifices that PRICE LEADERS may be called on to make. Inconsistency of moves can undermine the price leader's credibility.

In some industries, price leaders do more than just set prices. They can also share new technologies and new products, etc. Depending on the strategy of the price leader, all these things can make an industry more or less profitable than it would otherwise be.

Strategists for a business that is not a price leader should be sure that they know what the price leader's vision of the industry is and that they understand how the price leader sees its role. These strategists can then take advantage of that understanding to benefit their businesses.

Price Policy: a business's approach to setting prices for its products. PRICE POLICY is a key aspect of a business's MARKETING POLICY. Price policy is governed by two characteristics: the competitive characteristics of the industry and the GOALS and STRATEGY of the individual business.

The number of businesses in an industry and the significance of each, the nature of the product and the existence of SUBSTITUTES, together with the number and characteristics of the buyers, determine the scope each business in the industry has to change and adjust its prices. In a perfectly competitive market, businesses are price takers. No individual business is large enough to influence the MARKET PRICE. At the other extreme, a business occupying a MONOPOLY position has complete freedom to select a level of output and price that maximizes its profitability. In most industries, however, competitors are classified as OLIGOPOLISTIC or MONOPOLISTIC. The PRICE POLICIES of the businesses in these industries are highly interdependent. That is, the price one business charges is likely not only to be a function of what its buyers will pay but also to be a function of what competitors are charging. RIVALRY in many industries leads competitors to influence and respond to each other's prices. In addition, PRICE POLICIES are influenced by price-to-performance trends relative to SUBSTITUTE PRODUCTS and the effect of price on ENTRY BARRIERS and MOBILITY BARRIERS.

When evaluating and formulating PRICE POLICIES then, a strategist is interested in INDUSTRY STRUCTURE and the cost structure of the business and its competitors. COST ANALYSIS should reveal MARGINAL COSTS, COST DRIVERS, relative COST ADVANTAGES, and also how these are changing.

The price a buyer is willing to pay is an expression of the value of the product. That value is the sum of the UTILITY of the product itself, the image and information that are conveyed through the advertising and promotion of the product, the availability of the product through wholesale and retail distribution systems, and the service that goes with it. The price a business sets for its products is its estimate of what all this is worth to its selected BUYER GROUPS. In assessing value to the buyer, one must understand the UTILITY of the product to the buyer, the buyer's PRICE SENSITIVITY, the degree of intrinsic BUYER POWER, and the ELASTICITY OF DEMAND.

Although the limits to a business's freedom to set price are determined by INDUSTRY STRUCTURE and the value of the product to the buyer, PRICE POLICIES are modified to reflect the goals and strategy of the individual business as well. Different objectives for profit, MARKET SHARE, or PRICE LEADERSHIP translate into different PRICE POLICIES. In addition, although PRICE POLICY is always an important part of a COMPETITIVE STRATEGY, it is more important to some strategies than to others. For example, it is going to be very important to a business following EXPERIENCE-BASED PRICING as part of a COST LEADERSHIP STRATEGY.

Price Pyramid: a technique for illustrating the trade-off between price and volume for a given company's products or for competitive products in an industry. Products at the top of the pyramid have the highest price and the lowest sales volume. Products at the base of the pyramid have the lowest price and the greatest sales volume.

Price/Quality Matrix: one of a number of charts used to analyze a portfolio of businesses. The matrix displays the relationship between RELATIVE PRICE and relative PRODUCT QUALITY in the products of the businesses in the company's portfolio. The matrix also shows the company's distribution of sales or profits along those two dimensions.

The circles on the BUBBLE CHART are drawn in proportion to the sales or profit of each business. Most strategists follow such a chart with a summary exhibit showing what percentage of the company's sales and earnings fall in each cell and how these have changed over time. Businesses that fall in either the bottom right or the upper left cell deserve further analysis to see why the expected positive correlation between price and quality is not holding. The matrix also provides an indicator of the consistency of strategy among businesses in a portfolio. For example, the business of a company trying to build FORMULA FIT around a generic DIFFERENTIATION STRATEGY should be clustered in the upper right-hand cell.

PRICE/QUALITY MATRICES can also be developed for products within a business.

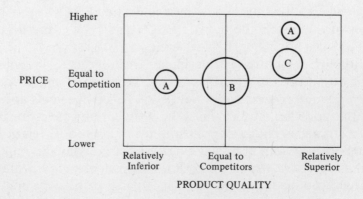

Price Sensitivity: responsiveness of a buyer to changes in the price of a product. A buyer or a BUYER GROUP is considered price-sensitive about a given product when the price of the product significantly affects whether the buyer will buy the product or how much of the product the buyer will buy. The term can refer to the price ELASTICITY OF DEMAND for a generic product but usually refers to cross-elasticities of demand between competing brands. In general, buyers tend to be price-sensitive when the purchase of the product is a significant percentage of the buyer's total purchases over some time period. Buyers may also be price-sensitive if the product is perceived as a COMMODITY and, therefore, not a product about which a wrong choice could negatively affect the buyer.

Strategists are concerned with the PRICE SENSITIVITY of different BUYER GROUPS because of the effect it can have on BUYER POWER.

Price-to-Performance Ratio: a ratio used to compare products in terms of their RELATIVE PRICE and relative UTILITY. The product that offers more UTILITY for a given price is often said to have a higher PRICE-TO-PERFORMANCE RATIO than the other. There is no standard way of actually calculating a ratio per se because performance dimensions vary from product to product. Different industries do it differently, and some do not quantify the ratio at all. However, in general, a business tries to compare its product with another on some common basis.

Many industries calculate a PRICE-TO-PERFORMANCE RATIO by taking a measure of how a given product performs at a specific price and dividing that by a measure of how a competing product performs at the same price. For example, exterior house paint and exterior house stain can be compared in terms of coverage. If $20 worth of paint covers 400 square feet and $20 worth of stain covers only 300 square feet, then paint must have a higher PRICE-TO-PERFORMANCE RATIO of 1.33 (400 sq. ft./300 sq. ft.) as compared to stain's ratio of .75 (300 sq. ft./400 sq. ft.). On the other hand, a stain company might argue that stain lasts six years for every four years that paint lasts. Therefore, the stain company might compare area covered times years and argue that it had the higher PRICE-TO-PERFORMANCE RATIO of 1.12 as compared to paint's ratio of .88.

Strategists are concerned with PRICE-TO-PERFORMANCE RATIOS when comparing their products to those of their competitors as well as to potential SUBSTITUTE PRODUCTS. Strategists also follow changes in PRICE-TO-PERFORMANCE RATIOS over time.

Price Umbrella: the protection from price competition afforded by a business or a group of businesses that resists downward price pressure from existing sellers. A business that prices its products above an equilibrium price is said to be providing a PRICE UMBRELLA. Sometimes most of the competitors in an industry will be pricing high enough to provide a PRICE UMBRELLA for the whole industry. Usually, industrywide PRICE UMBRELLAS are the result of one business's having assumed the role of PRICE LEADER.

To the extent that RIVALRY can be controlled, PRICE UMBRELLAS may increase an industry's profitability for the short term. However, to the extent that either RIVALRY cannot be controlled or ENTRY and MOBILITY BARRIERS are low, PRICE UMBRELLAS can, in the long term, reduce the profitability of an industry by attracting new entrants.

Some strategists feel that most PRICE UMBRELLAS are really cost umbrellas. That is, they occur when the prices charged by a competitor in a HIGH-COST POSITION allow high returns for its lower-cost competitors. Industries with price umbrellas that result from cost umbrellas may be especially vulnerable to ENTRY.

Prisoner's Dilemma: a GAME THEORY concept that is relevant to PRICE POLICY. In the PRISONER'S DILEMMA, two armed robbers, Prisoner A and Prisoner B, have been captured and charged. However, the prosecutor concludes that there is insufficient evidence to convict either Prisoner A or Prisoner B without confessions. Therefore, the prosecutor sets up the following situation in order to manipulate A or B into confessing. First, the prosecutor isolates each prisoner in a cell. The prosecutor then visits Prisoner A and explains that if Prisoner A will confess, the prosecutor will ensure only a five-year sentence for A and put B in jail for life. However, the prosecutor continues, if A refuses to confess and B does confess, then A will get the life imprisonment and B will get only five years. The prosecutor visits B and presents the same proposition. The prosecutor also tells each of the prisoners that the other seems very likely to confess. The choices and outcomes for each prisoner are shown on page 259.

This is a problem of communication and information. If the prisoners can communicate, then they can agree not to confess and both go free. However, in the absence of that communication, both prisoners will probably confess, and, therefore, they are both likely to be sentenced to five years. They each choose the option with the least odious outcome.

Price competition in an OLIGOPOLY is often considered to be

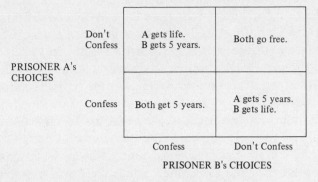

PRISONER'S DILEMMA

		Don't Confess	A gets life. B gets 5 years.	Both go free.
PRISONER A's CHOICES				
		Confess	Both get 5 years.	A gets 5 years. B gets life.
			Confess	Don't Confess

PRISONER B's CHOICES

analogous to the PRISONER'S DILEMMA. For example, if the competitors can agree on a high price and communicate often enough to trust each other to maintain it, they will probably be better off. However, if each competitor expects the others to cut price, then they are all likely to end up doing so.

For this reason, oligopolistic businesses have a strong incentive to collude and to fix prices although antitrust laws prohibit price-fixing. Strategists with businesses in oligopolistic industries may use MARKET SIGNALS to communicate their intention not to cut price legally or be otherwise aggressive. Some strategists will adopt a price leadership role for their business to cope with this situation. Unlike the prisoners facing a onetime decision, businesses setting prices continually repeat the process so that learned cooperation is possible.

Private Label: *see* BRAND IDENTIFICATION.

Process Innovation: a change in the method by which a product is made. Significant PROCESS INNOVATIONS can change the profitability of a business by increasing or decreasing the level of CAPITAL INTENSITY or VERTICAL INTEGRATION, changing the FIXED-TO-VALUE ADDED RATIO, etc. Depending on the company's CORPORATE STRATEGY, such innovations can change the profitability of other businesses in the company by affecting the level of SHARED EXPERIENCE and by changing the BUSINESS INTERRELATIONSHIPS. Such innovations are likely to affect the profitability of the business's competitors to the extent that they affect INDUSTRY STRUCTURE.

Some strategists see PROCESS INNOVATION as being synonymous with TECHNOLOGICAL CHANGE.

Process Life Cycle: a concept that describes changes over time in the production methods used to make a product in terms of an evolution through four stages. The PROCESS LIFE CYCLE is analogous to and closely related to the PRODUCT LIFE CYCLE. The four stages are distinguished by differences in scale or volume, in the continuity of the process, in the labor requirements and skills, and in the degree of equipment specialization. The four stages or production methods are a job shop, a batch process, an assembly line, and a continuous flow.

In a typical job shop, each product is more or less unique or is being produced for the first time. A jumbled flow or job shop process is usually selected as being most effective in meeting those product requirements. Because units are produced in different forms and require different tasks, there is a tendency to use general-purpose equipment. The equipment also tends to be underutilized, for availability and capability are more important than CAPACITY UTILIZATION. The workers need a wide range of production skills, and each job takes much longer elapsed time than the total labor hours required.

A business moves to stage two as it develops a more standard line of similar products or as it increases the volume of its products to the point at which there is some continuity in production. This enables workers to move from a job shop to a flow pattern in which batches of a given model proceed irregularly through a series of work stations or possibly even along a low-volume assembly line. The disconnected line flow allows for some ECONOMIES OF SCALE.

A business whose products have sufficient demand to allow them to be produced in significant volume may choose to make only a few models and use a relatively mechanized and connected production process, such as a moving assembly line. Such a process allows the cost-saving economies available from a standardized and automated process.

Finally, a business such as refining, where the product is a COMMODITY, may choose a continuous process. However, such operations are highly specialized, inflexible, and capital-intensive. Still, their disadvantages may be more than offset by the low VARIABLE COSTS arising from a high volume passing through a standardized process.

According to the concept, as the process evolves from stage to stage, the business loses flexibility but gains in lower costs. There is also a more subtle suggestion that as the process evolves from stage one to stage four, the manufacturer may be less able to achieve high levels of PRODUCT QUALITY but will be able to get dependably consistent quality in a large volume. Not all products pass through four stages. The beginning and end points in the evolution of a production process are defined by the physical characteristics of the product. However, the concept does highlight the degree to which process technology is a policy choice and the importance of planning ahead for changing volume and quality requirements.

Product Attribute Curve: a graph used to illustrate the relationship between additional product features or attributes and the value a buyer places on a product. There is a tendency for the value of a product to a buyer to increase with cumulative product attributes until the buyer's needs have been satisfied and the buyer is unwilling to pay for any more additional features. A sample PRODUCT ATTRIBUTE CURVE is shown as follows.

The term "cumulative product attributes" refers to the augmented product, including all forms of UTILITY. The term "value to the buyer" refers to the amount the buyer is willing to pay for the product with those attributes. To analyze a product's UTILITY, the product is disassembled into its attributes, and then the attributes are cumulated in the order of the buyer's HIERARCHY OF NEEDS. For example, in buying a seat on an airplane, one set of buyers is most interested in safety and basic comforts and after that in departure time, flight time, and in-flight services. Those buyers are willing to pay some amount of money to leave at a specific time, more to arrive when they want, and more for good in-flight service. They may be willing to pay a little more to see a movie during the flight, but they

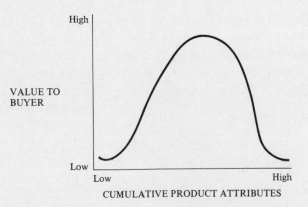

CUMULATIVE PRODUCT ATTRIBUTES

are unlikely to pay any more to have a full orchestra to entertain them, to have expensive art on the cabin walls, or to have astronauts as pilots, etc. As additional attributes continue to be added to the product, the price the buyer is willing to pay flattens out. Then at some point the product becomes unattractive to the buyer, and the price begins to fall.

It is evident that the shape of the PRODUCT ATTRIBUTE CURVE for a given product is going to depend on the BUYER GROUP analyzed. For example, a group of college students might not care at all when the flight departs or how long it takes. They may only be willing to pay to get to their destination safely some time within the next week. A group of traveling executives might feel that having to turn down the lights for a movie is an inconvenience.

Changes over time in BUYER INFORMATION can make buyers more or less willing to pay for a given product attribute. In an efficient market or a world of PERFECT COMPETITION, the buyer knows the price and usefulness of all the possible combinations of products available and can pick the combination that is most satisfying. In practice, it costs time and money for a buyer to find out all there is to know about everything that could be purchased, and the cost of this BUYER INFORMATION leads to imperfections in the market. As a result, buyers often pay for products that they don't need as well as pay more for product features than they need.

PRODUCT ATTRIBUTE CURVE analysis is often used in developing PRICE POLICY for a business. It can also be useful to identify a competitor's attributes and prices on the curve as part of a COMPETITOR ANALYSIS.

Product Change: *see* PRODUCT INNOVATION.

Product Design/Stage Matrix: a matrix based on the interaction of the PRODUCT LIFE CYCLE and product design specialization. The matrix is a two-by-two, drawn as follows.

The matrix shows four conditions under which competition oc-

| | | PRODUCT DESIGN SPECIALIZATION | |
		Standard	Custom
PRODUCT LIFE CYCLE STAGE	Mature	Condition 3	Condition 4
	Growth	Condition 2	Condition 1

curs and implies that over time changes occur that move an EMERG-
ING INDUSTRY from Condition 1 to Condition 2, then 3 and then 4.
Accordingly, most products come into being under Condition 1, attracted by the potential for growth and custom designed for the few
buyers that understand them. Over time the product becomes increasingly standardized as new competitors imitate the original producer, and the product moves to Condition 2. The product moves
to Condition 3 as the product is more widely understood, and market
growth slows with SATURATION. The product moves into Condition
4 when some producers decide to differentiate their products in order
to compete for the replacement market. DEMATURITY, through new
product design or new product uses, can return the product to Condition 1 and begin the cycle again.

Product Differences: variations in the features of the products offered by competitors in an industry. That is, PRODUCT DIFFERENCES
exist when one competitor's product offers the buyer different UTIL-
ITY from that of another competitor's product. The differences may
arise from variations in production technology, tailoring to fill particular applications, or attempts to appeal to different BUYER GROUPS.
They do not necessarily correlate with differences in PRODUCT
QUALITY.

Product Differentiation: the presence of any significant basis, other
than price, for choosing one company's product over another's.
Economists would include as examples of PRODUCT DIFFERENTIATION
the styling differences between two furriers' mink coats, the perceived difference between branded aspirin and private label aspirin,
and the cost of learning how to use another company's computer
instead of the computer one's own management is currently using.
However, strategists tend to separate PRODUCT DIFFERENTIATION into
PRODUCT DIFFERENCES, BRAND IDENTIFICATION, and SWITCHING
COSTS. Strategists may use combinations of those to develop a DIF-
FERENTIATION STRATEGY that builds their buyer's loyalty to their
company's products and entices new buyers away from other companies' products.

PRODUCT DIFFERENTIATION in an industry allows competitors to
charge different prices for their products. Competitors may be under
less pressure to follow each other's price changes because their buyers are loyal. Therefore, product differentiating tactics contribute to
profitability because they can reduce both RIVALRY and BUYER

POWER. However, sustaining a business's COMPETITIVE POSITION depends on its ability to maintain PRODUCT DIFFERENTIATION. Although MARKET SHARES are insulated from competitors' price changes, they may be quite vulnerable to changes in the features of competitors' products.

Differentiation is sometimes associated with strong ENTRY BARRIERS, for example, when brands are subject to heavy national advertising. In other markets, differentiation is associated with easy ENTRY because of the profuse ways of differentiating the product, for example, starting a new restaurant.

Product Innovation: a change that causes the buyers of a product to perceive that product as having new UTILITY. The UTILITY of the product has only to be perceived as new by its intended BUYER GROUP and may, in fact, be very familiar to other BUYER GROUPS.

PRODUCT INNOVATION is an EVOLUTIONARY PROCESS. For example, it can affect an industry's profitability by allowing it to serve new buyers, by making ENTRY more expensive, by changing supplier needs, and by improving the industry's position vis-à-vis SUBSTITUTE PRODUCTS.

Some strategists define product innovation broadly to include PROCESS INNOVATION and TECHNOLOGICAL CHANGE. Others agree that these TACTICS have comparable effects on INDUSTRY STRUCTURE but are sufficiently different to merit their own terminology.

Some strategists believe that the buyer's VALUE CHAIN and BUYER GROUP ANALYSIS are the key to PRODUCT INNOVATION. They point out that in some industries more than half the PRODUCT INNOVATIONS are based on buyer ideas.

Productivity: the number of units of output produced per unit of input. For a business, inputs are often classified as capital, labor, and purchased inputs. Total PRODUCTIVITY is maximized by combining labor efficiently with capital and purchased inputs and by using the minimum quantities of all of them.

The ratio of output to labor hours is the most commonly used measure of PRODUCTIVITY. Changes in this ratio over time are used to illustrate changes in labor productivity. Labor productivity is best thought of in terms of how efforts to motivate labor are working. That is, for given quantities of all other inputs, output varies with the effort supplied by a given quantity of labor. Capital productivity is measured by the ratio of output to the MARKET VALUE of the investment assets required to produce that output. Strategists very often use measures of relative PRODUCTIVITY when comparing their costs with those of their competitors.

Tactics for increasing PRODUCTIVITY are often part of a FIX PLAN.

Product Life Cycle: a concept for analyzing stages in the sales history of a product or line of products. The PRODUCT LIFE CYCLE is usually presented as a sales curve drawn over time from product introduction to product withdrawal, divided into five stages as shown in the graph below.

THE PRODUCT LIFE CYCLE

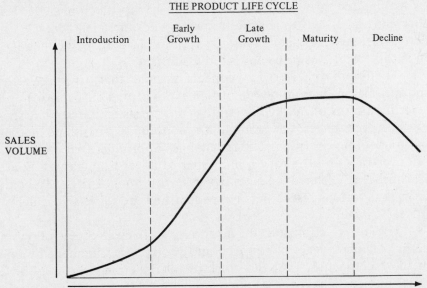

The PRODUCT LIFE CYCLE is often explained as being caused by the diffusion and adoption of innovations. During the introduction stage, sales typically start to build slowly. Management works to develop TACTICS directed at the purchasing DECISION-MAKING UNIT to stimulate awareness, interest, trial, and purchase of the new product but is likely to reach only a few of the potential buyer groups. Over time, if the TACTICS are successful, larger numbers of buyers are added to the market. Sales growth begins to accelerate at an increasing rate, and the product enters the early growth stage. In the late growth stage, sales continue to grow, but the rate of growth starts to slow down. Eventually, during the maturity stage, the rate of growth approaches zero, the point of saturation is reached, and sales become steady at the replacement purchase rate. Finally, in the decline stage, as new products appear and divert buyers from the existing product, sales drop until the product is withdrawn from the market.

The designation of the point at which one stage ends and another begins tends to be arbitrary. Some researchers have proposed specific boundary measures based on a normal distribution of percentage changes in REAL GROWTH from year to year; however, the stages are usually bounded by points at which changes in the rate of sales growth become pronounced. Sometimes the life cycle is drawn with only four stages. This is done by either combining the early growth stage and the late growth stage into a single growth stage or by making the early growth stage part of the introduction stage. Before plotting a sales time series to assess PRODUCT LIFE CYCLE characteristics, the sales data should be adjusted or deflated for changes in such variables as price and supply shortfalls.

The PRODUCT LIFE CYCLE concept assumes that, irrespective of the specific product involved, certain types of market behavior and certain patterns of marketing strategy are consistently found at specific life cycle stages. For example, the concept assumes that patterns of competitors' ENTRY and EXIT, changes in product UTILITY, levels of advertising to sales ratios, and types of advertising STRATEGY are all consistently related to stages in the PRODUCT LIFE CYCLE. The patterns that various researchers have identified are summarized below for each stage.

The introduction stage of a product's life cycle often follows a period of many years of research and product development by one or more competitors. At the point of introduction there may be a single pioneer. The pioneer may remain the sole competitor throughout the stage, or other competitors may enter and jointly contribute to developing the market. Competitors are likely to be attracted into the industry to the extent that it is perceived to be large or highly profitable. Competitors may also be interested if the new product threatens their existing businesses or if it seems to complement their existing businesses.

The introduction stage usually involves many uncertainties. Buyers may worry that the new product may not perform adequately, and manufacturers may be undecided as to the optimal MANUFACTURING and MARKETING POLICY. The resources necessary to develop the market and bring the product into the early growth stage can be very high, even exceeding the initial cost of developing the product.

During the introduction stage, there are usually few forms of the product as the competitors struggle to build volume to a BREAK-EVEN level. During this stage, advertising aims to educate customers about the product rather than to point out PRODUCT DIFFERENCES or build BRAND IDENTITY. Many products also require personal selling effort to educate buyers and distributors about the use of the product and its value. SKIM PRICING or PENETRATION PRICING may be used, depending on the competitor's need to recover costs and the strategist's assessment of the PRICE SENSITIVITY of the BUYER GROUPS.

The duration of the introduction stage depends on a number of factors and can range from a few months to many years. A major determinant is the NEW PRODUCT INTRODUCTION of each competitor and its effect on the development of the market. A decision on the part of any competitor to use EXPERIENCE-BASED PRICING will have a significant effect as well. In general, the more radical the required changes in buyers' habits, the greater the complexity of the product, the more difficult the demonstration of the benefits, and the greater the RISK of using the new product, the longer the introduction stage is likely to be. Even if the potential benefits of using the product are substantial, the introduction stage may be prolonged if its price is high relative to SUBSTITUTES or if the purchasing DECISION-MAKING PROCESS involves a number of people. Technical problems with the production process and early product failure can also retard market development. A more subtle point is that an inability to expand production CAPACITY to meet growing DEMAND can also slow things down. Some strategists consider the building of excess CAPACITY to be an effective TACTIC for encouraging market development and discouraging other entrants.

The early growth stage is characterized by an increasing rate of growth of sales. The increasing sales or an inability on the part of the pioneers to satisfy market DEMAND often attracts additional entrants, whose marketing efforts further stimulate the sales growth. During this stage, products introduced by new entrants tend to be ME-TOO products rather than new designs. New distribution channels may open up as competitors struggle for distribution, and promotional activity tends to remain at a high level. The nature of the advertising changes from an emphasis on stimulating first-time purchases to an emphasis on PRODUCT DIFFERENCES, BRAND IDENTITY, and MARKET SEGMENTATION. However, the ratio of marketing expenditure to sales may drop as the denominator, sales, increases. Prices, if not already very low, may fall in the early growth stage as cost declines, associated with increasing ECONOMIES OF SCALE and CUMULATIVE EXPERIENCE, allow for PRICE COMPETITION. However, this stage is not expected to be a period of intense RIVALRY. The rapid expansion of the market is expected to provide enough DEMAND to allow all competitors to have sufficient sales growth. One competitor's sales growth does not have to come at the expense of other competitors; however, as a business's sales increase, its MARKET SHARE may be decreasing. This is an important stage for the strategist to begin COMPETITOR ANALYSIS because the plans of each competitor are going to have a significant effect on the EVOLUTIONARY PROCESSES in the industry.

In the late growth stage, sales continue to increase, but the rate of growth decreases. By the end of this stage, REAL GROWTH will have dropped to near zero. The growth rates achieved by competitors in the early growth stage can no longer be maintained from growth in the market, and the stronger competitors tend to initiate tough competitive actions to maintain their past sales growth. Weaker competitors may begin to EXIT.

In contrast to the ME-TOO PRODUCTS offered in the early growth stage, some competitors may now introduce product changes and modifications in order to develop a COMPETITIVE ADVANTAGE through PRODUCT DIFFERENTIATION. These efforts as well as the efforts of competitors following a FOCUS STRATEGY may result in a proliferation of product variations as competitors adapt their products to specific BUYER GROUP requirements. Distribution channels may resist this to the extent that slower sales growth makes the outlets more selective, reducing the number of brands and the number of individual items of a given brand that they are willing to carry. In contrast to the early growth stage, price may become a frequent competitive weapon to the extent that some competitors seek a COMPETITIVE ADVANTAGE through a COST LEADERSHIP STRATEGY.

A business following a BUILD PLAN during this stage may increase the MARKET SHARE, but it is likely to cost more than it would have in an earlier stage. Competitors in the late growth stage face a trade-off between high MARKET SHARE and high current profit. By spending a lot of money on product improvement, promotion, and distribution, a business may be able to build a high share position; but it may have to lose some current profit in the hope of making it up in the next stage.

The maturity stage begins with an end to REAL GROWTH. During this stage, year-to-year changes are due to changes in basic macroeconomic factors. Most sales are to repeat users, and if economic conditions are depressed, replacement may be postponed.

Pricing is likely to be competitive, and if so, the low margins may limit MARKET SEGMENTATION. Therefore, TACTICS for developing buyer loyalty may rely more on packaging and promotional strategies than expensive PRODUCT DIFFERENCES. After the EXIT of weaker competitors, the industry becomes more CONCENTRATED, and MARKET SHARES become stabilized. Distribution can be critical during the maturity stage. This is especially true if a COMPETITIVE ADVANTAGE is difficult to achieve through either low cost or differentiation. Competitors often increase VALUE ADDED SHARE in distribution to build and protect their positions.

ENTRY is considered difficult during an industry's maturity stage because ENTRY BARRIERS are thought to be at their peak. If successful ENTRY does occur, it is usually because the entrenched competitors have not built sustainable COMPETITIVE ADVANTAGES and one or more untried GENERIC STRATEGIES remain economically plausible. Potential entrants during the maturity stage typically have significant resources to spend on achieving a LOW-COST STRATEGY, the resources and the know-how to achieve a DIFFERENTIATION STRATEGY, or the ability to recognize and serve a particular BUYER GROUP with a FOCUS STRATEGY.

Because MARKET SHARES achieved before or during the maturity stage are often sustained throughout the maturity stage and because the maturity stage may last many years, it is important to anticipate the amount of time it takes a product to reach maturity. Recent studies seem to indicate that the period of time from introduction to the peak of the life cycle curve is decreasing. Take, for example, a study of products in the home electric appliance industry. The products introduced before 1920, such as the electric range, refrigerator, and vacuum cleaner, took an average of over thirty years to reach their sales peak. Products introduced much later, including the electric frying pan and the toaster oven, took an average of less than ten years to reach their peak. To the extent that this example can be generalized to apply to other industries, it is important to strategists. A shortening of the PRODUCT LIFE CYCLE, which may result from such factors as improved technology, faster information dissemination, and greater buyer purchasing power, makes it even more important to enter an industry with the right strategy the first time.

Although the maturity stage of the PRODUCT LIFE CYCLE may

last many years, eventually sales are expected to turn downward and enter the decline stage. The sales decline may be gradual or steep. Usually, the decline stage is expected to be shorter than average when the product is being replaced by a SUBSTITUTE and longer than average when buyers' needs are changing in a way that makes the product obsolete.

As REAL GROWTH in sales continues to fall, overcapacity in the industry is expected to become a problem. PRICE COMPETITION may intensify as competitors try to increase their CAPACITY UTILIZATION although this is less likely if the EXIT BARRIERS are low enough to allow some competitors to get out. Marketing expenditures are expected to drop in the decline stage as competitors reduce support for declining products. Advertising effort may be directed away from mass media toward more specialized media in an effort to target the remaining BUYER GROUPS and reduce costs. Further cost reductions may be made by cutting back the product lines to achieve whatever ECONOMIES OF SCALE are still available.

Late in the decline stage there may be opportunities for profits if a group of loyal, relatively price-insensitive buyers remains and only a few competitors are left to compete for their business. Those remaining in the industry may be able to reduce the number of products in their lines, stop selling to the more powerful BUYER GROUPS, cut expenses, and earn good returns during this stage.

Not all products proceed along an identical PRODUCT LIFE CYCLE curve. Some products show such a rapid growth from the very beginning that they skip the slow sales start implied by the introduction stage. Other products may never experience rapid growth and, therefore, may go directly from introduction to maturity. Still other products move from the maturity stage to a second period of late growth or even DEMATURITY rather than into the decline stage. Therefore, a first step in using the PRODUCT LIFE CYCLE concept is to determine to what extent the idealized sequence of stages is followed as well as the typical length of each stage for a particular industry.

The measurement of a PRODUCT'S LIFE CYCLE also depends on how the product is defined. That is, the life cycle of a product such as fruit juice may be different from the life cycle of a product form such as frozen orange juice, as well as being different from the life cycle of a particular brand such as Minute Maid. In general, the life cycle of a product can be expected to be longer than that of a particular product form or brand. The mature stage of many broadly defined products such as appliances or writing instruments can be expected to continue for an indefinite period because they are always needed. Product forms, on the other hand, probably have more typical PRODUCT LIFE CYCLES. For example, product forms such as black and white portable TVs and cartridge fountain pens seem to pass through a regular sequence of introduction, early growth, late growth, maturity, and decline. An individual brand's life cycle is likely to be less typical because changing COMPETITIVE STRATEGIES and tactics can alter RIVALRY and SHARE BALANCE, producing ups and downs in sales that occur regardless of the product's life cycle stage.

In addition to anticipating the life cycle, some strategists also recognize the possibilities for manipulating it. For example, some strategists use strategy to postpone the maturity stage and maintain the growth stage. They do this by developing new uses for the product for new and existing BUYER GROUPS or by making changes in the product's UTILITY that will attract new buyers or generate greater usage from current users. Such changes usually involve increasing the actual or perceived PRODUCT QUALITY. Adding new features that expand the product's versatility, safety, or convenience is another variation of the preceding. A side benefit of these TACTICS is the possibility of building a company image of progressiveness and leadership. They can also lead to renewed sales force and distributors' enthusiasm and may generate free publicity. A disadvantage is that the changes may be imitable, and unless there is some advantage to being first, the investment in changes may not be justified.

Strategists who are comfortable with the PRODUCT LIFE CYCLE concept feel that it is useful in formulating COMPETITIVE STRATEGY. They may also use the concept as the basis for the LIFE CYCLE MATRIX in formulating CORPORATE STRATEGY. Other strategists argue that it attempts to standardize change in all industries when the important point is to understand the unique EVOLUTIONARY PROCESSES in specific industries.

Product/Market Certainty Matrix: a technique used to evaluate sales plans and to adjust them to reflect the uncertainty associated with the newness of the product or the market. The projected sales of each business in a company's portfolio are classified on the basis of whether the product sold is an existing product, a new but related product, or a new product and on the basis of whether the target market is an existing market, a new but related market, or a new

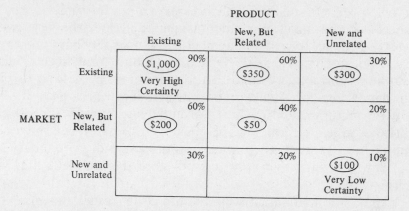

market. The sales figures are then arrayed on a matrix like the one above.

The technique is based on the assumption that the further the sales are from the upper left-hand corner of the matrix, the less certainty there is that they will be realized. That is, in general, it is more likely that a business will be able to generate a planned amount of sales from a product that already exists in a familiar market than it is that a business will be able to generate a planned amount of sales from a new and unrelated product that will be sold in a new and unrelated market.

On the basis of convention, rather than statistical insight, values of 3, 2, and 1 are assigned to existing, related, and unrelated categories. Multiples of these values times ten are assigned to each cell to indicate the probability of realizing the sales forecast. The probabilities range from a 90 percent chance of meeting plan in the upper left-hand cell to a 10 percent chance in the lower right-hand cell.

In the preceding example, a business has a five-year plan with estimated sales of $2,000,000 in year five. Analysis showed that $1,000,000 of those sales are expected to come from the sale of current products to current markets and that $350,000 are expected to come from the sales of related new products to those same markets, etc. Weighting the sales in each cell by the amount of uncertainty involved gives a certainty-adjusted year-five sales figure of $1,350,000. With much more effort, a more scientifically derived set of probabilities can be developed for each cell. Some strategists do that by analyzing the past history of their businesses. Certainty adjusted profits can also be calculated.

Strategists who use the matrix find that it is a good technique for highlighting the uncertainty in plans that rely on new products or new markets to reach their GOALS. The MARKETING CERTAINTY MATRIX is also used in this way.

Product Mix: a business's PRODUCT MIX is often classified as wide or narrow along a number of dimensions, including the number of different products, the diversity of applications and features, or the price range. Strategists often use COMPETITOR MAPS to compare one business's PRODUCT MIX with that of its competitors.

Product/Process Matrix: a matrix based on the interaction of the PRODUCT LIFE CYCLE and the PROCESS LIFE CYCLE that is used to call attention to the consistency of the MANUFACTURING POLICY and the PRODUCT POLICY of a business. The matrix is usually drawn with four rows and four columns as on page 274.

The rows of the matrix show the four major stages through which a production process is expected to pass in going from the jumbled flow in the top row to the continuous flow in the bottom row. The columns show the PRODUCT LIFE CYCLE stages going from the great variety associated with the introduction stage on the left-hand side to standardized commodity products associated with the decline stage on the right-hand side.

Each business in a company's portfolio can be located on the matrix on the basis of its stage in its PRODUCT'S LIFE CYCLE and on the basis of its stage in the LIFE CYCLE PROCESS. A business's stage of PRODUCT LIFE CYCLE and its stage of PROCESS LIFE CYCLE are expected to match so that each business should fall in one of the circles on the matrix's diagonal. Those that do fall in a circle are considered to have product structures and process structures that are compatible. Each circle is associated with a set of manufacturing OBJECTIVES and tasks involving more or less flexibility, quality, dependability, and cost control.

In diagonal position 1, the manufacturing OBJECTIVE is usually to produce high-margin, custom-designed products, using general-purpose machinery. These products are often required on short order. Key management tasks often involve preserving flexibility; estimating capacity, costs, and delivery times; breaking bottlenecks; and tracing and exploiting orders.

In diagonal position 2, the OBJECTIVE is to obtain high margins with a full line of products under conditions of quality control and often with associated services and fast delivery. The key management tasks for diagonal position 2 often involve developing standards, bal-

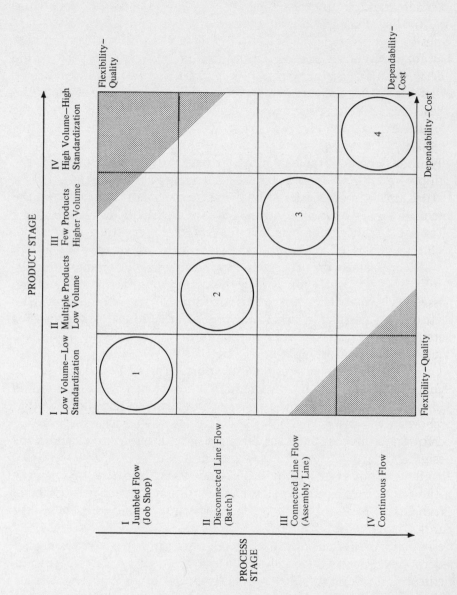

PRODUCT STAGE

I Low Volume—Low Standardization

II Multiple Products Low Volume

III Few Products Higher Volume

IV High Volume—High Standardization

Flexibility— Quality

Dependability— Cost

PROCESS STAGE

I Jumbled Flow (Job Shop)

II Disconnected Line Flow (Batch)

III Connected Line Flow (Assembly Line)

IV Continuous Flow

Flexibility—Quality

Dependability—Cost

1

2

3

4

ancing the process, and managing a growing and increasingly complex function.

In diagonal position 3, the OBJECTIVE is to produce high volumes of lower-margin products by standardizing the product to allow for long runs. This is often supported by multiple source suppliers and captive or dedicated distribution. The key manufacturing tasks are similar to those of diagonal position 2, with increasing emphasis on cost and inventory control.

In diagonal position 4, the OBJECTIVE is to produce very high volumes as cheaply as possible, given quality constraints. This is usually done with long runs of standardized products on specialized equipment, taking advantage of ECONOMIES OF SCALE and CUMULATIVE EXPERIENCE as well as VERTICAL INTEGRATION. The key management tasks on diagonal position 4 are to keep the plant running at peak efficiency and to decide how and when to invest in new technologies.

Businesses are not expected to fall in either of the shaded corners. Some strategists make a conscious choice to move their businesses off the expected diagonal, but this is rare. Usually, businesses drift off the diagonal without management's recognizing this or understanding its implications. The concept of the FOCUSED FACTORY is closely related to the PRODUCT/PROCESS MATRIX.

Product Quality: the beneficial attributes of a product as they really are or as they are perceived to be by the product's potential buyers or both. Evaluations of quality are often based on factors such as performance, dependability, durability, workmanship, materials, or design.

Some strategists say that a product can have high quality even if the buyer does not perceive it as such. Other strategists say that a product can have quality only if the potential buyer perceives it regardless of whether it really does have intrinsic quality in terms of design or materials, etc. However, all agree that the important consideration is the quality of the business's product relative to competitors. The strategist should be concerned if that relative position is inconsistent with the business's COMPETITIVE STRATEGY.

A relative product quality index for a given business can be developed in a number of ways. The most common is to ask the business to estimate what percentage of its sales is of products that its buyers would consider to be superior in quality to the products its competitors are selling and what percentage is from products considered inferior. The difference between those two percentages is often used as a relative product quality index. Take, for example, a business that estimated that 60 percent of its sales were from products that were relatively superior, 10 percent were from products that were relatively inferior, and 30 percent were from products that were considered equal to its competitors in quality. That business's relative product quality index would be 50 percent (60 percent less 10 percent).

In addition to being concerned with PRODUCT QUALITY on a business level, many strategists are concerned with the general level of PRODUCT QUALITY in the company's portfolio. These strategists often use a PRICE/QUALITY MATRIX as part of a portfolio analysis.

Product Quality Strategy: *see* DIFFERENTIATION STRATEGY.

Profitable Break-even: the volume at which a business both breaks even and earns its REQUIRED RETURN is called its PROFITABLE BREAK-EVEN point. A profitable break-even volume is usually determined by adding some amount of profit to the FIXED COST estimate of a standardized break-even calculation. The profit amount is based on the business's REQUIRED RETURN.

Profit Center: an entity in a company's ORGANIZATIONAL HIERARCHY for which the company's MEASUREMENT SYSTEMS measure both the revenues generated by their activities as well as the cost incurred in those activities. Managers of PROFIT CENTERS have what is called profit and loss or P and L responsibility. Those managers are responsible for achieving the combination of costs and revenues that generates the required return for that entity.

Some companies define what is a cost and what is a revenue on the basis of the span of the manager's authority. For example, a manager for a sales function who has the authority to set prices may be held responsible for total revenue minus STANDARD COST of manufacturing. A product marketing manager might be responsible for revenues minus standard manufacturing costs and minus advertising costs.

PROFIT CENTERS may contain COST CENTERS and REVENUE CENTERS.

Profit Maximization: an OBJECTIVE of seeking the largest number of dollars of profit. A business can maximize profits in a perfectly competitive market by increasing its output until the MARGINAL REVENUE from an additional unit equals the MARGINAL COST of producing that unit. Under other market conditions a business can change its prices until it finds the profit maximizing combination of price and output.

The preceding approach will yield a maximum profit at a specific level of investment, that is, when the business's CAPACITY is specified. CAPACITY additions will be profit maximizing when they are made on the condition that the expected ROI on the additional investment equals the relevant COST OF CAPITAL. Maximizing profit is only the same as maximizing ROI if CAPACITY is taken as given.

BUILD, HOLD, and HARVEST PLANS are usually based on different investment ASSUMPTIONS. Maximizing RETURN ON INVESTMENT, when faced with a choice of plans, requires an analysis of the different output levels given different amounts of investment.

Proprietary Experience: *see* EXPERIENCE CURVE.

Prosperity: *see* BUSINESS CYCLE.

Psychographic Needs: *see* BUYER GROUP.

Pull Through: tactics for promoting a product directly to the END USER, who then asks for it and draws it through the distribution channel. A product can either be pushed or pulled through its distribution channel to its END USER. With a PUSH THROUGH approach, the distribution channels are given incentives to push the product through. The two approaches are not mutually exclusive, and most businesses develop a MARKETING POLICY that combines the two. Still, some businesses tend to rely more on one approach than on the other.

PULL THROUGH tactics are commonly used in marketing CONSUMER GOODS. For example, advertising aimed at consumers can be used to generate demand for a nonprescription remedy. The consumers' requests for the product spur the druggist to carry it. In fact, if a manufacturer wants to sell its products through large food and mass merchandising outlets, which tend to be more powerful than drug stores, it will probably have to spend a considerable amount on consumer advertising in order to pull those products through.

In the marketing of industrial goods, it is also possible to develop PULL THROUGH for products. One common way to do this is to appeal directly to the specifying engineer. For example, industrial lighting manufacturers will advertise in architectural design trade magazines in order to get the architects to specify their products by brand so that the builder or contractor has to buy from them.

PULL THROUGH is a way to mitigate the BUYER POWER of one's

IMMEDIATE CUSTOMER by appealing to the next customer in the distribution channel or by appealing directly to the END USER.

Purchased Value: the value of the material inputs at any stage in a product's VALUE ADDED CHAIN. Take, for example, the VALUE ADDED CHAIN for a cotton dress. The cotton must be grown, spun, woven, dyed, cut into a pattern, sewn, sold to a wholesaler, sold to a retailer, displayed, advertised, and then sold to the END USER. From the dressmaker's perspective, the cost of the woven cotton is the product's PURCHASED VALUE, and the steps until it is sold to a wholesaler are the dressmaker's VALUE ADDED. From the retailer's perspective, the wholesale price of the dress is the PURCHASED VALUE, and all other following steps are VALUE ADDED.

For some types of analysis, PURCHASED VALUE is taken as a single cost in developing a VALUE ADDED CHAIN. For other types of analysis, such as the consideration of BACKWARD INTEGRATION, PURCHASE VALUE may be broken down into the supplier's value added stages.

Purchasing: *see* DECISION-MAKING PROCESS.

Pure Competition: an INDUSTRY STRUCTURE in which no competitor is able to influence MARKET PRICE by varying the SUPPLY or by affecting DEMAND. PERFECT COMPETITION requires even stricter conditions.

Push Through: tactics for promoting a product by encouraging the distribution channel to push the product through to the END USER. A product can either be pulled or pushed through its distribution channel to its END USER. With a PULL THROUGH approach, the product is usually promoted directly to the END USER. The two are not mutually exclusive, and businesses will combine the two. Still, some businesses tend to rely more on one approach than the other.

CONSUMER GOODS are very often pushed through by giving discounts to retailers or by giving them cooperative advertising budgets. INDUSTRIAL GOODS are often pushed through by providing outlets with attractive margins, service support, or engineering information. PUSH THROUGH tactics tend to be effective when the distributor's influence in the purchase decision is strong, for example, if the END USER is dependent on the distributor for information on how to use the product.

Q

Question Mark: a business in a company's portfolio that has a relatively weak COMPETITIVE POSITION but that is in a relatively fast-growing industry. The label is associated with one cell of the GROWTH/SHARE MATRIX. The attractiveness of the industry makes a BUILD PLAN interesting, but the low RELATIVE MARKET SHARE held by the business makes the cost and benefit of such a plan uncertain. QUESTION MARKS may have NEGATIVE ECONOMIC VALUE, but they may also have high potential for positive ECONOMIC VALUE with the right COMPETITIVE STRATEGY.

R

Real Growth: the rate of change in a nominal monetary value such as sales adjusted to eliminate the effect of changes in specific prices or changes in the general price level. When sales are adjusted for specific product price changes, REAL GROWTH measures the growth in the number of units sold. For example, if a business's sales have been growing at the rate of 15 percent per year in CURRENT DOLLARS and if prices have been increasing at 10 percent per year, then the REAL GROWTH in sales is 5 percent, which is the 15 percent current dollar growth minus the 10 percent growth in prices.

When the term REAL GROWTH is used to refer to growth over and above the general level of INFLATION, real growth is not synonymous with the change in the number of units. That is, if in the preceding example the rate of INFLATION over the same period had been 12 percent, then the REAL GROWTH in sales would be considered to be only 3 percent. The argument is that whereas the business has been able to increase its unit sales by 5 percent per year, it did not increase its prices enough to keep up with INFLATION; therefore, the business's REAL GROWTH in sales is only 3 percent.

Rebuild Plan: a type of FIX PLAN for a business that has had a large MARKET SHARE and lost it. A REBUILD PLAN is often considered when share has been lost because of complacency or because the company was to some extent harvesting the business for short-term profits.

Most strategists consider REBUILD PLANS to be very expensive because they require additional spending to reverse a trend and to win back the confidence of lost buyers, suppliers, etc. Therefore, many strategists only use a REBUILD PLAN when the business's market position is somehow important to the parent's CORPORATE STRATEGY, when it is very obvious that the business was premature in harvesting, and when there is a significant reward to rebuilding.

Recession: *see* BUSINESS CYCLE.

Redeployment: *see* EXIT.

Regional Brand: *see* BRAND IDENTIFICATION.

Regression Analysis: a statistical technique used to identify relationships between variables and to measure how closely the relationships hold. Simple regression analysis is used to explain the behavior of one variable, called the dependent variable, on the basis of changes in one other variable, called the independent variable. In multiple regression analysis, a number of independent variables are used to explain the behavior of the dependent variable. The information obtained from REGRESSION ANALYSIS is frequently used to forecast future values for the dependent variable. The computer is a valuable tool in REGRESSION ANALYSIS.

REGRESSION ANALYSIS can be thought of as a formal way of fitting a line to a series of dots. For example, to estimate the future demand for skis in a region, one might begin by looking at past DEMAND and past weather reports to see if there were any relationship between the two. To do so, one would look at the level of DEMAND for skis (the dependent variable) in various years and at the snowfall (the independent variable, also called the explanatory variable) in those same years. Ten years of DEMAND for skis and ten years of snowfall could be graphed on a scatter plot as shown in the following diagram, with ten dots, one for each year.

The analyst can inspect the scatter plot and draw a line that shows roughly the relationship between the two variables, or the analyst can calculate how much the demand goes up when the snowfall

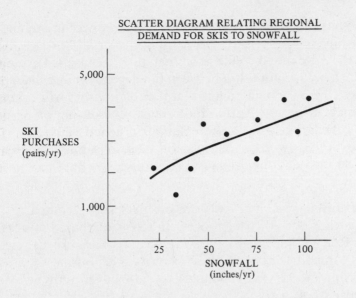

SCATTER DIAGRAM RELATING REGIONAL
DEMAND FOR SKIS TO SNOWFALL

goes up and how much the demand goes down when the snowfall goes down. But an easier and more sophisticated method is to enter the demand data and the snowfall data in a computer and let a regression analysis program estimate the relationship. The computer's efficiency increases when more data is added or the number of explanatory variables is increased.

The output from a regression analysis program is an equation that says that the demand for skis tends to equal a constant plus a coefficient times the snowfall. Given this equation, the future demand for skis can be estimated readily once predictions of the estimated future snowfall are entered.

In addition to the equation, a regression program will calculate a number of statistics indicating how closely the line fits the data or how well the equation explains the dependent variable. The most popular indicator is called the coefficient of determination or the R^2. The R^2 is a number that ranges from zero to one and can be thought of as indicating the proportion of the variation in the dependent variable, which can be "explained" by changes in the independent variables. An R^2 of 1.0 indicates that 100 percent of the variation in the dependent variable is accounted for, and an R^2 of .80 indicates that 80 percent of the past variation is accounted for. In the preceding example, there are certainly many other factors that determine the demand for skis, so the equation is not likely to have an R^2 near one. Other statistics generated in REGRESSION ANALYSIS provide estimates of how sensitive a dependent variable is to changes in any independent variable.

It is important to remember that just because an explanation indicates a past relationship between the dependent and independent variables, there is no guarantee that the relationship will continue in the future. Also, an equation indicates a relationship based on statistical correlation and not necessarily on actual causation. Therefore, to be trustworthy, REGRESSION ANALYSIS must be based on clearly defined and logical causal relations.

Related Businesses: two or more businesses in a company's portfolio that are related to each other in terms of shared FUNCTIONAL AREAS. RELATED BUSINESSES are the obvious basis for FUNCTIONAL FIT in a company's CORPORATE STRATEGY. Such businesses are likely to contribute to SHARED EXPERIENCE and can certainly be expected to involve SHARED COSTS.

Businesses selling products using similar technologies or with similar applications or selling to common buyer groups are often considered related, too.

Relative Costs: a given business's costs as compared with those of its competitors. RELATIVE COSTS are most often described roughly as being less than, equal to, or greater than the business's competitor's costs. However, relative costs can also be expressed as an index calculated by dividing the costs of the given business by the average costs of each of its competitors. In that case, an index of 1.0 is usually used to indicate that a given business has costs equal to that of its competitors, an index of less than 1.0 is used for a COST ADVANTAGE, and an index of greater than 1.0 for a cost disadvantage. For example, if a given business had a unit cost of $8.00 and it had three competitors with costs of $13.00, $9.00, and $8.00, then its relative cost index would be $8.00 divided by $10.00, or $.80.

Although the relative cost index does show that the business has lower than average costs compared to its competitors, the index does not show that there is one competitor with cost parity. Therefore, some strategists calculate a relative cost index in the same way a RELATIVE MARKET SHARE is calculated. That is, the low cost producer's costs are used as the denominator. In that way, the business in the preceding example would have an index of 1.0, showing that its costs are equal to those of its lowest cost competitor.

Relative costs can be analyzed for a single product, for lines of products, for businesses, and even for companies. The costs considered can include VARIABLE COSTS, total costs, or any combination of elements in the business's COST STRUCTURE.

Strategists usually find relative cost data very useful in COMPETITOR ANALYSIS. Finding out competitor costs can be extremely difficult. Still, even estimates of relative costs can provide helpful information.

Relative Market Share: the ratio of the sales of a given business to the sales of the competitor with the highest sales in that industry. If, for example, Company A has $125 million in sales and its largest rival, Company B, has $625 million in sales, then Company A's RELATIVE MARKET SHARE is $125 million divided by $625 million, which equals $.2x$. (Relative market share is usually expressed with an x to indicate, as just shown, the Company A's relative market share $= .2$ times Company B's.) Sales data is used in this example, but MARKET SHARE data can be used as well to generate the same ratio. If total industry sales are $5 billion, then Company A's share is 2.5 percent, and Company B's share is 12.5 percent. The ratio of Company A's share to Company B's share is again $.2x$. However, when market shares are used, it is important to make sure that both share calculations are based on the same figure for total industry sales.

The standard calculation of relative market share will not work for the largest competitor itself. In that case, the ratio of its sales to the sales of the next largest competitor is used. If, in the preceding example, Company C's sales of $400 million were the second highest in the industry, then Company B's relative market share would be $500 million divided by $400 million or $1.25x$. Therefore, a business with relative market share greater than $1.0x$ must have the highest sales in the industry, and the degree to which its relative market share exceeds $1.0x$ indicates how much higher its sales are than the number two business.

Many strategists use relative market share as an indicator of how strong a business is relative to competition. Although the calculation of relative market share involves only sales, the interpretation is often extended to profitability as well on the assumption that the bigger a business, the lower its RELATIVE COSTS and the higher its relative profits. This assumption is defended by appealing to the importance of the CUMULATIVE EXPERIENCE and ECONOMIES OF SCALE that the largest business enjoys.

However, associations between profits and relative market share must be made with care. For example, a business with a small relative market share in a relatively HIGH-COST POSITION may command a much higher price than its high-share, low-cost competitor. The higher price may allow the small-share business more profit than the large-share business. The determination of whether or not a high relative market share is profitable depends on INDUSTRY STRUCTURE. Nevertheless, assessing a business's COMPETITIVE POSITION in an industry is very difficult, and any measure such as relative market share that can be quantified is useful.

Relative Price: describes the relationship between the price charged by a business and the prices charged for competing products. The relationship is quantified by using a RELATIVE PRICE RATIO. Businesses with low relative prices have relative price ratios of less than 1.0, and those with high relative prices have ratios of greater than 1.0.

In most industries, maintaining a low RELATIVE PRICE requires a COST LEADERSHIP STRATEGY. A business following an EXPERIENCE-BASED PRICING policy may also be able to maintain a low RELATIVE PRICE. In some industries, a low RELATIVE PRICE may be difficult to maintain because competitors may follow a price cut and bring the business's RELATIVE PRICE RATIO back to 1.0. For example, if the buyers are very price-sensitive, many of them may buy from the low-price competitor, sharply reducing volume for the other competitors. This could leave those competitors with no choice but to cut their prices as well to prevent loss of MARKET SHARE. This kind of PRICE COMPETITION can lower the profitability of the industry as well as cause some competitors to EXIT.

In most industries, maintaining a high RELATIVE PRICE requires either a DIFFERENTIATION STRATEGY or a FOCUS STRATEGY. PRICE LEADERS very often maintain a slightly higher RELATIVE PRICE, especially during periods of low industry CAPACITY UTILIZATION. This usually results in a loss of share that the PRICE LEADER expects to regain when industry sales increase and is done to mitigate price RIVALRY by buffering the effect of a downturn on competitors. Although strategists recognize that a high RELATIVE PRICE may allow a business to increase its returns in the short term, most point out that unless the business has differentiated its product or enjoys the protection of ENTRY BARRIERS, a high RELATIVE PRICE may also provide a PRICE UMBRELLA that attracts new competitors and leads to decreased profitability in the long term.

Relative Price Ratio: the price of the business's product divided by the average price of its competitors' comparable products. RELATIVE PRICE RATIOS are used to quantify a business's PRICE POLICY relative to that of its competitors. If the ratio is greater than 1.0, the business has a high RELATIVE PRICE. If the ratio is less than 1.0, the business has a low RELATIVE PRICE, and if the ratio equals 1.0, the business's product is priced at the average for the industry. Sometimes RELATIVE PRICE RATIOS are measured with respect to the prices of the competitor with the highest MARKET SHARE. RELATIVE PRICE RATIOS can be calculated for individual products, for product lines, for businesses, and even for an entire company.

Strategists often look for trends in RELATIVE PRICE RATIOS within the portfolio of their own businesses as well as within the portfolios of competitors to identify trends and changes in pricing policy. BUBBLE CHARTS are frequently drawn of RELATIVE PRICE versus RELATIVE MARKET SHARE or some other discriminant.

Replacement Sales: *see* SATURATION.

Replacement Value: a value placed on an asset that is equal to the current MARKET PRICE of a comparable asset. The REPLACEMENT VALUE of an asset can be very different from the value based on the historical cost at which it is carried on a balance sheet. For example, a plant built ten years ago might have cost $25,000. Today it might cost $125,000 to build a plant of similar CAPACITY requiring a similar amount of maintenance and operating at a similar level of VARIABLE COSTS per unit. The REPLACEMENT VALUE of the asset would therefore be $125,000 even though the asset cost only $25,000 when it was bought. REPLACEMENT VALUE can also be below original cost. For example, the REPLACEMENT VALUE of a ten-year-old electronic calculator is probably less than its cost.

Required Return: the return on an investment that must be offered or expected in order to induce a given investor to undertake a particular investment. For example, REQUIRED RETURNS for corporations are often measured in terms of RETURN ON EQUITY, and REQUIRED RETURNS from businesses within corporations are often measured in terms of RETURN ON INVESTMENT. The level of the RE-QUIRED RETURN is often related to the OPPORTUNITY COST facing the investor.

One drawback to using a method such as BREAK-EVEN ANALYSIS to measure the payback period or additional sales required to recoup an investment is that the method implies a REQUIRED RETURN of zero. It is important to remember that funds are not free and that the cost of debt and the COST OF EQUITY must be accounted for when evaluating investment decisions.

Resource Allocation: the process by which a company decides how to distribute its resources among alternative uses. Although, in fact, this process applies to all RESOURCES, it is usually discussed as if only financial RESOURCES are involved.

The traditional approach to RESOURCE ALLOCATION assumes that all cash generated by the operations of the company's businesses belongs to the company and that the company has the right to allocate those RESOURCES among existing businesses and new businesses as it sees fit. The company decides how to allocate those resources by asking all its businesses to propose investments and to include in those proposals the expected future CASH FLOWS. The company calculates the PRESENT VALUE of those CASH FLOWS and ranks the investments by PRESENT VALUE. Then the company allocates its cash to those investments that have the highest PRESENT VALUE. The company keeps working down its list of investments until it has committed all the cash intended. If the company runs out of investments with positive CASH FLOW before it has allocated all its cash, the company looks for new businesses to invest in or returns that cash to its shareholders in the form of dividends.

Some strategists are very comfortable with this traditional approach. Others feel that it ignores a number of realities. For example, they argue that any group of managers can put together a proposal that will show a positive PRESENT VALUE. If those managers know beforehand what the cutoff level of PRESENT VALUE is going to be to get funded, they can probably come up with a proposal that shows at least that level of PRESENT VALUE. Also, those strategists argue that two investments may have the same PRESENT VALUE but that one may be much more risky than another. In support of this, they offer the following rule of thumb statistics on four types of investments and the probability of accurately forecasting the CASH FLOW:

Type of Investment Proposal	Probability of Forecast Accuracy
Invest to reduce costs in an existing business	100%
Invest to expand sales of an existing product	50%
Invest in developing and selling a new product	10%
Invest in acquiring a new business	5%

To compensate for the uncertainty of the FORECASTS, some strategists support a modified version of the traditional approach and adjust the discount rates for each investment to reflect the RISK involved in that investment.

Strategists who disagree with that approach argue that it assumes that the investments are independent of one another when, in fact, the nature of STRATEGIC LEVERAGE is to make investments that support and enhance one another. They point out that, in working its way down a list of internal investments using the traditional approach, a company is likely to miss more profitable opportunities to invest in new businesses. These strategists feel that RESOURCE ALLOCATION is the key to how a company creates ECONOMIC VALUE and is basic to the company's CONCEPT OF MANAGEMENT. Therefore, resources must be allocated within the context of the company's CORPORATE STRATEGY. They argue this may even require allocating cash to an investment that shows a negative PRESENT VALUE when analyzed independently.

Resources: inputs that are available for use. Economists group RESOURCES into four categories. The first is land, which includes all items that are provided by nature. The second is labor, which includes all efforts by humans, whether manual or mental. The third is capital, which includes everything that is made by humans to help them with their productive efforts. The fourth is entrepreneurial ability. This is a combination of innovativeness, risk-taking, need-analyzing, and other abilities that put life into an otherwise lifeless collection of land, labor, and capital and create ECONOMIC VALUE.

Many strategists feel that guiding the allocation of these RESOURCES among the businesses in a company is the key function of a CORPORATE STRATEGY.

Retaliation: *see* EXPECTED RETALIATION.

Return on Equity: a measure of how much a company has earned on the money invested by the shareholders. RETURN ON EQUITY is calculated by taking the ratio of net income to total shareholders' equity. Net income is defined as profits after interest expense and taxes, and total shareholders' equity includes capital stock and retained earnings. This ratio is one measure used by present or prospective investors to determine the profitability of the company and, therefore, the attractiveness of the investment. RETURN ON EQUITY is often abbreviated as ROE.

Return on Investment (ROI):   the ratio of income before taxes to the sum of net FIXED CAPITAL and net WORKING CAPITAL. ROI is often used by companies to evaluate BUSINESS UNIT performance and is considered, with variations, to be the standard PERFORMANCE MEASURE.

The reason ROI is considered a good measure of profitability for business units is that it focuses management's attention on managing the business's assets so as to yield a good return. The RETURN ON INVESTMENT ratio is often decomposed to highlight the different factors which combine to determine overall profitability. For example, ROI can be broken down as follows.

$$\frac{Return}{Sales} \times \frac{sales}{investment} = \frac{return}{investment}$$

The ratio of return to sales focuses attention on cost control and PRICE POLICY whereas the ratio of sales to investment focuses management attention on generating more sales per dollar of investment. Some companies also adjust the ROI of each business for RISK in order to focus management attention on the COST OF CAPITAL involved.

Criticisms of ROI as a single performance measure revolve around the assertion that it encourages managers to adopt a short-term perspective and may indeed encourage managers to HARVEST a business. This is because one of the easiest ways to increase ROI is to reduce the investment. By cutting back on new equipment or reducing inventory levels, a manager may well improve ROI in the short term only to undermine the long-term COMPETITIVE POSITION of the business.

Return on Sales: *see* RETURN ON INVESTMENT (ROI).

Revenue Center: an entity in a company's ORGANIZATIONAL HIER-ARCHY for which the company's MEASUREMENT SYSTEM measures the revenues generated by the entity's activity. The manager of a REV-ENUE CENTER generally has little or no control over costs or pricing. For example, a sales department whose manager is responsible for meeting or exceeding a sales goal without spending more than the department's budget for expenses would most likely be a REVENUE CENTER.

REVENUE CENTERS are usually part of a PROFIT CENTER or an INVESTMENT CENTER.

Risk: the probability of suffering damage or loss. More formally, RISK refers to the variability of an expected outcome. In the case of investors in companies, RISK is the probability that either the company will be unable to meet its financial obligations when due or demanded and the RISK that the CAPITAL MARKETS will adversely affect the value of the security.

The RISK attached to an investment in a given company reflects the net RISK of all the company's operations combined. But it is not equal to the sum of the risks because some RISKS offset one another. Theorists often divide a security's risk into SYSTEMATIC RISK and UN-SYSTEMATIC RISK depending on the source.

Because the perceived RISK involved in investing in a company affects the company's COST OF CAPITAL, RISK is an important factor in creating ECONOMIC VALUE. Therefore, strategists are concerned with the amount of RISK their companies are exposed to. Strategists must often try to mitigate RISK when formulating a CONCEPT OF FIT for a company's portfolio of businesses and when developing COM-PETITIVE STRATEGIES to protect the profitability of each business in the portfolio.

Risk Aversion: the degree to which an individual prefers a given return with complete certainty over a higher return with some RISK. Most individuals are assumed to be risk-averse. Therefore, in order to get individuals to put their money at RISK in an investment, one must promise them a RISK PREMIUM or reward in the form of a higher expected return.

Individuals or companies with a higher than average degree of RISK AVERSION can be expected to earn lower than average returns in the long term. This is because their RISK AVERSION will lead them to reject consistently investments that promise above-average returns for undertaking above-average RISK. Instead, those investments will be made by less risk-averse companies requiring a lower RISK PREMIUM.

Strategists have to take into consideration the RISK AVERSION of the individuals involved in formulating CORPORATE STRATEGY, especially as it relates to ACQUISITION and DIVESTMENT, and in formulating COMPETITIVE STRATEGIES, especially if they involve BUILD PLANS. The RISK AVERSION of corporate managers whose wealth depends heavily on the performance of their companies may differ from the RISK AVERSION of the company's financial investors who can diversify.

Risk-Free: *see* CAPITAL ASSET PRICING MODEL.

Risk Premium: an additional return on an investment that is offered to induce individuals or companies to put their money at RISK. The RISK PREMIUM of a given investment is usually measured by taking the promised return on that investment and subtracting the expected return on a risk-free investment. The difference is that investment's RISK PREMIUM. The expected return on a risk-free investment is often approximated by the return on U.S. government securities.

Rivalry: the pattern and intensity of competitive interaction among the businesses in an industry. RIVALRY is one of the five COMPETITIVE FORCES that determines the level and variance of profitability among industries. RIVALRY stems from the interdependence of the businesses in an industry. If one competitor's profits are highly sensitive to another's actions, RIVALRY will be higher than in an industry where competitors are more isolated from one another. Cycles of competitive moves and countermoves can be set off by actions taken by competitors to increase either their level of RETURN ON INVESTMENT or the scale of their investment. Several STRUCTURAL FACTORS have a particularly strong impact on industry RIVALRY. These include INDUSTRY CONCENTRATION, growth, COST STRUCTURE, DIVERSE COMPETITORS, and EXIT BARRIERS.

INDUSTRY CONCENTRATION tends to reduce RIVALRY, especially if there is a lack of SHARE BALANCE among the competitors and one is obviously the DOMINANT FIRM. In such industries, the competitors are likely to be familiar with one another, and the DOMINANT FIRM is likely to have the power to hold down RIVALRY. On the other hand, SHARE BALANCE in the industry may increase RIVALRY if all competitors perceive that they have similar strengths and may have equal chances to become the DOMINANT FIRM in the industry. Also, a low CONCENTRATION RATIO may foster certain patterns of RIVALRY because competitors may not be as aware of their mutual dependence.

In general, industry growth which is faster than expected tends to decrease RIVALRY, and slow industry growth tends to increase it. This is because fast growth reduces mutual dependence and slow growth increases it.

Industries in which many of the competitors have a high FIXED-TO-VALUE ADDED RATIO have the potential for a high level of RIVALRY. When capacity is underutilized, high FIXED COSTS can create pressure to cut prices in order to increase volume to cover those FIXED COSTS. The lower the level of industry CAPACITY UTILIZATION, the higher the pressure is likely to be. An industry where there is INTERMITTENT OVERCAPACITY is likely to have a high level of RIVALRY.

DIVERSE COMPETITORS can increase the potential for RIVALRY by making it more difficult for the competitors to understand one another. In the same way, CORPORATE STAKES can affect RIVALRY by making one business more aggressive than its competitors would expect because of the stakes its parent happens to have in that business. If more than one competitor has a parent company placing high CORPORATE STAKES on it, RIVALRY will be even higher.

EXIT BARRIERS increase RIVALRY by keeping businesses that would otherwise leave in the industry.

The presence of PRODUCT DIFFERENCES, BRAND IDENTIFICATION, and SWITCHING COSTS in an industry can reduce RIVALRY by binding the buyer to a particular competitor and stabilizing MARKET SHARES. As INDUSTRY STRUCTURES evolve and STRUCTURAL FACTORS change, rivalry also changes. Therefore, many strategists try to anticipate increases and decreases in rivalry and try to take advantage of that insight. Of the five COMPETITIVE FORCES, most strategists feel that rivalry is the one that requires the most monitoring and controlling. Rivalry is usually controlled by looking for TACTICS other than PRICE COMPETITION, such as exploiting MIXED MOTIVES and BLIND SPOTS, which are less damaging to industry profitability.

ROI/Cash Flow Matrix: one of a number of charts that is used to analyze a portfolio of businesses. This matrix is often used to show

how a company has been allocating its cash and to compare the business plan of each of the businesses in a portfolio with the plans prescribed for each cell. The matrix is usually drawn as follows.

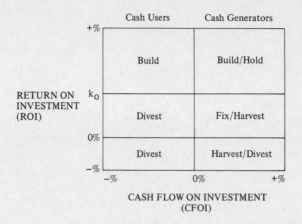

Businesses in the portfolio are located on the matrix on the basis of their RETURN ON INVESTMENT and their cash flow on investment. Cash flow on investment is calculated by dividing the amount of cash the business contributes to the company by the amount of investment the company has in the business. A business that is a CASH GENERATOR shows a positive cash flow on investment. A business that is a CASH USER has a negative amount of cash contributed to the company in the numerator and, therefore, a CFOI of less than 0 percent.

The matrix indicates that any cash user that is earning an ROI greater than the company's COST OF CAPITAL (k_o) should follow a BUILD PLAN and that more of the company's capital should be invested in those businesses. Businesses that are currently CASH GENERATORS and earning an ROI above the company's k_o are either not carrying out a sufficiently aggressive BUILD PLAN or they are at a point where they cannot profitably use any more investment and a HOLD PLAN is appropriate.

Any business earning less than the company's COST OF CAPITAL and continuing to use cash should probably be DIVESTED unless analysis shows that there is strong likelihood that a BUILD PLAN could bring its returns above the COST OF CAPITAL. A business earning a negative ROI and continuing to use cash requires the closest look of all. Again, without an assured near-term improvement, the business should be DIVESTED.

The matrix provides more options for businesses with low returns that are CASH GENERATORS. Businesses that have a positive ROI are given a choice between a FIX PLAN or a HARVEST PLAN to improve the business's profitability. Businesses that are earning a negative ROI are given a choice between improvement with a HARVEST PLAN or DIVESTMENT.

A basic premise of the recommendations of the matrix is the importance placed on the balance of CASH FLOW in a company's portfolio. Not all strategists place the same emphasis on preserving sources of internally generated funds.

ROI/Market Share Corridor: a chart that is used to show the degree of correlation between a given business's profitability and its MARKET SHARE. In the sample chart that follows, five competitors are plotted on the basis of their RETURN ON INVESTMENT and MARKET SHARE.

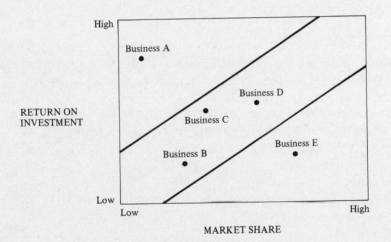

Strategists tend to use the chart to test for a relationship between ROI and MARKET SHARE and to generate discussion about the basis for that relationship in the industry. INTRA-INDUSTRY STRUCTURE is an important determinant of the degree of correlation as well as the number and success of the GENERIC STRATEGIES which are being followed.

Although the different levels of ROI found in different industries can undermine the comparisons, ROI/MARKET SHARE CORRIDORS are sometimes used to analyze the businesses within a company's portfolio, especially companies with strong FORMULA FIT.

S

Saturation: occurs when the needs of a MARKET SEGMENT or BUYER GROUP are satisfied. Saturation is reached when DEMAND for a product, usually a durable good, becomes quite price-inelastic after a certain number of units are purchased. At that point, most of the future sales of that product will be replacement sales. For example, almost 100 percent of all households in the United States have a refrigerator. Therefore, most new sales of refrigerators are replacement sales.

Strategists use TACTICS like SKIM PRICING, PLANNED OBSOLESCENCE, and TRADING UP, to resist SATURATION.

SBU: *see* STRATEGIC BUSINESS UNIT.

Scale Effects: reductions in UNIT COSTS that result from increasing the SCALE OF OPERATIONS of a function, a plant, a business, or an entire company. This phenomenon is called ECONOMIES OF SCALE.

Scale of Operation: the level of activity or output at which a business is operating in a given time period. For example, a business that has produced 5,000 units over the last five years in equal amounts per year has had a SCALE OF OPERATIONS of 1,000 units per year.

Although SCALE OF OPERATIONS usually refers to the business level where it is equal to the business's INTER-PLANT SCALE, it can also be used to describe a company. A company's SCALE OF OPERATIONS is equal to the sum of the operations of each of its businesses. However, for a diversified company, there may be no consistent basis for calculating an overall figure.

The SCALE OF OPERATIONS at an individual plant level is called INTRA-PLANT SCALE.

Scenario: a description of the future competitive environment of a business based on a selected combination of ASSUMPTIONS and FORECASTS about future events. Strategists develop SCENARIOS in order to identify and anticipate emerging or potential competitive threats and to stimulate thinking and discussion about STRATEGY.

The FORECASTS and ASSUMPTIONS on which a useful scenario is built must be internally consistent. In addition, they must deal with each of the factors that can have an impact on the profitability of the business, most of which cannot be controlled by the business. Usually, a strategist will vary the underlying ASSUMPTIONS and generate a set of SCENARIOS. Each scenario has a different outlook for the business, ranging from pessimistic to optimistic. The scenario based on the most likely set of ASSUMPTIONS and FORECASTS usually provides the foundation for devising a business's strategy whereas the optimistic and pessimistic SCENARIOS help the strategist to identify the factors which are likely to have the greatest impact on the future performance of the business. Some strategists use an IMPORTANCE/CONTROL GRID to identify the key events around which SCENARIOS should be built for a given business.

Scientific Management: a concept of management as a science with clearly defined principles, the application of which leads to high performance. The objective of SCIENTIFIC MANAGEMENT is the maximum prosperity for the employer together with maximum prosperity for the employee. Maximum prosperity for the employer was defined as ECONOMIC VALUE for the shareholders and the achievement of outstanding efficiency relative to competitors in order to sustain that value. Maximum prosperity for the employees was defined as higher compensation than competitors are paying and maximum efficiency to allow the highest grade of work, constrained only by the employees' abilities. SCIENTIFIC MANAGEMENT was based on the conviction that the interests of employee and employer were symbiotic and not antagonistic as commonly thought. The argument was that the interests had to be one and the same because the employer cannot exist over the long term unless its employees prosper and vice versa. Accordingly, the key to being able to pay more than competitors and still earn higher returns was PRODUCTIVITY.

Many strategists see the concept of SCIENTIFIC MANAGEMENT as the precursor of such current concepts as the EXPERIENCE CURVE and the COST LEADERSHIP STRATEGY.

Scope: *see* COMPETITIVE SCOPE.

Scope Grid: a matrix that contrasts any two of the four dimensions of COMPETITIVE SCOPE. For example, the range of VERTICAL INTEGRATION can be contrasted with degree of geographic scope.

The cells in a scope grid can be filled in to show the positions of competitors or the costs and benefits of each combination.

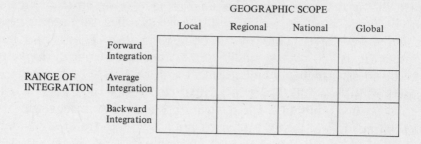

| | GEOGRAPHIC SCOPE | | | |
	Local	Regional	National	Global
RANGE OF INTEGRATION — Forward Integration				
Average Integration				
Backward Integration				

Screening: *see* ACQUISITION SCREENING.

Sector: a group of related industries or a major segment of an economy, such as an industrial sector, a government sector, or a private sector. In planning, a SECTOR is a level in the PLANNING HIERARCHY located between the corporate and the business levels and consists of groups of businesses. A SECTOR is a relatively new level in PLANNING HIERARCHIES, and strategists differ on the purpose and composition of a sector.

Some strategists form SECTORS on the basis of macro-industry classification. For example, a company might have an INDUSTRIAL GOODS sector and a CONSUMER GOODS sector. Managers at the sector level take an intermediate perspective. They review and augment the business's industry perspective before COMPETITIVE STRATEGIES are presented at the corporate level.

Some strategists feel that SECTORS should act as subcorporations with their own portfolio of businesses. The only rule for defining SECTOR is that every effort should be made to prevent one SECTOR from containing a business that is related to a business in another SECTOR. The corporate level would then invest, for its shareholders, in each of its SECTORS. The SECTOR would be responsible for RESOURCE ALLOCATION and for managing its own portfolio of businesses. Strategists who are uncomfortable with the role for the SECTOR argue that the company's RISK of suboptimization is too great. To counter this, other strategists have tried allocating debt and equity to the SECTOR'S portfolio.

A new role for the SECTOR that some strategists favor is as a combination of businesses with the same GENERIC STRATEGY. The SECTOR is then responsible for creating STRATEGIC LEVERAGE through FORMULA FIT and for developing an ORGANIZATIONAL STRUCTURE that supports the effective formulation and implementation of that GENERIC STRATEGY in each of its businesses. This role has developed as strategists have recognized that most companies have a hard time developing a CONCEPT OF MANAGEMENT that allows them to be effective at more than one GENERIC STRATEGY.

Segmentation: the process of dividing a company into BUSINESS UNITS with meaningfully identifiable competitors, suppliers, buyers, and substitutes. A BUSINESS UNIT is the basic entity for which a COMPETITIVE STRATEGY is developed and around which a PLANNING HIERARCHY is organized. The company's approach to STRATEGIC PLANNING determines how it is segmented, and competitors may segment their companies differently. These different approaches to SEGMENTATION shape the competitors' perceptions of the competitive environment and can either reveal or obscure OPPORTUNITIES and THREATS in the industry. Therefore, different approaches to SEGMENTATION lead to different strategies.

MARKET SEGMENTATION refers to the division of the potential purchasers of a product into BUYER GROUPS.

Segment Scope: *see* COMPETITIVE SCOPE.

Segment Spillover: occurs when buyers in one MARKET SEGMENT become aware of and demand the same VALUE that buyers in another market segment are getting. This can happen because one or more competitors have businesses in more than one MARKET SEGMENT or because UNCERTAINTY REDUCTION has otherwise occurred. Competitors in more than one segment are most likely to be subject to the effects of spillover, but it can also affect businesses with FOCUSED STRATEGIES whose competitors may be encouraging it.

Selective Demand: the DEMAND for a specific competitor's product as opposed to the DEMAND for that type of product. For example, in a given industry, the SELECTIVE DEMAND for the DOMINANT FIRM'S product is usually higher than the SELECTIVE DEMAND for any of its competitor's products.

Sensitivity Analysis: the process of testing a FORECAST to assess the impact of changes in the underlying ASSUMPTIONS on the accuracy of the FORECAST.

Take, for example, a forecast of $1 million in net income that may be sensitive to changes in the assumed inflation rate. The SENSITIVITY ANALYSIS might begin with an estimate of how far off the inflation rate assumption is likely to be, say, that inflation might be as low as 5 percent and as high as 15 percent. The proportional difference between the net income forecasts based on the inflation assumptions of 5 percent and 15 percent and the net income forecast based on the most likely assumption of 10 percent would indicate the degree of sensitivity. If the difference is too small or insignificant to change any decisions, the net income forecast is considered "robust" and not sensitive to changes in the inflation ASSUMPTION.

Because both ALTERNATIVE PLANS and SCENARIOS are based on FORECASTS, most strategists use SENSITIVITY ANALYSIS to evaluate both. At the very least, they do a simple SENSITIVITY ANALYSIS of any disputable ASSUMPTION underpinning a forecast and develop a ranking of the ASSUMPTIONS that are the most significant. That list, in turn, can be monitored during implementation of any strategy based on the FORECAST.

In applying probabilities to the range of assumed outcomes and using additional statistical methods, the process of SENSITIVITY ANALYSIS can become more sophisticated and complex.

Sequenced Strategy: a STRATEGY that begins with a narrow enough COMPETITIVE SCOPE to establish a STRATEGIC BEACHHEAD and then expands the scope. There are two common types of sequenced strategy: sequenced ENTRY and a sequenced OFFENSIVE STRATEGY. The two are often combined.

A sequenced ENTRY strategy often involves an initial ENTRY into one STRATEGIC GROUP and then overcoming MOBILITY BARRIERS to move to the subsequent groups.

A sequenced OFFENSIVE STRATEGY often involves CHERRY PICKING a product or MARKET SEGMENT with a FOCUS STRATEGY and then expanding COMPETITIVE SCOPE until segment scope is industrywide.

Strategists who favor SEQUENCED STRATEGIES feel that they lower the risk of retaliation, put less up-front investment at risk, and are less expensive than a full-blown attack even when the plan is to abandon the original beachhead once the desired STRATEGIC GROUP is reached.

Strategists who are uncomfortable with sequenced strategies feel that they make retaliation easier and that even when incumbents choose not to retaliate, the incumbent has time to build BLOCKING POSITIONS that are likely to hinder expansion. Furthermore, they argue that although the up-front investment may be lower, the beachhead may suffer from the lack of a full strategy, the latter being the optimal choice for building COMPETITIVE ADVANTAGE.

Served Market: the portion of the total potential market that a business serves. It is the particular combination of BUYER GROUPS to which the business promotes its products and for which the business designs its products. For example, the SERVED MARKET of a roofing shingle manufacturer might lie in the northeast region of the United States. In serving its market, the manufacturer would make its shingle in the specific weight and colors that are considered desirable in the northeast and would advertise in media that reach buyers located in the northeast.

A business's SERVED MARKET is often used as the denominator in calculating MARKET SHARE.

Seven-S Framework: a framework for understanding the options in changing an organization. The seven S's are divided into three "hard S's": strategy, structure, and systems; and four "soft S's": skills, staff, style of management, and shared values. Accordingly, the "Hard S's" are the most likely areas for strategists to attempt change in because they appear more susceptible to analysis. However, actual change may well be implemented much more effectively through the "soft S's." Therefore, effective change requires managers who are comfortable with all seven dimensions.

Strategists who use the SEVEN-S FRAMEWORK point to the importance of CORPORATE CULTURE and MARKET SIGNALS in effecting implementation.

Share Balance: the degree of equality in MARKET SHARES of the significant competitors in an industry. Shares are considered in balance if competitors have RELATIVE MARKET SHARES of approximately $1.0x$. The question of SHARE BALANCE is important in analyzing OLIGOPOLIES. Balance in MARKET SHARE tends to increase RIVALRY in an industry. In general, for tempering RIVALRY there has to be sufficient imbalance in shares to allow one business to take a leadership position as the DOMINANT FIRM or the PRICE LEADER.

Strategists usually consider it advantageous to push for SHARE BALANCE in adjacent industries. For example, SUPPLIER POWER may be mitigated by SHARE BALANCE in supplier industries. Buyers will often try to preserve that balance by distributing their purchases so as to prevent any one supplier from becoming disproportionately large. Businesses may also try to preserve SHARE BALANCE in their buyers, but the advantages and TACTICS are less obvious.

Shared Cost: a cost incurred by a FUNCTIONAL AREA that serves two or more businesses in a company's portfolio. For example, the cost of a sales force that is used for more than one business is a SHARED COST as is the cost of shared production facilities, etc.

Sometimes costs that are shared by two or more products within a business are also called SHARED COSTS. Economists refer to SHARED COSTS as joint costs. SHARED COSTS make the MARGINAL COST of one business dependent on the operating scale of another.

SHARED EXPERIENCE may translate into declining SHARED COSTS, and the businesses may benefit from ECONOMIES OF SCALE as well. However, SHARED COSTS can cause problems for a company if one business is in trouble or is being divested.

Shared Experience: the proficiency and competency gained and enjoyed by two or more businesses in a company which produce a product or perform a function jointly. For example, a company that makes air conditioning units and heating units that incorporate the same basic electric motor has the potential for developing SHARED

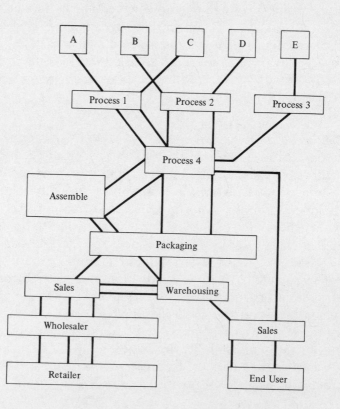

EXPERIENCE in making the motor. By consolidating its motor manufacturing function, it can accelerate its CUMULATIVE EXPERIENCE in
that function beyond that of a company making air conditioning or
heating units on a similar scale. Although the example points to the
manufacturing function, SHARED EXPERIENCE can be developed at
any point in a product's VALUE ADDED CHAIN.

Strategists often diagram a business or company to reveal potential for SHARED EXPERIENCE. In the diagram on page 300, the
business that makes products A, B, C, D, and E may gain significant
SHARED EXPERIENCE in process 4 and in packaging.

Strategists use and develop opportunities for SHARED EXPERI-
ENCE in order to take advantage of FUNCTIONAL FIT in a CORPORATE
STRATEGY.

Shared Experience Matrix: a matrix showing the potential COST AD-
VANTAGE of SHARED EXPERIENCE by comparing the relative cost of
an activity with the potential cost for reduction. RELATIVE COSTS are
determined as the cost of the activity as a percent of total relevant
UNIT COSTS or assets of the business or company. Potential for cost
reduction is measured by the activity's sensitivity to ECONOMIES OF
SCALE, LEARNING, or utilization. The following is a simple SHARED
EXPERIENCE MATRIX.

SENSITIVITY OF THE ACTIVITY
TO SCALE, LEARNING, OR UTILIZATION

	Low	High
High	Potentially important if sensitivity changes	Important activity for shared experience
Low	Unimportant activity for shared experience	Potentially important if cost structure changes

ACTIVITY
COST AS A
PERCENTAGE
OF UNIT COSTS
OR ASSETS

SHARED EXPERIENCE MATRICES are often used to evaluate which
activities in a business's VALUE CHAIN should be exploited with a
HORIZONTAL STRATEGY.

Shareholder Wealth: *see* ECONOMIC VALUE.

Share of Voice: a measure of the relative amount of information one competitor is providing to the buyers in its industry. SHARE OF VOICE is usually calculated by dividing the amount a business is spending on informing buyers about its products by the sum of all similar expenditures of all competitors in the industry. For example, if Business A spends $1 million per year on advertising and Business A's competitors spend a total of $3 million more, then Business A has a 25 percent SHARE OF VOICE. SHARE OF VOICE can be measured for a specific brand, for a type of product, for a business, or even for a company. Also, the numerator and denominator in the SHARE OF VOICE calculation can include specific types of information related expenditures, such as media advertising, point of purchase merchandising, or the entire marketing budget.

Relative SHARE OF VOICE can also be calculated in the same way RELATIVE MARKET SHARE is calculated. That is, a given business's SHARE OF VOICE is divided by the largest SHARE OF VOICE in the industry.

Many strategists find it useful to make comparisons between SHARE OF VOICE data and MARKET SHARE data. A BUILD PLAN usually calls for an increase in SHARE OF VOICE to lead an increase in MARKET SHARE.

Shopping Goods: *see* CONSUMER GOOD.

Shrinkage Barrier: a characteristic of a STRATEGY that raises the cost of narrowing COMPETITIVE SCOPE or otherwise cutting back output or disposing of excess capacity. SHRINKAGE BARRIERS can arise from both COMPETITIVE STRATEGIES and CORPORATE STRATEGIES. They result when the performance of a business or company is tied to its current COMPETITIVE SCOPE or from emotional responses. For example, a business may have LINKAGES across market segments that give it COMPETITIVE ADVANTAGES, or a company's BUSINESS INTER-RELATIONSHIPS may make those businesses dependent on one another for COMPETITIVE ADVANTAGE. Reluctance to idle SPECIALIZED ASSETS or resistance to giving up a skilled work force are two examples of emotional SHRINKAGE BARRIERS.

SHRINKAGE BARRIERS may make it hard to develop an effective EXIT or END GAME STRATEGY. SHRINKAGE BARRIERS may also increase the likelihood of retaliation when faced with an OFFENSIVE STRATEGY.

SIC Code: *see* STANDARD INDUSTRIAL CLASSIFICATION.

Signaling: *see* MARKET SIGNAL.

Signal of Value: *see* VALUE SIGNAL.

Skim Pricing: a policy establishing the current prices of a product at a level that is significantly higher than the expected EQUILIBRIUM PRICE. SKIM PRICING is usually done to take advantage of current ENTRY and MOBILITY BARRIERS. For example, a pharmaceutical business that has recently spent heavily on R&D to develop a new product may use a SKIM PRICING policy to recoup that investment and to earn high returns until its competitors are able to match the product. Skimming can also be used initially to serve a less price-sensitive MARKET SEGMENT. For example, publishers often introduce a new book in an expensive hardcover edition to earn high margins from the less price-sensitive readers before publishing the cheaper paperback edition.

The RISK of SKIM PRICING is that the high initial price may attract competitors who might not otherwise be interested if they were aware of the expected long-run EQUILIBRIUM PRICE. Over the long term these additional competitors may increase the RIVALRY in the industry, offsetting whatever returns a business might have gained as a result of its initial high price.

PENETRATION PRICING is the opposite of SKIM PRICING.

Social Trends: *see* ENVIRONMENTAL SCANNING.

Specialized Asset: an asset that is specific to a given product or a given process. Usually SPECIALIZED ASSETS, such as plants, equipment, raw materials, or work in process inventories, cannot be used for another product or process without a significant amount of investment in modification.

Businesses often develop SPECIALIZED ASSETS as a result of following a COST LEADERSHIP STRATEGY or as a result of following a MANUFACTURING POLICY based on the FOCUSED FACTORY concept.

Because specialized assets can give rise to EXIT BARRIERS, strategists like to be aware of the degree to which their businesses are acquiring them. Specialized assets can also become a SHRINKAGE BARRIER by precluding alternative uses for excess CAPACITY. Strategists like to be aware of the extent of their competitors' specialized assets as well.

Specialized Competition: *see* POTENTIAL ADVANTAGE MATRIX.

Specialty Imperative: *see* COMMODITY SPECIALTY MATRIX.

Specialty Product: a product for which a buyer is willing to spend extra time or extra money to buy a particular brand over a competitor's more readily available or less expensive brand.

Specific Foe: the competitor against which a given business directs its STRATEGY. Sometimes a business can select a competitor as its SPECIFIC FOE, and sometimes a SPECIFIC FOE is simply the competitor that presents the greatest threat to the business.

Strategists who are comfortable with the concept of a SPECIFIC FOE feel that it avoids the confusion of worrying about all of a business's competitors and focuses attention on the most important one.

Strategists who are uncomfortable with the concept of a SPECIFIC FOE argue that most of their businesses tend to focus on a single competitor already and that regardless of whether that competitor is the correct choice of SPECIFIC FOE, an important job for the strategist is to get managers to think in terms of the RIVALRY in their industries. That implies understanding the dynamics of all competitors.

Spillover: *see* SEGMENT SPILLOVER.

Stability: *see* INDUSTRY STABILITY.

Stalemated Industry: an industry in which no one competitor seems to be any better off than the others. Industries become stalemated when no one competitor has devised a way to achieve a sufficient COMPETITIVE ADVANTAGE to carry out a GENERIC STRATEGY effectively. Perhaps no competitor has developed enough PRODUCT DIFFERENTIATION to pursue a DIFFERENTIATION STRATEGY, or competitors have been unable to keep experience proprietary. MINIMUM EFFICIENT SCALE may imply such a small MARKET SHARE that it is impossible to achieve a COST LEADERSHIP STRATEGY. There may be no targetable BUYER GROUPS.

Some strategists think that some industries are inherently stalemated and will never be otherwise. Other strategists feel that EVOLUTIONARY PROCESSES and insight on the part of competitors can break any stalemate such that at least one GENERIC STRATEGY can be effective.

Standard Cost: the expected cost of a product at a given level of production and under an assumed set of circumstances. The STANDARD COST of a product is established on the basis of past experience or research and includes the following elements: direct material; direct labor; manufacturing expenses; and, in some cases, selling and administrative expenses.

STANDARD COSTS are a basic element of a company's cost control system. Management compares actual costs with STANDARD COSTS, notes the variances in costs, determines their causes, and looks for ways to lower the STANDARD COSTS. For example, if actual labor costs for certain operations are substantially higher than the standard labor costs, the increase is investigated to determine why they are higher. The study of the differences between standard and actual costs is called variance analysis.

In some companies, variances become the profits and losses imputed to internal operations. Take, for example, a company in which $10 is set as the STANDARD COST for a unit of raw material. If the material is subsequently purchased at a price above or below the STANDARD COST, the difference represents a profit or loss in the company's purchasing operation. The STANDARD COST rather than the actual cost is still used to measure usage of the material by other FUNCTIONAL AREAS, so measures of their activity are not affected by purchasing's performance.

Strategists should be aware that to the extent that STANDARD COSTS are used as PERFORMANCE MEASURES, they will affect behavior. Therefore, it is important that the incentives implied in the cost system be consistent with the goals of a business's COMPETITIVE STRATEGY.

In addition to being used for cost control, STANDARD COSTS are used to develop UNIT COSTS for establishing selling prices, valuing inventories, or other purposes. The strategist should be aware of the effects of these on the MARKETING POLICY of the business, as well as on the INCENTIVE SYSTEM. Different competitors may measure STANDARD COSTS differently, and this can be expected to affect their PRICING POLICIES.

Standard Industrial Classification: the basis on which the Census Bureau provides data on industrial activity. Data is collected periodically from individual plants and aggregated into industries by assigning to each plant the SIC code of its principal product. This SIC system classifies industries on five levels of aggregation, starting with a two-digit number of the most broadly defined industry. Most strategists use data at the four-digit SIC code level for ENVIRONMENTAL SCANNING and for estimating industry size.

Star: a business in a company's portfolio that is currently making a significant positive contribution to ECONOMIC VALUE. Usually, STARS are businesses that have strong COMPETITIVE POSITIONS and are competing in attractive industries. The label is used in the GROWTH/ SHARE MATRIX to describe a business with a large MARKET SHARE in a fast-growing industry.

Start-Up Business: a new business venture, whether begun as an independent company, developed internally in an existing company, or the result of a JOINT VENTURE, etc. Start-up businesses may be pioneers in an EMERGING INDUSTRY, or they may be ENTRANTS to an existing industry.

Management of a START-UP BUSINESS presents many challenges. Managing the new business often requires learning about new products, new processes, or new buyers. A START-UP BUSINESS is also likely to incur shakedown losses before becoming profitable. The appearance of a START-UP BUSINESS in an industry can change the competitive environment. The start-up is viewed as a new entrant by incumbent competitors and as a new source of supply by potential buyers.

Strategic Beachhead: an expansion of COMPETITIVE SCOPE into a new area. Beachheads often involve ENTRY into a new industry or STRATEGIC GROUP with the intention of building significant position. A STRATEGIC BEACHHEAD is often a key element of a SEQUENCED STRATEGY.

Strategic Business Unit (SBU):   a discrete BUSINESS UNIT which has identifiable competitors, competes in an external market, includes the relevant FUNCTIONAL AREAS for integrated planning, and has an identifiable COMPETITIVE STRATEGY. An SBU can produce a number of products, use a number of processes, and sell to a number of markets.

The label is often used interchangeably with the term BUSINESS UNIT. In some companies, the label is used to emphasize an entity's position in the PLANNING HIERARCHY and to distinguish it from other organizational entities.

Strategic Competition: a mode of competition in which the competitors formulate STRATEGIES and allocate RESOURCES with an awareness of INDUSTRY STRUCTURE and competitors' activities. Change in industries with STRATEGIC COMPETITION is a result of deliberate actions taken to alter the balance of COMPETITIVE ADVANTAGE in the industry. Depending on the aggressiveness involved in the COMPETITIVE STRATEGIES pursued, STRATEGIC COMPETITION can result in dramatic changes in an industry. Businesses competing in this mode can be expected to have a long-term perspective, to be willing to accumulate capital, and to commit a significant amount of resources to risky untried investment.

NATURAL COMPETITION is the opposite of STRATEGIC COMPETITION.

Strategic Condition Matrix: one of a number of charts that are used to analyze a portfolio of businesses. The STRATEGIC CONDITION MATRIX assumes that the CASH FLOW and profitability of a business are determined by the interaction of the business's COMPETITIVE POSITION and the life cycle stage of the industry in which the business competes. Furthermore, the concept assumes that a business's position in the matrix determines the range of effective strategies available to it.

Businesses are arrayed on the matrix on the basis of their industry's maturity and their COMPETITIVE POSITION. Usually, each business is represented as a circle drawn in proportion to that business's sales.

Industry maturity is based on the life cycle stage of the industry. That stage is determined by the levels and rates of change in a number of factors. Principally, those factors are the size and growth rate

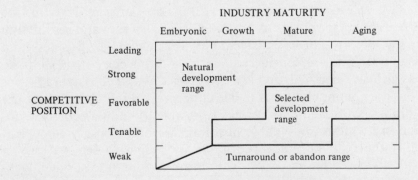

of industry sales, the breadth of the industry's product lines, the industry's degree of CONCENTRATION, the amount of buyer loyalty in the industry, SHARE BALANCE, ENTRY BARRIERS, and product and process technology. The stage of an industry's life cycle is expected to affect a business in that industry in three ways. First, the life cycle stage determines the type of STRATEGIC PLAN that is likely to be most effective for a business. For example, a BUILD PLAN is not considered appropriate in an aging industry. Second, stage affects the ability of the business to generate CASH FLOW. For example, businesses in mature stage industries are expected to generate higher CASH FLOW than businesses in embryonic stage or growth stage industries. Third, the life cycle stage is expected to determine the optimal way a business should be managed. For example, the ORGANIZATIONAL HIERARCHY of a business in a mature stage industry is likely to be different from that of a business in an embryonic stage industry.

Although the matrix does recognize that different industries move through their life cycle stages at different rates, the concept is considered applicable to any type of product in any industry. In addition, no stage is considered to be an inherently unattractive stage in which to have a business; any stage can be potentially attractive if the business's strategy and the company's expectations are appropriate.

COMPETITIVE POSITION is determined by a number of factors such as MARKET SHARE, ECONOMIES OF SCALE, technological strength, management flexibility, COST ADVANTAGES, and CAPACITY. The importance of these factors in determining COMPETITIVE POSITION varies with the life cycle stage. For example, MARKET SHARE and COST ADVANTAGES become increasingly important as the industry moves closer to its aging stage. Technological strength becomes less important at the same time.

Five categories of COMPETITIVE POSITION are employed in the matrix. Dominant positions are considered very rare and result from a monopoly or a protected technological advantage. Businesses in strong positions are considered less rare and occupy strategic positions well shielded by MOBILITY and ENTRY BARRIERS. Favorable positions are commonly found in less concentrated industries where the favorably positioned business has been able to build a protected position in its industry. Tenable positions are only considered acceptable if they can be made profitable by selling to selected BUYER GROUPS. Businesses in weak positions are too small to survive, lacking the ability or resources to serve the market, or unable to stake out a protected position.

The interaction of the life cycle stage and COMPETITIVE POSITION determines the range of strategic options available to a business. Businesses in the natural development range are considered to have a broad range of effective strategies available to them. Businesses in the selective development range are considered to have a narrower range of effective choices available to them. Businesses in the turn-around or abandon range are considered ready for either a FIX PLAN or DIVESTMENT.

The STRATEGIC CONDITION MATRIX is similar to the GROWTH/ SHARE MATRIX in that both are concerned with displaying a portfolio of businesses in terms of their expected returns. The STRATEGIC CON-DITION MATRIX is a derivative of the LIFE CYCLE MATRIX.

Strategic Diversity: the degree to which competitors in an industry have independent strategies. STRATEGIC DIVERSITY is likely to be high if TARGET MARKETS do not overlap or if PRODUCT DIFFERENTIATION can minimize the overlap and if there is a wide range of technologies and supplies available to produce the product. In general, STRATEGIC DI-VERSITY leads to low levels of RIVALRY.

STRATEGIC GROUPS are often analyzed with COMPETITOR MAPS to understand STRATEGIC DIVERSITY.

Strategic Field Map: a matrix of the relationships between products and VALUE ADDED steps that indicates the interdependencies across businesses within a company. The following is a simplified field map.

		PRODUCTS				
		Product A	Product B	Product C	Product D	Product E
	Distribution	O	X	X	X	X
	Marketing	X	X	X	O	O
VALUE ADDED STEPS	Manufacturing	O	X	X	X	O
	Raw Materials	O	X	X	O	Z
	Research & Development	X	X	X	X	X

The cells are used to indicate where BUSINESS INTERRELATION-SHIPS allow SHARED EXPERIENCE and KNOW-HOW to be exploited within a company. FIELD MAPS are also used to suggest new areas for ACQUISITION or internal development.

Strategic Game Board: *see* GAME GRID.

Strategic Group: a set of competitors in an industry following similar COMPETITIVE STRATEGIES. Because of the similarity of COMPETITIVE STRATEGY, businesses in a STRATEGIC GROUP are expected to earn similar returns. Differences in profitability among competitors within the same STRATEGIC GROUP result from differences in their ability to carry out the strategy or random elements of luck.

The STRUCTURAL FACTORS or capabilities which isolate one group of competitors from others are called MOBILITY BARRIERS. Differences in profitability between groups reflect differing heights of MOBILITY BARRIERS.

STRATEGIC GROUPS are often plotted on COMPETITOR MAPS for analysis.

Strategic Intelligence Grid: a matrix for deciding what type of information must be gathered and analyzed to develop a particular STRATEGY or TACTIC. The grid shows the relationship between the type of environment the data will come from and the type of intelligence the data will provide.

The grid indicates that there are six types of environments from

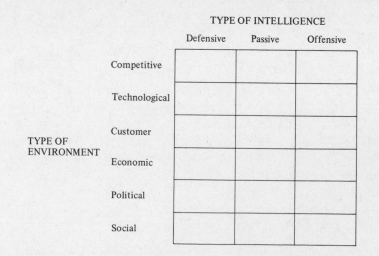

| | TYPE OF INTELLIGENCE | | |
	Defensive	Passive	Offensive
Competitive			
Technological			
Customer			
Economic			
Political			
Social			

TYPE OF ENVIRONMENT

which information can be collected. The first is COMPETITIVE ANAL-
YSIS about current and potential competitors. The second is the area
of current technology and the potential for TECHNOLOGICAL CHANGE
anywhere in the VALUE SYSTEM. Third is the customer. Collecting information on customers is likely to involve market surveys and BUYER
GROUP ANALYSES. ENVIRONMENTAL SCANNING is often used to collect
information from the last three environments.

The grid further indicates that information from these six types
of environments can be used to provide three types of intelligence.
Defensive intelligence is collected to avoid unanticipated THREATS
and for the development of contingency plans. Passive intelligence
is collected to provide benchmarks for MEASUREMENT SYSTEMS. And
OFFENSIVE INTELLIGENCE is collected to identify OPPORTUNITIES.

Strategists who use the STRATEGIC INFORMATION GRID say that it
avoids data overload and helps indicate what information is relevant
and useful.

Strategic Issue: *see* ISSUE MANAGEMENT.

Strategic Leverage: the use of effective STRATEGIES to increase the
ECONOMIC VALUE of a company. Strategists use STRATEGIC LEVERAGE
to build COMPETITIVE ADVANTAGES, and those, in turn, make the
company more profitable and less risky than it would be otherwise.
There are two general ways that strategists build STRATEGIC LEVER-
AGE. One is at the business level, by positioning a business within an
industry, and the other is at the corporate level, by managing and
assembling a portfolio of businesses.

Strategists build STRATEGIC LEVERAGE into the COMPETITIVE
STRATEGY of each business in order to build profitable protected positions in the industries in which the businesses compete. For example, a business may identify all its products with the same family
brand name so as to take advantage of advertising ECONOMIES OF
SCALE.

Strategists build STRATEGIC LEVERAGE into a CORPORATE STRAT-
EGY in order to make the businesses in that portfolio worth more as
part of the company's portfolio than they would be as stand-alone
companies. Take, for example, a CORPORATE STRATEGY based on
building FUNCTIONAL FIT in the manufacturing area. The benefits of
SHARED EXPERIENCE can be enjoyed by several businesses in the
portfolio.

Although the two ways to build STRATEGIC LEVERAGE are often

separated in order to discuss them, in practice they are very much linked. The STRATEGIC LEVERAGE that the company builds at the corporate level will probably translate into STRATEGIC LEVERAGE at the business level as well. If we take the preceding example, the businesses in the company's portfolio that use that particular manufacturing function may enjoy a COMPETITIVE ADVANTAGE that allows them to implement a COST LEADERSHIP STRATEGY effectively.

Building STRATEGIC LEVERAGE is what strategists get paid for.

Strategic Management: the process of administering an entity such that it carries out its purpose. The broadest definition of STRATEGIC MANAGEMENT is the management of COMPETITIVE ADVANTAGE and includes identifying goals and analyzing the environment, recognizing THREATS and OPPORTUNITIES, formulating strategies to protect against the threats and take advantage of the opportunities, and implementing and monitoring those strategies so as to sustain COMPETITIVE ADVANTAGES in the face of environmental change. Strategists who use this broad definition see STRATEGIC MANAGEMENT as a pervasive approach to managing all aspects of the company. They see the formulation of CORPORATE STRATEGY, the formulation of COMPETITIVE STRATEGY, the PLANNING PROCESS, and the implementation of all the preceding as being part of STRATEGIC MANAGEMENT.

The narrowest definition of STRATEGIC MANAGEMENT limits it to a definition analogous to operations management or marketing management but with the emphasis on achieving strategic rather than functional objectives.

Strategic Plan: the framework which details the TACTICS, timetables, RESOURCE ALLOCATION, pro forma financial statements, programs, and projects necessary to carry out a STRATEGY. A CORPORATE STRATEGY is embodied in a corporate plan, and a COMPETITIVE STRATEGY is embodied in a BUSINESS PLAN.

At the business level, the approach to competing in the industry is dictated by the COMPETITIVE STRATEGY. The COMPETITIVE STRATEGY can often be characterized as one of the three GENERIC STRATEGIES: LOW COST, DIFFERENTIATION, or FOCUS. The associated BUSINESS PLAN can usually be characterized as a BUILD PLAN, a HOLD PLAN, or a HARVEST PLAN on the basis of the underlying growth and market share goals. At the corporate level, the corporate plan should be related to the CORPORATE STRATEGY. In practice, the corporate plan tends to be the sum of all the company's BUSINESS PLANS.

Strategic Planning: a discipline that a company undertakes with a greater or lesser degree of formality to determine explicitly what it should do in the future. The objective of STRATEGIC PLANNING is to create real and increasing ECONOMIC VALUE for the company's shareholders and to determine how best to use the company's resources within its competitive environment.

Although there are many ways of looking at STRATEGIC PLANNING, it is helpful to view STRATEGIC PLANNING as a discipline comprised of three processes that take place with more or less emphasis at various levels of the company's hierarchy:

CORPORATE HIERARCHY	ANALYTICAL/CREATIVE PROCESS	ORGANIZATIONAL PROCESS	IMPLEMENTATION PROCESS
Corporate Group Division Business Function	• Analyzing Capital Markets, Industries and Competitors • Formulating a Corporate Strategy, Competitive Strategies, Strategic Plans, and Operating Policies	• Resource Allocation • Planning Cycles • Report Formats • Who Reports to Whom, and Who Is Responsible for What When	• Spending the Resources to Implement Projects, Programs, and Procedures to Carry Out the Strategies • Measurement Systems • Incentive Systems

The three processes are pulled together and integrated in the PLANNING PROCESS and carried out in a sequence and timetable called a PLANNING CYCLE. The individuals involved in the PLANNING PROCESS are found at various levels throughout an organization and form the PLANNING HIERARCHY.

Strategic Triangle: a theory of competitive strategy formulation and business unit SEGMENTATION based on three factors: the customer, the corporation, and the competitor. Accordingly, a good COMPETITIVE STRATEGY is characterized by a clearly defined market, an optimal use of CORPORATE STRENGTHS, and a COMPETITIVE ADVANTAGE.

Strategists who use the STRATEGIC TRIANGLE tend to emphasize the customer as being pivotal, and, therefore, MARKET SEGMENTATION becomes the basis for defining BUSINESS UNITS and formulating strategies. They argue that a COMPETITIVE STRATEGY in which corporate strengths or COMPETITOR ANALYSIS were pivotal may miss THREATS and OPPORTUNITIES in the market. Nevertheless, their STRATEGIES are based on maximizing the use of current corporate strengths, encouraging the development of needed corporate strengths, and establishing CONSTRUCTIVE CONFLICT with competitors.

Many strategists agree that the customer emphasis tends to be appropriate at the business level but that it remains a corporate level responsibility to control the companywide balance of the triangle.

Strategy: an approach to using resources within the constraints of a competitive environment in order to achieve a set of GOALS. In companies, different types of strategies are formulated at various levels of the organization which address different aspects of the environment. At the top, a company formulates a CORPORATE STRATEGY. A CORPORATE STRATEGY enumerates the economic and social goals to be attained by the company in order to meet the shareholder's expectations and outlines the principles around which the company will organize and manage its portfolio of businesses. The principles are described in the company's CONCEPT OF ASSEMBLY, CONCEPT OF FIT, and CONCEPT OF MANAGEMENT.

At the business level, a company formulates COMPETITIVE STRATEGIES for competing in each business's industry. A COMPETITIVE STRATEGY is based on a STRUCTURAL ANALYSIS of the industry and consists of a statement of the business's GOALS, a statement of how the business is going to compete, and a series of OPERATING POLICIES to guide its FUNCTIONAL AREAS.

A STRATEGY takes shape in the form of a STRATEGIC PLAN which details proforma financial statements, projects, programs, procedures, and the allocation of resources. Different types of plans correspond to different types of STRATEGIES. A BUSINESS PLAN is devised on the basis of the COMPETITIVE STRATEGY of each business. The BUSINESS PLANS of all the businesses in the company's portfolio comprise the CORPORATE PLAN and reflect the CORPORATE STRATEGY. The process of devising and carrying out STRATEGY is STRATEGIC PLANNING.

Strategy and Structure: a hypothesis that the ORGANIZATIONAL STRUCTURE of a company determines the range of strategies that the company is capable of effectively carrying out and that a given STRATEGY can best be carried out by a specific structure. Therefore, a company that is attempting to carry out a STRATEGY without an appropriate ORGANIZATIONAL STRUCTURE is suboptimizing its ability to create ECONOMIC VALUE for its shareholders. For this reason, a company's CORPORATE STRATEGY should set out the company's approach to its ORGANIZATIONAL STRUCTURE.

Strategy Audit: a review of past and current STRATEGY. The STRAT-
EGY AUDIT may be carried out to identify and articulate the STRATEGY
of a company which has done little explicit STRATEGIC PLANNING in
the past or to ascertain how faithfully a company is following its
proclaimed strategy. The STRATEGY AUDIT may include an evaluation
of the effectiveness of a strategy as well. STRATEGY AUDITS may be
performed at the corporate, SECTOR, or business level of a PLANNING
HIERARCHY. Consultants are very often used in STRATEGY AUDITS because of the need for objectivity.

In companies without a well-defined strategy, a corporate level
STRATEGY AUDIT involves a series of interviews with top management
to determine what the implicit CORPORATE STRATEGY has been. That
is, what has top management understood the corporate GOALS to be
and why? What types of businesses have they been acquiring, developing, and divesting and why? What kinds of strategies do they
think they are good at implementing and why? What advantages do
their businesses enjoy as compared to their competitors? How have
they organized, managed, and rewarded their businesses and why?
The results of the interviews combined with an analysis of quantitative industry data and corporate performance indicators form a
report on what a company's STRATEGY has been.

A business level STRATEGY AUDIT involves interviews with management and the collection of data that shows what the business and
each FUNCTIONAL AREA have been doing. The objective is to identify
the ASSUMPTIONS the business's managers are making about their OB-
JECTIVES, competitors, and INDUSTRY STRUCTURE that led them to
carry out their implicit STRATEGY.

STRATEGY AUDITS are very often used as the basis for formulating CORPORATE and COMPETITIVE STRATEGIES.

Strengths and Weaknesses: those attributes that affect an entity's
ability to carry out its GOALS. The STRENGTHS AND WEAKNESSES of
a business or company determine the company's ability to create real
and increasing ECONOMIC VALUE for its shareholders. Assessing these
STRENGTHS AND WEAKNESSES is a key step in formulating STRATEGY.
A business's STRENGTHS AND WEAKNESSES are based on the composition and quantity of its managerial, financial, and physical resources and also stem from experience or past STRATEGIES.

The attributes of a business must be assessed as STRENGTHS or
WEAKNESSES within the context of the business's INDUSTRY STRUC-

TURE and INTRA-INDUSTRY STRUCTURE. A business's strengths can be viewed as those attributes which protect it from the COMPETITIVE FORCES in its industry and those attributes which allow the business to build MOBILITY BARRIERS. In the same way, a business's weaknesses are those attributes that make it vulnerable to the COMPETITIVE FORCES in its industry and those attributes which lower its MOBILITY BARRIERS.

Many strategists like to begin the STRATEGY formulation process with a management assessment of STRENGTHS AND WEAKNESSES. Research into these assessments has shown a number of interesting findings. For example, the higher the management level of the assessors, the more likely they are to be optimistic about strengths and minimize weaknesses. Also, strengths are likely to involve descriptions of past performance rather than behavior relative to competitors.

Structural Analysis: the identification and examination of the characteristics of an industry which determine the level and variability of the profitability of the competitors. The characteristics are called STRUCTURAL FACTORS. A STRUCTURAL ANALYSIS investigates how these STRUCTURAL FACTORS influence the five COMPETITIVE FORCES in an industry. The five COMPETITIVE FORCES are usually diagrammed as shown below.

For the purpose of understanding STRUCTURAL ANALYSIS, industry profitability can be measured in terms of RETURN ON INVESTMENT. The objective of STRUCTURAL ANALYSIS is to understand for

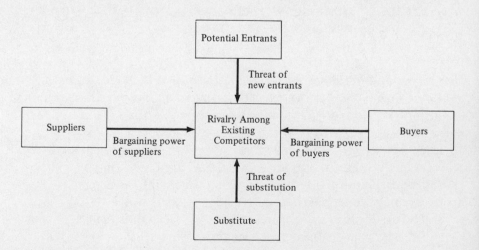

a given industry how each of those five forces affects both the numerator and the denominator in an industry's RETURN ON INVESTMENT.

For example, the threat of ENTRY from potential entrants can hold down returns by preventing the industry from raising its prices above the ENTRY DETERRING PRICE. It can also inflate expenses by forcing the industry to build expensive ENTRY BARRIERS like BRAND IDENTIFICATION. The threat of ENTRY can increase the level of investment by forcing the industry to invest in ENTRY BARRIERS such as ECONOMIES OF SCALE or proprietary technology.

RIVALRY affects the returns directly when the competitors in an industry engage in PRICE COMPETITION. RIVALRY can also affect returns when, for example, it involves promotion battles that cut into the industry's margins. RIVALRY can affect the level of investment, too. For example, NONPRICE COMPETITION based on prompt service can increase the industry's investment in inventory.

The bargaining power of buyers affects returns by constraining the industry's ability to raise prices. BUYER POWER can also force the industry to provide the buyers with expensive information on how to use the product, personalized sales help, and warrantees. BUYER POWER can affect investment in inventory and warehouses or in rental expenses if buyers can force the industry to warehouse its products and hold title until the buyers want them.

The threat of SUBSTITUTE PRODUCTS can affect the returns by putting a limit on how high a price the industry can charge. SUBSTITUTES can reduce returns if the industry has to spend to fend off the SUBSTITUTE PRODUCTS. For example, the industry might spend on collective advertising to inform the buyers of the industry's superiority to its SUBSTITUTE. Each competitor may also have to maintain its PRICE/PERFORMANCE RATIO vis-à-vis substitutes and may be forced to invest in new technology in order to do so.

Suppliers can affect the returns only with PULL THROUGH, and this is an unusual circumstance. For the most part, SUPPLIER POWER affects the returns by raising the price the industry pays for its supplies. Powerful suppliers can also force the industry to inventory its supplies or to invest to adapt to changes in the suppliers' product, etc.

Strategists comfortable with the concept of INDUSTRY STRUCTURE feel that understanding the level of RIVALRY, the effectiveness of ENTRY BARRIERS, the degree of BUYER POWER, the degree of SUPPLIER POWER, and the threat of SUBSTITUTE PRODUCTS in an industry is fundamental to understanding current profitability in an industry and, therefore, is fundamental to developing a COMPETITIVE STRATEGY for earning higher than average returns in that industry.

INTRA-INDUSTRY STRUCTURE is a concept which focuses on the variability of returns in an industry rather than on the level of returns for the industry overall. Many strategists find that it is quite difficult to do a STRUCTURAL ANALYSIS of an industry that has a complex INTRA-INDUSTRY STRUCTURE.

Structural Factor: a characteristic of an industry that affects the level and range of returns earned by competitors in that industry. A list of important STRUCTURAL FACTORS would include MARKET GROWTH, BUYER CONCENTRATION, BUYER VOLUME, INTERMITTENT OVERCAPACITY, INDUSTRY CONCENTRATION, CORPORATE STAKES, absolute COST ADVANTAGES, DIVERSE COMPETITORS, ECONOMIES OF SCALE, EXIT BARRIERS, FIXED COST–TO–VALUE ADDED RATIO, PRODUCT DIFFERENCES, BRAND IDENTIFICATION, SWITCHING COSTS, access to distribution, government policy, EXPECTED RETALIATION, BUYER INFORMATION, threat of BACKWARD INTEGRATION, SUBSTITUTE PRODUCTS, PULL THROUGH, COST STRUCTURE, DECISION-MAKING UNIT'S incentives, supplier CONCENTRATION, and threat of FORWARD INTEGRATION.

Identifying the impact of the STRUCTURAL FACTORS on each of the five COMPETITIVE FORCES which shape the competitive environment of a business is the foundation of a STRUCTURAL ANALYSIS of an industry and of building a COMPETITIVE STRATEGY.

Stuck-in-the-Middle: a term used to describe a business that has not been able to achieve one of the three GENERIC STRATEGIES and, therefore, is not benefiting from a sustainable COMPETITIVE ADVANTAGE. A business that is STUCK-IN-THE-MIDDLE loses the high-volume price-sensitive buyers to competitors with an effective COST LEADERSHIP STRATEGY and loses the utility-conscious buyers to either a competitor with an effective DIFFERENTIATION STRATEGY or a competitor with an effective FOCUSED STRATEGY. The business probably also suffers from a confused CORPORATE CULTURE and an ORGANIZATIONAL STRUCTURE with conflicting MANAGEMENT SYSTEMS.

Most strategists agree that it requires time and effort to redirect a STUCK-IN-THE-MIDDLE business toward an explicit STRATEGY. A common problem is that such businesses seem to flop back and forth between different STRATEGIES rather than develop a commitment to one or another.

Substitute Product: a product that can supplant another in performing one or more functions for the buyer. The presence of substitutes is one of the five COMPETITIVE FORCES comprising industry structure. SUBSTITUTE PRODUCTS both constrain the potential profitability of an industry and simultaneously determine the size of overall industry DEMAND. Because of this, it is important for the strategist to identify the SUBSTITUTE PRODUCTS that are relevant to the business and to assess their threat.

The key to identifying substitutes is to search for products that perform the same function or functions as the industry's product rather than products that take the same form. Furthermore, the function the product performs needs to be defined as broadly as possible in order to reveal the full range of substitution possibilities. For example, a manufacturer of metal tennis rackets faces substitution not only from wood or fiberglass rackets but also from squash rackets, other sports equipment, and other uses of leisure time. Therefore, the function of metal rackets most broadly defined is a provision for leisure-time activity. Products that satisfy the generalized function of the industry's product often look a great deal different from those that can perform the more literal function. MARKETING MYOPIA refers to an inability to recognize the full range of substitutes for a product.

It is important to examine the possibilities for substitution at all stages of the VALUE ADDED CHAIN. For example, suppose a business produces a paper filter which reaches the END USER in two ways. First, the paper filter is bought by an electronics components manufacturer who, in turn, uses the filter as a component in an appliance that is sold to consumers. Secondly, the filter is sold to original equipment manufacturers of a machine that is used to produce product A's or product B's, which are, in turn, sold to consumers. Most obviously, the availability of a different type of filter would affect demand for the paper filter. Somewhat less obviously, it would be affected by a change that eliminated the need for the filter in either the way the appliance was built or in the way the original equipment manufacturer's machine was built. But the DEMAND for the filter would also be affected by substitutes for the appliance as well as by substitutes for either product A or product B. In this way, substitution in the downstream stages of the VALUE ADDED CHAIN works its way backward to affect the DEMAND for the product of the industry.

A given product faces a range of substitutes that can be ranked by degree of substitutability. The degree of substitutability will depend on the quality-adjusted PRICE-PERFORMANCE of the substitute in performing the function relative to the industry's product. For example, a word processing machine may be an expensive substitute for a typewriter, but because it also substitutes for a range of other products, the quality adjustment lowers the cost for the buyer and increases its degree of substitutability. A similar example is an electronic cash register, which costs more than a mechanical one but allows the retailer to keep track of inventory as well as pricing and provides better sales slips for the consumer.

Therefore, when analyzing the PRICE-PERFORMANCE trends of substitutes, the strategist must consider a number of factors in addition to its relative purchase price. First, the cost per unit of function must be considered. This is the relative cost per unit of the function performed, which is not necessarily the purchase price. Also, the life cycle costs must be considered. This includes an assessment of the substitutes's relative maintenance costs, useful life, and any salvage value. The value to the buyer is also important. That is, the cost of the substitute may be adjusted to reflect any difference in its value to the buyer, such as improvements in productivity that result from switching to the substitute. For example, the substitute may have lower installation costs or reduce the need for quality control checks. Finally, any impact of the substitute on the performance of a buyer's product has to be considered. For example, the fact that a substitute form of displaying or packaging a product may attract more customers or give the product a higher-quality image that can command a higher price must be factored into the substitution calculation.

The comparison of the PRICE-PERFORMANCE trends of a given business's products with its substitutes often involves an analysis of SWITCHING COSTS. SWITCHING COSTS in substitution can include the cost of switching to a new type of supplier, as well as the costs of switching to the new way of performing the function. These SWITCHING COSTS are generally larger than the costs of switching brands of a given product. They are likely to include the cost of retraining employees, the costs of end-product redesign to incorporate the substitute input, the cost of any new ancillary equipment required, the costs of altering the manufacturing process to incorporate the SUB-STITUTE PRODUCT, the cost of new spare parts inventory, etc. SWITCHING COSTS may vary with different BUYER GROUPS. For some BUYER GROUPS, switching to a substitute may require significant technological capabilities that the group may not possess. The strategist may consider this in BUYER SELECTION to protect against substitutes.

Substitution Curve: *see* DIFFUSION THEORY.

Sunk Cost: a cost which has already been incurred and cannot be reversed or avoided. In evaluating investments, SUNK COSTS should be ignored because they are unavoidable outflows of cash that, therefore, should not be considered in making decisions. It is the PRESENT VALUE of avoidable future CASH FLOWS that are important.

Strategists often find that the larger the SUNK COST, the harder it is to ignore. For example, a decision maker might argue for continuing to spend to try to break even on a project that has already cost a million dollars. Another might argue that it makes no sense to keep investing in a project that will never earn its REQUIRED RE-TURN on the million dollars already sunk in it. Both are making the mistake of considering SUNK COSTS in their analysis.

Supplier Power: one of the five COMPETITIVE FORCES that determine the level and variance of profitability among industries. Suppliers can reduce the profitability of an industry by exercising their power to increase the cost of PURCHASED VALUE in the industry and by raising the amount of investment required to compete in the industry. Suppliers do this by charging more for their products, by forcing inventory on the industry, and by forcing the industry to invest to adapt to changes in the supplier's products, etc. The factors that affect SUPPLIER POWER can be classified into two types. The first type affects the intrinsic power of the supplier, and the second type affects the buyers' ability to trade suppliers off against one another.

The STRUCTURAL FACTORS that affect intrinsic SUPPLIER POWER are supplier CONCENTRATION, relative supplier volume, buyer information, and the threat of FORWARD INTEGRATION. For example, if there are fewer suppliers than there are buyers, the suppliers are much more likely to be intrinsically powerful than they would be if the buyers were more concentrated. If the suppliers' product is more important to the buyer than the buyers' business is to the supplier, then the supplier is likely to be powerful. For example, if half the buyers' VARIABLE COSTS consist of PURCHASED VALUE from the supplier and the buyer accounts for only 1 percent of the supplier's total sales, then the supplier is likely to be intrinsically powerful. In addition, the less the buyer knows about the supplier's business, the more powerful the supplier is apt to be. For example, if the buyer neither knows how the supplier makes its products nor how much that process should cost, that gives the supplier some intrinsic power. Finally, a supplier with a credible threat of FORWARD INTEGRATION also has intrinsic power.

However, even if STRUCTURAL FACTORS provide suppliers with intrinsic power, that power is likely to be mitigated by any OPPORTUNITY the buyers have to play the suppliers off against one another. Suppliers are susceptible to being played off against one another if they are unable to develop BRAND IDENTIFICATION, if they are unable to develop SWITCHING COSTS, if they are unable to develop PULL THROUGH, and if there are SUBSTITUTE PRODUCTS that the buyer could use instead.

Most strategists feel that it is very important both to control the intrinsic power of their suppliers and to look for ways to play them off against each other. For example, they deliberately try to keep their suppliers from becoming more concentrated than they are through multiple sourcing. Multiple sourcing also keeps down the amount of PRODUCT DIFFERENCES and works against BRAND IDENTIFICATION.

Many strategists find that their businesses are susceptible to supplier TACTICS that increase PULL THROUGH and SWITCHING COSTS. The TACTICS are likely to provide tangible benefits to the buyer, but they also contribute to SUPPLIER POWER. In the case of PULL THROUGH, the efforts on the part of the supplier to reach the END USER can seem to make it easier for the business to sell its products. For example, the effort of the supplier to make its nonstick coating brand known to the consumer may seem like a plus to the users of the coating because they can advertise their products as having that brand on them and take advantage of the supplier's advertising expenditures free of charge. However, the advertising link with the buyer's product gives the supplier more power. In the same way, supplier services which increase the ease of purchasing or lead to a customized approach to using the product can benefit the buyer and at the same time increase SWITCHING COSTS. For example, buyer access to a computerized ordering system can seem like a giveaway, when really it helps lock the buyer into one supplier and makes it more difficult for the buyer to switch to another.

Supply: the quantity of a product that sellers will provide at any given price. A SUPPLY curve represents the different quantities of a particular product that sellers will provide at different price levels. For the individual company, the supply function directly reflects its MARGINAL COSTS. As the plant utilization rate rises, shifts must be added eventually or less efficient facilities must be used so that it takes a higher price to warrant more output.

The industry supply curve, like the industry DEMAND curve, is the combination of the supply curves of all the companies in the industry. It may also incorporate the ENTRY of new sellers at higher prices. An industry supply curve is drawn as shown below.

Short-run industry supply, like industry demand, can be more or less elastic. In industries with high ELASTICITY OF SUPPLY, an increase in price will bring on a large increase in new output, and a decrease in price will have the opposite effect. This might be the case in industries where CAPACITY used to produce other products can be readily converted to producing the product or in industries with low ENTRY BARRIERS. In industries with inelastic supply, an increase in price has little effect in stimulating more output, and a decrease in price has little effect on discouraging output. This is usually because the FIXED COSTS are high and the capacity cannot easily be used to make another product.

The supply curves of competing sellers need not be identical.

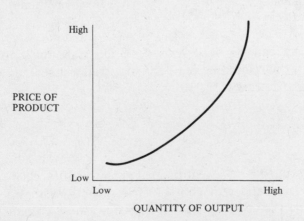

At a given price one may be in a position to expand utilization considerably, and another may be facing a capacity constraint.

In the long run, most of the elasticity of an industry supply curve comes from new entrants and new capacity constructed by going firms. How much time elapses before these processes are complete, therefore, determines the time horizons pertinent to the long run. The timing of the process need not be symmetrical when price falls. Long-run contraction comes from the exit of competitors and the scrapping of inefficient capacity. These processes depend on EXIT BARRIERS and other factors.

Industry supply curves can change or shift over time as a result of a wide variety of exogenous factors, such as technological change or change in the price or availability of factors of production or the impact of conditions like weather, which affect output. For example, TECHNOLOGICAL CHANGE can shift the supply curve downward if more efficient ways are discovered to produce the product. The EXPERIENCE CURVE is a downward shift in the supply curve over time. Technological changes can also make the supply curve more or less elastic. For example, a shift from high VARIABLE COST to high fixed cost production methods may make the supply curve much less elastic in the short run by raising the time lag for adding capacity and increasing the EXIT or SHRINKAGE BARRIERS to cutting back output.

Sustainable Growth: the growth in sales that a company can maintain at current levels of profitability with a given CAPITAL STRUCTURE. In its most general form, the formula for calculating the SUSTAINABLE GROWTH for a company is this.

$$\text{Sustainable growth} = \text{return on equity} \times \text{earnings retention rate}$$

The formula can be decomposed to illustrate the constraints to growth and the related policies for the strategist seeking to increase the sustainable growth rate.

$$\frac{\text{Pretax profits}}{\text{sales}} \times \frac{\text{sales}}{\text{assets}} \times \left(1 - \frac{\text{tax}}{\text{rate}}\right) \times \left(1 - \frac{\text{dividend payout rate}}{}\right) \times \frac{\text{assets}}{\text{net worth}} = \frac{\text{sustainable}}{\text{growth}}$$

The first term focuses attention on current profitability and policies such as pricing and cost control. The second highlights utilization and efficiency of the asset base. The final three emphasize the importance of three areas of financial policy: taxes, dividend policy, and the selection of the appropriate CAPITAL STRUCTURE. For a more sophisticated analysis, the SUSTAINABLE GROWTH rate equation can be further expanded to isolate the effect of WORKING CAPITAL management or INFLATION, etc.

The SUSTAINABLE GROWTH rate can also be used as a benchmark for evaluating how realistic the future growth plans put forward by a company are. The weighted average of the planned growth of all a company's businesses cannot exceed the company's SUSTAINABLE GROWTH rate unless the increase in sales is supported by higher profitability, better asset utilization, or changes in financial policies. Business growth plans are often related to a company's SUSTAINABLE GROWTH rate in PLAN PENETRATION CHARTS.

Strategists often calculate SUSTAINABLE GROWTH rates for competitors as part of a COMPETITOR ANALYSIS.

Switching Cost: a onetime cost facing the buyer when switching from one supplier's product to another. These costs are not related to the product itself but rather to how the product is purchased or used. For example, switching from one supplier's product to another's may require that the buyer incur the cost of retraining employees, the cost of new ancillary equipment, the cost and time in testing or qualifying a new source, the cost of redesigning its product, or even the psychic costs of severing a relationship. If these SWITCHING COSTS are high, then the new supplier must offer a major improvement in price or performance in order for the buyer to switch products.

SWITCHING COSTS are an important consideration in measuring the PRICE-PERFORMANCE of competing products and of SUBSTITUTE PRODUCTS. Some strategists feel that because SWITCHING COSTS are related to a specific onetime action, they should be evaluated as an investment decision. Therefore, the PRESENT VALUE of costs that occur over time, such as shaking down a new process, should be calculated; and they should be compared with the PRESENT VALUE of the benefits of switching.

Most strategists feel that it is important to build SWITCHING COSTS into their own products and to prevent suppliers from building them in their products.

Synergy: occurs when two or more businesses are combined in a company's portfolio so as to make the effect of their joint STRATEGY more beneficial than the sum of their individual strategies.

Many strategists feel that the term SYNERGY is too ill-defined and that its vagueness was the reason so many became disenchanted with the concept. They prefer to use terms like building financial and STRATEGIC LEVERAGE with an effective CONCEPT OF FIT or building superior performance with BUSINESS INTERRELATIONSHIPS.

Systematic Risk: RISK that affects all investments in the same way. For the investor in the stock of a company, SYSTEMATIC RISK results from events such as changes in government tax or interest rate policies that will affect that company as well as all others in the same way. (UNSYSTEMATIC RISK, by contrast, results from possible events that will affect that company differently from others.) The more a given company is likely to be affected by events that affect others, the more the investor is exposed to SYSTEMATIC RISK in buying the company's stock.

The CAPITAL ASSET PRICING MODEL says that the higher the exposure to the SYSTEMATIC RISK, the higher the REQUIRED RETURN on the investment should be. This is because SYSTEMATIC RISK cannot be diversified away. The CAPITAL ASSET PRICING MODEL uses the term BETA, a measure of the volatility in the return of a security associated with the volatility of the stock market as a whole, to quantify the SYSTEMATIC RISK of a company's stock.

SYSTEMATIC RISK is sometimes called market risk.

T

Tactic: the means with which STRATEGIES are carried out. Often the boundary between tactic and strategy becomes blurred. A given STRATEGY may be viewed as a TACTIC in carrying out a higher-order STRATEGY. Any STRATEGY may be only a TACTIC from the perspective of a larger STRATEGY, and everything may be just TACTICS with regard to the grandest STRATEGY. In STRATEGIC PLANNING, STRATEGIES are usually identified as being either a CORPORATE STRATEGY or a COMPETITIVE STRATEGY. Everything else is a TACTIC. For example, an OPERATING POLICY or program, procedure, or project would all be TACTICS. Still, even though one can appreciate the logic of the differences between TACTICS and STRATEGIES, most strategists find that the convenience of talking in terms of marketing STRATEGIES, financial STRATEGIES, and personal STRATEGIES, etc., overwhelms the logic.

Tangible Relationships: *see* BUSINESS INTERRELATIONSHIPS.

Tapered Integration: partial VERTICAL INTEGRATION. Tapered backward integration involves making some, but not all, of the PURCHASED VALUE accounted for by the previous stage in the VALUE ADDED CHAIN. In the same way, tapered forward integration involves doing some, but not all, of the next stage forward in the VALUE ADDED CHAIN.

Strategists increase their bargaining power over their suppliers with tapered BACKWARD INTEGRATION and over their buyers with tapered FORWARD INTEGRATION. TAPERED INTEGRATION also gives the business a high level of buyer information about its suppliers. In addition, TAPERED INTEGRATION can be used to assure some minimum level of SUPPLY and DEMAND. Also, if the industry is subject to fluctuations in DEMAND, a business may profit from keeping its own facilities utilized and letting independent suppliers and buyers deal with the fluctuations.

Targeted Strategy: *see* FOCUS STRATEGY.

Target Market: the selected BUYER GROUPS that a business's COMPETITIVE STRATEGY addresses. TARGET MARKETS are usually distinguished by buyer type, geographic location, product UTILITY needs, and distribution channel, etc. Potential TARGET MARKETS will change as competitors expand or contract their capabilities.

TARGET MARKETS are also called target market segments or target segments.

Target Portfolio: an ideal combination of businesses for a company with a particular set of corporate economic GOALS. A company often describes its TARGET PORTFOLIO of businesses along some selected dimensions, using the GROWTH/SHARE MATRIX, the BUSINESS/INDUSTRY MATRIX, or the LIFE CYCLE MATRIX. Other companies draw their own matrices in order to take into account additional dimensions such as political risk, geographic distribution, or the mix of CONSUMER and INDUSTRIAL GOODS.

Technological Change: a change in the process by which an activity is carried out. A significant technological change will affect a business's profitability. For example, it could result in lower costs, lower investment, higher MOBILITY BARRIERS, and increased PRODUCT DIFFERENTIATION.

Although technological change is most often thought of as involving manufacturing, many strategists consider OPPORTUNITIES for change in any step in a business's VALUE ADDED CHAIN or any activity in its VALUE CHAIN.

Some strategists define TECHNOLOGICAL CHANGE to mean specifically an increase in the relative sophistication of the methodologies involved in an activity. They feel that an understanding of the relative sophistication of a business's technologies, those of its competitors, those of potential entrants, and those of businesses in other industries can reveal OPPORTUNITIES for COMPETITIVE ADVANTAGES.

Some strategists also point out the differences between continuous and discontinuous TECHNOLOGICAL CHANGE. Continuous change is used to describe industries in which there are ongoing and more or less predictable changes in technology. Discontinuous TECHNOLOGICAL CHANGE involves significant and more or less unpredictable changes in technology. The latter can provide both THREATS and OPPORTUNITIES. For example, the potential for discontinuous change may very much increase the RISK of a pioneering ENTRY or even of a PREEMPTIVE TACTIC. Discontinuities can provide great OPPORTUNITIES for late ENTRANTS, especially those with ADJACENT EXPERIENCE.

Thin Industry: an industry in which almost all competitors earn the same below average return. Although there does not seem to be any one type of INDUSTRY STRUCTURE that always leads to a THIN INDUSTRY, THIN INDUSTRIES tend to be FRAGMENTED. Moreover, analysis of a THIN INDUSTRY often shows almost no differences between the COMPETITIVE STRATEGIES of the businesses in the industry.

Threat: a situation that can lessen a business's ability to protect and improve its COMPETITIVE POSITION in its industry. THREATS arise from potential changes in the business's INDUSTRY STRUCTURE and INTRA-INDUSTRY STRUCTURE that would depress the business's profitability in the absence of some action on the part of the business.

For a given business competing in an industry, a THREAT related to INDUSTRY STRUCTURE involves a change that unfavorably affects RIVALRY, that lowers ENTRY BARRIERS, that increases SUPPLIER

POWER or BUYER POWER, or that decreases the product's PRICE-PER-FORMANCE as compared to SUBSTITUTE PRODUCTS. A THREAT related to INTRA-INDUSTRY STRUCTURE involves a change that reduces the MOBILITY BARRIERS of the business's STRATEGIC GROUP or makes another STRATEGIC GROUP more attractive and less accessible.

Time Study: a technique for establishing PRODUCTIVITY standards by establishing an allowed time to complete a task. TIME STUDY can invoke current and historical data from stopwatches, motion studies, work sampling, etc. TIME STUDY, together with appropriate INCENTIVE SYSTEMS, can be used to increase PRODUCTIVITY. At the turn of the century, TIME STUDY was the basis for SCIENTIFIC MANAGEMENT.

Top-down Planning: the formulation of STRATEGIC PLANS by individuals at the top of the ORGANIZATIONAL HIERARCHY. The approach is based on the idea that those individuals at the top have the most perspective on the business and its competitive environment. A modified TOP-DOWN APPROACH involves a PLANNING PROCESS that both provides for a great deal of direction from top management and sets limits on the range of STRATEGIES that lower-level managers can consider. A company with a highly centralized organizational structure is more likely to take a top-down approach than a more decentralized company.

BOTTOM-UP PLANNING is the opposite of TOP-DOWN PLANNING.

Trade-offs: actions, outcomes, or choices that are in some way mutually exclusive. Strategists continually face TRADE-OFFS in making strategic choices. The most common usually involve cost vs. benefit, short-term vs. long-term goals, MARKET SHARE growth vs. RETURN ON INVESTMENT, and action vs. analysis.

Many strategists feel that effective trade-offs can be made only when ASSUMPTIONS are well understood.

Trading Up: the practice of inducing a current owner of a product to purchase a more expensive version of the same product. This tactic is quite common in selling such CONSUMER GOODS as cameras or stereo equipment. The tactic is also used by INDUSTRIAL GOODS manufacturers to soften the effect of BUSINESS CYCLES on their sales by making the purchase of the new version of a durable good too attractive to postpone.

Trade-up also refers to the practice of inducing a buyer to purchase a more expensive product during the DECISION-MAKING PROCESS. For example, an automobile dealer may begin the sales talk by discussing the stripped-down, low-price version the customer came in to see and then moving the discussion toward options and add-ons in the hope of trading the customer up to a more expensive version.

TRADING UP is a TACTIC that many strategists use to generate DEMAND for products in saturated markets. It is also used to encourage the purchase of replacement products that would otherwise be postponed.

Transborder Segments: MARKET SEGMENTS that are more or less homogeneous across national boundaries. Some strategists believe that worldwide markets are becoming increasingly homogeneous and that this INSIGHT can be taken advantage of with a GLOBAL STRATEGY. Other strategists also point out the advantages of a GLOBAL PERSPECTIVE but do so because they believe that it is TECHNOLOGICAL CHANGE that allows a business to overcome the costs associated with serving market segments that are more or less heterogeneous in different countries.

Transfer Price: the price used to value products traded among entities within a company. The objective of assigning TRANSFER PRICES is to provide a basis for deciding whether to carry out activities internally or to go to outside suppliers. If the entities are in different tax jurisdictions, transfer prices may be set to minimize taxes. In that case, the company generally tries either to minimize or maximize the "public" transfer price in order to minimize the tax bill. When the primary objective is to compare internal and external sources of supply, a market-based transfer price is the best test. When this is unavailable because the transferred product is distinctive, MARGINAL COST is the preferred basis for the transfer price. AVERAGE COST and UNIT COST are sometimes used as well but provide a less reliable basis for comparison.

Any PROFIT CENTER that sells products to other groups in the company has to have transfer pricing to account for that exchange. That transfer price will affect the individuals involved in buying and selling that product. The lower the transfer price is relative to the MARKET PRICE, the more interested the buying group is going to be in buying internally; and the higher the transfer price is relative to the market price, the more interested the seller group is going to be in selling internally. Therefore, because transfer prices affect behavior, strategists are often concerned with determining transfer prices. In some companies, transfer prices are directly related to the CORPORATE STRATEGY. Take, for example, a company that is trying to build CUMULATIVE EXPERIENCE in manufacturing a particular component. That company might use low transfer prices to encourage its other businesses to use as many of the company's components as possible despite the availability of cheaper alternatives.

Transitional Imperative: *see* COMMODITY/SPECIALTY MATRIX.

Transition Shift: *see* BUYER TRANSACTION CYCLE.

Turnaround Plan: a plan to restore profitability to a business or a company. A turnaround plan for a business is often called a FIX PLAN. The intent of a turnaround plan for an entire company is to restore the company's ability to create ECONOMIC VALUE. This usually involves efforts to develop FINANCIAL LEVERAGE, such as reorganizing the company's CAPITAL STRUCTURE, as well as efforts to develop STRATEGIC LEVERAGE. The latter may be built around a series of FIX PLANS for the company's businesses or a PORTFOLIO CLEANUP or an entirely new CORPORATE STRATEGY.

U

Unbundling: *see* BUNDLING.

Uncertainty Chart: a chart used to display the sources of RISK and the magnitude of the RISKS facing the businesses in a company's portfolio. The events which could influence the performance of the businesses are identified and ranked on the basis of the likelihood of their occurrence on the vertical axis of the chart. The businesses being analyzed are arrayed across the top. Usually, numerical indicators of risk are calculated for each business in a company's portfolio and then weighted to give an index for the entire company. In the example that follows, three businesses are analyzed with respect to six events.

The numerical indicators are calculated thus. Events with a high, medium, or low probability of occurring are given values of one, two, and three respectively. The potential impact of each event on the individual businesses is evaluated; and again high, medium, and low assessments are given values of one, two, and three respectively. The numerical indicator is the product of the two factors: the probability and the impact. For example, for Business A, the likelihood of a labor dispute is medium, and the potential impact is low, giving rise to an indicator of two. For Business B, the likelihood of a labor dispute is also medium, but the potential impact is high, giving rise to an indicator of six. For each business, indicators are calculated for each event, and the total is computed. The total is divided by the number of events to arrive at a RISK index for each business. Following that valuation scheme, Business A has an index of four, Business B has an index of five, and Business C has an index of three.

This type of chart is useful both for displaying the elements of uncertainty as well as for analyzing the source of the uncertainty.

Some strategists go further and show the relationship between the business's index and the company's investment in each business and each business's profitability. This kind of display shows, in ef-

IMPACT OF EVENT

		Business A			Business B			Business C		
		L	M	H	L	M	H	L	M	H
High	Higher inflation			9		6			6	
	Tighter credit		6				9		6	
Medium	Labor dispute	2					6	2		
	Dollar weakening		4			4			4	
	New Entrant		2				3			3
Low	Price controls	1				2		1		
	Business index		4			5			3	

LIKELIHOOD OF EVENT

fect, how much of the company's capital is invested in relatively risky businesses and how much of its profits come from relatively risky sources. The indices can also be weighted by investment, sales, or profitability, etc., to calculate a company's index. Corporate risk can also be analyzed in terms of SYSTEMATIC and UNSYSTEMATIC RISK.

UNCERTAINTY CHARTS can be used to analyze SCENARIOS together with IMPORTANCE/CONTROL GRIDS.

Uncertainty Reduction: a trend associated with increased certainty about an industry's structure as that industry evolves. For example, observers of the industry begin to understand how large the market will be, who the BUYER GROUPS are, how the product will be configured, what kind of MARKETING POLICY will be effective, and what technologies will work, etc.

Many strategists consider industries in which there has been little UNCERTAINTY REDUCTION to be risky industries in which to compete. They would rather let another company ENTER and reduce uncertainty so that they can follow later with less RISK. Other strategists consider such industries to be good OPPORTUNITIES and favor pioneering ENTRIES and even aggressive BUILD PLANS.

Undifferentiated Product: *see* COMMODITY.

Uniqueness Driver: a factor that affects the differentiation of an end product. The uniqueness of an end product is built up by the VALUE SYSTEM of activities that incorporate that end product. Research has identified nine major drivers of uniqueness: policy choices, LINKAGES, timing, location, business interrelationships, learning, VERTICAL INTEGRATION, SCALE OF OPERATIONS, and institutional factors. For example, a highly differentiated product like expensive cosmetics will derive its uniqueness from policies emphasizing quality materials, from LINKAGES between advertising and package design, with trained salespeople in the channels, with carefully timed premium offers, with counters well located in high-end stores, with a sharing of its company's high-quality IMAGE, by learning to be the best in new product development, by controlling any value step needed, by being big enough for efficient distribution, and by working with government regulations.

Uniqueness drivers vary across activities, businesses, competitors, and industries. Uniqueness drivers also vary in cost. Managing uniqueness drivers is essential to carrying out a DIFFEREN-

TIATION STRATEGY and cannot be ignored in carrying out any STRATEGY.

COST DRIVERS are analogous drivers that affect the cost of an end product.

Unit Cost: the sum of FIXED COSTS and VARIABLE COSTS of a unit of output at a certain volume of business activity. For example, the UNIT COSTS of widgets at three levels of activity are as follows.

	VOLUME OF ACTIVITY (Number of widget units produced)		
	100 units	*125 units*	*150 units*
Total fixed costs	$300	$300	$300
Total variable costs ($4 per unit)	400	500	600
Fixed costs (per unit)	$3.00	$2.40	$2.00
Variable cost (per unit)	4.00	4.00	4.00
UNIT COST	$7.00	$6.40	$6.00

Notice that the UNIT COST depends on the number of units produced. In this example, it is because of the ECONOMIES OF SCALE involved in spreading the FIXED COST of $300 over more units. The FIXED COST per unit can change depending on the volume of activity and on the CUMULATIVE EXPERIENCE of business activity.

The relative size of the fixed and variable portions of UNIT COSTS can have a significant effect on PRICE COMPETITION and RIVALRY in the industry.

Unmatched Leverage: occurs when a competitor is benefiting from STRATEGIC LEVERAGE that a business has not or cannot duplicate. UNMATCHED LEVERAGE usually arises when the competitor is part of a company that has a CORPORATE STRATEGY which provides some significant form of STRATEGIC LEVERAGE that the business's company does not provide.

Examples of unmatched leverage are often found in the distribution stage of the VALUE ADDED CHAIN. For example, a competitor may be part of a company that has a number of businesses that distribute products through the same channel. That competitor may have significant unmatched leverage vis-à-vis a competing business that is part of a company that has no other businesses using the same distribution channel.

A company with a number of businesses facing competitors with unmatched leverage is usually a company without a well-thought-out CONCEPT OF FIT. Therefore, some strategists consider the analysis of unmatched leverage to be a good indicator of the effectiveness of a corporate strategy.

Unsystematic Risk: the risk that is associated with a particular investment. In the case of the stock of a specific company, the UN-SYSTEMATIC RISK of that investment arises from events that specifically affect that company and not the overall economy. Examples would be labor strikes, plane crashes, or the invention of a new SUB-STITUTE PRODUCT. UNSYSTEMATIC RISK is contrasted with SYSTEM-ATIC RISK, which is related to events that affect all companies to a greater or lesser extent and is sometimes referred to as market risk.

The CAPITAL ASSET PRICING MODEL is based on the premise that DIVERSIFICATION can eliminate unsystematic risk and not systematic risk. Therefore, investors are rewarded only for the systematic risk associated with an investment and are not rewarded for the unsystematic risk.

Upstream Value: *see* VALUE STREAM.

Upswing: *see* BUSINESS CYCLE.

Utility: a hypothetical measure of the total satisfaction obtained from consuming a given quantity of a commodity. This is the formal economic definition of UTILITY. Strategists define the term more loosely as the usefulness of a product in satisfying a need of a buyer and differentiate among "types" of utility arising from particular attributes or features of a product.

These types of utility can be classified with respect to form, time, location, and control. Form utility is increased when products are augmented to make them more useful or attractive. Time utility is increased when products are augmented to make them available when wanted. Location utility is increased when products are augmented to make them more conveniently available. Control utility is increased when products are made more available in a type of ownership that is more attractive to the buyer. For example, form utility might be added to a car with options, time utility might be added with quick delivery, location utility might be added with a nearby dealership, and control utility might be added by making the car rentable.

Analyzing the utility of a product is important in understanding PRODUCT DIFFERENTIATION. The PRODUCT ATTRIBUTE CURVE is one tool used to analyze the utility of a product.

Many strategists see BUYER VALUE as being determined by a product's combination of price and utility.

Utility Curve: a curve illustrating the relationship between the quantity of a good consumed and the total satisfaction derived. The basic premise is that total UTILITY increases as each additional unit of a good is consumed but that the MARGINAL UTILITY added by each successive unit decreases. As a result, the curve takes the shape shown in the graph that follows, rising but at a decreasing rate. Notice that the UTILITY added as the fourth unit of the good is consumed is much less than that gained when the first unit is consumed.

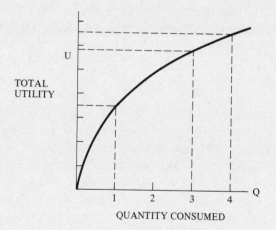

The notion of UTILITY plays a central role in economists' descriptions of consumer behavior and in their explanations of the downward slope of the DEMAND curve.

V

Value: the accrued benefit derived from owning a product, business, or company. A product's VALUE is based on a COST ADVANTAGE or the ability to provide UTILITY or both. A business's VALUE is reflected in its ability to add to the ECONOMIC VALUE of the company by contributing to its level of STRATEGIC LEVERAGE. A company's VALUE is determined by the social and ECONOMIC VALUE it offers its shareholders.

Value Added: the difference between the selling price of a flow of output and the costs of the purchased inputs used in making it. VALUE ADDED arises from the activities of a business which add UTILITY to the product or provide information to the buyer. For example, form UTILITY is added to sugar when raw sugar is refined. Therefore, refined sugar has more VALUE ADDED than raw sugar. Additional form UTILITY is added when the refined sugar is packaged. VALUE can also be added when a company provides the buyer with information about the product. For example, an advertised brand of sugar which carries a higher price is considered to have more VALUE ADDED than a lower priced nonadvertised brand. Note that VALUE ADDED is the additional amount the buyer is willing to pay for the end product over and above the business's purchased value. Therefore, by definition, VALUE ADDED includes profits. A VALUE ADDED CHAIN is a graphic representation of the activities which add VALUE as a product is transformed from raw material and delivered to the END USER. A business may be involved in any number of activities in the VALUE ADDED CHAIN. For example, an integrated food processor may be involved in a number of VALUE ADDED steps from growing the raw materials to advertising the finished product. On the other hand, a retailer may add VALUE by just purchasing products from a wholesaler and making them available in stores. The greater the number of VALUE ADDED stages a business participates in, the greater its VERTICAL INTEGRATION. The degree of VERTICAL INTEGRATION in an industry and the variation in degree among the competitors are key aspects of INDUSTRY STRUCTURE.

Value Added Advantage: a technique for identifying a business's potential STRENGTHS by analyzing its COST STRUCTURE. Diagrams of VALUE ADDED CHAINS are usually annotated to show the business's advantages and disadvantages and then compared with similar diagrams of the business's competitors. For example:

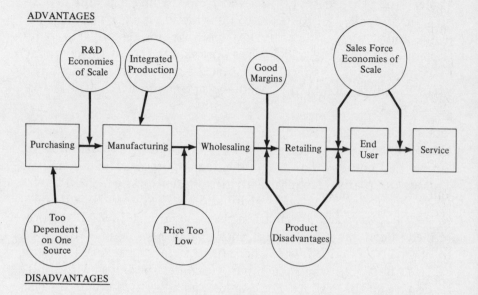

Note that the advantages or disadvantages can be expressed in short phrases, as in the diagram, or can be quantified by using measures such as VALUE ADDED SHARE.

Value Added Chain: the sequence of activities performed as raw materials are transformed into products and delivered to the END USER.

The term also refers to a graphic representation of the product's COST STRUCTURE from the purchase of raw materials to the final sale to END USER. VALUE ADDED CHAINS can be developed in more or less detail and can be drawn in relative scale to illustrate the relevant points about the UNIT COSTS of manufacturing and selling a given product.

Purchasing Costs 2%	Raw Materials 10%	Fixed Manufacturing 20%	Variable Manufacturing 8%	Overhead 5%	Advertising Costs 20%	Promotion Costs 12%	Sales Costs 10%	Warehousing Costs 5%	Distributing Costs 8%

VALUE ADDED CHAINS are drawn to illustrate the costs incurred during one value added stage as a proportion of total costs rather than sales dollars, ignoring the profits of the business. As a result, comparisons of competitors' VALUE ADDED CHAINS are not affected by differences in pricing policies.

VALUE ADDED CHAINS can be drawn to cover only the stages in which a given business participates, or they can be drawn for the entire chain of the product. The latter allows the comparison of the extent of one business's participation with its more or less VERTICALLY INTEGRATED competitors.

VALUE ADDED CHAINS can also be drawn to emphasize the fixed and variable components of the COST STRUCTURE as well as to emphasize the various stages of the chain and their related effect on total costs. VALUE ADDED CHAINS play an important role in COST ANALYSIS.

Value Added Share: an indicator of COST ADVANTAGES or STRATEGIC LEVERAGE enjoyed by a business at a particular VALUE ADDED stage due to SHARED COSTS, SHARED EXPERIENCE, or FUNCTIONAL FIT with other businesses in a company's portfolio. VALUE ADDED SHARE focuses attention on the expenditures of the company as a whole for goods or services in a particular activity and measures the importance of the company as a consumer or buyer of these goods or services. Consider two manufacturers of roofing shingles of roughly equal size which sell their product through building material distributors. One is a stand-alone business, and the other is part of a company which manufactures other building supplies that it also sells through the same channel. A comparison of their VALUE ADDED SHARES, that is, the ratio of the companywide expenditures of each competitor to the total received by the building supply distributors, may shed light on differences between the competitors. The higher VALUE ADDED SHARE enjoyed by the second business as part of a larger company may be reflected as a COST ADVANTAGE at the distribution stage of the VALUE ADDED CHAIN.

Value Analysis: an explicit cost-cutting program based on the identification of components that can be redesigned, standardized, or made by cheaper methods of production. A purchasing agent who is acting as a value analyst will carefully examine the high-cost components in a given product, often finding that 20 percent of the parts will comprise about 80 percent of the costs. The examination involves five considerations.

1. Can a nonstandardized part be slightly redesigned into a standardized part? If so, competitive bids can be solicited, and this generally leads to lower prices.
2. Can a nonstandardized part's function be modified to allow use of a standardized part?
3. Can two or more parts be combined into one?
4. Can cheaper substitute materials be used or materials that allow savings in the costs of molds and dies?
5. Can suppliers make certain parts for less by improving their tooling, by grouping similar work, or by increasing quantities?

Some companies have similar programs called value engineering. This type of program can be important in implementing a COST LEADERSHIP STRATEGY or an EXPERIENCE-BASED PRICING POLICY.

Value-Based Strategy: another name for a DIFFERENTIATION STRATEGY. The COMPETITIVE STRATEGY is called value-based because it often includes a MARKETING POLICY based on giving the buyer more value at a LIFE CYCLE PRICE than the competition. It often includes a MANUFACTURING POLICY based on looking for ways to modify the product to provide even more VALUE.

Value Chain: a diagram of the activities of a BUSINESS UNIT in designing, producing, marketing, and distributing its product which is used to understand the behavior of costs and the existing and potential sources of differentiation. The activities of a business are divided into the nine generic categories displayed on the VALUE CHAIN (page 341). The nine categories include five primary or direct activities (inbound logistics, operations, outbound logistics, marketing and sales, and service) and four support or indirect activities (firm infrastructure, human resource management, technology development, and procurement). By extending the support activities horizontally across all five of the primary activities, the VALUE CHAIN emphasizes the fact that each activity of a business, often referred to as a value activity, employs purchased inputs, human resources, technology, and information.

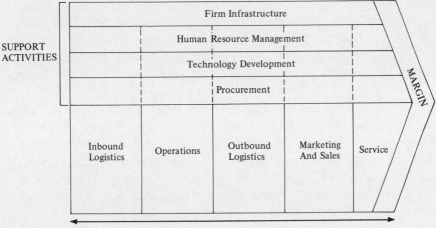

SUPPORT
ACTIVITIES

| Firm Infrastructure |
| Human Resource Management |
| Technology Development |
| Procurement |

| Inbound Logistics | Operations | Outbound Logistics | Marketing And Sales | Service |

MARGIN

Upstream Value Activities   Downstream Value Activities

PRIMARY ACTIVITIES

This treatment of purchased inputs and the distinction between primary and support activities distinguish the VALUE CHAIN from the VALUE ADDED CHAIN. The generic activities can be subdivided further in cases when activities have different economics, when they have a strong impact on the business's differentiation, or when they represent a significant or growing proportion of total costs.

The VALUE CHAIN itself can be drawn to emphasize several aspects of the underlying analysis of the business's activities. The area on the diagram devoted to each activity is frequently drawn in proportion to the distribution of operation costs or assets involved in each activity. When presented in this way, the VALUE CHAIN approach highlights the activities with the greatest significance and counteracts the tendency to focus on manufacturing activities alone when analyzing costs. The VALUE CHAIN is also used to display the COST DRIVERS behind each activity. Identification of the COST DRIVERS in this fashion gives insight into the LINKAGES between value activities.

Exploiting LINKAGES between activities and discovering new ways to configure the VALUE CHAIN of a business are a means of creating COMPETITIVE ADVANTAGE for the strategist. The VALUE CHAIN approach is also valuable in COMPETITOR ANALYSIS. Differences in the configuration of the VALUE CHAINS of individual competitors often indicate the sources of COST ADVANTAGE or DIFFERENTIATION within an industry.

The series of VALUE CHAINS, including those of the suppliers to the business itself, and the buyers served by the business are referred to as the VALUE STREAM. The vertical LINKAGES between these chains can present a business with OPPORTUNITIES to reconfigure its VALUE CHAIN by taking on new activities or by shifting current activities either upstream to suppliers or downstream to distributors or buyers.

Value Creation: the generation of ECONOMIC VALUE by companies for their shareholders through FINANCIAL LEVERAGE and STRATEGIC LEVERAGE. A company's blueprint for VALUE CREATION through STRATEGIC LEVERAGE is called a CORPORATE STRATEGY at the corporate level and is called a COMPETITIVE STRATEGY at the business level. Finding ways to build STRATEGIC LEVERAGE is the prime responsibility of the strategist.

Value Curve: a graph used to identify and examine the relationship between a company's stock price and its profitability. The graph is drawn using the company's MARKET-TO-BOOK RATIO as a measure of the elevation of its stock price and the ratio of RETURN ON EQUITY to its COST OF EQUITY as a measure of the ECONOMIC VALUE being generated by the company.

A VALUE CURVE is drawn for a group of companies which are growing at the same rate with the assumption that this growth rate is both a stable one and an indicator of future growth potential. The exhibit that follows shows a typical VALUE CURVE for eight companies.

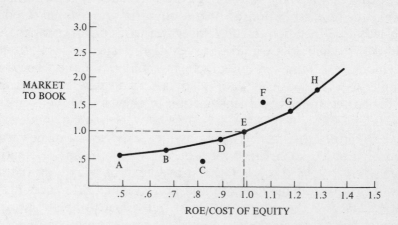

The position and shape of the curve are explained by two assertions: (1) that shareholders will pay an increasing amount over the BOOK

VALUE of the company for returns in excess of their REQUIRED RE-TURN and (2) that shareholders will only pay BOOK VALUE for a company that is earning their REQUIRED RETURN.

Some theorists feel that there is a normal VALUE CURVE that applies to all companies at a given level of growth. Others are more comfortable drawing VALUE CURVES for companies that have businesses competing in similar industries, for companies with a similar level of corporate sales, for companies with similar amounts of assets, or for an individual company at different points in time.

The eight companies were located on the graph in the exhibit on the basis of their MARKET-TO-BOOK RATIO and on the basis of their RETURN ON EQUITY to their COST OF EQUITY. Note that Company E's RETURN ON EQUITY was equal to its COST OF EQUITY, and so its ratio of ROE/cost of equity is 1.0. Therefore, its MARKET-TO-BOOK RATIO is also 1.0. Also note that the four companies that were returning less than their COST OF EQUITY have a MARKET-TO-BOOK RATIO of less than one and that the three companies that were returning more than their COST OF EQUITY have a MARKET-TO-BOOK RATIO of greater than one.

Companies like C that fall below the curve and companies like F that fall above it require further analysis in order to explain why the investor values them disproportionately to their returns. The first question is whether the company's COST OF EQUITY was correctly estimated. If, after further analysis, the COST OF EQUITY still seems right, then the answer is expected to lie with the investor's perception of the company or the assumption that the company's current growth rate is indicative of its future growth. In the case of companies like Company C, the investors doubt either the company's reported RE-TURN ON EQUITY or its ability to maintain that return within the investor's time frame. In the case of companies like Company F, the investors have some reason to think that the company is going to earn an even higher RETURN ON EQUITY during the investor's time frame.

Deviations from the VALUE CURVE can be explained by such extraordinary events as a major acquisition or DIVESTMENT, a significant strike in one or more of the company's businesses, the effects of CYCLICALITY, or the fact that the company has a number of businesses with aggressive BUILD PLANS in high MARKET GROWTH industries that are incurring high near-term expenses, etc.

The horizontal axis for the VALUE CURVE shown earlier was based on the ratio of each company's RETURN ON EQUITY to its COST OF

EQUITY. VALUE CURVES are also drawn using the difference between the company's ROE and its COST OF EQUITY or simply RETURN ON EQUITY.

Those theorists who feel that the appropriate VALUE CURVE for each company must be estimated individually suggest three approaches. The first is to plot a historical VALUE CURVE for the company by using its MARKET-TO-BOOK RATIO and some measure of its return taken at different points in time. The second is to plot a VALUE CURVE for a number of companies that are somehow similar to the given company. The third is to plot industry VALUE CURVES for each industry the company's business competes in. The data for industry VALUE CURVES is very difficult to collect because there are rarely enough undiversified companies in an industry. Therefore, the relevant data for competitors has to be estimated from data for their diversified parents. Once the series of industry VALUE CURVES is drawn, each curve must be weighted by the sales or assets that the company has in each industry to get a composite VALUE CURVE. Strategists who agree with these theorists use whatever combination of the three approaches seems to give them the most information.

Theorists also debate the use of BOOK VALUE in a MARKET-TO-BOOK RATIO. Some feel that VALUE CURVES are not relevant unless the data has been adjusted for REPLACEMENT VALUE. They point out that a company may have a high MARKET-TO-BOOK RATIO simply because the BOOK VALUE of its assets is very low relative to the REPLACEMENT VALUE. Other theorists feel that this sort of adjustment is unnecessary.

Strategists who use VALUE CURVES feel that they provide a basis for relating their company's performance with the reaction of their shareholders. The curve gives them an idea of what kind of stock price they can expect if they earn a given RETURN ON EQUITY or what kind of RETURN ON EQUITY they will have to earn if they want a given stock price.

Strategists who are uncomfortable with the VALUE CURVE concept usually argue that there is too much uncertainty involved in developing the data points to make the curve useful. They point to the problem with REPLACEMENT VALUE in the MARKET-TO-BOOK RATIO, and they point to the number of estimates that are involved in determining a company's COST OF EQUITY or REQUIRED RETURN. Finally, they argue that the assumption that a group of companies can be selected that have a similar level of stable growth potential is unrealistic.

Value Leverage Ratio: the ratio of RETURN ON EQUITY to its COST OF CAPITAL. VALUE LEVERAGE RATIOS can be calculated at the company or business level. For example, a company that has a 25 percent RETURN ON EQUITY and a 20 percent COST OF CAPITAL would have a VALUE LEVERAGE RATIO of 1.25. That company level ratio is used as one way to express ECONOMIC VALUE. Company level VALUE LEVERAGE RATIOS are used to compare the ECONOMIC VALUE of a company at different points in time and to compare one company's ECONOMIC VALUE with that of a number of other companies. Some strategists use a company level VALUE LEVERAGE RATIO on the vertical axis in drawing a VALUE CURVE.

Business level VALUE LEVERAGE RATIOS can be calculated for each business in a company's portfolio. This is easiest to do in a company that has no long-term debt in its CAPITAL STRUCTURE. In that case, the company's equity is usually allocated to each business on the basis of relative amount of assets employed in that business. The return on equity is then calculated for each business. Some strategists then use the company's COST OF EQUITY as the denominator for each business's VALUE LEVERAGE RATIO. Other strategists attempt to develop a COST OF EQUITY based on an assessment of the RISK for each business or based on COST OF EQUITY estimates for companies that generate most of their sales from the business's industry. If the company has debt, then the calculation is somewhat more difficult. The debt must be allocated to each business, and each business's returns must be adjusted accordingly for the cost of its allocated debt. Some strategists allocate that debt on the basis of an assessment of the credit worthiness of each business. However, there is no obvious way to do it.

Business level VALUE LEVERAGE RATIOS are used to assess which businesses in the company's portfolio are contributing to the company's ability to create ECONOMIC VALUE and which businesses are not.

Value Signal: a MARKET SIGNAL which buyers use to weigh the BUYER VALUE of a business's products. VALUE SIGNALS include advertising, reputation, information provided by the business, and the appearance of employees or facilities. COMPLEMENTARY PRODUCTS can also serve as VALUE SIGNALS to buyers. The strategist must be aware of the factors which affect the buyer's perception of a product's value and must often search for ways to influence those factors over which the business has no direct control. This is important for a business pursuing any GENERIC STRATEGY but is especially important when differentiation is the COMPETITIVE ADVANTAGE.

Value Stream: the range of activities that add value to a product from the procurement of supplies to purchase by the END USER. A VALUE STREAM is often illustrated as a series of VALUE ADDED CHAINS as follows.

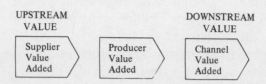

An analysis of the VALUE ADDED in each of these stages helps to understand the relative profitability of companies with businesses competing in each stage or combinations thereof.

The VALUE SYSTEM is a more sophisticated approach to understanding upstream and DOWNSTREAM VALUE and the COMPETITIVE SCOPE of the companies involved.

Value System: a technique for analyzing the stream of activities that add VALUE to a product. A typical VALUE SYSTEM arrays VALUE CHAINS for all activities from the mining of raw materials to consumption by the END USER. Such a VALUE SYSTEM is often illustrated as follows.

Strategists who work with value systems emphasize the importance of understanding the value system context in which a given business operates. They also emphasize the importance of understanding upstream value in supplier chains and the DOWNSTREAM VALUE in buyer value chains as a means of building and maintaining COMPETITIVE ADVANTAGE.

Basic value systems can be expanded horizontally to indicate the COMPETITIVE SCOPE of the companies with businesses competing in the industry and upstream or downstream of the industry. For example, a complex value system designed to show participation in upstream activities of each of four companies might be illustrated as follows.

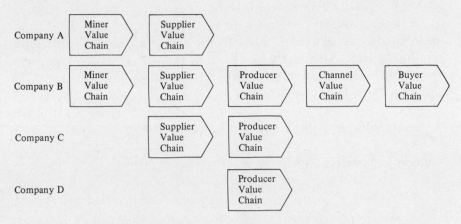

That value system could be further expanded to show value chains for each channel or group of channels or to show value chains for each buyer group or individual buyer. Most strategists start with a general illustration of the value system and then build an increasing amount of detail into each value chain as needed.

Some strategists add that in many industries it is becoming important to go beyond the END USER to the disposer and include a value chain of that disposer or salvager in order to have a complete system.

Variable Cost: a cost that varies proportionately with changes in the volume of production or the level of activity. Manufacturing VARIABLE COSTS often include direct labor, direct materials, and energy costs. By strict definition, VARIABLE COSTS should vary proportionately, but in practice they may not. For example, a 10 percent increase in production may require less than a 10 percent increase in energy required. Costs that do change but do not vary proportionately with changes in volume are often called semivariable or semifixed costs.

FIXED COSTS are the opposite of VARIABLE COSTS.

Vertical Integration: occurs when a business participates in more than one stage of a product's VALUE ADDED CHAIN. For example, a manufacturing company that is completely integrated participates in all stages of its product's VALUE ADDED CHAIN from the extraction of the raw materials through all stages of manufacturing, marketing, distributing, right up to delivering the finished product to the END USER.

A business which moves into activities closer to the beginning of the VALUE ADDED CHAIN is said to be integrating backward, and one moving into activities closer to the END USER is said to be integrating forward. The degree of VERTICAL INTEGRATION in an industry has a major impact on its structure, particularly on the relationships with suppliers and buyers.

Vertical Linkage: *see* LINKAGE.

Volume Industries: *see* POTENTIAL ADVANTAGE MATRIX.

W

Weaknesses: *see* STRENGTHS AND WEAKNESSES.

Working Capital: a company's current assets minus its current liabilities. (Sometimes WORKING CAPITAL refers only to the current assets, and the term "net working capital" is used to mean the difference between current assets and current liabilities.) Current assets are comprised primarily of cash, short-term securities, accounts receivable, and inventories. The level of investment in these assets is closely related to the level of sales generated by a business. Some types of current liabilities, such as accounts payable and accruals, also tend to increase with sales whereas the level of bank loans and the balance between long- and short-term borrowings are determined by the company's financial policies.

Because there is an OPPORTUNITY COST to the use of WORKING CAPITAL, many strategists feel that it is important to analyze the WORKING CAPITAL requirements of the businesses in a company's portfolio. Balancing the WORKING CAPITAL needs of the businesses in the company's portfolio as an element of FINANCIAL FIT can reduce overall financing requirements. To this end, strategists often analyze the mix of businesses in their portfolios to determine the extent to which they offset each other's seasonal and cyclical trends or requirements for growth. The GROWTH/SHARE MATRIX is often used as part of such an analysis.

Z

Zero-Base Budgeting: a budgeting process in which all expenditures (and the underlying programs) are reviewed each period, not just incremental amounts or expenditures. Under a nonzero-based budget system, most historical expenditures are assumed to continue, and only incremental expenditures are reviewed.

Some strategists favor ZERO-BASE BUDGETING because they feel that it requires the business to analyze its total competitive situation in order to justify all its expenditures. They argue that marginal programs are less likely to be carried from year to year and that alternative, more cost-effective ways of carrying out programs are more likely to be put forward. Others feel that the cost of spending the additional time required exceeds the benefits.

Zero-Sum Game: a situation in GAME THEORY in which one player's gain is another player's loss. It is a game in which it is impossible for both competitors to do well. Strategists often refer to the competitive situation in some industries as being ZERO-SUM. They are implying that in such an industry any gain in the profitability of one competitor must come at the expense of another. This description is often used to describe RIVALRY in an industry with low or no growth, where a business considering a BUILD PLAN can increase sales only if competitors' sales slow or drop.

Bibliography

AAKER, DAVID A. *Developing Business Strategies.* New York: Wiley, 1984.

ABELL, DEREK F. *Defining the Business.* Englewood Cliffs, N.J.: Prentice-Hall, 1980.

——, and JOHN S. HAMMOND. *Strategic Market Planning.* Englewood Cliffs, N.J.: Prentice-Hall, 1979.

ABERNATHY, W. J. "The Limits of the Learning Curve." *Harvard Business Review,* September–October 1974.

——, KIM B. CLARK, and ALAN M. KANTROW. *Industrial Renaissance.* New York: Basic Books, 1983.

ACKOFF, RUSSELL L. *A Concept of Corporate Planning.* New York: Wiley, 1970.

——. *Creating the Corporate Future: Plan or Be Planned For.* New York: Wiley, 1981.

AGUILAR, FRANCIS J. *Scanning the Business Environment.* New York: Macmillan, 1967.

ALLEN, MICHAEL. "The Corporate Strategy Gaps." *Management Today,* September 1980.

——, ALEXANDER R. OLIVER, and EDWARD H. SCHWALLIE. "The Key to Successful Acquisitions." *Journal of Business Strategy,* Fall 1981.

351

ALLIO, ROBERT J., and MALCOLM W. PENNINGTON, eds. *Corporate Planning*. New York: AMACON, American Management Association, 1979.

AMES, CHARLES B. "Marketing Planning for Industrial Products." *Harvard Business Review,* September–October 1958.

ANDREWS, KENNETH R. *The Concept of Corporate Strategy.* Homewood, Ill.: Irwin, 1980.

ANSOFF, H. IGOR. *Corporate Strategy: An Analytic Approach to Business Policy for Growth and Expansion.* New York: McGraw-Hill, 1965.

———. *Strategic Management.* New York: Wiley, 1979.

———, ROGER P. DECLERK, and ROBERT L. HAYS. *From Strategic Planning to Strategic Management.* New York: Wiley, 1976.

ANTHONY, ROBERT N., and JAMES S. REECE. *Management Accounting Principles.* Homewood, Ill.: Irwin, 1975.

BAIN, JOE S. *Industrial Organization.* New York: Wiley, 1959.

BAKER, EDWIN L. "Managing Organizational Culture." *The McKinsey Quarterly,* Autumn 1980.

BALL, BEN C., JR., and PETER LORANGE. "Managing Your Strategic Responsiveness to the Environment." *Managerial Planning,* November–December 1979.

BECKER, JANE. "Programming for Profit." *Executive,* February 1979.

BENJAMIN, ROBERT I., JOHN F. ROCKART, MICHAEL S. SCOTT MORTON, and JOHN WYMAN. "Information Technology: A Strategic Opportunity." *Sloan Management Review,* Spring 1984.

BETTIS, RICHARD A., and WILLIAM K. HALL. "Strategic Portfolio Management in the Multibusiness Firm." *California Management Review,* Fall 1981.

BIERMAN, HAROLD, JR. *Strategic Financial Planning.* New York: Free Press, 1980.

BIGGADIKE, RALPH. "Entry Strategy and Performance." Strategic Planning Institute, August, 1976.

BONGE, JOHN W., and BRUCE P. COLEMAN. *Concepts for Corporate Strategy.* New York: Macmillan, 1972.

BONOMA, THOMAS V. *The Marketing Edge.* New York: Free Press, 1985.

———, and BENSON P. SHAPIRO. *Segmenting the Industrial Market.* Lexington, Mass.: Lexington Books, 1983.

Boston Consulting Group. *Perspectives on Experience.* Cambridge, Mass.: Boston Consulting Group, 1972.

BOULTON, WILLIAM R., et al. "How Are Companies Planning Now?—A Survey." *Long Range Planning,* 15, 1982.

BOWER, JOSEPH L. "Solving the Problems of Business Planning." *Journal of Business Strategy,* Winter 1982.

———. *The Two Faces of Management.* Boston: Houghton Mifflin, 1983.

BOWMAN, EDWARD H. "A Risk/Return Paradox for Strategic Management." *Sloan Management Review,* Spring 1980.

BRADLEY, JAMES W., and DONALD H. KORN. *Acquisition and Corporate Development.* Lexington, Mass.: Lexington Books, 1981.

BRANCH, MELVILLE C. *The Corporate Planning Process.* New York: American Management Association, 1962.

BREALEY, RICHARD, and STEWART MYERS. *Principles of Corporate Finance.* New York: McGraw-Hill, 1981.

BROOKE, MICHAEL Z., and MARK VAN BUESEKUM. *International Corporate Planning.* London: Pitman, 1979.

BUARON, ROBERTO. "How to Win the Market-Share Game? Try Changing the Rules." *Management Review,* January 1981.

———. "New-Game Strategies." *The McKinsey Quarterly,* Spring 1981.

BUFFA, ELWOOD SPENCER. *Essentials of Management Science.* New York: Wiley, 1978.

BURNETT, C. DON, DENNIS P. YESKEY, and DAVID RICHARDSON. "New Roles for Corporate Planners in the 1980s." *Journal of Business Strategy,* Spring 1984.

BUTTERS, KEITH J., WILLIAM E. FRUHAN, and THOMAS R. PIPER, eds. *Case Problems in Finance.* Homewood, Ill.: Irwin, 1975.

BUZZELL, ROBERT D. "Are There Natural Market Structures?" *Journal of Marketing,* Winter 1981.

———, BRADLEY T. GALE, and R. G. SULTAN. "Market Share—A Key to Profitability." *Harvard Business Review,* January–February 1975.

———, ROBERT E. M. NOURSE, JOHN B. MATTHEWS, JR., and THEODORE LEVITT. *Marketing a Contemporary Analysis.* New York: McGraw-Hill, 1972.

CAPON, NOEL, JOHN U. FARLEY, and JAMES HULBERT. "International Diffusion of Corporate and Strategic Planning Practices." *Columbia Journal of World Business,* Fall 1980.

CANNON, J. THOMAS. *Business Strategy and Policy.* New York: Harcourt, 1968.

CARROLL, GLENN R. "The Specialist Strategy." *California Management Review,* Spring 1984.

CARROLL, PETER J. "The Link Between Performance and Strategy." *Journal of Business Strategy,* Spring 1982.

CAVES, RICHARD. "Corporate Strategy and Structure." *Journal of Economic Literature,* 1B, 1980.

——. *American Industry: Structure, Conduct, Performance.* Englewood Cliffs, N.J.: Prentice-Hall, 1982.

CHAMBERLAIN, NEIL. *Social Strategy and Corporate Culture.* New York: Free Press, 1982.

CHANDLER, ALFRED D. *Strategy and Structure, Chapters in the History of the Industrial Enterprise.* Cambridge, Mass.: The MIT Press, 1962.

——. *The Visible Hand.* Cambridge, Mass.: Belknap Press, 1977.

CHANNON, DEREK F., with MICHAEL JALLAND. *Multinational Strategic Planning.* London: Macmillan, 1979.

CHARAN, RAM. "How to Strengthen Your Strategy Review Process." *Journal of Business Strategy,* Winter 1982.

CHRISTENSEN, C. ROLAND. *Policy Formulation and Administration.* Homewood, Ill.: Irwin, 1980.

——, KENNETH R. ANDREWS, JOSEPH L. BONER, RICHARD G. HAMMERMESH, and MICHAEL E. PORTER. *Business Policy: Texts and Cases.* Homewood, Ill.: Irwin, 1982.

CLARK, J. M. *Competition as a Dynamic Process.* Washington, D.C.: Brookings, 1961.

COLLIER, DON. "Strategic Management in Diversified, Decentralized Companies." *Journal of Business Strategy,* Summer 1982.

COLLIER, JAMES R. *Effective Long Range Business Planning.* Englewood Cliffs, N.J.: Prentice-Hall, 1968.

COOPERS & LYBRAND. "Acquisitions Candidate-Product Lines and Markets." *Management Advisory Services,* April 1982.

COREY, E. RAYMOND. *Industrial Marketing.* Englewood Cliffs, N.J.: Prentice-Hall, 1976.

COX, CONNIE A. "Gap Analysis: A New Business Planning Essential." *Business Marketing,* May 1983.

CRAVENS, DAVID W., GERALD E. HILLS, and ROBERT B. WOODRUFF. *Marketing Decision Making: Concepts and Strategy.* Homewood, Ill.: Irwin, 1980.

CUNNINGHAM, MARY E. "Planning for Humanism." *Journal of Business Strategy,* Spring 1983.

CUSHMAN, ROBERT. "Corporate Strategy: Planning for the Future." Boston: North American Society for Corporate Planners, 1978.

DAVIDSON, KENNETH M. "Looking at the Strategic Impact of Mergers." *Journal of Business Strategy,* Summer 1981.

DAVIDSON, SIDNEY, JAMES S. SCHINDLER, CLYDE P. STICKNEY, and ROMAN

L. WEIL. *Accounting: The Language of Business.* Glen Ridge, N.J.: Thomas Horton, 1975–1976.

DAY, GEORGE S. "Diagnosing the Product Portfolio." *Journal of Marketing,* April 1977.

———. "Gaining Insights Through Strategy Analysis." *Journal of Business Strategy,* Summer 1983.

DEAN, JOEL. "Pricing Policies for New Products." *Harvard Business Review,* November 1950.

DENNING, BASIL W. *Corporate Planning.* New York: McGraw-Hill, 1971.

DIMMA, WILLIAM A. "A Perspective on Presidents and Planning." Remarks to the Annual Conference of the North American Society for Corporate Planning, June 1981.

DOLAN, PATRICK F. "A Four-Phased Rescue Plan for Today's Troubled Companies." *Journal of Business Strategy,* Summer 1983.

DONALDSON, GORDON. "Financial Goals and Strategic Consequences." *Harvard Business Review,* May–June 1985.

DONHAM, WALLACE BRETT. *Business Adrift.* New York: McGraw-Hill, 1931.

DOZ, YVES L. "Strategic Management in Multinational Companies." *Sloan Management Review,* Winter 1980.

DRUCKER, PETER F. *The Concept of the Corporation.* New York: Day, 1946.

DYER, WILLIAM G. *Contemporary Issues on Management and Organization Development.* Reading, Mass.: Addison-Wesley, 1983.

EBELING, H. WILLIAM, JR., and THOMAS DOORLEY. "A Strategic Approach to Acquisitions." *Journal of Business Strategy,* Winter 1983.

ECCLES, ROBERT G. *The Transfer Pricing Problem.* Lexington, Mass.: Lexington Books, 1985.

ELFREY, PRISCILLA. *The Hidden Agenda.* New York: Wiley, 1982.

ENIS, BEN M. "GE, PIMS, BCG, and the PLC." *Business,* May–June 1980.

ENSHOFF, J. R., and A. FINNEL. "Defining Corporate Strategy: A Case Study Using Strategic Assumptives." *Sloan Management Review,* Spring 1979.

EWING, DAVID W. *Long-Range Planning for Management.* New York: Harper & Row, 1972.

FOLLET, MARY PARKER. *Dynamic Administration: The Collected Papers of Mary Parker Follet.* Edited by Henry C. Metcalf and L. Urwick. New York: Harper, 1942.

FOMBURN, CHARLES, and W. GRAHAM ASTLEY. "Beyond Corporate Strategy." *Journal of Business Strategy,* Spring 1983.

FORBIS, JOHN L., and NITIN T. MEHTA. "Value-Based Strategy for Industrial Products." *The McKinsey Quarterly,* Summer 1981.

FOURAKER, LAURENCE E., and SIDNEY SIEGEL. *Bargaining Behavior.* New York: McGraw-Hill, 1963.

FREIER, JEROLD L. "Acquisition Search Programs." *Mergers and Acquisitions,* Summer 1981.

FROHMAN, ALAN L. "Putting Technology into Strategic Planning." *California Management Review,* Winter 1985.

FRUHAN, WILLIAM E., JR. *Financial Strategy.* Homewood, Ill.: Irwin, 1979.

———. "How Fast Should Your Company Grow?" *Harvard Business Review,* January–February 1984.

GALBRAITH, JAY R., and DANIEL A. NATHANSON. *Strategy Implementation: The Role of Structure and Process.* St. Paul, Minn.: West Publishing, 1978.

GALBRAITH, JOHN K. *American Capitalism: The Concept of Countervailing Power.* Cambridge, Mass.: Houghton Mifflin, 1952.

GARVIN, DAVID A. "What Does Product Quality Really Mean?" *Sloan Management Review,* Fall 1984.

GEORGE, CLAUDE S. *The History of Management Thought.* Englewood Cliffs, N.J.: Prentice-Hall, 1972.

GHEMAWAT, PANKAJ. "Building Strategy on the Experience Curve." *Harvard Business Review,* March–April 1985.

GLEUCK, WILLIAM F. *Strategic Management and Business Policy: A Book of Readings.* New York: McGraw-Hill, 1980.

GLUCK, FREDERICK W. "Strategic Choice and Resource Allocation." *The McKinsey Quarterly,* Winter 1980.

———. "Meeting the Challenge of Global Competition." *The McKinsey Quarterly,* Autumn 1982.

———, STEPHEN KAUFMAN, and STEVEN A. WALLECK. "The Four Phases of Strategic Management." *Journal of Business Strategy,* Winter 1982.

GOLDHAR, JOEL D., and MARIANN JELINEK. "The Interface Between Strategy and Manufacturing Technology." *Columbia Journal of World Business,* Spring 1983.

GRANT, JOHN, and WILLIAM R. KING. *The Logic of Strategic Planning.* Boston: Little, Brown, 1982.

GRAY, EDMUND R., ed. *Business Policy and Strategy: Selected Readings.* Austin, Tex.: Austin Press, 1979.

GUP, BENTON E. *Guide to Strategic Planning.* New York: McGraw-Hill, 1980.

GUPTA, ANIL K., and V. GOVINDARAJAN. "Build, Hold, Harvest: Converting Strategic Intentions into Reality." *Journal of Business Strategy,* Winter 1984.

HALL, WILLIAM K. "SBU's: Hot, New Topic in the Management of Diversification." *Business Horizons,* February 1978.

HAMMERMESH, RICHARD G., ed. *Strategic Management.* New York: Wiley, 1983.

——, and RODERICK E. WHITE. "Manage Beyond Portfolio Analysis." *Harvard Business Review,* January–February 1984.

HANER, FREDERICK T. *Global Business Strategy for the 1980s.* New York: Praeger, 1980.

HARRIGAN, KATHRYN RUDIE. *Strategies for Declining Industries.* Lexington, Mass.: Lexington Books, 1980.

——. *Strategic Flexibility.* Lexington, Mass.: Lexington Books, 1985.

HASPESLAGH, P. "Portfolio Planning: Uses and Limits." *Harvard Business Review,* January–February 1982.

HATTEN, MARY LOUISE. *Microeconomics for Management.* Englewood Cliffs, N.J.: Prentice-Hall, 1981.

HAX, ARNOLDO C., and NICOLAS S. MAJLUF. *Strategic Management: An Integrative Perspective.* Englewood Cliffs, N.J.: Prentice-Hall, 1984.

HEANY, DONALD F. "Degrees of Product Innovation." *Journal of Business Strategy,* Spring 1983.

HELFERT, ERIC. *Techniques of Financial Analysis.* Homewood, Ill.: Irwin, 1977.

HENDERSON, BRUCE D. *Henderson on Corporate Strategy.* Cambridge, Mass.: Abt Books, 1979.

——. "Understanding the Forces of Strategic and Natural Competition." *Journal of Business Strategy,* Winter 1981.

——. *The Logic of Business Strategy.* Cambridge, Mass.: Ballinger, 1984.

——. "Strategic and Natural Competition." *Perspectives.* Boston: Boston Consulting Group.

HENRY, HAROLD W. *Long Range Planning Practices in 45 Industrial Companies.* Englewood Cliffs, N.J.: Prentice-Hall, 1967.

——. "Then and Now: A Look at Strategic Planning Systems." *Journal of Business Strategy,* Winter 1981.

HENZLER, HERBERT. "Functional Dogmas That Frustrate Strategy." *The McKinsey Quarterly,* Winter 1982.

HERTZ, DAVID B., and THOMAS HOWARD. "Evaluating the Risks in Acquisition." *Long Range Planning,* 15(6), 1982.

HESKETT, JAMES L. *Marketing.* New York: Macmillan, 1976.

HOFER, CHARLES W., and DAN SCHENDEL. *Strategy Formulation: Analytical Concepts.* St. Paul, Minn.: West Publishing, 1978.

HUFF, ANNE S. "Strategic Intelligence Systems." *Information and Management,* November 1979.

HUNSICKER, J. QUINCY. "The Malaise of Strategic Planning." *Management Review,* March 1980.

HUSSEY, DAVID E. *Corporate Planning Theory and Practice.* New York: Pergamon, 1982.

JACKSON, BARBARA B. *Computer Models in Management.* New York: Irwin, 1979.

————. *Winning and Keeping Industrial Customers: The Dynamics of Customer Relationships.* Lexington, Mass.: Lexington, 1985.

JACKSON, DONALD W., JR., and BRUCE J. WALKER. "The Channels Manager: Marketing's Newest Aide?" *California Management Review,* Winter 1980.

JANIS, IRVING L., and LEON MANN. *Decision Making.* New York: Free Press, 1977.

JOHNSON, BRUCE W., ASHOK NATARAJAN, and ALFRED RAPPAPORT. "Shareholder Returns and Corporate Excellence." *Journal of Business Strategy,* Fall 1985.

JUSTIS, ROBERT T., RICHARD J. JUDD, and DAVID B. STEPHENS. *Strategic Management and Policy—Concepts and Cases.* Englewood Cliffs, N.J.: Prentice-Hall, 1985.

KASTENS, MERRITT L. *Long-Range Planning for Your Business: An Operating Manual.* New York: AMACON, American Management Association, 1976.

KATZ, ROBERT L. *Cases and Concepts on Corporate Strategy.* Englewood Cliffs, N.J.: Prentice-Hall, 1970.

KERIN, ROGER A., and ROBERT A. PETERSON. *Perspectives on Strategic Marketing Management.* Boston: Allyn and Bacon, 1980.

KING, WILLIAM R., and DAVID I. CLELAND, *Strategic Planning and Policy.* New York: Van Nostrand, 1978.

KIERALFF, HERBERT E. "Finding the Best Acquisition Candidates." *Harvard Business Review,* 1981.

KIECHEL, WALTER, III. "Playing by the Rules of the Corporate Strategy Game." *Fortune,* September 24, 1979.

————. "The Decline of the Experience Curve." *Fortune,* October 5, 1981.

————. "Three (or Four, or More) Ways to Win." *Fortune,* October 19, 1981.

————. "Playing the Global Game." *Fortune,* November 16, 1981.

————. "Corporate Strategies Under Fire." *Fortune,* December 27, 1982.

KOGUT, BRUCE. "Designing Global Strategies: Comparative and Competitive Value Added Chains." *Sloan Management Review,* Summer 1985.

KOTLER, PHILIP. *Marketing Management.* Englewood Cliffs, N.J.: Prentice-Hall, 1976.

——. *Marketing Essentials.* New York: Prentice Hall, 1984.

KOTTER, JOHN P. *Power and Influence.* New York: Free Press, 1985.

——, LEONARD A. SCHLESINGER, and VIJAY SATHE. *Organization.* Homewood, Ill.: Irwin, 1979.

KREIKEN, J. "Formulating and Implementing a More Systematic Approach to Strategic Management." *Management Review,* July 1980.

KUEHN, ALFRED A., and RALPH L. DAY. "Strategy of Product Quality." *Harvard Business Review,* November–December 1962.

LAMB, ROBERT B., ed. *Competitive Strategic Management.* Englewood Cliffs, N.J.: Prentice-Hall, 1984.

LEAF, ROBIN H. "Learning from Your Competitors." *The McKinsey Quarterly,* Spring 1978.

LEFTWICH, RICHARD H. *The Price System and Resource Allocation.* 5th ed. Hinsdale, Ill.: Dryden, 1970.

LEONTIADES, MILTON. *Management Policy, Strategy and Plans.* Boston: Little, Brown, 1982.

——. *Strategies for Diversification and Change.* Boston: Little, Brown, 1980.

LEVITT, THEODORE. *Industrial Purchasing Behavior.* Boston: Harvard University, Graduate School of Business Administration, Division of Research, 1965.

LEVY, F. K., G. L. THOMPSON, and J. D. WIEST. "The ABCs of the Critical Path Method." *Harvard Business Review,* September–October 1963.

LEWIS, WALKER. "Strategic Planning Systems, Design and Operation." *Journal of Business Strategy,* Summer 1981.

LIGHT, J. O., and WILLIAM L. WHITE. *The Financial System.* Homewood, Ill.: Irwin, 1979.

LIPSEY, RICHARD G., and PETER O. STEINER. *Economics.* 5th. ed. New York: Harper & Row, 1978.

LORANGE, PETER. *Corporate Planning: An Executive Viewpoint.* Englewood Cliffs, N.J.: Prentice-Hall, 1980.

——, and RICHARD F. VANCIL. *Strategic Planning Systems.* Englewood Cliffs, N.J.: Prentice-Hall, 1977.

LORIE, JAMES H., and MARY T. HAMILTON. *The Stock Market.* Homewood, Ill.: Irwin, 1979.

LORSCH, JAY W., "Managing Diversity and Interdependence." Boston: Harvard University Graduate School of Business Administration, Division of Research, 1973.

LUCK, DAVID JOHNSTON. *Marketing Strategy and Plans.* Englewood Cliffs, N.J.: Prentice-Hall, 1979.

LYNCH, JACQUELINE MARA, compiler. *Student's Economic Dictionary.* Marblehead, Mass.: Mara, 1979.

MACAVOY, ROBERT E. "Corporate Strategy and the Power of Competitive Analysis." *Management Review,* July 1983.

MACMILLAN, IAN C. "Preemptive Strategies." *Journal of Business Strategies,* Fall 1983.

MAILANDT, PETER. "Simplifying the Search for Four-Leaf Clovers." *Harvard Business Review,* July–August 1982.

MARGOLIS, DIANE R. *The Managers.* New York: Morrow, 1979.

MARSH, TERRY A., and DOUGLAS S. SWANSON. "Risk-Return Trade-Offs for Strategic Management." *Sloan Management Review,* Spring 1984.

MARSHALL, LEON CARROLL. *Business Administration.* Chicago: University of Chicago Press, 1921.

MATHUR, SHIV SAHAI. "Competitive Industrial Marketing Strategies." *The McKinsey Quarterly,* Winter 1985.

MATZ, ADOLPH, and MILTON F. USRY. *Cost Accounting: Planning and Control.* 7th ed. Cincinnati: South-Western, 1980.

McCARTHY, DANIEL J., ROBERT J. MINICHIELLO, and JOSEPH R. CURRAN. *Business Policy and Strategy Concepts and Readings.* Homewood, Ill.: Irwin, 1979.

McDONALD, JOHN. *The Game of Business.* New York: Doubleday, 1975.

McFARLAN, F. WARREN. *Corporate Information Systems.* New York: Irwin, 1983.

McGINNIS, MICHAEL A. "The Key to Strategic Planning: Integrating Analysts and Intuition." *Sloan Management Review,* Fall 1984.

McLAGAN, DONALD L. "Improving on Seven Inadequacies of Traditional Cash Flow Analysis." *Data Resources,* June 1976.

———, and BEN BUFFA. "How to Grow in a Slow Growth Decade." *Journal of Business Strategy,* Winter 1982.

———, and PETER ZIESMER. "Analyzing Strategic Cost in a High-Inflation Economy." *Journal of Business Strategy,* Summer 1982.

McNAIR, MALCOLM PERRINE, and HOWARD T. LEWIS. *Business and Modern Society: Papers by Members of the Faculty of the Graduate School of Business Administration, Harvard University.* Cambridge, Mass.: Harvard University, 1938.

MILLS, D. QUINN. *The New Competitors.* New York: Wiley, 1985.

MINTZBERY, HENRY. *The Structuring of Organizations.* Englewood Cliffs, N.J.: Prentice-Hall, 1979.

MOFFAT, DONALD W., ed. *Concise Desk Book of Business Finance.* Englewood Cliffs, N.J.: Prentice-Hall, 1978.

MONTGOMERY, DAVID B., and CHARLES B. WEINBERG. "Toward Strategic Intelligence Systems." *Journal of Marketing,* Fall 1979.

MORIARTY, ROWLAND T. *Industrial Buyer Behavior: Concepts, Issues and Applications.* Lexington, Mass.: Lexington Books, 1983.

MOSKOWITZ, MILTON, MICHAEL KATZ, and ROBERT LEVERING, eds. *Everybody's Business.* San Francisco: Harper & Row, 1980.

NAYLOR, THOMAS H. *Corporate Planning Models.* Reading, Mass.: Addison-Wesley, 1979.

———. *Strategic Planning Management.* Ohio: Planning Executives Institute, 1980.

OHMAE, KENICHI. *The Mind of the Strategist.* New York: McGraw-Hill, 1982.

———. "The Strategic Triangle and Business Unit Strategy." *The McKinsey Quarterly,* Winter 1983.

———. *Triad Power, the Coming Shape of Global Competition.* New York: Free Press, 1985.

OXENFELDT, ALFRED R. "How to Use Market-Share Measurement." *Harvard Business Review,* January–February 1959.

———, and WILLIAM L. MOORE. "Competitor Analysis—A Price-Centered Approach." *Management Review,* May 1981.

PEARCE, JOHN A., II. *Strategic Management.* New York: Irwin, 1982.

PENROSE, EDITH T. *The Theory of Growth of the Firm.* Oxford: Blackwell, 1959.

PETERS, THOMAS, and NANCY AUSTIN. *A Passion for Excellence.* New York: Random House, 1985.

———, and ROBERT H. WATERMAN, JR. *In Search of Excellence: Lessons from America's Best Run Companies.* New York: Harper & Row, 1982.

POLLARD, HAROLD R. *Trends in Management Thinking 1960–1970.* New York: Gulf Publishing, 1978.

PORTER, MICHAEL E. *Interbrand Choice, Strategy and Bilateral Market Power.* Cambridge, Mass.: Harvard University Press, 1976.

———. *Competitive Strategy.* New York: Free Press, 1980.

———. *Competitive Advantage: Creating and Sustaining Superior Performance.* New York: Free Press, 1985.

———, ed. *Competition in Global Industries.* Cambridge, Mass.: Harvard Graduate School of Business Administration, forthcoming.

PRICE, ROBERT M. "Uncertainty and Strategic Opportunity." *Journal of Business Strategy,* Winter 1982.

QUINN, JAMES BRIAN. *Strategies for Change: Logical Incrementalism.* Homewood, Ill.: Irwin, 1980.

———. "Formulating Strategy One Step at a Time." *Journal of Business Strategy,* Winter 1981.

RAMOND, CHARLES. *The Art of Using Science in Marketing.* New York: Harper & Row, 1974.

REILLY, ROBERT F. "Planning for an Acquisition Strategy." *Managerial Planning,* March–April 1980.

REYNOLDS, LLOYD G. *Macroeconomics: Analysis and Policy.* Homewood, Ill.: Irwin, 1979.

ROACH, JOHN D. C. "From Strategic Planning to Strategic Performance: Closing the Achievement Gap." *Outlook,* Spring 1981.

ROBERTS, EDWARD B., and CHARLES A. BERRY. "Entering New Businesses: Selecting Strategies for Success." *Sloan Management Review,* Spring 1985.

ROBINSON, E. A. G. *The Structure of Competitive Industry.* Chicago: University of Chicago Press, 1958.

ROBINSON, JOAN. *The Economics of Imperfect Competition.* London: Macmillan, 1934.

ROETHLISBERGER, F. J., and WILLIAM J. DICKSON. *Management and the Worker.* Cambridge, Mass.: Harvard University Press, 1939, 1976.

ROGERS, DAVID C. D. *Business Policy and Planning: Text and Cases.* Englewood Cliffs, N.J.: Prentice-Hall, 1977.

ROGERS, EVERETT M. *Diffusion of Innovations.* 3rd ed. New York: Free Press, 1982.

ROSENKRANZ, FRIEDRICH. *An Introduction to Corporate Modeling.* Durham, N.C.: Duke University Press, 1979.

ROSS, ELLIOT B. "Making Money with Proactive Pricing." *Harvard Business Review,* November–December 1984.

ROTH, WILLIAM F., JR. *Problem Solving for Managers.* New York: Praeger, 1985.

ROTHCHILD, WILLIAM E. *Putting It All Together.* New York: AMACOM, American Management Association, 1979.

———. *How to Gain (and Maintain) the Competitive Advantage in Business.* New York: McGraw-Hill, 1984.

RUBY, LUCIEN. "Objectives for Start-Up Businesses," Strategic Planning Institute, PIMS Letter Series, 1978.

SALTER, MALCOLM S., and WOLF A. WEINHOLD. *Diversification Through Acquisition.* New York: Free Press, 1979.

SASSER, WILLIAM EARL, PAUL OLSEN, and DARRYL WYCKOFF. *Management of Service Operations.* New York: Allyn and Bacon, 1978.

SCHELLING, THOMAS C. *The Strategy of Conflict.* Cambridge, Mass.: Harvard University Press, 1960.

SCHENDEL, DAN E. *Strategic Management: A New View of Business Policy and Planning.* Boston: Little, Brown, 1979.

SCHERER, F. M. *Industrial Market Structure and Economic Performance.* Chicago: Rand McNally, 1970.

SCHMENNER, ROGER W. *Production/Operations Management, Concepts and Situations.* Chicago: Science Research Associates, 1981.

SCHOEFFLER, SIDNEY, ROBERT D. BUZZELL, and DONALD F. HEANY. "Impact of Strategic Planning on Profit Performance." *Harvard Business Review,* March–April 1974.

SEED, ALLEN H., III. "Winning Strategies for Shareholder Value Creation." *The Journal of Business Strategy,* Fall 1985.

SHANKLIN, WILLIAM L., and JOHN K. RYANS, JR. "Is the International Cash Cow Really a Prize Heifer?" *Business Horizons,* March–April 1981.

SHAPIRO, BENSON P. *Sales Program Management: Formulation and Implementation.* New York: McGraw-Hill, 1977.

———, and THOMAS V. BONOMA. "How to Segment Industrial Markets." *Harvard Business Review,* May–June 1984.

———, ROBERT J. DOLAN, and JOHN A. QUELCH. *Marketing Management.* Homewood, Ill.: Irwin, 1985.

SHIRLEY, ROBERT C., MICHAEL H. PETERS, and ADEL I. EL-ANSARY. *Strategy and Policy Formulation: A Multifunctional Orientation.* New York: Wiley, 1981.

SKINNER, WICKHAM. *Manufacturing: The Formidable Competitive Weapon.* New York: Wiley, 1985.

SLATTER, STUART ST. P. "Common Pitfalls in Using the BCG Portfolio Matrix." *London Business School Journal,* Winter 1980.

SOLOMONS, DAVID. *Divisional Performance.* Homewood, Ill.: Irwin, 1965.

SOMMERS, WILLIAM P. "Directing Strategy at the Corporate Level." *Outlook,* Spring 1980.

SOUTH, STEPHEN E. "Competitive Advantage, the Cornerstone of Strategic Thinking." *Journal of Business Strategy,* Spring 1981.

SPENCE, A. MICHAEL. *Market Signaling.* Cambridge, Mass.: Harvard University Press, 1974.

STEINER, GEORGE A. *Top Management Planning.* New York: Macmillan, 1969.

———. *Strategic Planning: What Every Manager Must Know.* New York: Free Press, 1979.

———, and JOHN B. MINER. *Management Policy and Strategy.* New York: Macmillan, 1982.

STEVENSON, HOWARD H. "Defining Corporate Strengths and Weaknesses." *Sloan Management Review,* Spring 1976.

STRATEGIC PLANNING ASSOCIATION, INC. *Strategy and Shareholder Value: The Value Curve.* Washington, D.C.: Strategic Planning Associates, 1981.

TAYLOR, FREDERICK WINSLOW. *The Principles of Scientific Management.* New York: Harper & Row, 1971.

TEECE, DAVID J. "Economic Analysis and Strategic Management." *California Management Review,* Spring 1984.

———. "The Multinational Enterprise: Market Failure and Market Power Considerations." *Sloan Management Review,* Spring 1981.

THOMPSON, ARTHUR A., JR. "Strategies for Staying Cost Competitive." *Harvard Business Review,* January–February 1984.

———, and A. J. STRICKLAND III. *Strategy Formulation and Implementation: Task of the General Managers.* Dallas: Business Publication, 1980.

TOURANGEAU, KEVIN W. *Strategy Management: How to Plan, Execute and Control Strategic Plans for Your Business.* New York: McGraw-Hill, 1981.

TREGOE, BENJAMIN B., and JOHN W. ZIMMERMAN. "The New Strategic Manager." *Business,* May–June 1981.

UYTERHAVEN, HUGO. *Strategy and Organization.* New York: Irwin, 1977.

VAN HORN, JAMES C. *Financial Management Policy.* Englewood Cliffs, N.J.: Prentice-Hall, 1974.

VANCIL, RICHARD F., ed. *Financial Executive's Handbook.* Homewood, Ill.: Dow-Jones, Irwin, 1978.

———, and P. LORANGE. "Strategic Planning in Diversified Companies." *Harvard Business Review,* January–February 1975.

VARADARAJAN, POONDI. "Intensive Growth Opportunities: An Extended Classification." *California Management Review,* Spring 1983.

VATTER, PAUL A., STEPHEN A. BRADLEY, SHERWOOD C. FREY, JR., and BARBARA JACKSON. *Quantitative Methods in Management: Text and Cases.* Homewood, Ill.: Irwin, 1978.

VITOROVICH, NICHOLAS. "Higher Productivity Through Shared Scale." *The McKinsey Quarterly,* Spring 1983.

VON NEUMANN, JOHN, and OSKUR MORGENSTERN. *Theory of Games and Economic Behavior.* Princeton: Princeton University Press, 1944.

WATERMAN, ROBERT H., JR., THOMAS J. PETERS, and JULIEN R. PHILIPS. "Structure Is Not Organization." *Business Horizons,* June 1980.

WELLS, LOUIS T., ed. *The Product Life Cycle and International Trade.* Cambridge, Mass.: Harvard University, Graduate School of Business Administration, Division of Research, 1972.

WENSLEY, ROBIN. "PIMS and BCG: New Horizons or False Dawn?" *Strategic Management Journal,* April–June 1982.

WESTON, J. FRED, and EUGENE F. BRIGHAM. *Managerial Finance.* 6th ed. Hinsdale, Ill.: Dryden, 1978.

WHEELWRIGHT, STEVEN C. "Restoring the Competitive Edge in U.S. Manufacturing." *California Management Review,* Spring 1985.

——, and SPYROS MAKRIDAKIS. *Forecasting Methods for Management.* New York: Wiley, 1973.

WHITTAKER, JAMES B. *Strategic Planning in a Rapidly Changing Environment.* Lexington, Mass.: D. C. Heath, 1978.

WILLIAMS, JEFFREY R. "Competitive Strategy Valuation." *Journal of Business,* Spring 1984.

WILLIAMSON, OLIVER E. *Markets and Hierarchies.* New York: Free Press, 1975.

WILSON, IAN H., WILLIAM GENGE, and PAUL J. SOLOMAN. "Strategic Planning for Marketers." *Business Horizons,* December 1978.

WILSON, J. TYLEE. "Strategic Planning at R. J. Reynolds Industries." *Journal of Business Strategy,* Fall 1985.

YAVITZ, BORIS, and WILLIAM H. NEWMAN. "What the Corporation Should Provide Its Business Units." *Journal of Business Strategy,* Summer 1982.

YIP, GEORGE. *Barriers to Entry: A Corporate Strategy Perspective.* Lexington, Mass.: Lexington Books, 1982.

Index and Cross-Reference